The Pictorial Story of Ships

The Pictorial Story of
Ships

NEW ENGLISH LIBRARY
TIMES MIRROR

Editor: Richard H. Stuart
Compiler: Robert G. Gray
Copy Editor: William J. Howell
Art Editor: Deborah Miles
Designers: Mark Holt, Nykola Stoakes
Picture Research: Rosemary L. Lister, Penelope Grant,
Jane O'Farrell

ACKNOWLEDGEMENTS
Much of the material in this book first appeared in the
partwork, HISTORY OF SHIPS, and I should like to thank
the editor of that publication, E. L. Cornwell, for making my
editorial task much simpler than it might otherwise have been.
I also wish to extend my thanks to Bill Howell, who compiled
the index, to Eileen Murphy for her administrative help, and
to all those whose work appears in this book.

R.S.

This edition published in 1977 by
New English Library Limited,
Barnard's Inn
Holborn,
London EC1N 2JR,
England

Set in 11/12pt Monotype Times New Roman by South Bucks
Typesetters Limited
Printed by Fratelli Spada, Ciampino, Rome, Italy

45003430 5

Contents

Early Ships

Left: **Danish medieval craft of 1350.**
MARITIME MUSEUM, KRONBORG

Above: Thor Heyerdahl's balsa raft 'Kon-Tiki' under way.
KON-TIKI MUSEUM

THE earliest forms of water-craft known to archaeologists are the primitive dug-out canoes, fragments of which have been excavated from the swamps and bogs of the British Isles, from the Stone Age lake-dwellings of Switzerland, and from the east and west coasts of North America. Some researchers believe that Stone Age folk probably also used the small circular coracle: a simple craft which is light enough to be carried on a man's back. Originally constructed from basketwork made watertight with skins, and now partly of more modern materials, coracles can still be seen in the hands of fishermen on Welsh rivers.

Another type of craft of indeterminate age is the balsa raft of South America. Although extremely light – lighter even than cork – balsa wood is a sappy timber and absorbs water over a long period. Its positive qualities, however, were triumphantly demonstrated by the Norwegian Thor Heyerdahl in 1947, when he sailed his *Kon-Tiki* across the Pacific from Peru, having built her from balsa without iron nails or wire ropes. He made another experimental voyage some years

later, sailing across the North Atlantic to the West Indies from the Mediterranean in a replica of a papyrus boat of ancient Egypt. The material of which the boat was built, *Cyperus Papyrus*, was a sedge-like plant growing in great profusion in Egypt at that time.

Thousands of years ago, its stems were not only made into paper, but for long it was the chief material used for building serviceable boats. Since Egypt had no timber except for short lengths of stunted acacia, sycamore-fig and tamarisk trees, she concentrated on developing her papyrus craft.

Strictly speaking, as they had no keel or stem and sternposts, they were closer to rafts than boats. They were built by wrapping papyrus stems together in a tightly-lashed bundle, forming a long slim shape with high upturned ends curved nearly at right angles. To prevent the boat from hogging, or arching up in the middle, a strong rope was stretched from end to end and strained taut over crutches above the heads of the crew.

At some early time the boat was given a simple sail which was loose-footed, or free along the bottom edge. The sail and its cordage were all made from papyrus stems too. Sometimes a mast was contrived by fixing a leaning spar on each side and tying them together at the top to form a tall triangle. On this a smaller spar, a yard, was slung crossways

Above: Model of Thor Heyerdahl's reed boat 'Ra II' in the Science Museum, London. D. RUDKIN

Left: Model of an Egyptian ship dating from the time of Queen Hatshepsut. MARINE MUSEUM, LISBON

Left below: An Egyptian shipyard of the Old Kingdom, on the Nile, taken from an ancient relief. LALANCE

Right: Model of a Phoenician galley with mast and sail, besides oars which were probably manned by freemen and not by slaves. MARINE MUSEUM, LISBON

to carry the sail. Later, as a protection against spray, a rectangular screen was added well aft and to one side. Among other improvements, the sail was given a second spar at the foot and, to take the strain of a larger sail, a web of cords was stretched out fanwise from the mast down to the lower yard.

The first known picture of any sailing craft comes from Egypt on a painted vase of about BC 3100. The Nile being the life-blood of Egyptian commerce, boats were a vital necessity to everyday life. Though for centuries most of them were constructed from papyrus, the number of those built in wood was steadily increasing. They had their short lengths of timber skilfully linked together and secured with mortises and tenons. In build, they were shaped in imitation of the spoon-shaped papyrus craft, and this similarity was taken to the extreme of painting the wood in the same green as the fresh papyrus reed.

For the building of the pyramids and other great monuments, the heavy loads of stone were transported on huge rafts of papyrus. They were aided by the Nile itself, for since the wind in Egypt blows from the north on nearly every day of the year, vessels can sail up-river with the wind, and then be carried back by the current. In fact, this was so much a part of the Egyptian way of life that the words for 'go south' were shown in the hieroglyphics as a boat with a sail, 'go north' being simply represented as a boat without one.

In the tomb of Cheops, the builder of the Great Pyramid, a large wooden boat was found which was over 160 feet in length and twenty feet in beam. It had been carefully stripped down to its component parts, but nearly all of them were intact and formed into a shapely decked vessel, not intended for sailing, and with more than a hint of the papyrus style. In the hermetically sealed tomb, a slight scent still lingered: the scent of the cedarwood of which the boat had been made.

With the discovery of the tomb of Queen Hatshepsut (BC 1503) there were found some excellent bas-reliefs of her ships. Five of them are depicted sailing to the mysterious land of Punt, somewhere to the south. The other five, with furled sails, are loading cargo. The ships were about seventy feet long and, in the absence of local timber of any size, were probably constructed from short lengths dovetailed together with wedges.

It was probably in the thirteenth century BC that Egypt began building ships for two distinct purposes, namely fighting and trading. One was the warship, with a stout metal ram at her bows, and the other, the trading vessel, was broader and deeper in the water with a square hold for carrying cargo.

The idea spread throughout the Mediterranean. From about the same period, the Phoenicians have left us a very clear impression of one of their war-galleys: a model in terracotta which was found at Babylus. Unlike the Egyptian ships, the Phoenician and Greek galleys probably developed from the primitive dug-out, becoming more refined as skill increased. Much later, an artist portrayed King Luli of Sidon in a bas-relief of BC 701. The king's fleet is escaping to Tyre and his ships are biremes, propelled by two banks of oars which are apparently staggered, one above the other. The rowers of Phoenicia were free men, not slaves, and their ship carried the large square sail of the Mediterranean. This relief also shows warships as being distinct from the merchant ships.

Many decorative pictures have been found on vases and in wall-paintings from Egypt and Greece, some of which prove the use at that time of a crow's-nest which was reached by ladders attached to the mast. Not only Phoenician but also Egyptian ships are believed to have traded with ports on the south-western coast of India, and it is thought that the present village of Puvar could be the mysterious Ophir.

Between 610 and 595 BC Pharoah Necho decided to re-open a canal long since silted up, linking the Nile and the Red Sea. The Pharoah suggested that a Phoenician ship should sail down it to explore, and the ship left on a three-year voyage. About half-way through their mission, the crew made an astonishing discovery. They suddenly noticed that when they were facing forward the sun was beginning to rise over their right shoulders instead of over their left. Unknowingly, they had begun to circumnavigate the continent of Africa.

The ships of Assyria looked much the same as those of Phoenicia, but the Etruscans, of whom so little is known, have left one surprise. A wall-painting found in 1954, dating from 470 BC, clearly shows a two-masted ship, although it had been believed that no vessel had more than a single sail for a number of centuries. The ship's second mast was short and stepped well forward of her mainmast, with a small sail spread on it. She had a deep hull and bulwarks like many a later vessel.

By then the Greek shipbuilders had strengthened the none-too-stout narrow hull of the war-galley with thick planks along the sides from end to end of the ship. The huge pointed ram was supported throughout her length, and unmistakably Greek was the large eye painted on each bow. At both bow and stern was built a solid deck and, linking them, there was a light decking fore and aft which covered the rowers.

The merchant ship had a rounded hull with definite stem and stern. Her mast, stepped amidships, was steadied by one shroud on each side and the sail halyard was led aft to act as a backstay. She had developed into a sailing ship rather than a galley, being deeper and broader in the beam, but oars (or sweeps) still remained the more important means of propulsion.

A larger ship, the trireme, with three banks of oars,

appeared after the bireme. How her oars were arranged is a puzzle which has led to much speculation and argument. If the oarsmen sat in three rows, one above the other, the oars of those in the uppermost tier would have had to be too long and too steeply angled to be handled at all. One theory is simply that three rowers sat side by side working at the same oar, but there are numerous other explanations.

The problem becomes even more complicated when one looks at the still larger ships – the quinqueremes and the hepteremes, with five and six banks of oars each. Greek vessels of all kinds were engaged in trade along various routes, but the most regular traffic was with the cargoes of the large corn ships which maintained food supplies to Rome. In time the distinction between Greek and Roman ships became thin. They both adopted as a decoration for their sterns a great carving of a swan with a down-curved neck. Round it, thrusting out over the water, was a light stern-walk or gallery. It appears to have been a Roman who invented the tiny headsail called the artemon. This was spread beyond the ship's bows on a short spar that was canted well forward to aid steering. It was completely forgotten after the fall of Rome and did not come into use again until the early Middle Ages.

With the emergence of the warship as a breed in its own right, it was likely that naval warfare would soon take place on a large scale. When Xerxes set out from Asia Minor in BC 480 with a massive army to humble the Greeks, he assembled the largest fleet of warships that had then been seen. His ships were joined by two hundred long low Phoenician war galleys from Tyre and Sidon, by a squadron from Egypt, and by other vessels from four rebellious Greek states which had thrown in their lot with the Persians. This made a total of over 1,500 ships, including fighting vessels and cargo carriers, intended to run parallel to the gigantic army.

In order to cross the Dardanelles, Xerxes had built a floating bridge composed of covered boats and small ships. His engineers built two bridges in the event, as the first one collapsed, killing a number of troops. The first team of engineers having been beheaded, the second bridge was well constructed and held firm for a full week.

In Athens, the chief magistrate, a man called Themistocles, was urging every man capable of bearing arms to join a ship. He knew that no army they could raise would have any chance of resisting the might of Persia and her allies. The only hope for Greece, he maintained, was to destroy the enemy's fleet. His idea was to make the Persians fight in a narrow channel that would allow them no room for manoeuvre, thus depriving them of the chance to deploy their full power.

The dawn following the arrival of the Persian warships a

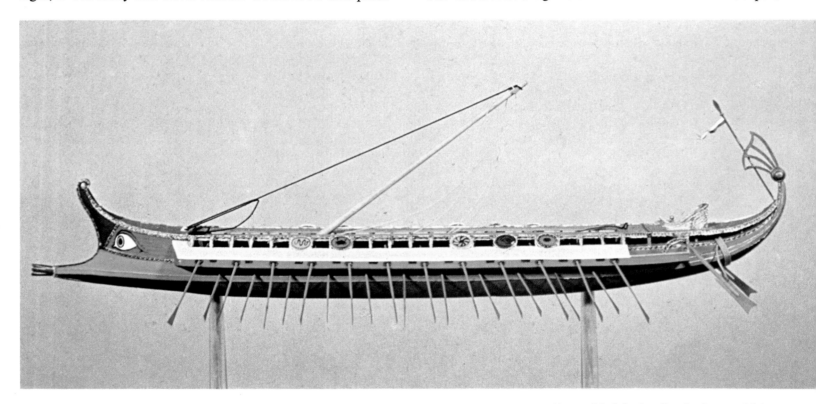

Above: Model of a Greek bireme which clearly shows the two banks of oars, the ram and the characteristic eye at the bow. MARINE MUSEUM, LISBON

Left: A Greek warship of 500 BC equipped with two banks of oars, a mast stepped amidships and a powerful, decorated ram.
NATIONAL MARITIME MUSEUM, HAIFA

Above right: A model of a Roman trireme, in the Naval Museum at La Spezia, shows the down-curved swan neck, auxiliary mast and sails, and the arrangement of rowers seated side-by-side for each oar. M. PUCCIARELLI

freak storm flung scores of vessels ashore, damaging some of them beyond repair. A large number had previously been despatched to sail up from the farther end of the channel to catch the Greeks between themselves and the main fleet. They also suffered in the gale, and almost half of Xerxes' great armada was lost. With the coming of quieter weather there was a little fighting, but on the third morning there was no Greek ship in sight. Themistocles, hearing news of the forcing of Thermopylae, had taken his fleet down through the channel and, rounding the southernmost point of Attica, turned north to shelter in the strait behind Salamis. He had with him 366 ships, roughly half the total of the Persians, who were following him and preparing for battle.

Although now divided into two groups, the Persians at the eastern entrance to the channel still had the larger force of ships and men. Their numbers could not be used to much advantage, however, because of the narrowness of their only route towards the Greeks. As the eager Persian line advanced, the Greek ships suddenly attempted to break through, and hand-to-hand fighting broke out all around. Ships were rammed and turned over, some were boarded and their crews slain to a man. The savage fighting went on for twelve hours, and despite being so heavily outnumbered, the Greeks gradually gained the upper hand.

Its navy having been destroyed by its own size in the cramped channel, the Persian army was left without support and the campaign collapsed. The small remnant was defeated in a battle the following year, and Greece suffered no further invasion from outside for 1,500 years.

By the ninth century AD Persian fleets, operating from naval bases in Syria and Crete, were making a steady but gradual invasion of the Mediterranean waters. The change was quite striking, for the Persian craft of that time were very different from any earlier Mediterranean shipping. Called the dhow, a word which has since come to be applied to almost any Arab ship, the shape of their vessel was modelled on the whale, and below the water-line its design was remarkably advanced. The smaller dhows went through an outstanding period of development from open boats into decked or half-decked craft. This resulted in them being planked as a permanent fixture, either all over, or sometimes only at the bow and stern with a cargo hold in between.

These dhows were usually one-masters with a yard of enormous length. They were regularly engaged in coastal trading, though in the main they ran a lucrative slave-trade. The characteristic rig comprised a long yard – the same length as the dhow herself – slung on a mast positioned well forward. The Arabs had found that height above the water-line had much to do with the efficiency of the sail, and theirs could be hoisted high above the masthead. The tacking of this ship is fascinating to watch, and in smaller dhows – which still operate today – this involves bringing the yard upright and some of the crew running forward with the sheet (the master-rope controlling the sail), while others swing the yard round, so that yard and sail have been reversed. Dhows are still being built, mainly in India, but types are becoming fewer and there is an indication of European influence in them. Nevertheless, the Arab dhow, which is often still a sailing vessel pure and simple, is probably the last direct survivor from the remotest chapters of maritime history.

Changes in the building materials used for these early ships came less frequently than the dramatic improvements in design, but one significant step was in the introduction of iron fastenings. The earliest evidence of iron nails being used in shipbuilding comes from the wreck of a ship of the third century BC found off the coast of Sicily. There is a distinct possibility that she might have been a Punic ship, and the iron nails had been driven into her planks through dowels, or round wooden pegs, which had been inserted first.

Modern techniques of undersea exploration have led to the finding and examination of many wrecks on the sea-bed of the Mediterranean. Nearly all of those early remains are of Greek or Roman merchantmen of the fourth and fifth centuries, laden with cargoes of amphoras, the large two-handled wine jars of the Roman period. The wrecks show that their shipwrights had used copper nails which had first been forced through wooden pegs.

A second-century sailing barge recovered in England from the Thames also revealed a number of large iron nails. They vary in length up to as much as twenty-nine inches, but are all of the same shape for holding the side-planks to the floor timbers. They have hollow conical heads, and rounded shanks that become square in section at their pointed ends. To drive them home, a hole was drilled into the plank and a dowel driven through it. This is precisely the same principle used today for fixing a screw into a wall with a plug fitted into a hole drilled in the plaster.

Also in England, the Sutton Hoo ship proved to be a highly significant find. She had nearly 2,000 little dark blobs of raised sand in the grave-mound, showing where each rivet had once hung. Only some three hundred have survived in any substance. The vessel was a large open boat with a high

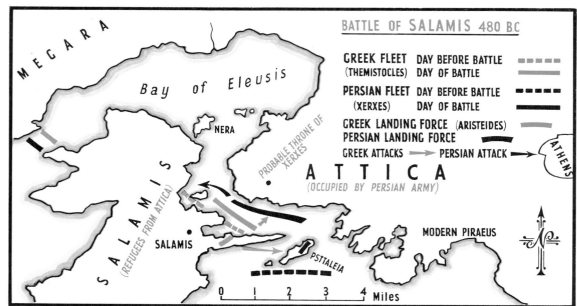

BATTLE OF SALAMIS 480 BC

GREEK FLEET (THEMISTOCLES)	DAY BEFORE BATTLE	-----
	DAY OF BATTLE	
PERSIAN FLEET (XERXES)	DAY BEFORE BATTLE	-----
	DAY OF BATTLE	
GREEK LANDING FORCE (ARISTEIDES)		
PERSIAN LANDING FORCE		
GREEK ATTACKS	→	PERSIAN ATTACK →

Left: Map of the naval movements at the Battle of Salamis in 480 BC which left Xerxes' army without support. P. F. WINDING

Below: Old print of Greek triremes in action at Salamis. MARY EVANS PICTURE LIBRARY

stern-piece, eighty feet long, fourteen feet across the beam, and four and a half feet deep. There was no mast, for she was entirely dependent on oars. There were thirty-eight wooden rowlocks for the oarsmen with a steering-oar on the starboard side. Clinker-built with broad planking, the vessel had twenty-six ribs which made a clear impression on the sandy soil before the processes of erosion had done their work. The excavation work begun in 1938 was suspended at the outbreak of war, and during the Second World War the site was used as a training area for British tanks. Some damage was done, but in the circumstances, it is astonishing how much has survived.

Vikings and
North Europeans

IN the late eighth century, the Vikings from Norway began to make their increasingly frequent raids on the English coasts. Soon they had established bases in the Orkneys and Shetlands and made raids on the Welsh coast from the Isle of Man. One Norwegian chief, Turgeis, made his way to Ireland and founded the city of Dublin. After ten years he tried to convert the Irish to his own form of paganism, but they rose in anger and managed to drown him. He was succeeded by the famous Olaf the White who brought his own fleet with him. From time to time both Norwegians

and Danes found their way to various parts of Ireland, though they never really settled there. After their numbers had grown, they made occasional raids into France, using southern Ireland as a base.

From Norway itself and from Denmark there were repeated attacks by sea up the Seine on Quentoric (Paris); Rouen and Nantes were also targets for Viking hostility, and the rich Rhine port of Dorestad in Holland was plundered again and again. The Vikings, however, did not always have their own way in France. Twice they were defeated in Paris and turned their attention to ravaging the countryside to the north. There many of them settled in what they called Normandy: later they were to conquer England at Hastings.

Although some Swedes took part in these attacks, in general they struck out on their own towards Latvia and Estonia. They ventured down the Dnieper in 862 and defeated a Russian army. As a result, Rurik, their chief, founded a dynasty and created the Russian state. Savagely cruel though they could be, the Vikings had a regulated society with recognised ethics, and they had their courts at the Althing, or parliament, to dispense their own peculiar form of justice. In their society women were not chattels, but had privileges and an established status. It is astonishing that in only three centuries the Vikings should have spread all over Europe and as far as Constantinople and North America, but whatever may have been the urge that drove them so far afield, they had the craft to make it possible.

The Gokstad longship which was found near Oslo in 1880 can be taken as a typical war-galley of the later ninth century. She was clinker-built with overlapping oak planks lashed, not riveted, to the ribs. The planks rested on wooden cleats, or projections, and were bound to the ribs with strips of lime bark. She was over seventy-nine feet in length and sixteen and a half feet in beam, and could have been either rowed or sailed, having square oarports fitted in the second board below the gunwale. The large square sail was coloured red or striped, and attached to a single, very long yard. The sail could also be spread over the ship to serve as a tent or awning while she was moored or at anchor. She had fine lines, and when under sail she must have looked superb, with sixteen round shields on each side, painted alternately yellow and black.

Above: 'The Landing of Leif Ericsson in the New World', a painting by Moran.
BY COURTESY OF THE US NAVAL ACADEMY MUSEUM

Facing page:
Top: The preserved Gokstad longship in the Viking Ship Museum, Oslo. PAUL POPPER LTD

Centre left: An ornate carved figurehead from the ninth-century Norwegian Oseberg ship. VIKING SHIP MUSEUM, OSLO

Bottom left: A drawing by E. Weienshislef shows Finn Arnesonn, a Viking ruler, in a threatening attitude.
ROYAL NORWEGIAN EMBASSY

Bottom right: An impression from A. E. Wood's engraving of a fleet of Viking warships headed by the Danish 'Raven'.
MARY EVANS PICTURE LIBRARY

But by no means all Viking ships were fighting ships. The knarr, built in much the same way as the longship, though larger, deeper and more rounded, was designed for trading. For almost three hundred years it was the ocean-going knarr, gradually developing with time, that kept the settlers in Greenland supplied.

For the overseas voyages, navigation was a vital factor, and the Norsemen relied largely on the sun and the stars. There is no doubt that their navigational skills were highly advanced, for their achievements rank among the most remarkable feats of navigation and seamanship ever recorded.

Perhaps the most famous descendant of the Norwegian Vikings was Leif Ericsson. Leif had been converted to Christianity in Norway by King Olaf, who had sent him back to Greenland to do the same for the settlers. On his arrival, Leif heard a great deal about Bjarni Herjulfsson's discovery of a wooded country, the islands now known as Labrador and Baffin. This trader had not gone ashore in the unknown territory, but sailed away and eventually made a good landfall on the Greenland coast.

At the prospect of bringing cargoes of timber to treeless Greenland, Leif was all eagerness. He bought Bjarni's boat, a large knarr, and set off with a crew of thirty-five men in the summer of the year 1001. Finding Bjarni's island, he persevered until he saw a better coast with a freshwater stream, plenty of timber for building and an abundance of salmon. There were also masses of wild berries, which led him to name the country Vinland, or Wineland, from Vimber, a wine-berry. Perhaps he was copying his father, who had called his new country Greenland to entice new settlers to that forbidding land.

Leif and his men spent the winter, a mild season, in collecting berries and felling the precious timber to take back with them in the ship in spring. They had a triumphant return to Greenland, and ever afterwards Leif was known as Leif the Lucky. There were several more expeditions, but each had to return, partly because of shortage of food and partly to avoid the antagonism of the *skraelings*, as the Norsemen called the Red Indians and Eskimos.

The last recorded attempt to colonise was in 1013 in two ships; it was ruined by a woman named Freydis, Leif's half-sister. By lying and cheating, she incited her husband to kill all the men who were not of her crew, while she murdered the women. She herself survived to return to Greenland, where, it seems, she suffered little or no retribution.

In Greenland the Norse settlement in the west vanished completely at some unknown time, apparently destroyed by the Eskimos. The eastern one was long supported by a ship which was fairly regularly sent with supplies from Norway. Then, because of a war in Scandinavia, no ship arrived, and the colony was eventually forgotten. It seems to have lingered on, gradually weakening from semi-starvation until the last of them died. The crew of a ship which went in for shelter between 1406 and 1410 could find no people: only cattle running wild. Bodies were, however, discovered in the 1920s, preserved in the ice of Greenland, still wearing the clothes of a century long gone by.

Many suggestions have been made as to the whereabouts of Vinland. Of them, New England has been one of the most favoured, but in 1960 a Norwegian archaeologist discovered a site which seems to fit the description of the place described in the sagas. It was at L'Anse aux Meadows in northern Newfoundland, and excavations supported the argument that this was Leif's original settlement. Two great houses were found; the biggest was seventy feet long and fifty-five feet wide, with walls of turf and a roof covered with sods. There was a fireplace in the centre and benches of turf along each wall. The charred roof timber gave a date of AD 1000, with a possible error of 100 years each way, which is exactly what one would expect. There can be little doubt that Leif discovered the New World some five hundred years before Columbus.

Compasses

THE invention of the compass has been ascribed to the Chinese, although, as there was little if any communication between the several ancient civilisations, it is probable that an appreciation of the properties of the magnetised needle was born independently in various maritime societies during the first millenium AD. There is evidence in Scandinavian records that the mariner's compass as a practical navigational aid was probably developed in northern Europe between the years 868 and 1100 AD.

In its earliest form the compass consisted merely of a suspended bar of lodestone, a magnetic oxide of iron found in China, Bengal, Arabia and (of lower quality) in Germany, Scandinavia and the west of England. Presumably its use stemmed from the realisation that its directional properties could be related to the bearing of some celestial body, in particular in the northern seas to the Pole Star which occupied an apparently fixed position in the heavens. The crude use of lodestone was soon overtaken by the technique of magnetising an iron needle.

The early crude method of floating the needle, supported by a piece of cork or straw, on water was soon replaced by mounting it on a pivot. The compass card, eight to ten inches in diameter and marked with the thirty-two points, to which the needle was affixed, came next, possibly in the fifteenth century and certainly in the sixteenth; also by the sixteenth century the complete compass was being mounted on pivots in a wooden box fitted with a glass lid, so that it was protected from the elements. The whole assembly was supported in brass gimbals so that it might remain level irrespective of pitching and rolling movements of the ship.

It was soon realised that although in Mediterranean waters the compass indicated something near the magnetic north, elsewhere it was subject to differing amounts of error, called compass variation. In Britain and France, variation was allowed for by offsetting the needle half a point to the eastward of the meridian line of the card, but as ships moved elsewhere it led to considerable navigational errors. Moreover, the design and manufacture of the compasses themselves were crude until the middle of the eighteenth century when Dr Gowan Knight applied himself to the task of designing a compass on well-engineered scientific principles.

Knight's compass was adopted as standard for the Royal Navy and served well until the advent of iron-hulled ships in the nineteenth century. Already it had been appreciated that substantial masses of iron, such as guns and stanchions, had a marked effect on the accuracy of the compass and that the anomaly was itself subject to change with alteration of course. The error, or deviation, formed the subject of an investigation by Matthew Flinders, who devised means to correct the compass by the use of vertical soft iron bars usually placed abaft the bowl. In 1840 an important improvement was made to compasses by the Admiralty. This was the use of four parallel magnetised needles, and it overcame much of the problem.

An iron hull made matters worse but the work of the Astronomer Royal, Sir George Airey, produced an answer in the form of a mass of soft iron placed on each side of the compass which was itself placed high up in the ship as far removed as possible from the effects of the iron structure. The modern magnetic compass derives from the work of Sir William Thompson (Lord Kelvin), 1824-1907, who assimilated that of Flinders and Airey and produced a well-engineered instrument, the design of which has changed little during the past hundred years.

For naval purposes, however, the Kelvin compass had drawbacks. Warships have always had to steam harder than merchant ships, and the resulting vibration affected the compass. Kelvin's compasses used a 'dry card', i.e. the magnet and card were hung in an airtight box; this system simplified manufacture and reduced weight, and provided the compass was hung in gimbals it was not unduly affected by the motion of the ship in normal conditions. It was assumed that in really violent motion precise bearings would be of little use. A warship, on the other hand, could be steaming hard or firing her guns in the mildest of weather, and would need just the degree of precision that was lacking.

Dissatisfaction with the standard magnetic compasses produced late in the nineteenth century led the Admiralty to start its own research programme into compass-design. A talented naval officer, Captain Louis Chetwynd (1866-1914) solved the problem by 'damping' the card's wild swinging; the magnet and card were hung in a bowl filled with liquid. The choice of liquid was important, and eventually alcohol was used because it behaved better under extremes of temperature. By the time Chetwynd's improvements had been incorporated into naval compasses he became so well known that his name was given to all liquid-bowl compasses thereafter.

The early years of the present century brought new developments which made unnecessary complete reliance upon the magnetic compass. The principle of the gyroscope and the laws of precession had been long known and it could be shown mathematically that a suitably constrained gyroscope would precess until the axis of spin lay horizontal in the plane of the earth's axis. Thus, unlike the magnetic compass, it would indicate true north. Practical development of the theory led to the design of the gyro compass, the first seaworthy version of which was produced by the German firm, Hermann Anschütz, in 1908.

In the gyro compass the effect of precession is applied by fixing a semi-circular tube weighted with mercury to the frame in which the wheel is suspended, when the axis of the gyroscope seeks the north-south meridian by oscillating on each side of it. These oscillations are damped out by the exertion of precessional pressure on the vertical axis, which causes the gyroscope to settle steadily on the north-south meridian.

In the meantime, Elmer A. Sperry in the United States had developed another design of gyro compass which was easier to manufacture and much bigger than the Anschütz type. The Sperry design employed a gyro rotor weighing 52lb which was driven electrically at 6,000rpm. It was adopted by the British Admiralty and for fifty years the Sperry design and successive developments have served as the standard gyro compass in HM ships.

The first Royal Navy ships fitted with the Sperry gyro compass were the capital ships of the Home Fleet just before the outbreak of the First World War. The two battle-cruisers *Invincible* and *Inflexible* sent out to the Falkland Islands in November 1914 to track down Admiral Spee's

A mariner's compass, with a simple card showing only eight points, in the Naval Museum at Genova-Pegli. M. PUCCIARELLI

cruisers had to complete the installation of their gyro compasses at breakneck speed.

A third type, designed by S. G. Brown in England, first appeared in 1916 and has since been employed extensively both in merchant ships and warships.

Between the wars the usual fit for a warship comprised one, or in large vessels two, gyro compasses, a 'standard' magnetic compass, placed high in the ship to minimise the effects of permanent and induced hull magnetism, and secondary magnetic compasses on the bridge (pelorus) and at the emergency conning position. Wartime needs led, however, to the development of the Admiralty Transmitting Magnetic Compass, and subsequently the Admiralty Gyro Magnetic Compass, to meet the needs of new-construction ships and craft.

The latest development is the Ship's Inertial Navigation System (SINS) derived from inertial navigation systems produced in the 1950s for use in ballistic missiles and giving not only an indication of true north (and hence ship's heading) but also ship's position, in terms of latitude and longitude, and ship's speed over the ground. The use of this sophisticated equipment is confined to major warships, however, other vessels being fitted with modern developments of the Anschüzt, Sperry Arma or Brown gyro compasses.

SINS is in reality only an extended application of the gyro compass. Using a gyro compass to find true north, and accelerometers to measure the movement of the ship's hull, the system plots the continuous movement relative to a known point of departure. Without SINS nuclear submarines could not navigate for long periods underwater, and it is the heart of the Polaris underwater-launched ballistic missile system. As Polaris and its derivatives are ballistic weapons, the range and bearing of the target must be known within quite strict limits. The latitude and longitude of the point of departure and the target are known, and the SINS continuously updates the fire-control computer to ensure that the missile will follow a ballistic path once it leaves the water.

The magnetic compass also continues to be fitted in many small craft, although for larger vessels it is now regarded as an anachronism. No doubt new developments will ease further the task of the ship's navigator, but in the meantime the modern gyro compass is an accurate and reliable instrument.

The Development of Ship Forms

THE great fleet which King Richard Coeur-de-Lion collected for his voyage to the Holy Land in 1191 to join the Third Crusade – gay with banners and pennons – must have been a sight to remember. The ships made up a total of well over a hundred, with hired vessels added to the nucleus of the King's ships, including thirty-nine galleys and a few of a larger and heavier new type of round ship called a cog.

Their voyage down to the Strait of Gibraltar and into the Mediterranean seems to have been without much incident, until Richard turned aside on the way and conquered Cyprus. Off the coast of Syria, however, they fell in with a monster; an enormous ship with no fewer than three tall masts and packed with hundreds of fierce Saracens. Richard's ships attacked the stranger from all sides but without making much impression against her height. Then the galleys were ordered in. They dashed at her with their rams, holed her sides and sank her.

The galleys, low and slim and chiefly dependent on their oars, formed a class of vessel by themselves, but the bulk of the other ships had a strong family resemblance to those of the Vikings of the past. Although they relied almost entirely on their sails, they were still clinker-built, with overlapped planking.

The vessels of the Mediterranean came of a different tradition to that of the North. A large number of them, all carvel-built, with planks edge to edge, were hired or bought from the shipyards in the southern ports, especially in Venice and Genoa, by Crusaders who had journeyed overland.

Different again were the later two-masted ships that King Louis of France ordered from Venice in 1268. They were to have keels twenty-seven metres long and stem- and stern-posts nearly nine metres high. In addition to having two complete decks from end to end of the ship, they had a half-deck extending from the bow to amidships and extra decking at the stern to provide cabins. Similar ships were ordered from Genoa and although they were rather smaller, the mainyard, the spar which carried the larger sail, was of greater length than the ship's hull.

In spite of all the variations in design of ships in general, there was a basic underwater form of hull which accords with the eighth-century Arab's maxim that it should imitate the shape of the whale. (Now, at last, that long-held tenet has lapsed in the technology of the twentieth century.) The results of the Crusades from the maritime point of view did not include only the opening up of the Mediterranean to trade with the North but also the fusion, to some extent, of shipbuilding ideas. It might be more than a coincidence that the final Crusade was coming to its end just at the time of the most important development in the history of seafaring. Some nautical genius invented the stern-rudder, which had a direct effect on the shape of the hull.

For thousands of years every kind of sailing craft, from the papyrus boat of Ancient Egypt to the majestic quin-queremes of Greece or the longships of the Norsemen, had used some form of steering-oar worked over the vessel's quarter(s). The number of them varied; once, the Ancient Egyptians had tried using as many as six of the oars, three on each quarter, and for centuries Mediterranean ships in general used two oars, one on each quarter, but no arrangement could be really satisfactory. The steering-oar worked well enough in vessels that were sailing with a following wind; the difficulty came with the discovery of how to tack and to make use of a wind on the beam when the ship was heeling over.

The new-fangled stern-rudder was probably the result of much experiment before it came to be hung in its most effective position on a vertical, or nearly vertical, sternpost. Then, in addition to simplifying matters for the helmsman, it also made possible a number of improvements, not least in the form of the hull, in designing ships.

It is fairly safe to assume that the Chinese had already developed their own type of rudder hung at the stern in their own way, but in Europe, the first indication of one in place and functioning is on the civic seal of the town of Elbing in Germany, in 1242. In English waters it did not appear until the fourteenth century, according to the evidence of the civic seals of several seaport towns. The Dover seal, for instance, dated as late as 1284, shows a vessel still using a steering-oar; incidentally, the artist has pictured it incorrectly on the port and not the starboard quarter.

There is a surprising point in both the Dover seal and one from Sandwich of 1238. Their ships have a bowsprit, which was then a sprit for holding the bow line, and, in addition, both have considerably more than their fair share of shrouds and stays supporting the masts.

In 1340, Edward III wrote to the Black Prince to describe his victory at Sluys 'from our ship *Cogge Thomas*'. With the straight stern, the rudder had made it possible for the new-style cog to be built larger and of an altered shape, giving her more stowage room both for trade purposes and for war. She was shortened and widened in the hull, ultimately reducing her length from five times the width of beam down to three times the beam, a proportion that was carried on for years, while the size of most ships continued to grow. The deck at the forward end of the cog had become nearly triangular but in spite of all that was being done to bring her up to date, she could not reign supreme for ever in the face of the swelling demand for bigger and bigger vessels.

It was evident that clinker would have to give way to the southern carvel style before long and, around the shipyards, there was talk of the coming of ships with two masts and even with three. King Henry V, it was said, had started to build a great vessel at Bayonne which would be 186 feet long from stem to stern as early as 1419! Who knew what the next few years would bring?

Right: A miniature from Froissart's 'Chronicles' showing ships at the Battle of Sluys about which Edward III wrote to the Black Prince, then ten years old.
NATIONAL LIBRARY, PARIS (M. PUCCIARELLI)

Following spread: Nicola Božidarević's painting depicts Dubrovnik in 1499 when, after development in the 13th and 14th centuries, the city had become a major maritime centre.
POMORSKIMUSEJ DUBROVNIK

uint se roy dan
gleterre z ses ma
reschaulx eurent
ordonnees leurs
batailles et leurs nauires
moult richement z rangent
Ilz furent tendre et traire
les voiles contremôt et vin
drent au vent de quartier
sur dextre pour au lauantage
du souleil qui en venant
leur estoit ou visaige. Si
sauuperent que ce se pouoit
troy mueure et detraict vng

uil et tournoyrent tant ilz
leurent a leur vouleute. Les
normans qui les vouient
tourner se merueilloient
pour quoy ilz le faisoient z
disoient ilz resongnet et
reculent Car ilz ne sont
pas gens pour combattre a
nous. Bn vouent les nor
mans pur ses lumieres que le
roy dangleterre y estoit par
sommelement. Si mirent
leurs vuisseaulx en bô estat
Car Ilz estoient faiges en

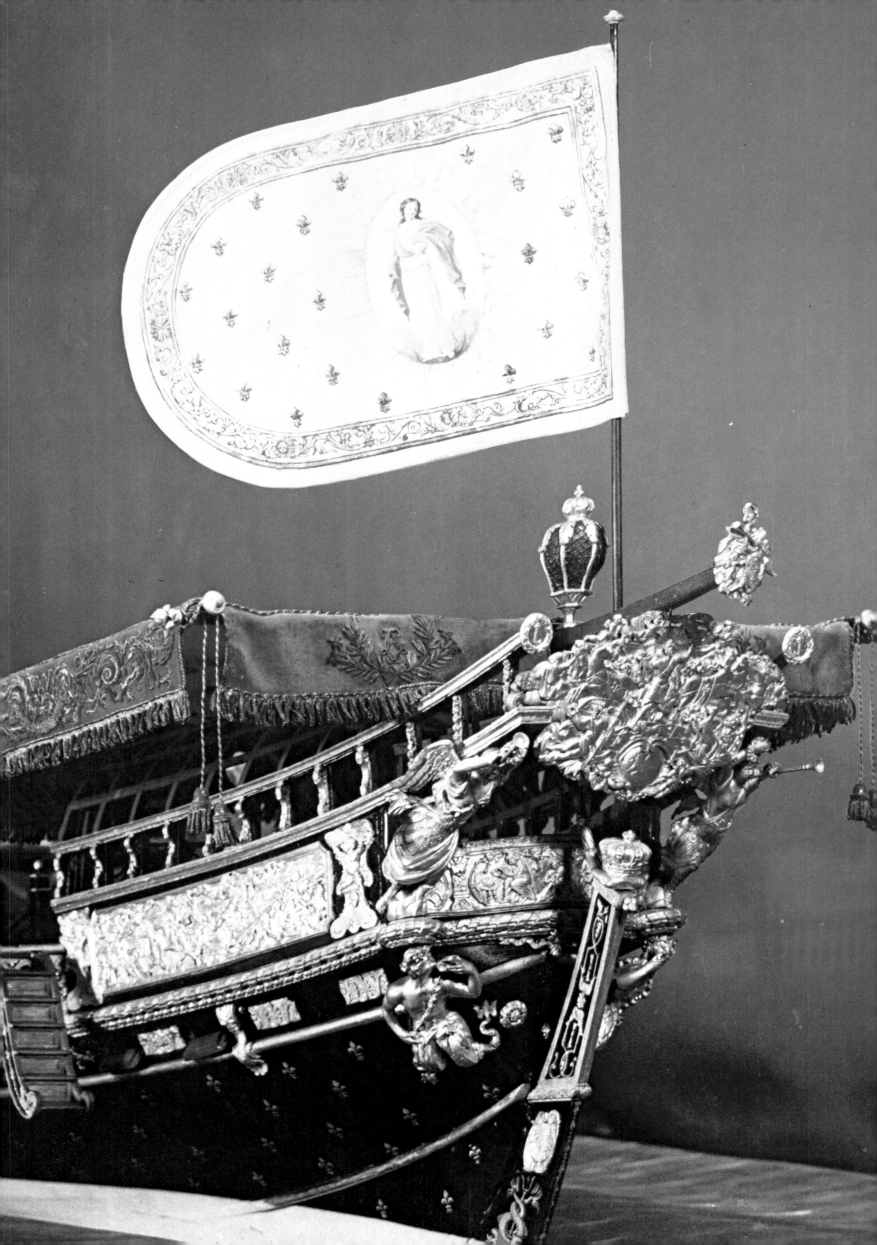

Galleys
and Galleasses

THE mere mention of a war-galley can conjure up visions of galley-slaves collapsing over their oars. Usually, of course, in antiquity the oars were manned by slaves and in later times either by criminals or by prisoners of war, when conditions were much the same. In favourable weather the shapely vessel could also travel swiftly under sail alone. Long, very long, lean and low in the water, with shallow draught, the galley was in a class by itself, changing little over the years in build and rig.

The galley was not robust, in fact, it was lightly built; but it was at home in the short choppy seas of the Mediterranean as it would never have been in the open Atlantic. From early in the fifteenth century onward, every state and country of any consequence in the Mediterranean basin, from Turkey to the Knights of St John, had its fleet of war-galleys, though decorated to varying degrees of magnificence.

The largest numbers of them were those of Venice and Spain, both of which could at one time muster a hundred. The Spanish galleys were based on Catagena, chiefly to protect shipping from the Turkish and Berber pirates. There,

the Spaniards had started manning their craft with infantry soldiers as oarsmen but quickly found the idea to be unworkable. Then convicts or other wrongdoers took their place on the benches and, it was reported, were 'treated like volunteers'. Judging from the later reputation of the Spanish galleys, the volunteer spirit does not appear to have been at all long-lived.

In the fifteenth century the oars were ranged in groups of three, with one man to each, until it was found to be more efficient and simpler to have several rowers on one oar, which was made much longer and heavier. By the seventeenth century, French galleys at least were equipped with as many as thirty-three pairs for five, six, or seven men pulling together on each bench. Usually the looms, or handles, of the oars had wooden cleats nailed to them in series of six or seven handgrips. Otherwise the wretched rowers had scanty consideration. They were chained to the bench, which was about ten feet long and four wide, and there they sat, perhaps all day long with one naked foot on the stretcher and the other raised and on the bench in front. On those benches, covered with sacking and stuffed with wool, men rowed, suffered and died.

One Frenchman, Jean Marteille de Bergerac, who had the misfortune to be sentenced in 1707 to his country's galleys, for the crime of being a Protestant, so he declares, wrote an account of his experiences. He describes how, when at sea, the master of the galleys was positioned aft beside

Left: The magnificent poop of the 17th-century French galley 'Réale'. MARINE MUSEUM, PARIS

Above: Venetian-style galley of the 16th century that served as a pattern for the Mediterranean powers of the time.
LA SPEZIA NAVAL MUSEUM (M. PUCCIARELLI)

the captain to hear his orders, while two under-officers were positioned one amidships and the other at the bows. All carried and used whips for flogging the entirely nude bodies of the rowers, who had to be kept alert for the sound of a whistle which gave them various orders to be obeyed at once.

The writer states that the men, including of course himself, had to row ten, twelve and even over twenty hours at a stretch. Any rowers who collapsed were given pieces of bread soaked in wine as a stimulant, but if all efforts failed to rouse them they were flogged and thrown overboard. He adds that the galley was not as fast as he expected and he estimated her speed as being no more than four-and-a-half knots, or rather less than five miles an hour.

Another French victim has given some additional details of his short but horrible time when chained to a bench. In his case, each oar had seven rowers. He was surprised to see the large number of men there were on board in such a remarkably small space and he mentions that few of the oarsmen had room to sleep at full length. Up forward were thirty sailors on a platform which he guessed to be about ten by eight feet. They were carried chiefly to fight off an enemy at the bows and to tend the two large lateen sails, which could give some respite to the rowers from their grinding labour at the oars.

At the other end of the vessel the captain and officers lived in a cabin on the poop, where their cramped state and general conditions were not so much better than those of the seamen. They had a canopy spread overhead to give some protection from sun and spray but it had to be taken in during spells of bad weather, when the continual fling of water on board brought misery to all.

The lengthening of the galleys' oars for handling by several rowers together made it necessary to have the benches turned slightly athwartships in order not to foul the innermost rower. At about the same time the vessel was encircled by a wooden outrigger which carried tholes, or pivots, for the oars to work on, giving more powerful leverage, and which would also help to ward off an attack. A much greater innovation however was the arrival of guns as the main weapon in place of the ferocious-looking ram-bow.

At first a gun of fairly large calibre was laid on a bed of well-filled sacks in the eyes of the vessel, in other words right forward, in the bows. Its weight rested on the end of the corsia, an upward extension of the galley's keel which, added primarily for strength, served also as a gangway along the full length of the vessel.

The gun was a great advantage, although it had limitations. It could not be trained either laterally or vertically, and otherwise only by aiming the galley itself at the target. Later on, it was joined by two smaller guns on each side of it in the bows, making a total of five chase guns, as they were called, all pointing forward.

The French had found that sentencing unwanted citizens to the galleys was an extremely handy and useful way of obtaining free labour, which perhaps explains why they finally owned one of the largest fleets in the Mediterranean and also why they continued to build galleys until 1720. Even England at one time experimented with ten of the type, but only to learn their shortcomings in the Channel and let them end their days in the role of tugs on the Thames.

In spite of all they achieved, galleys were really under a severe handicap in a fight. They could attack only end-on, whether with the earlier ram or the later gun, and owing to their length they were unable to manoeuvre quickly. To turn at all meant making a wide arc and, in the process, exposing their barely protected sides to the enemy.

In a set-piece fleet battle there would, of course, be no such problem, provided that the flanks of the fleet could be effectively covered, and galleys would line up side to side with each screening the next. And they had above all the precious facility of being largely independent of the wind, having both oars and sail.

Another handicap, one that was due to their crowded

state and the shortage of storage space on board, was that they were unable to stow any quantity of provisions which would allow them to keep the sea. Generally their cruises had to be of short duration.

It was perhaps thinking along these lines that set some early and unknown naval architect evolving a new idea. What was needed, he saw, was a big vessel which would have all the advantages of the galley and of the normal ship without any of the disadvantages of either. It would be fast, capable of being rowed by a large number of oarsmen, rigged to carry three large sails, able to turn and manoeuvre without fuss, two-decked and armed with guns along the sides.

This paragon of ships was given the name of galleass. She, or more probably a later version, was about 160 feet long in the hull, 130 feet on the keel, 30 feet in the beam and had a sternpost 20 feet high. Besides lateen sails, she had thirty banks of oars, each bank composed of two oars and every oar managed by six slaves who were in chains.

Five galleasses more or less answering to that description took part among the galleys in the battle of Lepanto in 1571 and they gave a good account of themselves. But nothing could give them the grace of line that distinguishes a good ship. The profile was low and, without sails set, the galleass looked a monstrosity, an unhappy compromise.

In 1588 it was a different story from that of Lepanto. The four galleasses that were prominent in the battle of the Armada fought bravely and well but apparently no one had foreseen what would be the effect of heavy gunshot on those

great splintering oars. The galleass was clearly not a success for a fleet battle, but in the hands of the Venetians it became a useful merchant ship.

Britain's Henry VIII had once had a galleass built on the Thames, but he soon had it completely rebuilt as a normal ship of war. He also at one time owned two war-galleys, the *Galley Subtle* and the *Galley Blanchard*. They had been captured from the French and with a touch of true economy they were kept manned by their own crews. The English captain who was first appointed to the *Subtle*, however, seems to have had language trouble and was replaced by a Spanish captain with a Venetian as patron, or sailing master, who were presumably linguists.

In 1638 a Spanish and a French fleet, each of fifteen galleys, met and fought close inshore at Genoa. It was a strangely transitional affair, with guns firing in prelude to a savage hand-to-hand fight between men in armour using muskets and pistols, swords and daggers. At the end, the French had captured three galleys and the Spaniards two but in reality it was practically a drawn battle, which was fitting enough, as it was the last great fight between Mediterranean galleys.

While they were slowly ending their days, galleys were finding fresh life farther afield. The Swedes, guided by Henrik af Chapman, and Russians were building numbers in the Baltic on the French model. With them they made furious forays, and the galley survived for another hundred years, although they were never really popular as fighting ships.

Facing page: Henrik af Chapman who led the Swedes in adopting French-style galleys. JOHN R. FREEMAN & CO

Top: The galley 'Réale' as engraved by Martier. M. PUCCIARELLI

Above: Martier's engraving of a bomb ketch with guns along the sides. M. PUCCIARELLI

Figureheads

THE origin of figureheads lies beyond history, but recent customs in some parts of the world and prehistoric carvings in others provide clues. The beginning was magical and later religious, as was head-hunting. Possession of a human head gave one power over the dead man's spirit and until very recently in some parts of Borneo rice fields were guarded from harm by the enslaved spirits of unfortunate enemies whose heads, impaled on posts, stood in the fields.

Rock carvings about 6,000 years old have been found in Nubia showing canoes with bulls' skulls on the sterns, evidently to give strength to the frail craft, as a bull was the ancient symbol of strength. In war, a victorious tribe returned with enemy heads on its spears and after a successful canoe raid the heads would be carried on the stems. Indeed, as late as 1718 Lieutenant Robert Maynard, RN, after defeating and killing the notorious and particularly bloodthirsty pirate Edward Teach (Blackbeard), returned to Bath Town, North Carolina, with Teach's head nailed to the bowsprit of his sloop, the *Ranger*. The head was then set up on a pole ashore as a warning to other pirates, just as the heads of malefactors were exposed at Temple Bar or on Old London Bridge.

Cretan ships of about 2000 BC had fish figures on the very high stem or sternpost (which end went first is debatable) and Egyptian river boats often had lotus-bud terminations at stem and stern; funeral barges had statues of the hunting god Horus; and fighting ships of 1190 BC had a lion's head on a prolongation of the keel which was used for ramming. The ships of their enemies at that time had birds' heads on both stem and sternpost.

Archaic Greek ships in drawings on pottery have stags' antlers on the bows, to give them swiftness, and Phoenician merchant ships were easily recognised by the horses' heads on their stems. Ancient ships of the Mediterranean world and the Far East, when they had no figurehead, had eyes painted on both sides of the bows so that the ship could see her way. Still found in many parts of the world today, they probably derive from the ancient Egyptian Sacred Eye of Ra which appears in tomb carvings of sea-going ships as early as 2700 BC.

Ships of classical Greece often had warriors' helmets as terminations of the stems, while others had animals or mythical figures. Roman merchantmen merely had carved and painted panels on each side of the stem, their main guardian at the stern being the cheniscus, the figure of a goose, thought to be particularly lucky for sailors for 'they swim on top of the water and sink not'. Roman war-galleys were elaborately provided with figureheads of bronze to reduce damage to the bows when ramming. In addition to the ram (often representing a fierce animal's head) there would be projecting swords or heads above it to protect the wooden stem. There was also a sacred bust or statue of the god or goddess into whose care the vessel was entrusted. The ships were topped by a carved or painted picture, sometimes carried on a pole, to identify the individual galley; a tree, a mountain, animal or any other suitable subject. The figureheads of ships taken in battle were often lodged in the temples dedicated to the gods who were credited with having bestowed the victory.

When a Greek ship entered port her figurehead was removed and taken ashore to salute the local deity, and there were special altars to stranger gods for sacrifices on behalf of the figureheads and their ships, wherever they came from.

Many centuries later, in Iceland, ships of the Viking period wishing to enter port had to take down their dragon or serpent heads lest they alarm the spirits of the place with

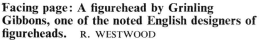

Facing page: A figurehead by Grinling Gibbons, one of the noted English designers of figureheads. R. WESTWOOD

Above: Ferocious-looking head from HMS 'Warrior', a 3rd Rate warship of 1781, now displayed in the Victory Museum, Portsmouth. R. WESTWOOD

Above right: Small Roman ship's figurehead decorated with a bronze bust of Ceres, the patron divinity of the ship which she adorned. M. PUCCIARELLI

Right: Carved rudderhead from a Danish ship of 1700. KRONBORG MUSEUM, DENMARK

their 'gaping heads and yawning snouts'. The reason is made clear by passages in the *Egissaga*, written in Iceland in the early thirteenth century but dealing with events of the mid-tenth century. The magic mentioned was being practised on land, but longships' heads were only a more permanent way of bringing curses and ill-fortune on the enemy. Briefly, an Icelandic chieftain fixed a horse's head on the top of a post and whichever way he turned it the guardian spirits of the land fled in terror and curses descended upon the country. Another instance dealt with a carving of a human head which, when set up on a post planted in the body of a sacrificed horse, was turned towards the enemy's home and brought bad luck to it. The connection with a horse strangely echoes the horse figureheads of ancient Phoenicia.

Norman ships carried on the Viking tradition but the heads shown in the Bayeux Tapestry seem intended to represent real as well as mythical beasts, including lions. It is curious how the lion recurs through thousands of years as a favourite subject for figureheads. In the Middle Ages, when a ship was prepared for war service her figurehead had to be removed to make way for the forward platform which, in time, became permanent as the forecastle. Then, when the forecastle became the carrack head, projecting far ahead of the stem, figureheads vanished and for a while were replaced by badges with coats of arms on the bows below the carrack head. However, that did not satisfy mariners, so a beak was added jutting well out in front of the forecastle and terminated by a small head, usually of an animal or reptile.

In Henry VIII's Navy only some carracks had those features, the others having a small head on the forecastle. It was not until the galleon reached perfection in Elizabeth's reign that the English began to mount figureheads at the end of the beakhead which had developed from the spur. Usually they had no connection with the ship's name and the queen's ships favoured the supporters of the Tudor Arms, the lion and the dragon of Wales. An exception was in the *White Bear*; when she was rebuilt in 1598 she was given Jupiter and his eagle. Very occasionally a tiger or a unicorn was used.

During the seventeenth and eighteenth centuries the lion was so generally used, in foreign as well as in English ships, that the figurehead – whatever its subject – was called the lion. Throughout the seventeenth century the main difference between English and Dutch lion figureheads was that the former were gilded and the latter were painted red. The French rarely used the lion, even when their ships were built in Holland. Their taste ran to classical mythology, such as Neptune with his seahorses, tritons, mermaids (French mermaids had two fish tails, one in place of each leg), or the reigning monarch. In the eighteenth century figures of Greek and Roman heroes were frequent, and the images of living royal personages were used for important ships. French figureheads were generally of higher aesthetic value than those of other nations, although in the late seventeenth century Grinling Gibbons did some superb work for the English Navy.

Spanish ships favoured lion heads until well into the

eighteenth century. Then they occasionally used royal portraits, and towards the end of the century there was an outburst of figures of saints, even the entire Holy Trinity for the four-decker *Santisima Trinidad* (1769-1805).

In England the lion was no longer used for the most important ships. Thus the *Prince Royal* (1610-1666), the finest ship of James I's fleet, had a mounted figure of St George riding down the dragon, and Charles I's masterpiece, the *Sovereign of the Seas* (1637-1696), had a mounted figure of King Edgar trampling seven kings. When the triumphant Cromwell had the *Naseby* (1655-1673) built he copied the *Sovereign of the Seas*' figurehead, but with great tactlessness had himself represented on horseback riding over the bodies of an Englishman, a Scotsman, an Irishman, a Frenchman, a Spaniard and a Dutchman, while the figure of Fame held a laurel wreath with the words 'God With Us'.

At the Restoration it was removed and hung from a gibbet, and then burnt on Coronation Day. Mr Pepys was annoyed because the new figure of Neptune cost £100 and he thought that people would soon have forgotten that the old one represented Cromwell and would have accepted it. The ship was renamed *Royal Charles*, but she was taken by the Dutch in their 1667 raid on the Medway and carried off to Holland, where relics of her are still preserved.

The Admiralty decreed in 1703 that all figureheads in future would be lions, but from the start the rule was broken for particular ships, so other subjects continued to be used, much as before. Even after the order was cancelled in 1727 the lion still remained the usual subject, including a period when Chinese lions were fashionable.

Owners of merchant ships with beakhead bows, similar to men-of-war, made an effort to provide suitable figureheads, but they were expensive and most of the smaller merchantmen had vertical stems anyway which were unsuited to the fitting of figureheads. Many of the smaller classes, both naval and merchant, with suitable bows, had fiddleheads and billetheads. They were curled terminations like a violin, the former turned inwards and the latter outwards from the ship.

Figureheads were occasionally gilded or painted entirely white, but were usually in natural colours. Unless the captain could afford to buy suitable paints, colours issued for other purposes might have had to be used. Lower-deck taste ran towards gaudy colour schemes, especially for female heads. The facial colouring was reputed to be inspired by the make-up worn by seaport prostitutes. One frigate captain was so ashamed of the way his men had painted the figurehead that he dug deeply into his own pocket and had it gilded, to the

Far left: Figurehead from the ship 'Supply' at Chatham on the River Medway. R. WESTWOOD

Centre: The patriotic figure of Brittania. R. WESTWOOD

Left: Well-preserved figure of 'Nymphe' at Chatham. R. WESTWOOD

great pride of all hands. Later, on the South American station, the men, bored by prolonged cruising, began to quarrel among themselves. Summoning them to the quarterdeck, the captain announced, 'Now, my lads, if this is not put an end to and hearty goodwill restored, by the Lord Harry I'll paint your figurehead black and put the ship into mourning!' That terrible threat ended the trouble.

Since figureheads were the personification of a ship, sailors lavished loving care upon them. Parts liable to damage, such as arms, were unshipped at sea, and to make repair easier they were never all in one piece.

The *Royal George* (1756-1782) had a mounted figure of George II and when, in 1778, the fleet had to retreat before a vastly superior Franco-Spanish force, a bosun's mate tied his hammock over its head, lest the figure see a British fleet retreating. At the Glorious First of June 1794, the *Brunswick*'s head, representing the Duke, had its hat shot away and a deputation came aft, under very heavy fire, and asked Captain Harvey (he was already twice wounded and would soon receive a third and mortal wound) to give them his cocked hat for the Duke. He did, and the carpenter nailed it to the figure's head. The ship's honour being thus saved, the deputation went back to their posts and sank their opponent, the *Vengeur*.

When the *Atlas*, launched in February 1782, was being masted for service it was found that the globe of the world the figure was supporting was too high and prevented the shipping of the bowsprit. The top was therefore sawn off and it was noticed that the American Colonies had gone. In March the Tory government fell and was replaced by a Whig administration composed of politicians sympathetic to the Americans, who ordered the British forces to stop fighting the colonists. By then the tide had turned and prospects of final victory were bright, but the new government made peace and granted independence to the future United States. Coincidences of that kind are not uncommon in the history of figureheads, and it all added to the mystique surrounding them.

One of the most curious figureheads borne by a ship of the Royal Navy was that of the 18-gun sloop-of-war *Termagant* (1796-1819), which had a double head with a woman on one side and a man on the other. The woman was equipped with a real broom and was belabouring the man, all painted in appropriate colours, including a bleeding nose. In its own way, it must have looked quite impressive, but it was unusual for such a small ship. In 1796 an attempt was made to abolish figureheads and replace them with scrolls. Because of unpopularity the order was never enforced; instead ships such as frigates and lower rates were permitted only busts and whole figures were reserved for ships of the line.

In France an attempt to abolish figureheads had been made in 1785 and an escutcheon with the fleur-de-lys was ordered, but figures crept back, and during the Revolution some very unusual ones appeared. The frigate *Carmagnole* (1793-1800) had a guillotine, and the *Ça Ira* (formerly *La Couronne*) of 1749-1795, when she took her new name, got a new figurehead – the lanterne of the Place de Grève from which many people were hanged during the Terror. Other renamed ships were given the busts of revolutionary leaders. The classicism fashionable under Napoleon brought back many figures from Greek and Roman history or mythology.

Pegasus was popular in clipper ship days, for the flying horse suggested the speed on which they prided themselves. Other clippers had portraits of the owner's family or of

characters from literature, oriental subjects, or heroes of the wars in India. The most famous merchant ship figurehead is the witch in Burns's *Tam o' Shanter*, carried by the *Cutty Sark* of 1869.

Figureheads lingered on in warships as long as their bows provided suitable mounts. Those of the first two iron-built ironclads, the *Warrior* of 1860 and *Black Prince* (1861-1923) were especially fine and still survive; but the advent of ram bows caused figureheads to be replaced by escutcheons and supporting decorations. Some were very elaborate, especially in German warships built in the 1880s and 1890s. The last battleships built for the British Navy to have such a decoration were of the Royal Sovereign class of 1891-92, but at the end of 1903 the two light battleships *Constitution* (1903-1915) and *Libertad* (1903-1920), which were building in England for Chile, were taken over and added to the Royal Navy as the *Triumph* and *Swiftsure*. They carried elaborate bow decorations to the end of their days.

The favourite Chilean escutcheon bore the Lone Star, while the National Arms, or other national symbols, were usual in various navies. The Chinese decoration was the dragon, and the Japanese used their national flower, the chrysanthemum, until far into the twentieth century. Most US sailing warships had billetheads but especially important ships were given figureheads. The three super-frigates, *Constitution* of 1797, *President* (1800-1817) and *United States* (1797-1866) had, respectively, Hercules, George Washington and the Goddess of Liberty. In 1807 the *Constitution*'s Hercules was replaced by Neptune, then in 1812 by a billethead, but in 1833 she received a portrait of President Andrew Jackson. Political opponents sawed it off one night and it was a year before it was replaced. Finally she returned to a billethead.

At the turn of the present century US midshipmen touched their caps every time they passed the figurehead of the Indian chief Tecumseh in the grounds of the Naval Academy at Annapolis. It had belonged to the 74-gun ship *Delaware* (1817-1861) and there was a tradition that midshipmen who did not salute it would fail in their examinations. The custom has long since died out and been forgotten by later generations of midshipmen.

American pre-dreadnought battleships had a decoration supporting a Stars and Stripes shield, but the *Massachusetts* (1893-1920) was presented by her name-state with a life-size bronze statue of Winged Victory with the inscription 'With Duty Done is Honour Won'. It was fixed to the fore turret, between the pair of 13-inch guns. In some navies the decorations were abolished and the stem left plain; instead there was an escutcheon on each side of the bow. The Germans were especially fond of that form and continued it for their major warships right through the days of Hitler's Navy.

Figureheads and escutcheons have long gone from the British Navy, yet the need for something personal to the ship remains. It was found, unofficially at first, in badges with an individual crest for each ship. They were carried on the gun tampions, but with the coming of missile armament they are now worn in a prominent place on board, accompanied by the ship's motto and scrolls with the battle honours of the name across the centuries. It is a naval version of the military custom of wearing each regiment's battle honours on its Colours, and a fitting conclusion to the long history of naval figureheads.

Similarly with some merchantmen, tradition, modified to suit modern conditions, lingers on. The common use of the soft-nosed bow since the Second World War has permitted owners frequently to repeat company insignia on bows and funnel, which can be a useful guide to the true owner of a ship whose funnel bears the colours of a charterer. Not all modern bow designs are company-orientated. For example, Orient liner motifs are inspired by individual ships' names and Ellerman Citys bear the escutcheon of the city after which each is named. Some, notably those on Fred Olsen ships' bows, are just attractive creations.

Left: The striking, immaculately painted figurehead of HMS 'Rodney'. R. WESTWOOD

Piracy

JUST as theft has always been a fact of life ashore, so has piracy always existed at sea. But as early as the seventh century BC, piracy in the Mediterranean and the Persian Gulf was becoming a recognised institution. Criminals, refugees, landless men and escaped slaves stole ships and formed colonies on the coasts to prey on shipping of all kinds. These maritime mafiosi were flourishing when Julius Caesar, at that time an arrogant young man, was captured in BC 78 during a voyage in a slow merchantman to Rhodes. He was well treated and was duly ransomed but, being Caesar, his first act when freed was to borrow four war-galleys and five hundred soldiers to turn the tables on his late hosts. He later fulfilled his firm promise to behead all the prisoners he took.

Early in the second century AD, the Emperor Trajan sailed into the Persian Gulf and dealt out retribution to the pirate fraternity there with fire and the sword. Then, in the fourth century, King Shapur of Persia came with the same intention, but with added savagery. Having captured a number of Arabs, he had holes pierced through their shoulders so that they could be strung together on ropes, thereby gaining himself the name of Lord of the Shoulders among Arab historians.

Piracy in the Mediterranean had its ups and downs until,

in 695, the Arabs flooded in from the east, bringing a new threat to shipping. But whatever the nationality and status of the pirate, he had a considerable advantage in plying his trade. At that date, when there was neither chart nor compass, the shipmaster would navigate chiefly by rule of thumb, hugging the coast and steering from headland to headland. The waiting corsair, lurking close inshore, could choose his moment to dash out and take his quarry by surprise, probably without much need for a chase.

The advent of the crusades, which produced a glut on the slave-market through the hordes of prisoners, had a depressing effect on the economy of the pirates. It was a century and a half before the slave-trading piracy came back to the foreground with the dhows of Algiers, Tunis and Barbary. Those were the days when hawk-like men in flowing robes sailed their outlandish craft up the English Channel to snatch a cargo of comely girls from villages on the Cornish coast, or even from the banks of the Thames.

Northern Europe, France and the countries of the British Isles had their fair share of piracy, but off the north coast of Germany it was particularly rife. The pirates' outrages on shipping became so alarming that German merchants in a number of settlements, from Bruges to Novgorod, banded

Left: A painting by Peter Wood of a Barbary corsair attacking a Dutch ship in the 17th century.

Above: An engraving of German trading ships of the Hanseatic League. MARY EVANS PICTURE LIBRARY

Overleaf: George Chambers' painting which depicts the bombardment of Algiers by Admiral Pellew in 1816 that virtually destroyed the hold of the Barbary pirates.
NATIONAL MARITIME MUSEUM, LONDON (GREENWICH HOSPITAL COLLECTION)

together early in the twelfth century to form a loose federation for mutual protection and benefit which was eventually called the Hanseatic League, or Hansa for short. The League developed into a close corporation, with Cologne at the head, although the important city of Lübeck was refused entry until nearly a century later.

The Hanseatic League's early days were full of hazard. Much mercantile traffic sailed to and fro in the Baltic from France, Holland, Norway and England, and though the Viking age was on the wane, there was still the likelihood of encountering marauding Danes or Swedes.

By 1390 Tunisian pirates had become such a menace to

shipping that Genoa recruited 'a great number of lords, knights and gentlemen of France and England' under command of Henry of Gloucester with English longbowmen, to wipe them out. After besieging the pirates in a fortress on the Tunis shore for a month, disease drove the attackers to come to terms.

Just a century later, the flood of Moors who had been driven from Spain by Ferdinand and Isabella took to the sea and, before long, the Spanish coast became a hunting-ground for pirates and slave-traders. However, the exploits of mere raiders such as these were overshadowed by the exploits of the Greek renegade Barbarossa. Having adopted Mohammedanism, he made his home in Tunisia, and rapidly made himself famous by capturing two war-galleys owned by the Pope, which were laden with very valuable cargoes.

Ferdinand of Spain, horrified by such deeds, made attack after attack on the coastal towns of Barbary and its shipping. In the end, however, all his forces were driven out except for those in the fort at the entrance to Algiers, who controlled the shipping in the harbour. Barbarossa launched a ferocious assault on the fort, preceded by two weeks of heavy gunfire. The survivors of the garrison surrendered, and Barbarossa, (a notoriously cruel man), watched while the wounded

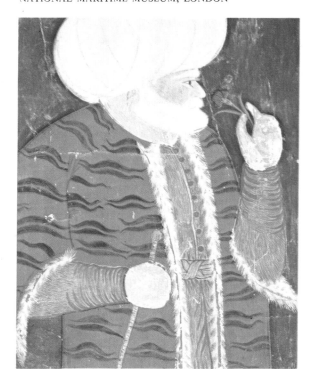

Below: A portrait by Nigari of Barbarossa, the pirate and naval commander.
M. PUCCIARELLI

Right: An engraving of the execution in Hamburg in 1402 of the famous pirate Stoertebeck and his 70 accomplices.
MARY EVANS PICTURE LIBRARY

Below right: The 'Kingfisher' engaging Barbary pirates in 1681 from a painting by W. van de Velde the Younger.
NATIONAL MARITIME MUSEUM, LONDON

governor of the fort was put to death for his stubborn defence. The fort was destroyed by Barbarossa's orders, and work was begun on the great mole of Algiers, which took thousands of Christian slaves two years to build and is still in existence. Two weeks after the fort had been destroyed, nine Spanish ships bringing troops, and unaware of the change in fortunes, sailed towards Algiers. Their crews were puzzling over the ruins of the fort, when they found themselves surrounded by the corsairs' galleys. They were captured and provided a total of 3,000 to swell the slave market.

In 1534 Barbarossa led sixty-one galleys through the Strait of Messina, stripped the harbour clear of all the ships there and took them away with the inevitable number of Christian slaves. He seems to have had a special feud with the Knights of Malta and, when he captured a vessel twice the size of his own in one fight, he was rowed triumphantly back to Algiers with the Knights as his galley-slaves.

A surprisingly high number of European renegades distinguished themselves as pirate leaders. For example, in 1588 thirty-five Algerian galleys had as their captains eleven Turks and no fewer than twenty-four Europeans. Two Englishmen at least are known by name: Sir Francis Verney of Buckinghamshire, and a naval deserter known simply as Ward. Between 1569 and 1616, these vessels captured a total of 466 British ships and sold their crews into slavery.

The daring of the Barbary pirates continued to grow. As many as thirty of their ships were used in abducting people from the shores of the Atlantic coast, and merchant vessels were captured in the English Channel. The inhabitants of south-west England were so nervous that they had the light at the Lizard put out in case it attracted the attention of pirates. Oliver Cromwell was the first Briton to take really decisive action. He sent the redoubtable Captain Blake with a fleet to deal with the Barbary Coast. In 1655 Blake took his fleet into the Bay of Tunis in two squadrons and, finding the pirate leader, the dey, beyond reasonable negotiation, opened fire in response to cannonading from the shore.

In a short time the harbour forts were in ruin, the guns dismounted and the moles cleared of men. When the fire from

the batteries had died away, boats were driven through the cannon-smoke directly at the corsairs' ships. After brief hand-to-hand fights on their decks, they were set on fire and destroyed. The next day Blake sailed to Algiers and collected all the British slaves for passage home.

Several other punitive squadrons of various navies sailed to the Barbary coast during the next twenty years, but without much lasting effect, until 1671 when Sir Edward Spragge burnt the Algerian fleet in Bougie harbour. In consequence a mob seized and decapitated the Chief Officer, and displayed his head to signify that they wanted peace. France, which had been in some kind of alliance with the Moors until late in the seventeenth century, now adopted a hostile attitude with some surprising results.

In 1683, a squadron sent to discipline Algiers under the command of the Marquis Duquesne, fired 6,000 shells into the town and port. It is estimated that 8,000 people were killed, and many buildings were destroyed. The Algerians rose in protest, assassinated the dey, and elected the Captain of the Galleys in his place. The new dey sent word to the French that if the bombardment was not stopped at once, he would blow every Frenchman in Algiers from his big mortars.

The shelling went on, and the dey chose for his first hostage the Vicar Apostolic, a much-loved priest. He was taken to the mole, lashed to the mouth of a mortar and shot towards the French fleet: but the French carried on firing until their ammunition was finished. Meanwhile, twenty other Frenchmen were blown from mortars or guns. At this time, a young United States entered the arena, but it was only in 1803, after years of paying tribute in arms and cash to the pirates, that a force under Commodore Edward Peeble, led to the surrender of the slave-traders. A strict blockade was maintained for two years, but then Tripoli drifted back into its old ways.

In 1820 the French sent a large fleet with an army of 37,000 troops to sort out the situation once and for all. They landed and steadily fought their way into Algiers. The dey was sent off to Naples in a frigate, and soon Tunis was taken in hand. The Barbary coast had finally been tamed.

Ships' Castles

THE Arabian Fleet, locked in a long-drawn-out war with the Greeks of Constantinople in the eighth century, had two main classes of fighting-ships. Their historian tells of the difference between those that were 'castellated' and the others that were not, meaning the castellated ones had battlemented little castles or castle-like contrivances fitted half-way up the masts. He describes them as having been in the nature of wooden boxes from which large stones or arrows could be thrown or shot at enemy ships, or, in a form of attack not unlike some aspects of modern warfare, as a vantage point for the flinging of 'white naphtha' down-wind at the enemy.

The historian goes on to give an illuminating, if somewhat highly coloured, picture of the Moslem fleets: 'Their ships regularly sailed in the Mediterranean and pounced upon the Christians as a lion seizes his prey. The whole sea was full of Moslem ships, whilst the Christians could no longer float a plank on it.'

Below: A model of a late-16th-century warship which shows a stage in the development of permanent castles.
ROYAL SCOTTISH MUSEUM, EDINBURGH

The use of some form of fort, strongpoint or castle on board ship was an adaptation of a very old idea, much older than is generally thought, and it came early to Europe. Even in the latter days of the Vikings, the larger vessels had a fighting platform at the bows. The use of the ship's castle that succeeded it was widespread in English waters in the activities of the Cinque Ports during the four centuries after the Norman Conquest.

When the Confederation of the Cinque Ports had taken shape as the defender of the south-east coast – the keeper of the gateway of England, so to speak – the individual ports undertook in return for their special privileges equally special obligations. The so-called Barons of the Ports undertook to furnish the king once a year, whenever called upon, with twenty ships for a period of fifteen days and with a crew of twenty-one men in each vessel. In order to fulfil that duty, the 'Portsmen' usually had to take ships and their crews off their normal occupation of fishing and coastal trading.

If the ships were needed to swell the king's fleet in time of war, as was likely to be the case, they would have to be suitably equipped for immediate service by their owners. At first, temporary fighting platforms were added to the bows and the stern for the use of the knights and men-at-arms who might be taken on board. Then a round or square fighting-top, originally made of wickerwork and then of wood, was secured to the mast, though not half-way up in the old Arabian style but at the masthead.

The evidence of ships in civic seals is generally apt to be a little suspect in matters of detail, since the artist, faced with the problem of fitting the length of a vessel into a circular frame, was apparently inclined to express his feelings by indulging his fancy (as some marine artists are tempted to do today). Nonetheless, a number of English seals of the thirteenth century concur in representing both the fore- and after-castles as square boxes. They are often elaborately carved and painted, without roofing or covering, and are raised high above the level of the deck with their inboard sides supported by stout posts.

After the vessel had completed her term of duty, such additions were removed before she returned to peacetime work. But as time went on, they were enlarged and improved until, when the ship was in use, they became prominent features. From giving the impression of large boxes open to the sky, they were roofed over, probably with coloured fabrics, giving a greater decorative effect in tune with the rich array of the banners and pennons of nobles and knights.

At last the castles became too unwieldy to be carried on board and fitted into place in sockets, so they ended by being built in as a permanent part of the ship. This was probably felt to be a welcome move by the Portsmen, who were carrying on a sanguinary and seemingly endless feud with the men of Yarmouth. Not content with that, they, with Dutch, Irish and Gascon allies, once fought a private battle against Normans, Frenchmen and Genoese at a pre-arranged meeting-place in the Channel.

In the later period, the forecastle was heightened in order

38

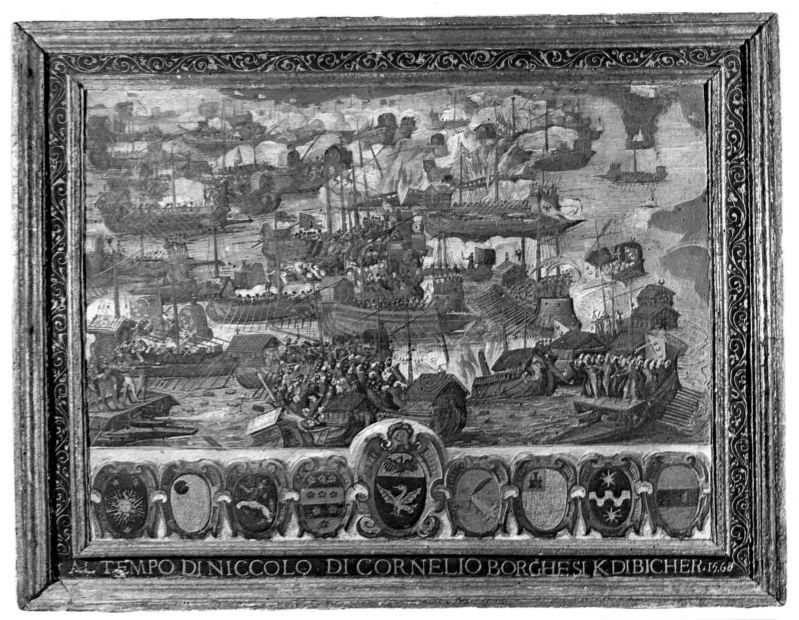

AL TEMPO DI NICCOLO DI CORNELIO BORGHESI K DI BICHER. 15.68

Left: In this model of a
Mediterranean merchant ship of the
16th century the forecastle overlapping
the bows is characteristic of the carrack.
NATIONAL MARITIME MUSEUM, HAIFA

Above: A 16th-century painting of
vessels with castles, rams, guns and
fighting men on platforms, from the
State Archives of Siena.
M. PUCCIARELLI

Right: An old idea – castle and access
ladder amidships in a Roman warship.
MARINE MUSEUM, LISBON

to achieve a good level for hand-to-hand fighting and it was perpetuated in the modern name of foc's'le. The after-castle at the stern, the summer castle as it used to be known, was also made higher, though not to the same extent. It had begun to prove its value for cabins and cabin-space. The fighting-top, on the mast, had also developed a dual purpose, as a crow's-nest for the look-out in time of peace and for the dropping of missiles or for pouring down hot pitch or Greek fire when the ship was in action.

Ship's castles were obviously familiar both in northern European waters and in the Mediterranean. In some cases, the practice of shipping and unshipping them into and out of sockets on the decks still lingered. There is an incomplete report, lacking the date as well as an explanation, that tells of a large number of vessels from Normandy which, disguised as peaceful wine-ships, sailed into the Gironde on the Biscay coast of France. There, in the mouth of the river, they mounted their fore- and after-castles, manned their tops and sailed out to raid and ravish.

The time came when ship's castles lost their usefulness in the great outbursts of building larger and larger ships. Decks were raised even higher and higher until, in a matter of only a few years, the era of multi-decks and triple masts had arrived. Then the castles were found a fresh purpose in the role of gun turrets, with the muzzles of a few small cannon peeping out of their sides. But that is another story.

Ships of Old China

Top: Colourful carvel-built Foochow junk, a sea-going trading vessel which showed little European influence in its design and remained virtually unchanged for 500 years. SCIENCE MUSEUM, LONDON

Above: Model of a Chinese trading junk in the Science Museum, London. D. J. KINGSTON

IF there be one thing in the world that this extraordinary craft is not at all like, that thing is a ship of any kind. So narrow, so long, so grotesque, so low in the middle, so high at each end . . . with mats for sails, great warped cigars for masts . . . As for the Chinese lounging on deck, the most extravagant imagination would never suppose them to be mariners'.

So wrote Charles Dickens of the junk *Keying*, brought to the Thames in 1848. Dickens's patronising description illustrates the confident assumption of superiority that characterised European attitudes to all things oriental at the time. Later study and further knowledge taught Europeans that far from being backward in nautical matters and water transport, the Chinese were, in fact, pioneers. They were using the rudder, including excellently proportioned balanced types, paddle-wheels, watertight bulkheads, simple types of compass, fore-and-aft rigs, tankers, and free-flooding compartments of the hull to reduce pounding or to keep fish fresh, long before the West. Moreover, their inland waterways and great river navigations were linked into a system that extended from Canton to where the Yellow River crosses the 40th parallel – about fifteen degrees of latitude – as long ago as the third century BC. That vast system of inland transport boasted pound locks around AD 1000, several hundreds of years before they were common in Britain.

The imperial control of the successive dynasties in China conceived all transport – land, waterway and sea – as an integrated system; it was a highly organised communication system which did much to ensure the continuity of political and cultural tradition. The efficient transport system had a powerful motive other than political expediency and that was the easier collection of the imperial grain tax (tribute rice) and other levies. The continuity of tradition in a largely illiterate population resulted in an evolution of ships and craft which was gentle, a slow refinement based on trial and error. But, through the millenia, special adaptation to local purpose and local weather or navigational conditions produced an amazing variety of ships and craft, all collectively dubbed junks or sampans.

Britain is fortunate in possessing, in the Science Museum, London, a unique collection of models of twenty-seven types of Chinese vessels. One of them, a remarkable crooked-stern junk of the upper Yangtze, spent the Second World War concealed from the Japanese buried in a crate in the garden of the Customs Reference Library and eventually came to Britain by troopship. The whole collection is mainly the work of several outstanding experts on Chinese shipping, notably Sir Frederick Maze, for many years head of the remarkable Chinese Maritime Customs organisation, after whom the collection is named; Mr G. R. G. Worcester, who spent a lifetime in the River Inspectorate of the Maritime Customs and made a detailed study of sea and inland waterway craft of all kinds; and Lt-Cdr D. Waters. Other models have been donated from private sources.

Chinese ship and boat building shows how Chinese ideas of structure are almost instinctively based on the incredible bamboo, the plant so intimately connected with almost every aspect of Chinese life. The largest species can grow to almost 100ft in height and be almost a foot in diameter. At intervals, the bamboo has transverse bulkheads, called septa. It is exceedingly light and strong and has a thousand uses. Not surprisingly, Chinese ship and craft builders copied the structure deriving its strength from cylindrical form reinforced at intervals by bulkheads. So they achieved a hull form resembling that of a curved half-section of bamboo. Indeed, in the Ma-yang-tzu, a river junk of the upper Yangtze which may be from about 30ft up to more than 100ft in length, the very marked tumble-home makes a hull which has an elliptical section, giving the immense strength necessary for the turbulent waters it navigates.

In Chinese hulls, then, the backbone of keel, stempost and sternpost as we know it in western shipbuilding is absent. Instead, strength comes from stout carvel planking, often interspersed with wales running the whole length of the ship, fastened to very strong bulkheads, which are frequently made watertight. Just as the wales increase longitudinal strength, frames between the bulkheads are added to reinforce the hull. The ends are closed off, in most types, by transoms which are well above the waterline by reason of the very marked sheer. In some types of craft the forward transom is analogous to the western swim-bow, as in the Thames barge. In some sampans the after swim is often overhung by a superstructure built on after extensions of the side members of the hull. Sampan is a word meaning three planks, a significant philological pointer to the simple origins of the ubiquitous little craft of that name.

In the larger junks, the overhanging superstructures at bow and stern give what, to western eyes, is an ungainly appearance, and which for long centuries diverted western attention from the superior underwater form of Chinese hulls. Westerners thought that a hull should be shaped like a fish – broader forward and slimmer aft; and so it was until the famous schooner *America* in the late nineteenth century made sailing men think again. The theory, of course, ignores the fact that a fish is totally submerged whereas a sailing ship meets a different set of hydrodynamic conditions at the surface. Chinese shipbuilders as long ago as the thirteenth century knew that the greatest hull fullness, the master

couple, should be aft of midships of the waterline profile, just like aquatic birds, as they pointed out.

Junks and sampans had their origins in the bamboo rafts used on rivers and at sea. Taiwan (Formosa) developed quite a sophisticated sailing type having a hull with sheer and some hollowness athwartships. Thor Heyerdahl found that the raft *Kon-Tiki* could be made to go to windward by suitable use of multiple daggerboards, a fact which was already known in the East; leeboards and centreboards were used by many types of river craft in China. References to leeboards occur as early as the eighth century, nearly a thousand years before they were used in Europe, first by the Portuguese and then by the Dutch.

A typical Chinese sampan belonging to a fishing family in Hong Kong. R. ADSHEAD

China pioneered big decked ocean-going sailing vessels. In 1291, when the biggest European vessel was the open longship, Marco Polo described a passage from China to Persia in a junk so big that there were 600 other passengers, along with a crew of 250. He also described the watertight bulkhead, a device that gave the Orient tankships for the sea transport of fresh water and oils centuries ago, but which was not adopted in the West until the nineteenth century. Appropriately enough, the first steamer with watertight bulkheads, the *Nemesis*, was built in China in 1840.

Big seagoing junks for both trading and naval purposes had been specialised into a wide variety of types by the fifth and sixth centuries. There is good evidence that Chinese traders had reached the Red Sea, Aden and even parts of the eastern African coast by that time and there are literary references to big battleships of the sixth century, with five decks and carrying archers. About two hundred years later naval vessels were classified in varieties of about six or seven categories ranging from big battleships to small assault craft. It is worth mentioning, in passing, that Chinese ideas of naval warfare have favoured fighting with projectiles – arrows, crossbow bolts and, a little later, a kind of mortar bomb – from the earliest times, whereas in the West sea

battles continued to be hand-to-hand melées until medieval times.

Junks continued to develop in size between the ninth and twelfth centuries. The biggest of the eighth century were around 600 tons, undoubtedly the world's biggest ships at the time. Size increased up to the fifteenth century when the great Ming Navy yards at Nanking were turning out the biggest ever built. Those gigantic junks were the treasure ships of the Ming Navy which consisted of thousands of all kinds of vessels. The big treasure ships had displacements calculated to have been 3,000 tons and more! They were over 400ft long, had nine masts and were crewed by over 1,000 men. The scale of Ming Navy thinking is perhaps indicated in that ships with only eight masts were reckoned as lower category, or Second-Rates as the West might term them.

That ships of such great size existed was confirmed in 1962 by the finding of a rudder-post on the site of one of the old Ming shipyards in Nanking. It measured 36ft long and the position of the point where the top of the blade was obviously fitted showed that the blade alone was nearly 18ft high. Experts calculated that the ship for which such a rudder was intended must have been between 480ft and 536ft long, depending on whether she was of shallow or deep draught.

Marco Polo's descriptions of the great junk in which he sailed from China to Persia have been dismissed as fanciful but there is not the slightest reason to doubt them. They are confirmed by the writings of the Arab traveller, Ibn Battuta (1304-78), who sailed in a big junk in 1350. He describes a vessel with innumerable cabins for travellers, crews of six hundred men plus about four hundred armed men (marines) and sailors, with their families on board, growing vegetables and herbs in tubs. He writes with obvious amazement at the great ship's five decks and twelve sails, the flotilla of smaller but nevertheless quite sizeable vessels which attended it as tenders and supporting supply ships.

Above: Junk in full sail off Hong Kong. R. ADSHEAD

Below: A Chinese junk of the type used chiefly for trade and suitable for sailing in the open sea.
MARY-EVANS PICTURE LIBRARY

Literary sources make it clear that long voyages of several months were not exceptional even as early as the eighth century. By the fourteenth and fifteenth centuries, Chinese trading junks were making regular voyages to destinations well down the eastern African coast, north as far as Kamchatka and east to Java, with conjectural landings on the Australian coast. It is also thought that they probably rounded the Cape from east to west into the Atlantic before Europeans rounded it from the opposite direction. Their ships were certainly capable of crossing the Atlantic or Pacific but lacked any commercial incentive to do so. Europe had nothing that China particularly wanted, whereas the wealth of the Orient had been a magnet to European merchants since ancient times. For them a sea route, cutting out the middlemen on the land caravan routes, was a great attraction.

Moreover, just when European ships were beginning to discover the world, the seagoing junks were quite suddenly almost completely swept from the seas by one of the most curious events in Chinese history, a deliberate abandonment of seapower by the Ming dynasty in 1435. By 1500 it was illegal even to build a junk with more than two masts for seagoing purposes. It all derived from an odd Confucius-inspired semi-mystical agrarian philosophy which regarded sea-borne trade as an unnecessary and even sinful extravagance and junk and navy building as reckless squandering of money and effort. Before dismissing that as a bit of cranky Chinese fanaticism, let us recollect twentieth-century ecological problems; conservationist thinking is not so far from Confucian and our ships of the future will be obliged to take account of the world energy crisis.

Gradually, over the centuries, China's sea-borne trade was restored and shipbuilding again flourished but China never regained her pre-eminence as a sea power and junks were never so big again as they had been in the great days of the Ming dynasty. The Yuan Mongol dynasty which followed encouraged sea-borne trade and Chinese shipping continued to develop, with certain modifications resulting from contact with Portuguese and, later, Dutch and English shipping.

The result was the slimmer finer-lined lorcha, a European-inspired hull form with modified Chinese stem and stern, but still with the characteristic junk rig – the balanced lugsail.

The junk rig will sail a boat four points (forty-five degrees) to the wind but how close to that a junk could get in making good a course depended on the skill of the sailing master, the *laodah*. The continuous battening of the Chinese lugsail kept it much flatter and increased its aerodynamic efficiency. Those Europeans who had experience of junks and junk rig, from John Meares in 1788 to Joshua Slocum in 1888 and Lt-Col Hasler in 1960, were enthusiastic about its efficiency and handiness – the 'most convenient boat rig in the whole world' according to Slocum.

The great Ming ships apart, the biggest seagoing junks had up to five masts, not all of them stepped on the ship's centreline, and each having a balanced lugsail. (A few exceptional types, such as the little Chusan fishing junk, had spritsails.) The leach of the sail was connected to a multiple sheet system at each batten and a parrel-like rope held each batten to the mast. Taking in sail was simply a matter of dropping it. The battens ensured that the sail fell in folds and the double topping lifts contained the lot. Matting was used for sails until canvas was imported from the West.

The masts had no shrouds but were immensely thick and stepped in massive fastenings. The 750-ton *Keying*, which was 160ft long, had a mainmast of solid teak ninety-five feet high and three feet in diameter at the base. Her mainsail weighed nine tons and took thirty men, using a capstan, two hours to hoist.

Seagoing junks lowered their rudders when in deep water; *Keying*'s was lowered twelve feet below the bottom of the ship and needed fifteen men with luffing tackle on the control cables. Those deep rudders were probably intended to help the keel-less hull when going to windward (leeboards were often used in river and canal craft).

The northern five-masted Shantung junk was an example of one with extra offset foremast and a similar extra mizen, both stepped well to port. In the attractive little Amoy fishing junk, a three-masted type, the single mizen was stepped well to starboard. The reasons are lost in antiquity but reasons there were, distilled from centuries of practical experience. Lugsails tended to be peaked in junks used at sea or in open inland waters, such as the wide Yangtze. However, where navigation was more confined the sails were taller and more square cut.

China's vast system of canals and navigable rivers kept tens of thousands of craft employed, bewildering in their diversity and ranging from the exotic pleasure boats of the Mandarins, the floating hotels and flower boats of the courtesans to the astonishing crooked-bow and crooked-stern junks of the upper Yangtze. The great harbours had virtual floating cities of sampan dwellers and on the canals and rivers everything was transported in all kinds of specially adapted craft. There were even articulated junks, which could be divided in the middle to cope with the navigational difficulties of the Grand Canal. By far the most amazing example of adaptation to special purpose are the crooked-bow and crooked-stern junks which were used in the great salt trade of the upper Yangtze and Kunthang rivers, where navigation is made terrifying by fast currents and great rapids.

Powerful, instantaneous and precise steering control is vital to survival and great steering sweeps are used. The larger, as long as the junks themselves, up to a hundred feet, is mounted on the deliberately twisted stern where it is on the centreline of the hull. The asymmetric hull form produced by the twisted stern is said to give the steering control necessary when riding rapids. A second and smaller sweep, up to fifty feet long, is also mounted on the stern but in such a way that neither sweep interferes with the other at any point of use. The crooked-bow type is used to bring the salt down a river west of the Kwanthan which westerners would dismiss as unnavigable. The twisted bow is said by the watermen to deflect the racing current in just the right way when the boats are being tracked upstream. The twist in the hulls is achieved by fire and steam after building.

The other great propulsion device of Chinese vessels, even more remarkable than the battened lugsail, is the *yulloh*, whose principle is an astonishing refinement of sculling over the stern. It produces the same results as a self-feathering and reversible screw propeller, and has been in use in China for more than two thousand years. It takes the form of a great stern sweep, curved at both blade and loom ends and fastened to the deck with a short length of rope. Children, sampan girls and almost any Chinese person who messes about in boats, uses it with ease. Eight-man teams, four on the oar and four on the rope, can drive quite big junks on the Yangtze at speeds up to four knots. The wandering Ibn Battuta declares that fifteen-man *yulloh* teams moved even the big Ming junks – incredible but not to be dismissed as impossible. No other country is so full of amazing examples of the achievements of human muscle power.

Perhaps the overall lesson of Chinese maritime history lies in the demonstration of human strength and of the unbelievably subtle technical artefacts which even a largely illiterate population was able to develop from the simplest of materials when the pace of life gave technology almost as much time for refinement and adaptation as biological evolution. Chinese technical history is a continuous and unified process. Ships, chariots, roads, canals, bridges, rivers, lakes and the sea were different aspects and products of the unified conception of practical life. The tracker toiling in the Yangtze gorges was the same human engine as the sailor heaving at the capstans of Ming junks. Nothing was too big for them to tackle, too difficult to solve. And if proof is needed, their amazing maritime history provides it.

Rounding the Cape

PRINCE Henry the Navigator stands alone in the annals of the sea. No other man could claim to have been responsible, directly or indirectly, for the discovery of half the world in a single century. That is Henry's unique distinction.

Born of an English mother – the daughter of John of Gaunt, with the King of Portugal as his father – he won his spurs at the age of twenty fighting against the Moors at the siege of Ceuta in 1415. In 1419 he was made governor of the Algarve and later resided at the town of Sagres, near Cape St Vincent, where he studied navigation. While his brother Pedro toured Europe for nautical books and charts, he gathered round him a number of would-be explorers, teaching and advising them, and filling them with enthusiasm.

The time was ripe and the prospect bright for voyages of discovery. Portugal was in a rare interlude of peace at a time when Prince Henry and his companions could handle improved navigational instruments and new charts at their leisure. Below them they might see against the blue of the Atlantic the pictured sails of the latest type of light caravel – square-sterned, seaworthy and capable of sailing within five points of the compass, fit surely for long voyaging.

Those were the exciting days when the old-style cartographer would fill blank areas on his chart with pictures of ferocious beasts that never were on sea or land. He might lure the explorer with fish-tailed beauties and some such statement as, 'Here be mermaydens which some do call syrens'. Then there was the magic Island of the Seven Cities to find, somewhere out in the Atlantic, and the lone isle of Antilia, though the hunt for the latter was to go on for centuries.

Prince Henry must have felt the excitement but he had no intention himself of leaving his quiet Sagres for the open sea, although he nursed an ambition to make contact with the semi-mythical Prester John, the Christian ruler among the African mountains. The Prince appears to have thought it his duty to remain on shore, developing his religious and commercial plans while encouraging and financing fresh expeditions. He spent the greater part of his life studying the possibilities of the uncharted world and of overseeing the creation of new trade routes. It was under his direction that the lost Azores were rediscovered, but still more promising was the rounding of the Moroccan Cape Bojador in 1434. The first cargo of West African slaves and gold reached Portugal in 1441 and from then on his captains worked their way farther down the West African coast, bringing back more unhappy slaves to develop the barren soil of the southern province of Alga.

Then, in 1461, came the tragedy of Prince Henry's death. By one year he had missed the triumph of hearing the report of a Portuguese ship sailing into the Gulf of Guinea. An interval of some years was followed by the successful voyage of one Diego Cam, who found the mouth of the Congo River and set up a pillar to mark his progress. He made a second voyage along the coast, setting up another pillar and collecting more negroes for slavery on the way. In all, he explored 1,450 miles of West African coastline.

Bartolomeu Diaz was next on the scene. In 1487 he sailed from Lisbon with two ships in an attempt to find Prester John. The currents inshore proved so troublesome, however,

that he stood well out to sea and sailed far to the southward. Looking in vain for land, he altered course and steered eastward, perhaps wondering what grim mystery might lie ahead. Without knowing it he had achieved fame for all time by doubling the Cape of Good Hope, the first European to do so. His crews were growing mutinous, however, after their exertions, so he was forced to turn for home.

The currents that had beset him on his outward voyage gave him little difficulty and he had a fair wind for much of the way, except while rounding the Cape. He named it the Cape of Storms but his king later renamed it to give a hint of welcome.

Following in the wake of Diaz went Vasco da Gama. He was a mariner of much experience who had also fought as a soldier. Born in 1460 of an aristocratic family, he is described by a contemporary as being 'very disdainful, ready to anger and very rash'. He had equipped himself for an ambitious voyage to discover a sea route to India with all the latest information in books and charts and with the best navigational instruments, while, of the four ships he took, two had been specially built for the voyage. Diaz had given him much sound advice from his own experience, which, rather surprisingly, da Gama took. He was recommended to build square-rigged vessels of broad beam and light draught instead

record of the homeward voyage, which took three months. With the outward passage, more than 24,000 nautical miles had been covered.

At Lisbon da Gama was greeted as the triumphant hero, the creator of new greatness and wealth-to-be for Portugal. King Manuel ennobled him and ordered the holding of great fêtes in all the principal cities in his honour.

In order to take early advantage of da Gama's achievement, a fleet of thirteen ships was made ready to sail to India. It was commanded by Pedros Alvarez Cabral, a navigator born in 1467, with a distinguished record. His fleet sailed from Lisbon in 1499, the year after da Gama returned.

of caravels, which had insufficient space for stores. Diaz also advised an offshore route to avoid calms and fierce local storms.

As a result, da Gama took the new *São Raphael* and *São Gabriel* with a small vessel and a big storeship. On a July day in 1497 all officers and crews attended a religious ceremony in the presence of the king and his court immediately before they set sail from the Tagus to prepare for the coming perils. The weather was fine and remained fine, although there was a sad lack of wind. Thomas Stevens, an Englishman on board the flagship, who wrote a good letter, described how 'sometime the ship standeth still sometime she goeth but in such order that it was almost as good to stand still'.

However, at last, she and her consorts arrived at the Cape, doubled it without mishap, and followed the coast northward. At Mossel Bay, near Georgetown, the natives entertained the ships' companies with music and dancing 'in the style of negroes'. Sailing on, they passed the last pillar Diaz had set up and reached Melinda, North of Zanzibar, where da Gama had the good fortune to obtain from some Moorish merchants an Indian pilot, who brought his ships to Calicut. There, he was not welcomed, largely owing to some more Moorish merchants who forcibly resented any competition and stirred up the natives. Da Gama himself was caught by Indians and had to fight his way out of imprisonment and out of the harbour. He decided to return to Portugal.

He had to discard his smallest vessel at Mozambique as his crews, depleted by illness and accident, were not enough to man the ships even though the storeship had been scuttled, having outlived her usefulness. Otherwise there is little to

Left: Prince Henry the Navigator – detail from the St Vincent Panels in the Portuguese Museum of Ancient Arts, Lisbon.
M. PUCCIARELLI

Top: The 'São Gabriel', one of Vasco da Gama's ships of the 1490s.
MARINE MUSEUM, LISBON

Above right: A portrait of Vasco da Gama by Lopez painted in 1524.
M. PUCCIARELLI

Right: The Cape of Good Hope: engraved by Mortier in 1700, more than 200 years after Bartolomeu Diaz first doubled the Cape.
M. PUCCIARELLI

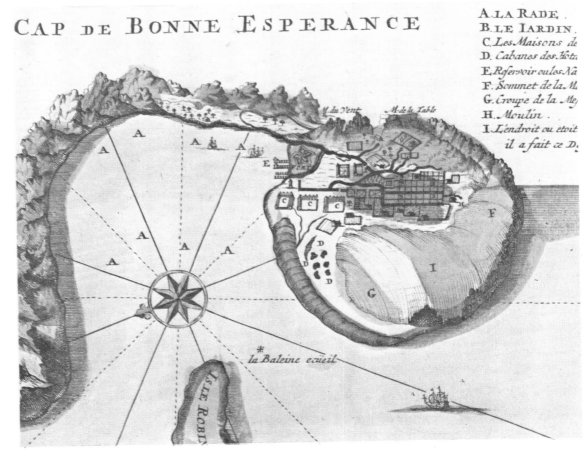

and he had taken possession in his sovereign's name. Cabral, in blissful ignorance, also took possession in his king's name.

From Brazil he started off again for India, but on a voyage that was dogged by misfortune. One of his ships came to grief near the Cape Verde Islands, four others were sunk by storms in the South Atlantic and one went hopelessly astray. To add to the list, a crew mutinied and as a result the ship and her rich cargo were lost. With the remaining six ships of his fleet, Cabral managed to arrive at Calicut, where he built a factory, with another at Cochin, to the south. He left a sufficient staff and sailed away. Almost at once the natives rose and massacred every person he had left behind.

When the news reached the king, he at once ordered a fleet to be fitted out to take punitive action and appointed Cabral to take command. Da Gama, however, intervened and begged for the command, so that he could avenge his own personal insults. In consequence, he sailed off with a fleet of twenty ships to Calicut and bombarded the town immediately on arrival. He did not deal gently with the townsfolk.

On his return to Lisbon with his vessels laden with gold and rich treasures, for the second time he was given a hero's welcome by the king and created 'Admiral of the Ships for

Right: Portrait of Pedro Alvarez Cabral from Sousa Macedo's 'Retratos e Elogios' in the Academy of Sciences Library, Lisbon.
M. PUCCIARELLI

Below: A model of a lateen-sailed caravel, from the time of Emanuel I, that would have been familiar to da Gama.
MARINE MUSEUM, LISBON

PEDRO ALVA RES CABRAL,
SENHOR DE BELMONTE,
ALCAIDE MÓR D' AZURARA,
DESCOBRIDOR DO BRAZIL,

For some reason he led his ships too far to the south-west. He might perhaps have been anxious to avoid the calms of the Gulf of Guinea or to carry out instructions from King Manuel. The king might have wanted to make sure that the newly-born sea route via the Cape did not run foul of the Treaty of Tordesilla, which, in 1494, had laid down the respective spheres of Portugal and Spain under the aegis of the Pope. Whatever the reason, there was no mistaking the fact that one morning the look-outs sighted the crest of a most intrusive mountain where no mountain should be. Cabral by accident had discovered Brazil. Actually he was not the first European discoverer, although he did not know it. In the previous year a Spaniard, Vicente Yañez Pinzon, a companion of Columbus, had happened upon the country

Ever'. But great as his achievements were, his reputation is marred, even in the violence current at the time, by stories that were quite horrific; tales of Portuguese women being flogged through the streets of Calicut watched by the Indians, of tortures with boiling oil and worse.

As for the unfortunate Cabral, the run of ill luck that had latterly clouded his successes remained with him to the end. In 1520, while on a voyage in the North Atlantic, his ship was overwhelmed in a storm and sank with all hands.

But the fact remains: da Gama, Cabral, Prince Henry the Navigator and Bartolomeu Diaz, four men widely different, between them opened up the world for the generations to come.

Columbus
and Magellan

CHRISTOPHER Columbus had lived with a vision and a dream. He had spent long hours studying charts and aids to navigation and, in the face of all denials, he knew that the world was round. Assuredly, he would explain, if a ship sailed far enough to the westward she would arrive in Cathay or Cipangu, China or Japan; wonders and riches were there, as Marco Polo had told all those years ago.

Columbus, born in Genoa, had first gone to sea as a boy and his voyaging had taken him to Iceland, England, the Guinea Coast and the Aegean Islands. He had fought and captured a Venetian galley and he had made his name known.

For more than ten years he tried to interest people in his plans for a voyage of discovery, in one European country after another. After he had been refused by the Senate of Genoa, he had approached John II of Portugal, Ferdinand and Isabella of Spain, Henry VII of England and lastly Charles of France; but all in vain. Then, suddenly, Queen Isabella changed her mind and sent for him. Though his pockets were empty, the terms he proposed were hardly modest. He stipulated that he should be provided with three ships, that he should have the rank of admiral and be made viceroy of all he discovered. Also he was to have one-tenth of the proceeds of the expedition.

He was at first refused but, so infectious was his enthusiasm, that he was granted all he asked for, including the three ships. The largest, the *Santa Maria* (though herself only about 75 feet in length and 25 feet in beam) was a three-masted ship – known as a *não* – which could set four square sails and a lateen mizen. The other two, the *Pinta* and *Nina*, were of a type which had originated in Portugal and were used for fishing or coastal trading; they were sturdy little craft originally lateen-rigged on their three masts, perhaps taking their name of caravel from the carvel style of build. Columbus had no great opinion of his ships. He declared that they were old and rotten, 'pierced with worm-holes like a beehive'.

The main trouble, however, was in finding enough men to sail them. Even crooks could not be tempted by good money. To many a mind the voyage was plain madness. Who could guess what horrors might lurk in those unknown seas?

Top: Christopher Columbus; a painting attributed to Ghirlandaio, and now in the Naval Museum at Genova-Pegli.
M. PUCCIARELLI

Above: A portrait of Ferdinand Magellan which now hangs in the Uffizi Gallery in Florence. M. PUCCIARELLI

Yet in the end, by one means or another, crews were collected; fifty officers and men for the *Santa Maria*, thirty for the *Pinta* which had been re-rigged with square sails before the start of the voyage, and twenty-four for the *Nina*. One August morning in 1492, the little squadron hoisted sail in the Andalusian port of Palos de la Frontera and got under way for the great venture. They did not get far that month. Three days out, the *Pinta* lost her rudder and they had to put in to Tenerife to refit her. Columbus seized the opportunity also to change the rig of the *Nina* to enable her to set square sails on her masts instead of the lateens.

There were no further mishaps after they had started off again, trying to keep to the latitude of the Canaries, twenty-eight degrees north, but there was repeated and growing trouble among the motley crews. They were weary of seeing, day after day, for sixty-nine days, nothing all round the ships but empty sea and sky. Suddenly, almost unbelieving, a man sighted land. Land! Land! Land it was, but not Cathay, only an island. Actually they had come upon one of the Bahamas.

Columbus, obsessed with the thought of China and Japan, though marvelling at the tropical plant-life and the bright scenery, led his ships to explore from island to island and on to Cuba. He finished at Haiti where his poor old *Santa Maria* went aground and was wrecked. Columbus named it La Isla Española – the Spanish Island – later corrupted to Hispaniola. He made the best of the situation by building a fort from the wreckage and garrisoning it with forty men who had to be left behind while he sailed back to Spain, to drop anchor eventually at Seville.

Fascinated by all that Columbus had brought with him, from parrots and strange plants to copper-skinned natives, King Ferdinand conferred on him the status of a grandee of Spain and furnished a whole fleet for a second voyage. That time, Columbus went as the admiral in command of seventeen ships, including two carracks and many caravels. He discovered and explored a large number of islands, from Dominica to Jamaica, in the attempt to locate China and he once landed on the mainland of South America.

He tried again on a third voyage, when his efforts nearly

wore him out. He seemed unable to control his men and was evidently a far better navigator than an administrator. In his sick state, he sent home a ship with a cargo of natives for slaves, and a dispatch for Queen Isabella, who sent out Commissioner Francisco de Bobadilla to report on him. Bobadilla promptly clapped him in irons and shipped him home in disgrace, but Isabella, not the most soft-hearted of queens, released him from his captivity and restored him to favour. He made one further voyage, but the heart had gone out of him and he returned to Spain only a shadow of the great Columbus.

It was twenty-seven years after Columbus discovered the New World that another navigator set sail on a famous voyage of exploration. Ferdinand Magellan, a Portuguese of knightly stock who had spent seven active years in India and the East Indies, had planned to circumnavigate the globe. He hoped to sail southward and westward to find some kind of channel that would take him from the Atlantic into the South Sea to find the Spice Islands (south of the Philippines). From there he intended to return home round the Cape of Good Hope.

Magellan, who appears to have been quick tempered, had a dispute with the Portuguese King John II, and had at once gone to Spain and had taken Spanish nationality. In 1519 he had shared in the command of ships which had been sent to discover the Spice Islands but had failed. The new enterprise had a far more ambitious aim, but one that was fully underwritten by money-lenders and grandees alike. The main problem was manning, as it had been with Columbus. Five ships were to form his fleet, ranging in size from the flagship *Trinidad* of 100 tons to the *Santiago* of only seventy-five tons. Their crews had to be made up with men of more than a dozen different nationalities, including Orientals and negroes. In all, with officers, they numbered 239 souls.

After a stormy passage, Magellan made a landfall north of Rio de Janeiro and he followed the coast southward slowly, keeping a good look-out for any opening to the west. He found not a channel but an anchorage on the coast of Patagonia which he named Puerto San Julian. There he set up a court of summary justice to deal with a mutiny, which had its origin soon after the ships had sailed from Spain. Trouble had started between Magellan and his second in command, Juan del Catagena, captain of the *San Antonio*; as the voyage progressed del Catagena's discourtesy turned to disobedience and finally to open mutiny. It then transpired that he was the ringleader of three mutinous captains. He found that Magellan was not the man to treat such behaviour lightly; after a session in the hold in irons,

with a number of mutineers, he and another culprit were marooned and a third executed.

Magellan spent five months in San Julian where he overhauled his ships, careening them onto their sides to 'bream', or burn, the marine growths from their bottoms. By then, he had lost two of the caravels, one wrecked without loss of life and the other worn out and unserviceable. With the remaining three ships in good trim, he carried on southward and rounding a cape, which he named the Cape of 11,000 Virgins, he sighted a bay widening out before him. Though he was not to know it for many an anxious day to come, he had found his strait, his gateway to Cathay.

But that strait was three hundred and ten miles in length – three hundred and ten tortuous miles of sudden fierce squalls and storms, of hidden shoals, of racing tides and false channels. For Magellan's ships, it meant literally hundreds of tacks and reversals of course; and his wretched crews were weak from starvation and the onset of scurvy. Only an immense determination and superlative skill drove him on to win through. One of his trusted men, Gomez, the pilot of the big *San Antonio*, could not stand the strain. He incited a mutiny on board, vanished from the strait and took the ship back to Seville, where he was promptly gaoled.

Magellan, who was not, strictly, the first to circumnavigate the world, was killed at Mactan in the Philippines in 1521, before he could complete the voyage. It was one of his captains, Juan Sebastian del Cano, of the *Vittoria*, who brought home the eighteen men, all that were left of the 239 who had sailed from Seville three years before. But the triumph can never be taken from Magellan, one of the greatest navigators of all time.

Top left: A map of the Straits of Magellan from a book by Antonio Pigafetta, Magellan's Italian secretary.
M. PUCCIARELLI

Top centre: Also from Pigafetta's book, a map of islands (now part of the Marianas) where natives stole a longboat from Magellan and which were nicknamed the Island of Thieves.
M. PUCCIARELLI

Top right: Pigafetta's map of the island Mactan, where Magellan was killed by natives. M. PUCCIARELLI

Facing page: A model of Columbus's 'Santa Maria', now in the Naval Museum at Genova-Pigli. M. PUCCIARELLI

Following spread: A flamboyant painting depicting ships built during the reign of Portugal's Emanuel I, around the first quarter of the 16th century. M. PUCCIARELLI

Quest for the North-East Passage

ON 10 May 1553, the day three ships left Radcliffe Dock, Stepney, there was great excitement on the banks of London's river. As the vessels passed Greenwich, where young King Edward VI lay dying, 'courtiers came running out and the common people flocked together, standing very thick upon the shore . . .' To quote Richard Hakluyt, chronicler of English voyages of exploration, 'it was a very triumph in all respects to the beholders'.

For some, though, the departure of the ships for unknown and uncharted seas meant more than just another romantic river spectacle. For several years, demand for woollen cloth – England's chief export – had been declining, and the need to find new markets becoming more and more important. England's merchants were also growing impatient of the monopoly that the Hanseatic League of German merchanst enjoyed in northern Europe, a monopoly which bound the

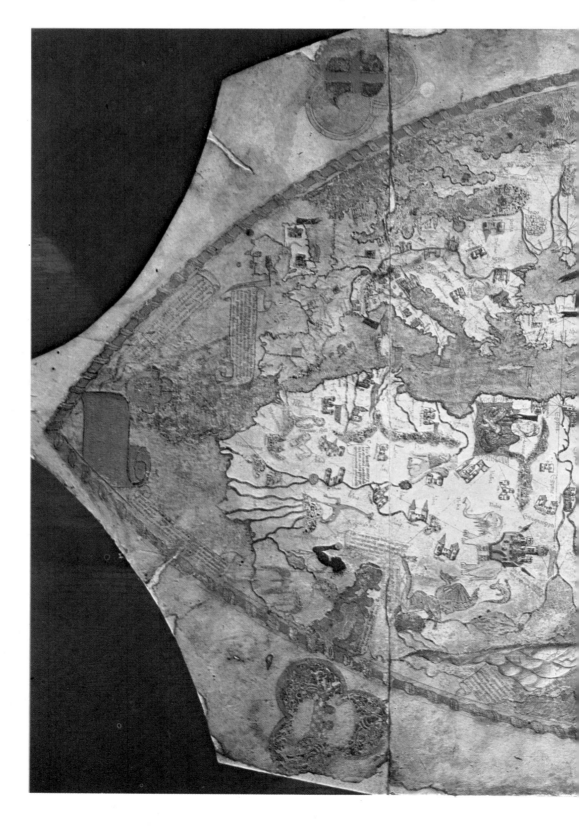

A 16th-century Genoese map, rich in decorative motifs and faithful in detail to the Mediterranean, which shows the contemporary impression of the expanse of Asia and the vastness of Russia. Maps such as this were well-known to Richard Chancellor and his companions, and to Richard Hakluyt the English geographer and chronicler of voyages in 'The Principall Navigations, Voiages and Discoveries of the English Nation' and 'Divers Voyages Touching the Discoverie of America' which give fascinating accounts of the voyages, privations and discoveries of the great English navigators and adventurers of the times.
M. PUCCIARELLI

English to trade only through Hansa agents.

Those facts were among the inspirations behind the audacious spirit which first stirred in the 1550s, and later exploded in that blaze of maritime enterprise characterised by the exploits of John Hawkins, Francis Drake, John Davis, Martin Frobisher and others. An older inspiration was the lure of the supposedly treasure-laden East. Ever since the thirteenth century, when Marco Polo had so temptingly described them, European imagination had been titillated by the gold-roofed cities of Cipangu (Japan) and the spices of Cathay (China).

In trying to reach that eastern Eldorado, Columbus, sailing westwards in the service of Spain, had stumbled on America, while the Portuguese were pioneering a route to the East round the coast of Africa. Excluded by the Iberian monopoly from the obvious routes, north Europeans began to seek the East through a North-West Passage along the north coast of America. Only when that eluded them did attention focus in the opposite direction, on a route along the Arctic coast of Asia. It was to find a North-East Passage, as well as to establish in the colder countries along the way new markets for English cloth, that a Merchant Venturers company was formed in 1552. The sum of £6,000 was raised to equip a fleet, and the company appointed Sir Hugh Willoughby to lead the expedition. By a unanimous vote, Bristol-born Richard Chancellor was picked as pilot-general.

Little is known about Chancellor and even less about Willoughby, a tall, well-born gentleman who might have fought in King Henry VIII's Scottish wars. Of the two, the merchants thought more of Chancellor, whom they regarded as 'a man of great estimation . . . in whom alone great hope for the performance of this business rested'. Such confidence was well founded. Sebastian Cabot, governor of the company, had seen Chancellor's capabilities on a voyage to the Levant, and John Dee, another driving force behind the expedition, knew of his skill in tackling problems of navigation and in improving navigational instruments.

The vessel *Bona Esperanza* (120 tons) was given to Willoughby and Chancellor was put in command of *Edward Bonaventure* (160 tons). The captain of the 90-ton *Bona Confidentia* was Cornelius Durfoorth. In all, 108 men and eleven merchants went with the ships, which carried provisions for eighteen months.

The preparations went ahead in a mood of high confidence,

for the merchants never seriously doubted that the expedition would reach Cathay. That view was apparently shared by the authorities, for King Edward provided letters addressed, grandiosely, to the 'Kings, Princes and other Potentates inhabiting the north-east parts of the world toward the mighty Empire of Cathay'. Such optimism derived from the gross inaccuracy which characterised geographical knowledge at that time. There was a widespread belief in the theories that the northern coast of Asia sloped steadily south-eastwards from the North Cape to China, and that somewhere in the Arctic ice lay a channel of temperate water through which ships could pass unhindered. To prepare for what was envisaged as a voyage through near-tropical seas, the bottoms of the ships were sheathed in lead. Sheathing was a precaution common in Spain, used to thwart the marine worms which thrived in the tropics and could bore through the toughest wood.

One person who had a different view was Sir Henry Sidney, father of Sir Philip, and patron of Richard Chancellor. Loath to part with his protégé, he told the merchants, 'How many perils for your sakes ... Chancellor is now to run ... He shall seek strange and unknown kingdoms ... commit his safety to barbarous and cruel people ... hazard his life among the monstrous and terrible beasts of the sea ...'

Such dangers were doubtless in the minds of those seamen who wept to see familiar shores slip from sight on the day the ships cleared Orford Ness and struck north-eastwards for Norway. Sighting the Norwegian coast at latitude 66°, the ships turned north and sailed towards the Lofoten Islands. There, Willoughby, Chancellor and Durfoorth agreed that, should a storm scatter the fleet, each was to make his way independently to Vardö. It was a prophetic arrangement. Hours later, a violent storm blew up. As the tiny ships were tossed about on heavy seas, Willoughby bellowed to Chancellor to keep close. Almost in the same moment, Willoughby's *Bona Esperanza* began to draw away and, with *Bona Confidentia*, disappeared from sight in the poor visibility.

Chancellor, left alone, steered *Edward Bonaventure* on a difficult course to Vardö, which he reached safely to find that nothing was known of the other two ships. For an anxious week, Chancellor waited in Vardö, little knowing that Willoughby and Durfoorth were hundreds of miles away, having been blown past the North Cape towards Novaya Zemlya. Without Chancellor, they were utterly lost. For weeks, they scoured the inhospitable coastline but, as Willoughby plaintively put it, 'the land lay not as the Globe made mention', and Vardö eluded him. It was, by then, early September, and with winter fast approaching, Willoughby gave up the search and anchored on the east Lapland coast near the mouth of the Arzina River. There, he decided to spend the winter.

By that time Chancellor was well on his way towards a totally unexpected adventure. Despairing of a rendezvous with Willoughby, Chancellor had left Vardö to sail north-eastwards across 'a huge and mighty sea' in the last of the perpetual sunlight the Arctic summer had to offer. Then, turning south, he entered a great bay called, as he learned from some fishermen, the Bay of St Nicholas. He had sailed into the White Sea, and late in August anchored at the mouth of Dvina River, in a remote corner of the land then ruled by the Czar who became known to history as Ivan the Terrible.

Chancellor and his crew had arrived in a country which many Englishmen believed implicitly to be inhabited by barbarians and cannibals, whose behaviour had hardly improved since the days of their savage Tartar ancestors. Even the venturesome Chancellor was extremely wary when, on 2 September, he went ashore at the point where Archangel now stands. His suspicions deepened when, despite initial friendliness, the Russians refused to trade or do more than send a message to Czar Ivan about the English ship's arrival. For days, the authorities demurred while Chancellor grew more and more impatient at the delay. Finally, after forcing the Russians to give him sledges and guides, he set out to travel the 1,500 snow-covered miles to Moscow. He was not many days out, however, before he met the Czar's messengers, who were speeding northwards with Ivan's express command to bring the visitors to the Russian capital immediately.

The sanction of their Czar was what the Russians had been waiting for. Their attitude changed completely, and they began to fight among themselves to be of service to the Englishmen, who arrived in Moscow to find a welcome hardly less overwhelming. Chancellor was summoned into Ivan's presence, to find the Czar seated in splendour, wearing a 'long garment of beaten gold, an imperial crown upon his head, a staff of crystal and gold in his right hand ...'

Chancellor presented to Ivan King Edward's letters requesting 'free passage, help and trade for these our servants' and two hours later received a singular mark of honour for so complete a stranger – Ivan's invitation to dinner. It was there that the Englishman saw the pomp of the Russian court in full display, as a hundred and forty servants in gold livery waited on two hundred richly robed nobles. As he ate roast swan off solid gold plates and drank wine from a massive gold cup, Chancellor also observed that, however uncouth his nobles seemed, the Czar himself was no barbarian. It was on Ivan's qualities of statesmanship and intelligence that Chancellor worked during the long winter he passed at the Kremlin.

Chancellor's arrival had been fortuitous, for he had come at a time when Ivan was anxious to extend contacts with the West, and it was only the influence of Western civilisation, he felt, that could help raise his country from its depths of barbarity and backwardness. When Chancellor left Moscow in February 1554, he carried with him letters from the Czar requesting King Edward to send a member of his council to conclude a formal trade agreement. However, unknown to Chancellor, King Edward VI had been dead for seven months, and England was now ruled by his half-sister, Queen Mary. Also unknown to Chancellor was the fate of Willoughby and his companions who, with their ships imprisoned in the ice, had frozen to death in the fearsome Arctic cold by January 1554.

Although he had failed to find the North-East Passage to Cathay, the news Chancellor brought home to London in the late summer of 1554 aroused considerable excitement. His discovery of the new direct and potentially fruitful Russian market more than compensated the merchants for

Above left: An engraving after a contemporary portrait of Ivan the Terrible by N. Ntkin in the 'Book of Titles'.
RUSSIAN STATE ARCHIVES

Above: Portrayal by A. Litochenko of Ivan the Terrible showing his treasures to a visiting English ambassador; a scene that might have been experienced by Chancellor at the Czar's court.
NOVOSTI PRESS AGENCY

their thwarted dreams of Eastern treasure. The Merchant Venturers reformed as the Muscovy Company, and were granted a monopoly of the Russian trade by Queen Mary and her Spanish husband Philip. Quickly, a second fleet was organised and equipped and, on 1 May 1555, Chancellor sailed with two ships, *Edward Bonaventure* and *Philip and Mary*, taking with him a cargo of sugar and cloth as well as two Muscovy Company agents.

Chancellor's brief for the voyage included orders to find Willoughby, as well as to 'learn by all ways and means possible how men may pass from Russia either by land or sea to Cathay . . .' The merchants doubtless hoped that Willoughby had already found his way there, for a two-year silence like his was not unusual in that age of slow communications. However, such hope did not long survive the arrival of *Edward Bonaventure* and *Philip and Mary* in Vardö, for by the summer of 1555, Russian fishermen had already found Willoughby's ships locked in the ice, their ill-clad emaciated crews dead and decomposed.

Leaving her companion ship at Vardö, *Edward Bonaventure* sailed alone to the Dvina River, where Chancellor and a trading party disembarked to make their way to Vologda, 550 miles from Moscow. After seventeen days at Vologda, where they warehoused their goods, Chancellor, George Killingworth and three others continued to Moscow, which they reached on 4 October. Six days later, when the Englishmen presented to him their letters from Mary and Philip, there was no doubt that Czar Ivan was immensely pleased to see them. As Killingworth later wrote, 'His Grace did ask how our Queen's Grace did, calling her cousin, saying he was glad we were come in health to his realm . . . And we went one by one unto him, and took him by the hand, and

then his Grace did bid us go in health and come to dinner . . .'

At a banquet as dazzling as the one Chancellor had attended in 1553, the Englishmen sat in the place of honour, in the centre of the hall, and though warned by some Italians to beware whom they trusted, they soon found that Russian friendliness was no façade. On 20 November they concluded a trading agreement with the Czar which granted English merchants free use of Russian ports, free trade within the country, and freedom to be ruled by their own laws. Three trading centres were to be set up – at Colmogro, Vologda and Moscow – and Ivan even guaranteed reparations should any English ship engaged in the Russian trade be set upon and robbed by pirates.

While those negotiations were going on, *Edward Bonaventure* and *Philip and Mary* had sailed back to England, taking with them the bodies of Willoughby and his companions. Within hours of their arrival, in early November 1555, grisly versions of the Lapland tragedy were current in London. The merchants of the Muscovy Company were, however, too hard-headed to pay attention to tales of the weird attitudes in which Willoughby and his men had been found frozen, and within five months, had organised and equipped a third fleet. On 23 April 1556, *Edward Bonaventure* and *Philip and Mary* sailed from Radcliffe Dock, carrying extra crews to man Willoughby's ships. Accompanying them was the tiny ten-man pinnace *Serchthrift*. While *Philip and Mary* sailed to Lapland to recover Willoughby's ships, the other vessels headed for the White Sea where, in early June, they parted. To the thunder of farewell salvoes, *Serchthrift* set off alone to follow instructions to find the still-elusive passage to Cathay.

On 20 July, Chancellor left Moscow accompanied by Osep Nepea, the Czar's ambassador, and his suite of sixteen attendants. Together, they travelled towards the Dvina River, where *Edward Bonaventure* had anchored to await them. When the ship had been loaded with a cargo of train oil, tallow, furs, felt and yarn, she set sail for England accompanied by *Bona Esperanza* and *Bona Confidentia* and their new crews, and also by *Philip and Mary*. However, as they skirted the coast of Norway, the four ships ran into a raging storm which only *Edward Bonaventure* managed to ride out. *Bona Confidentia* was shattered to pieces on the rocky coast, and the other ships were driven ashore at Trondheim. *Philip and Mary* survived to reach London, but *Bona Esperanza* disappeared and was never seen again.

Four months passed before Chancellor was able to struggle within sight of home, but even when, in mid-November 1556, he arrived off Pitsligo Bay, it was to meet violent winds and heavy seas which dragged his ship towards the rocks. Ground tackles were laid, but the cables snapped. With a hideous smashing of timbers, *Edward Bonaventure* disintegrated on the rocky shore. As she did so, Chancellor made a desperate effort to save the Russian ambassador. He launched a small boat, and with Nepea and his suite aboard, tried to row for the shore. But the craft capsized and Chancellor, together with seven Russians, was thrown into the swirling waters to drown.

Ambassador Nepea was saved by some Scots, who looted the wrecked ship and held the Russian prisoner for about four months. When he was eventually released, and entered London on 26 March 1557, he was the first Russian ambassador to be seen there. The trade he came to cement lasted for more than thirty years, to the immense profit of English merchants, who had to wait far longer to reap similar riches in Cathay.

The Magellan Strait

THE southernmost reaches of America are bleak regions of desolation and death where the elements are engaged in a desperate struggle. The tortured land, thrown up by the internal fire and by the crumpling of the earth's crust, is carved by the gales and blizzards of the Howling Fifties, by ice and glaciers and by the relentless swell and tides of the Southern Ocean which invade it through countless fjords and channels.

Barren islands to windward of the Magellan Strait, sombre and lifeless forests in the middle reaches, and rocks, bogs and tussock grass to the east discourage land travel while currents, eddies, fog, sleet and williwaws are nightmares to the mariner. Even the albatross, the penguins, the skuas and the sea-lions find it a difficult place, yet a few Indian tribes had been living there for ages unknown, eking out a wretched and primitive existence. Those desolate lands and windswept waters were to prove just as mean and inhospitable to European seamen.

In 1494 the Treaty of Tordesillas shared the world between Portugal and Spain. Everything to the west of 46° 37′ W was Spanish; all lands to the east were Portuguese. For Spain, it was a matter of reaching the Spice Islands by the western route, and Columbus had not solved that problem. Ferdinand Magellan, a Portuguese navigator snubbed by his king, was to be Spain's instrument of discovery. He knew some Portuguese secrets which hinted at a passage south of America into the South Sea – the maps of Behaim and of Schoner, and the reconnaissance journey of João de Lisboa in 1514. There was also the voyage in 1515 of the Spaniard Juan Diaz de Solis, who spoke of a strait.

Magellan set sail from San Lucar on 20 September 1519, as captain-general of 265 men and five ships for his voyage that would lead to his discovery of the Strait of Patagonia (the name Magellan Strait only came into use in 1534), and his death in the Philippines.

In 1525, Garcia de Loaysa and del Cano went on another expedition to the Moluccas by way of the strait. Whereas Magellan was favoured by the weather when he navigated his strait, the real character of the place was only revealed on the later voyage. They traversed it, but met a bad end at their destination and a relief expedition was sent out in 1527 under Alvaro de Saavedra; he inaugurated the safer Spanish route to the East – following the trade winds to Mexico, thence overland to the Pacific and following the trades to the Orient. The overland route was seen to be the obvious way after several other expeditions got mauled in or near the strait.

In 1540, Don Alonso de Camargo reached Peru from Spain by the strait, also at a high cost in ships and men; overland by the Panama Isthmus was the better way to and from Peru. So it happened that the Magellan Strait was almost forgotten by the Spaniards when Valparaiso was sacked by pirates who came out of the blue in 1578.

On 15 September 1577, Francis Drake made sail for a pretended voyage to Alexandria, but his real aim was to sail through the strait and to plunder the fat Spanish possessions on the Pacific. There were many parallels with Magellan's journey, with his discovery of what came to be named Cape Horn.

Taken by surprise, the incensed Spaniards, unaware of Drake Strait (the Cape Horn route), decided that the Magel-

lan Strait needed fortifying to prevent further raids. Pedro Sarmiento de Gambóa was sent with two ships from Peru to assess the military and colonial possibilities of the strait. It took him three months to reach the western entrance and on the way his consort deserted back to Callao. The strait was crossed in a mere three weeks and three native 'interpreters' were kidnapped on the way, sowing the seeds of the future hostility of the Indians.

Sarmiento sailed on to Spain, where he fitted out an expedition of twenty-three ships but the command was given to an incapable court favourite, Diego Flores. On 15 September 1581 3,000 souls embarked – mariners, friars, soldiers, colonists with wives and children, blacksmiths, masons, stone-cutters and even trumpeters. Five ships were lost before even leaving the coast of Spain and many more Spaniards died of a plague during the crossing of the Atlantic and the lengthy stop in Brazil. On the way to Argentina three worm-eaten ships foundered and intelligence was gathered about the passing of new English privateers; the race for the strait appeared to be lost and there were arguments about the suitability of pushing on.

They did push on and after hideous hardships the remnants of the expedition eventually reached the target in the narrows of the strait and the fort of Don Felipe was built and seeds were planted. A settlement was also started at Nombre de Jesus. Thomas Cavendish, who left Plymouth in July 1586 for Magellan Strait, passed Nombre de Jesus and found it a ghost town. He also called at Don Felipe to salvage the guns; because of the starved bodies littering the place he called it Port Famine – a name which has stuck.

By the end of the sixteenth century, Holland, having shaken off the Spanish yoke, was becoming an international power with interests in the East. She sent two expeditions by way of the Magellan Strait in 1598, under Simon de Cordes and Oliver van Noort. They met the usual gales, starvation and mutinies and only one ship limped back to tell the tale – without even making a profit.

France was still out of the picture, but a private Frenchman, Malherbe, sailed through the strait in the early seventeenth century on a round-the-world voyage – mostly overland – which took him twenty-five years.

In 1614-1617 a Dutch East India Company expedition under Joris Spilbergen sailed round the world, through the strait, at last achieving a success. The Dutch East India Company monopolised the eastern trade, forbidding any other Dutchman to use either the way of Good Hope or of Magellan (Drake Strait still remaining an unused English secret). But there were interlopers intent on beating the monopoly; in 1616 Cornelius Schouten and le Maire discovered the loophole – Cape Horn. That route was not a great improvement on the strait; the weather was just as bad, the sea worse, and one could not water or stock up with salt penguins as in the strait; but there was more sea room.

In 1669-1671, Narborough and Wood surveyed the strait in greater detail than their predecessors. In 1714, Legentil Labartinais, a French merchant and privateer, navigated the strait from east to west. In 1740, England and Spain were at war again and Commodore Anson was sent to the Pacific. He chose the Cape Horn way and his expedition was successful. In 1764, Commodore Byron was sent out to discover new lands thought to lie to the south (the myth of the Southern Continent lasted until Cook). After claiming the Falklands for England he sailed through the strait. The quest for 'Terra Australis' went on; Wallis and Carteret left Plymouth in 1766 and spent four miserable months in the strait with winds, rain and scurvy. The ships became separated on the Pacific side and made independent returns, Wallis discovering Tahiti on the way. The Frenchman Bougainville, on the same quest, entered the strait on 2 December 1767 with two ships and experienced the usual rains, fogs and currents. He had friendly contacts with the Indians but they ended in grief.

After Bougainville, Cape Horn was preferred by the

Facing page: Engraving showing Magellan using navigational instruments during a voyage of exploration.
MARY EVANS PICTURE LIBRARY

Left: Engraving from 'Moore's Voyages and Travels' of Louis de Bougainville hoisting the French colours on a rock in the 'Maghellan Streights'.
JOHN R. FREEMAN & CO

Right: Figurehead of Admiral Lord Anson, the British circumnavigator. R. WESTWOOD

explorers, Cook and Lapérouse. The Spaniards' last exploratory effort was then made by Cordoba, who updated the chart of the strait but still left all the side channels in blank – gaps that were filled by the British survey ships *Adventure* and *Beagle* in 1828. The captain of HMS *Beagle*, Prengles Stokes, became a victim of the curse of the strait; the storm-swept solitudes he was surveying combined with the loneliness inherent in his rank drove him out of his mind and he committed suicide. His grave can still be seen near Port Famine.

He was succeeded by Robert FitzRoy, who completed the expedition and who led the next surveying journey. The *Beagle* returned in 1832 to chart the Fuegian Archipelago, so that the naturalist Darwin, who was aboard, skirted the strait proper, but many of his observations on the Fuegian natural history and Indians also apply to the strait. It is an irony of fate that Darwin, the greatest proponent of the theory of evolution, was specifically taken on the *Beagle* by FitzRoy (who was a strict believer in the scriptures) to help dispel the 'unholy' ideas which were already emerging; at the time Darwin was considering entering the Church. That disappointment of FitzRoy was instrumental in his own death; he cut his throat in 1865. The *Beagle* seems to have had a jinx for her commanders.

The last great expedition to sail through the strait was that of Dumont d'Urville, in 1837, on his way to outline the coast of Antarctica. But that was the age of the Cape Horn trade; the faster ships did not need to stop midway on their journeys to water and they preferred sea room, so

the strait saw little merchant shipping. The strait town of Punta Arenas was founded in 1849, after a short abortive settlement at Puerto Bulnes. It was used as a coaling station for the few steamers which ventured around South America, but the economics of wind and coal still favoured the Cape Horn windjammers. They, however, suffered severe casualties and in 1906 it was suggested that steam tugs be based at Punta Arenas to tow the sailing ships through the strait. But a single day's tow would have cost as much as two weeks under sail off the horn.

In those days the Royal Navy was often seen in the strait; in 1881 HMS *Doterel* blew up in Punta Arenas harbour with the loss of 143 crew (there were only twelve survivors). In the early 1880s the harbour was used as a base for the French hydrographical naval survey of the *Romanche*, under Capitaine Martial. The first proper navigational markers were erected in the strait in the early 1860s and the first lighthouses were built at the end of the century. A famous lighthouse is the one perched on the Evangelistas Island in the middle of the Pacific entrance. It was built in 1896 by the British engineer Slaight and is manned by five men. It is exposed to every westerly gale and the relief is done by a tender which sometimes has to wait for up to forty days for amenable conditions, during which time the tender shelters by a landward island in a cove named Forty Day Harbour. Even then, getting on the lighthouse is a perilous matter, as it must be done by jumping from a boat to a rope ladder and the swell is always huge.

Left: The 'Beagle' in which Fitzroy and Darwin sailed to chart the Fuegian Archipelago.
NATIONAL MARITIME MUSEUM, LONDON

Right: Robert Fitzroy companion of Darwin in the 'Beagle' but who later committed suicide when he found Darwin's theory of evolution insupportable.
NATIONAL MARITIME MUSEUM, LONDON

Below: A picture by O. W. Brierly depicting the discovery of the Straits of Magellan in 1520.
ILLUSTRATED LONDON NEWS

Punta Arenas became a whaling port in 1894 when Chileans of Norwegian origin started the Magellan Whaling Society. In those days whales were to be found in the strait, but soon the whalers had to range farther afield. Whaling activities were pursued up to well after the Second World War.

In 1896 the strait was navigated by a gallant small sloop – the *Spray*, from Boston. Her skipper, Captain Joshua Slocum, a real seaman with salt water and Stockholm tar in his veins, was accomplishing the first solo circumnavigation. He got a true Magellanic greeting just as he had rounded Cape Virgins, on 11 February, and finally reached Punta Arenas.

The next historical event was during the First World War. Admiral von Spee's Far East Squadron had smashed a British squadron under Rear-Admiral Cradock at Coronel, off the Chilean coast. Admiral Sturdee was quickly dispatched with a new fleet consisting of the battleship *Canopus*, the battlecruisers *Invincible* and *Inflexible*, the cruisers *Carnarvon, Cornwall, Kent* and *Macedonia*, the light cruisers *Bristol* and *Glasgow* and the armed merchantman *Orama*, with the mission to patrol both ends of the Magellan and Drake Straits. While the squadron was preparing for the blockade by refuelling at Port Stanley on East Falkland island, von Spee's ships inadvertently bumped into the English force and the chase was on (8 December 1914). The Falkland battle resulted in the sinking of all the German ships except the cruiser *Dresden*, which succeeded in getting away and making Punta Arenas.

Under the laws of neutrality, she left within twenty-four hours and thereafter for many months played a game of hide-and-seek with the *Glasgow, Carnarvon* and *Kent*. She hid in various inlets and bays (such as Sepulveda's Bay and the Dresden's Inlet near Cape Horn) and was victualled during that time from Punta Arenas by a German national, Captain Pagels, who owned a tug used in peace time for ferrying passengers to and from their ships anchored off Punta Arenas. The British consul offered a large sum of money to Pagels if he was willing to disclose the whereabouts of the *Dresden*, but he refused to do so. Eventually the *Dresden* was caught by the *Kent* and *Glasgow* at Cumberland Bay in Juan Fernandez Island (of Robinson Crusoe-Alexander Selkirk fame). After a brief exchange of fire the German master scuttled his ship by blowing her up.

Meanwhile another drama was being enacted far to the south. The expedition led by Ernest Shackleton had sailed to the Antarctic on the *Endurance* in 1914; the ship got caught in the ice in the Weddel Sea and was eventually crushed on 27 October 1915. The twenty-eight men of the party took to camping on the ice after unsuccessful attempts to sledge the boats, but they were drifting with the pack. They finally managed to jury-sail and pull the boats to Elephant Island, where the best boat – a 22-foot whaler – was jury-rigged and Shackleton and five other men sailed her across 800 miles of the most miserable sea in the world to South Georgia, a distance they covered in twenty-five days – a most extraordinary feat of seamanship and endurance.

After crossing the island overland (which has only been done once since by well-equipped mountaineers), Shackleton reached the whaling station of Stromness on 20 May 1916. He unsuccessfully tried to reach Elephant Island with a Stromness trawler, and again on a Uruguayan fisheries vessel, from the Falklands. He finally went to Punta Arenas, where the British colony and some Chileans chartered the schooner *Emma*, which was also beaten back by the ice and weather. Then the Chilean Navy provided the Punta Arenas ocean-going tug *Yelcho*, which left on 25 August, reached Elephant Island on the 30th, picked up the shipwrecked colony and landed them at Punta Arenas on 3 September The most remarkable fact is that all the *Endurance*'s crew survived.

The Chilean Navy at Punta Arenas has many times since been involved in Antarctic rescues (as well as in expeditions and surveys), the latest being two evacuations of scientific parties on Deception Island when it erupted in the late 1960s and the picking up of the tourist passengers of the *Linblad Explorer*, which ran aground on an Antarctic island.

The opening of the Panama Canal in 1914 rang the death knell of the square-riggers and depressed the bunkering activities of Punta Arenas. However, the town has grown to 70,000 inhabitants, who live mainly from the export of wool and mutton, primarily to Britain. It is the administrative capital city of Chile's province of Magallanes and it is also a naval base. The town has a shipyard and is the centre for mining operations (lignite and gold) and for oil exploration in Tierra del Fuego. Oilfields are in production near Manantiales and a new oil port has been built at Caleta Clarence on Gente Grande Bay, Tierra del Fuego, providing about a third of Chile's requirements.

The increase in the size of merchant ships, particularly of tankers, means a renewed traffic through the strait or round the horn of those vessels too big for the Panama Canal. During the southern summer cruise ships on round-the-world tours call at Punta Arenas and visit the fjords.

The strait is now well charted, and has an excellent buoyage and beaconage; there are about 100 lighthouses in the waterway and adjacent canals. Even so, the weather is the same as of old; Puntarenians still have to fight frequent 'panteoneros' blowing at 100 knots or more (the Panteon is the town's cemetery), and the fogs, blizzards and williwaws can be just as dangerous in those narrow waters nowadays as they were in the days of sail. The tidal range at Dungeness Point Lighthouse (near Cape Virgins) reaches eleven metres and the first and second narrows can have spring-tide currents of nine knots; there are many races and also maelstroms where the Pacific and Atlantic tides meet. There is no need to ask why the Magellan Strait is such a graveyard of ships, both old windjammers and modern steamers.

However, safety has been greatly improved by the navigational aids and the introduction of compulsory pilotage organised by Chile (even though the strait is considered an international waterway). For west-bound ships the pilots are picked up off Dungeness Point and are carried all the way to Talcahuano or Valparaiso – the north-bound shipping now follows the more protected inland route of interlocking fjords and channels which link the strait to 'Middle' Chile. The weather is so unpredictable near the Evangelistas that pilots are flown to Australia or New Zealand to board east-bound ships. Since it takes more than a day to cross the strait, two pilots are carried so that there is always one on the bridge; even today mariners tackle the strait with a healthy respect.

Von Spee's flagship 'Scharnhorst' in the foreground sinking during the Battle of Falkland; a painting by W. C. Wyllie. NATIONAL MARITIME MUSEUM, LONDON

Privateer

Howard knighting Frobisher board the Ark Royal 1588.

Left: The British explorer and adventurer Martin Frobisher being knighted by Lord Howard on board 'Ark Royal' in 1588; an illustration from a book by Raphael Tuck.
D. CAPPER COLLECTION

Above An engraving of Queen Elizabeth bidding farewell to Frobisher. R. BROWN

THE Jolly Roger, the skull and crossbones flag of the pirate, was not flown by a privateer, although the line between the two classes of seagoing adventurers was thin. The privateer was more respectable, though he might conveniently forget the simple rules of his trade. As the owner of a ship in time of war he could arm her, collect a crew and freely sail away, provided he could show a commission to 'annoy the king's enemies'.

The arrival of peace meant that a privateer saw his livelihood vanish at a stroke. It was then that he might be tempted to relieve other ships of their cargoes whatever their nationalities. But privateering was an ancient calling for English seamen and part of their heritage. It is recorded that King Henry III gave commissions to seafaring folk to attack any enemy ships on condition that the proceeds went into the royal purse.

Another Henry, Bluff King Hal, had words to say in 1544 to the mayors of Newcastle-upon-Tyne, Scarborough and Hull on their slackness in not sending out enough ships. Helping his men-of-war, he said, were twelve or sixteen vessels in the west of the country which had gathered more than £10,000 and, he declared, 'It were burdensome that the king should set ships to defend all parts of the realm and keep the narrow seas withal'.

Besides the privateers, there was another category of adventurers – those bearing Letters of Marque, which authorised ship-owners who had been robbed in peacetime to seize the value of their goods, by force if necessary, from ships of the robbers' country. Eventually they became con-fused with privateering and faded away as a separate class. Several other countries supported privateers, notably the French.

One famous British explorer and adventurer was Sir Martin Frobisher, described as 'of great spirit and bould courage and natural hardness of body'. Frobisher was born in Yorkshire and, on the death of his father, he went to his uncle, a merchant-adventurer in London. At the age of fourteen he sailed in a disastrous expedition to West Africa which he was lucky to survive. Then for a while he fought as a soldier in Ireland. In 1562 he was at sea again on a voyage to Guinea and on his return he became a privateer captain. His captures included Spanish as well as French vessels and, as England was not yet at war with Spain, he was not popular with the authorities. He then started to have a profitable time with various kinds of dubious seafaring errands, which ended for a time in gaol for taking a London merchant's cargo of wine.

Ever since boyhood, Frobisher had hoped to have the chance of finding the elusive North-West Passage to the Far East and the riches of Cathay. After much planning and scheming, at the age of thirty-seven he saw the dream of his life come true. He had persuaded some friends to finance an expedition as partners and, at long last, on a June day in 1576, he hoisted sail at Blackwall and set off eagerly on the voyage, with a farewell message and wave from the queen. The expedition was a very small one and had only two 'barks' – little three-masted ships; the *Gabriel* captained by Frobisher, with a crew of eighteen, and the *Michael*,

A portrayal of the death of Sir Humphrey Gilbert in the sinking of the pinnace 'Squirrel' in a storm at sea north of the Azores in 1580. Gilbert, a half-brother of Sir Walter Raleigh, was an enthusiast in the search for a North-West Passage.
MARY EVANS PICTURE LIBRARY

with seventeen – and a pinnace manned by four seamen.

The expedition arrived at the Shetlands at the start of an eight-day gale, which whisked the pinnace away with her crew doomed, but Frobisher carried on after the weather improved and sighted the eastern coast of Greenland. They were forced to keep clear of the coast by pack-ice, which proved too much for the *Michael*'s captain, who took his ship home. The *Gabriel* went on to reach the coast of Labrador and, several days later, sailing northward, Frobisher found a 'great gutte, bay or passage', which he took to be the division between the continents of Europe and Asia. He gave it his name and sailed up it for 150 miles. Then Eskimos, not too friendly, appeared and he grappled one and heaved him on board, together with his kayak, to act as pilot.

Five of his crew had been carried off by the Eskimos, so, with only thirteen left and those worn out, he decided to return to England. First, he sent parties ashore to collect souvenirs. Among the items brought was a piece of black stone. A month afterwards, the *Gabriel* was back in the Thames 'with the great admiration of the people', in the belief that he had found the North-West Passage. When the black stone was examined by experts, verdicts differed; two of them declared it to be iron pyrites and the third found in it a speck of gold-dust. It was enough; Frobisher had seen a land of gold ore.

The immediate result was the merging of the original subscribers in a joint-stock Cathay Company, with Frobisher at the head as 'High Admiral of all seas and waters, land and isles' and all the rest, including Cathay. The queen actually produced £1,000 and lent a splendid ship, the *Aid*.

The North-West Passage was put aside; it was the gold that mattered, waiting to be dug, and on his next voyage Frobisher took thirty miners and refiners. With the *Aid* and two pinnaces, he left the Thames in May of 1577, arriving in Frobisher Strait in July. He brought back 200 tons of the black stone, so pleasing the Cathay Company that they raised money for a large fleet for the next voyage. Queen Elizabeth found well over £3,000 as her share and lent two more ships, making a total of fifteen to sail with the Captain-General in June of 1578.

But Frobisher Strait gave them no welcome. In an unusually stormy and cold summer, ice-floes and bergs caused much damage in the fleet and sank one of the barks. No great quantity of the black rock was loaded before the bitter weather, including blizzards, drove the fleet back to England. There Frobisher met the staggering news that his ore was iron pyrites and utterly worthless. All the effort had been wasted.

He could do little else but resume privateering until, in 1585, he sailed as Drake's vice-admiral to harry the West Indies. Four years later, by then Sir Martin Frobisher, he captured two treasure-ships off the Azores while commanding five of the Queen's vessels. He was on shore attacking a Spanish fort in 1594 when he was mortally wounded and he died later at Plymouth, mourned as being at heart a simple upright man.

Another enthusiast in the search for the North-West Passage was Sir Humphrey Gilbert, courtier, fighting soldier and coloniser. Born in 1539, a Devonian, he was a half-brother of Sir Walter Raleigh. He had many gifts, marred unfortunately by a quick temper that led to fierce rages. He was knighted for bravery some time before he went to sea in 1578. Caught by November gales, he made only a short cruise. It was two years later when he made his second attempt. He persuaded the queen to grant letters patent of wide scope, giving him authority over any lands not already occupied by Christians. Colonisation was to be his main object.

He could find funds for only four small vessels and a little pinnace and on the second day at sea the largest of his ships deserted and went elsewhere. The others crossed the North Atlantic and made a landfall on the Newfoundland coast and headed south to St Johns. There they found a mixed coterie of fishing craft – Spanish, Portuguese, French and English, thirty-six of them. Gilbert formally took possession of Newfoundland and established good relations with the fishermen, finding them cheerful and friendly. Soon they were sharing food and frolics for a happy fortnight.

Then two of Gilbert's captains decided that they were too ill to carry on. Finding them not too sick to sail home, he let them go in one of the smaller ships. He himself took command of the pinnace *Squirrel*, small though she was, and refused to take the *Hind*, the larger and safer vessel. He made for Sable Island, off the coast of Nova Scotia, to stock up with meat from the wild cattle and pigs that French seamen had left there to breed. But in dense fog the only ship of any size left struck a shoal and quickly sank. Nearly all her crew were drowned.

The combined effects of the dwindling of the fleet, the shortage of provisions and the approach of winter had such a disheartening effect on the ships' companies that at last Gilbert agreed to turn homeward. But nothing could persuade him to leave the pinnace for the *Hind*. They were north of the Azores in furious weather when the *Hind* surged up alongside Gilbert so that her captain could hail and ask how he fared. Gilbert's shouted reply was 'We are as near to heaven by sea as by land'. That night, with the sea still wilder, watchers saw the *Squirrel*'s lights suddenly go out and they knew that they had seen the last of their Captain-General.

The Spanish Flotas

SEVEN centuries after the Moors conquered Spain they were finally expelled in 1492 and the country, naturally poor, was left devastated by warfare. That same year Columbus reached the New World of the Americas and was followed by swarms of needy but proud adventurers whose livelihood was gone in their homeland as they knew no trade but arms. Generations of conflict with Muslim enemies had produced a breed of men who were totally ruthless, incredibly brave and fanatically Christian. Before them the Indian civilisations of central and south America went crashing down, and those lands, so rich in gold, silver and emeralds, became at once the salvation and the ruin of Spain.

Without the 'treasures of the Indies' the nation could hardly have survived, and certainly could never have taken a foremost place among the European States. But the imported wealth which saved Spain's economy became a liability when other countries wanted a share and were prepared to fight to get it. Spain speedily became so dependent on the annual import of treasure that even a short break in the flow across the Atlantic could bankrupt the government and merchants, a condition relieved only by the arrival of more treasure from the Americas.

During the sixteenth century Spain towered like a glittering colossus over the rest of Europe and was defended by the finest soldiers of the age. Yet the glamour and the glory rested on a very fragile base, for everything depended on sea-power, which Spain did not possess. There was indeed no national navy at all, only galley squadrons in the Mediterranean, and even those served only the provinces, not the country as a whole. Each time a galley fleet was needed it had to be formed from the various provincial squadrons by temporary arrangements to cover the particular campaign envisaged. Even the provinces were not themselves the galleys' owners; they merely appointed a commander and he had to provide the galleys and crews. The system continued when Spain did build ocean-going warships and did not end until the early eighteenth century, when a national navy was finally formed on the French model. The reform was then too late.

From 1504 the Casa de Contractación was the authority responsible for everything connected with the Indies trade, and it was based on Seville. The carracks and caravels it used were built on contracts with its generals and admirals, not by the Crown or State. They sailed either independently or two or three together, as that reduced delays while waiting for a larger number to assemble and avoided flooding the market with the cargoes of numerous ships all arriving at the same time.

A painting by M. J. Barton of a Spanish treasure galleon and escort.

French corsairs were the first to succumb to the temptations of the Indies trade, and, most of all, those from Normandy and Brittany. They began to lurk off the Azores and Cape St Vincent, the landfalls of Spanish ships homeward bound from the Americas, to waylay the rich carracks and caravels, sometimes with success. Fast, powerfully armed ships of moderate size were needed for the work, and French builders were equal to the demand. It was said that a Dieppe corsair prayer ran: 'Oh Lord, we do not ask for riches; only show us where they are!'

In 1522 that prayer was granted to a squadron of corsair ships under Jean Fleury of Dieppe. They fell in with three caravels and captured two laden with the Aztec treasures taken by Hernando Cortés in his conquest of Mexico. There were idols and vessels of solid gold, chests filled with jewels, treasure worth millions; but worth much more was the fact that the officers of one of the caravels had failed to destroy the secret papers and charts. The Frenchmen found laid before them the entire system for collecting and transporting the treasures, all the land and sea routes, the ports used, points of departure and landfall, all carefully laid down by the Casa for the captains of treasure ships. No corsair could ask for more than that! They had indeed been shown where riches were to be found.

It was a disaster that brought Spain to a standstill, causing widespread distress and financial collapse. Official Spain was stunned, although some time seems to have elapsed before the loss of the vital secrets was known. The Casa hastily issued orders that in future no ship of less than 100 tons would be allowed in the Americas trade, and every one must have at least four guns, six gunners and not less than twenty soldiers equipped with pikes, swords, arquebuses and cuirasses. Weapons for the seamen must also be carried, and all male passengers must provide arms for themselves and take a full part in the defence of the ship in the event of attack.

Losses increased rather than diminished, so in 1526 all Indies ships were ordered to sail in company, which was unpopular with both merchants and shipmasters for it had all the disadvantages of convoy without giving adequate protection. Large carracks were then selected as suitable for carrying a heavy armament and, named the Armada of Cantabria, after the district in north-western Spain where they would usually be based, patrolled in groups in the areas most favoured by corsairs, and particularly off Cape St Vincent and the Azores at the times when treasure fleets were due.

To worsen matters, relations with England had deteriorated from the former alliance to deep mutual suspicion and religious enmity. It was known in Spain, too, that English seamen were enviously watching the French corsairs and were only with difficulty being held back by their government which did not want a complete rupture with Spain. The marriage of Philip and the Catholic Mary of England for a time restored the alliance but the strong hold Protestants had on the English masses suggested that there could be serious trouble between Spain and England in the future.

By 1543 the patrol system had proved only partially effective, for the French in reply improved the sea-keeping qualities of their corsair ships and hunted farther out in the Atlantic. Some of the Armada of Cantabria were withdrawn from that service to form a flota guard, with the larger carracks of the Indies trade fully armed as warships. Protection was thus provided right across the Atlantic, and the flotas of history had come into existence. As time passed and corsairs continued to harass the Spaniards in mid-ocean and cut off stragglers, more and more of the finest carracks had to be turned over to escort duty. The building of new ones and providing the soldiers and guns for them became an increasing burden on the national economy. Even worse than the losses to human enemies were those to the elements, and especially the West Indies hurricanes.

For the first twelve years that the Casa kept records 222 out of 391 ships were wrecked or went down. In 1553 a flota from Vera Cruz was flung by a sudden violent storm on the Gulf Coast (now Texas), and most of the 1567 flota was lost on the rocks and cays of the Antilles. It was a melancholy story, two centuries long, and did at least as much as the operations of corsairs to ruin Spain. The cost of the annual flotas became increasingly difficult to meet, yet without them Spain could not survive as a major European state, or even provide adequately for its citizens. Then after the accession of Elizabeth to the English throne things got even worse, for with or without her permission her seamen emulated the French and also became corsairs; soon they were the worst and most daring of the lot.

By the mid-sixteenth century the operations of the flotas had been reduced to a system. All ships had to be registered and pay an *averia* (convoy tax) from which not even the royal ships were exempt. They had to have two captains, a *capitan de mar* to sail the ship and a *capitan de guerra* to command the soldiers and to lead in battle. The high command of the flota was held for a single round voyage, which normally took about eight months as the flotas lay for long periods in port awaiting good weather and trying to miss the hurricane seasons.

A captain-general, often a distinguished soldier rather than a sailor, was in supreme command and his ship was called the *capitana* of the flota; she was one of the largest and best of the flota guard. In charge of the treasure ships and merchantmen – for most of the ships carried the cargoes of ordinary trade – was the admiral and his ship was the *almiranta*, or second flagship. The large carracks carried up to 700 people – crew, soldiers and passengers. Living conditions were cramped and insanitary, so outbreaks of sickness were frequent. Certain parts of the ship were reserved for women passengers only, but even they had little comfort.

The original assembly point for the flotas was San Lucar, but as the ships got larger they drew too much water for the river and Cadiz then became the flota port. At first there was only one flota which went first to Cartagena and Nombre de Dios to load the South American cargoes, then on to Vera Cruz for those of Central America. Later there were two flotas, although they sometimes did the Atlantic

Above: Spanish galleys and English corsairs in conflict off Peru in 1628, from an engraving in the National Maritime Museum, Greenwich. K. FENWICK COLLECTION

Left: A map by Lazaro Luis, in the Lisbon Academy of Sciences, showing the coast of Florida and Cuba in 1563: a passage much used despite frequent hurricanes. M. PUCCIARELLI

crossing both ways in company. One was for New Spain (Mexico) and the other for Tierre Firme (the Spanish Main [land]). They stood south to the Canary Islands to pick up the trade winds and entered the Caribbean through the Mona Passage (between Hispaniola and Puerto Rico) and there, if they were in company, they separated. The New Spain flota dropped off ships at various islands as it headed for Vera Cruz, in the Gulf of Campeche. The Tierre Firme flota turned south-west across the Caribbean for Cartagena, 'the capital of the Spanish Main', and Nombre de Dios, or, after about 1600, to Portobello, when the older ports were allowed to decline.

The arrival of a flota was the occasion for a fair at which the products of Europe and the Americas were exchanged. From Europe came those luxuries the colonists missed most in their distant outposts: books, velvets, wines, musical instruments and linens, as well as letters and news. In return, apart from gold, silver and jewels (which were supposed to be crown property, but there was smuggling on a considerable scale), the Americas produced hides for bookbinding, saddlery and boots, logwood, mahogany, lignum vitae, cacao, indigo, cochineal and tobacco. The flota fairs were the great festivals of the colonies and were eagerly awaited in the months between.

After the sailing of a flota preparations for the next began throughout Spanish America as treasure and more humble products were amassed. In early days they came to the ports as they were garnered and stored in warehouses; but the raids of corsairs, including Drake, enforced the deliberate holding back of everything worth the corsairs' taking until the flotas were either due or had already arrived. The Mexican routes were by land or river, but the main sources of the Tierre Firme trade were down the western coast of South America. Pacific flotas assembled at Callao, where the Lima treasure was embarked and where ships from farther south joined. As the flota headed northwards it would pick up more ships and cargoes from the places it passed. There was a halt at Guayaquil, where more treasure would be waiting, and the final destination was Panama.

Pacific flotas did not need heavy guards, for few corsairs rounded Cape Horn, although small numbers (usually English) sometimes did. The first corsair raid into the Pacific

Left: Spanish galleons as depicted in a contemporary engraving now in the British Museum.
K. FENWICK COLLECTION

Above: Men engaged in building Spanish galleons; an engraving of 1898 by Paul Hardy.
K. FENWICK COLLECTION

was John Oxenham's, and that was not until 1575. There was thus a long period when the Pacific flotas needed no protection at all. Even after the capture and execution of the Oxenham expedition, few precautions were taken until Drake suddenly appeared off the coast in 1579.

From 1571 onwards galley squadrons were based at Havana, Vera Cruz and Cartagena in the Caribbean, and later a few were kept in the Pacific ports. They proved of great value for preventing local smuggling and also for examining inlets and river mouths where corsairs might be lurking; they made more captures than the big ships and were more feared by the corsairs as they were independent of the wind.

The cargoes from Panama crossed the Isthmus by mule train to a wretched fever-ridden outpost up the River Chagre called Venta Cruces, whence it went on by sea to Cartagena and Nombre de Dios; but after the corsairs began to probe up the Chagre and hover along the coastal route, important cargoes and treasures went all the way to the Tierre Firme ports by mule train.

Having taken in cargoes and passengers for Spain, the flota ships sailed for Havana. Those of the New Spain flota picked up on the way the ships they had detached at islands on the outward passage. Usually the two flotas united at Havana for the Atlantic crossing, but quite often they sailed separately. In either case they went through the Florida Straits despite its reputation for hurricanes, carefully trying to avoid the hurricane season but not always succeeding. The route north of Bermuda to the Azores and then to Cadiz was necessary because the prevailing winds of the North Atlantic blow clockwise round the areas of calm, so the anti-trade winds were as important in sailing-ship days for returning as the trades were for the outward voyage.

The regulations for returning flotas were strict. All ships had to be provisioned for eighty days, and no port must be entered except in dire emergency. When approaching Portugal and Spain there must be no communication with the shore by boat on pain of 200 lashes and ten years as a galley-slave. On reaching Cadiz no one could step out of the ship before officials from the Casa had searched the ship and examined all on board. Anyone trying to send a letter on shore before the royal dispatches had left was liable to be flogged or heavily fined. The rules were made necessary by the Casa's well-founded conviction that somehow or other much private treasure was in fact smuggled into Spain.

Corsairs rarely hunted alone and with numbers of them hovering round a flota the defence could easily become bewildered, not knowing where a real attack might fall and which threats were feints intended to draw the flota guards away from selected victims. With a crowd of ships varying in size and speed, all trying to keep close together, there was bound to be confusion, for sailing in close order was very difficult for large square-rigged ships wholly dependent on the wind. With corsairs harassing the flanks like packs of hungry wolves there were bound to be losses, especially in darkness or fog, and even in clear daylight no straggler was safe.

From 1550 things began to improve, thanks to two great Spanish seamen. Álvaro de Bazan, better known as the Marquis of Santa Cruz, although galley trained, had eyes to see beyond the confines of the Mediterranean. When only twenty-four years old he produced designs for a new type of ship especially for the flotas. His galleons, as he named them, would be faster and more weatherly than carracks and larger than caravels. All were to carry heavy guns and, as they would sail in company, they would be a formidable fighting force, carrying heavier metal than the agile corsairs could mount on their slim fast hulls. At least two in each flota were to sacrifice cargo for extra armament – thirty-six to fifty guns, he suggested – so that they would be, in effect, genuine men-of-war well able to take the brunt of flota defence against even the most powerful warships then afloat. Bazan's proposals were approved and twelve of his galleons were built as a beginning. After that the flotas suffered less from corsairs.

Pedro Menéndez de Avilés came of good family but ran away to sea at the age of fourteen and spent the next sixteen years of his life in corsair ships. He therefore knew the minds and methods of corsair captains better than most Spaniards ever did. When he became the captain-general of a flota, which he was on three occasions, he devised improved convoy systems and drew on the Armada of Cantabria to add to the flota guard. The combination of Bazan's galleons and the Avilés system proved to be effective and from 1567 to 1627 losses of ships in flota became rare. By the 1570s the English had become the leading corsairs, so Avilés proposed seizing the Scilly Isles as a base whence fast fighting ships of his own design could patrol the south and south-west coast of England and the entrance to the Channel to interrupt English corsair activities at their source. After his death in 1574 nothing more was heard of the project.

Unfortunately for Spain, his early life had not endeared him to the Casa, which tried to prevent the crown from appointing him captain-general; then his refusal to accept bribes from merchants engaged in smuggling alienated them as well. In 1563 the Casa had him imprisoned on unrecorded charges; it took twenty months and two royal commands to get him freed. Such was the Casa's attitude to one of the men who made the flotas almost impregnable.

Some 'loose' ships, as they were called, had always been used for carrying dispatches. They were simply unusually fast caravels which sailed unescorted and kept the Crown and Casa in touch with the American colonies. Improvements had from time to time been made, copying French or English galleon types. Open war with England broke out in 1585 and Bazan (by then Santa Cruz) suggested the sending of a great armada against it. Getting enough ships and soldiers was a major problem, and the only way to do it was by drawing on the flota guards, yet without the treasure they escorted across the Atlantic the project was impossible. Juan de Texeda, a fortification expert, went to the Indies as Governor of Havana and to supervise the strengthening of the port defences of the Indies and the Mainland, while at home Santa Cruz faced the problem of getting ships for his Great Armada and still keeping the flotas.

The solution was provided in a letter from the Duke of Medina Sidonia and Antonio de Guevara. They suggested building a dozen small fast ships of corsair type which would depend on speed instead of force. They would provide a 'light armada' to bring the treasure, while the ordinary and less important cargoes could come in any ships available after Santa Cruz had taken his pick for the 'enterprise of England'. Thus the 1588 treasure could be transported safely, yet the floating fortresses so far favoured would be available for service in the Great Armada.

Despite the warnings of many experts, the scheme was tried and proved a complete success. The fast treasure ships were safely home before their enemies had even sailed in search of the expected flota, and a rearrangement of schedules caused them also to miss the ordinary flota as well. Spain was therefore able to press on with the preparations for invading England.

The disaster to the Great Armada accounted for many of the finest and most powerful ships upon which the flotas had formerly depended for their protection. New galleons, with improvements copied from the victorious English galleons, were put in hand in the Spanish dockyards but two or three years had to pass before the losses could be made good. Meanwhile, the wealth of the Indies was more desperately needed than ever if Spanish power was to recover. The light armada of gallizabras was the only means immediately available, and once again they brought the treasure safely from America.

The year 1590 found the English very active in the Caribbean and off the Azores. Juan de Texeda was impressed by the gallizabras in their new role as treasure ships rather than dispatch vessels and he set about improving them, with the aid of Havana dockyard. By lengthening the keels and making the underwater hulls more galley-like, he greatly increased their speed. Fear for the safety of the treasure led to the postponement of the 1590 flota until 1591. In February 1591 four of the new treasure frigates were ready and on the 10th they left Havana with the most precious items of treasure, reaching Portugal on 12 March.

The combined flotas for the two years sailed later, only to meet a disastrous storm off the Azores, after the covering force that had come out to meet them had captured Sir Richard Grenville's *Revenge*. For the rest of the flota era the most precious and vital cargoes crossed in exceptionally fast ships, and there is no record that one was ever taken, although some treasure was often found in ordinary flota ships that were captured.

In 1628 a galleon flota in the Caribbean, taking silver to Havana for transfer to treasure frigates for the Atlantic crossing, was scattered by a storm. Part of it had reassembled to the number of four large galleons and eleven small ones when a large Dutch fleet under Piet Heijn (also spelt Hein and Heyn) sighted the galleons and chased them. The Spaniards, greatly outnumbered, sought refuge in Matanzas Bay, Cuba, hoping to land the silver and dispatch it for Havana before the Dutch could prevent them. In vain. Heijn went into the bay after them and captured the galleons with the silver, valued at four million ducats, still on board.

The end of the flotas came in the first half of the eighteenth century. By then most of the ships and crews were foreign, and it was also a bad time for disasters. Of the 1715 flota only one ship out of eleven survived a hurricane and in 1733 more than twenty were wrecked on the Florida Keys. The bones of hundreds of flota ships strew the floors of the Caribbean and Atlantic; the Florida Straits, the sea round Bermuda and the Azores, are vast flota graveyards; their story is little known today. Yet in their great sixteenth-century days it used to be said that enough treasure passed through Seville each year from the annual flotas to pave the entire city with gold; it was probably true.

A painting of the city and port of Seville where, it was said, enough treasure passed through each year from the flotas to pave the city with gold.
BY COURTESY OF MARTIN SANSCHEZ (D. RUDKIN)

Lepanto

Above: Charles V, Emperor of the Holy Roman Empire; a portrait of 1584.
MARY EVANS PICTURE LIBRARY

Right: Portrait of Philip II of Spain.
NATIONAL MARITIME MUSEUM, LONDON

ON 16 September 1571, a fleet sailed from Messina carrying with it the hopes of Christian Europe. While the papal nuncio stood on the shore, blessing each ship as it passed, prayers were offered up all over the Continent by people fearfully aware that their culture, their religion and perhaps their very lives depended on the fleet's success.

The crisis which caused such universal trepidation had been threatening Christendom ever since 1453, when the Ottoman Turks captured Constantinople. Until then, the hostility of Christian and Moslem had found its battleground at what seemed a safe distance from Europe. Crusades to the Holy Land had been for most Europeans a vicarious experience, an activity to be idealised as a proving-ground of Christian manhood and knightly chivalry. The fall of Constantinople, however, shattered that rather complacent concept, and replaced it with the realisation that the heartland of Christendom was in very grave danger.

Alarm increased over the following century, as Islam spread deeper and deeper into Europe and infiltrated the Mediterranean. During that time, the Turks conquered the Balkans, Egypt, Syria and parts of Russia, and extended their power southwards into Iraq and down to the Persian Gulf and Aden, where they challenged the supremacy of the Portuguese in the Indian Ocean.

There was considerable danger for the Christian States of Europe in Turkish dominance of the Aegean and the Black Sea and their spread along the North African coast, where the corsair kings of Algiers, Tunis and Tripoli acknowledged Ottoman Turkish suzerainty. Christian shipping was at the mercy of such pirates, and risks of capture, murder, torture or slavery were so great that it was virtually an act of courage for crews and captains, let alone passengers, to put to sea.

The Turkish Mediterranean fleet behaved with arrogant confidence. Among their more illustrious victims were the Knights of St John, who were driven from their base in Rhodes in 1523 after a heroic six-month resistance. The Knights' new home in Malta, granted to them by Emperor Charles V in 1530, carried with it the obligation to defend the Spanish possession of Tripoli; the Knights failed to hold it in 1551 and in 1556 they were attacked in Malta by a force that outnumbered them by nearly three to one. For almost four months, the Knights threw back repeated Turkish assaults, and were finally rescued by an expedition sent by King Philip II of Spain.

Philip was well aware of just how serious the Turkish danger was. It had been amply demonstrated to him early in his reign, in 1560, when he authorised an attack on Djerba, the island guarding the approaches to Tripoli. As soon as news of the attack reached Constantinople, eighty-five galleys were ordered to sea and covered the thousand miles to Djerba in the then phenomenal time of twenty days. When they sighted the Turks, the Christian crews panicked and tried to escape. They failed·dismally. The Turks seized twenty-seven of their forty-seven galleys and half the Christian force of 12,000 men.

Philip learned the harsh lesson very thoroughly. He embarked on an extensive galley-building programme and, in 1564, was able to send out a much-strengthened and technically superior fleet to discipline the North African pirates and regain initiative in the western Mediterranean.

The fleet consisted of a hundred galleys, of which seventy were Spanish, a vast improvement on the mere sixty-four which Philip, his Italian allies and the Knights of St John had possessed between them in 1560.

The situation, however, was still fraught with risk. The Turks were still dangerous in central and eastern Mediterranean; there was little to check them for, throughout the 1560s, Spain, the only power that could hope to challenge them successfully, was too occupied elsewhere to pay very much attention to Mediterranean affairs. It was fortunate that the major confrontation of Christian and Turk did not take place in that decade. That it did not was due partly to the Turks' preoccupation with the southward spread of Russian power, partly to the influence exercised over them by the French.

One effect of the situation was to preserve the island of Cyprus in the possession of the great mercantile empire of Venice for more than eighty years. Cyprus had been ceded to the Venetians in 1488 by the mother of the island's last Lusignan king, who hoped by the move to keep it from the Moslem Turkish grasp. As far as Venice was concerned, Cyprus proved a supremely lucrative, but at the same time highly dangerous, acquisition. Its strategic position, across the important sea route from Constantinople to Alexandria, made the island a potential source of trouble so long as it remained in Christian hands.

The danger did not materialise until 1569. In that year, the Turks abandoned the last of several plans for dealing with Russia, and the influence of the French began to wane as they became embroiled in civil war. King Philip was faced with a serious revolt of the Moriscos, the remnants of the Moors who had once ruled Spain, and in a massive explosion, the arsenal at Venice blew up. News of the latter event reached the Turks in greatly exaggerated form; the disaster, it was said, had wrecked most of the Venetian fleet.

The various factors combined to convince the Turks that the time had come to acquire Cyprus. Their first move, in February 1570, was to demand from Venice the immediate cession of the island. The Venetians refused. They were encouraged to do so by the papal nuncio, whose master, Pius V, had his own reasons for wanting to kindle a crusading spirit against the Turks. Ever since his election in 1566, Pius had been striving to forge Spain, France, Venice and the Italian States into a Holy League. When first mooted, the idea had aroused little enthusiasm, for rivalries and jealousies between those Christian nations were particularly strong.

The crisis over Cyprus changed their mood dramatically, and its gravity was underlined in July 1570, when the Turks invaded the island, stormed and sacked Nicosia, took Kyrenia without a fight and laid seige to Famagusta. The Venetians appealed to the Pope, who at once sent word to Philip. With uncharacteristic speed, Philip agreed within eight days to join Pius's cherished Holy League.

Despite the seriousness of the renewed Turkish onslaught on Christendom, the would-be allies of the League brought

A map from the Catalan atlas of the eastern Mediterranean and Black Seas which shows how Cyprus dominated the sea route from Alexandria to Constantinople. BRITISH MUSEUM (D. RUDKIN)

old animosities to their negotiation of the treaty. They argued over the composition of the joint fleet, over the rewards each State was to reap, over the nationality of the commander-in-chief, and even over the purpose of their efforts. Venice regarded the League as a device to help regain Cyprus; Spain looked upon it as the means of recovering her possessions in North Africa.

As a result, six months elapsed before terms were agreed, and the treaty was not ratified until 24 May 1571. It provided for a force of about 200 galleys, 100 transports and other vessels, 50,000 soldiers and 4,500 cavalry, to be gathered every year by the beginning of April. They were to fight not only against the Turks, but also against the Moslems of North Africa. One-sixth of the cost was to be borne by the Pope, one-third by Venice and one-half by Spain. The Spaniards, as the major contributors, were allowed to choose the commander-in-chief. Philip named his illegitimate half-brother Don John of Austria for the post.

Don John was an impetuous twenty-four-year old, who had first tasted battle only three years before, and he was a good choice to lead what was, in effect, a latter-day crusade.

On 25 August 1571, Don John sailed into Messina in his magnificent sixty-oar *Reale*, accompanied by twenty-three other galleys. They and the fifty-seven other Spanish galleys were the best-equipped, best-manned and best-built of the entire Christian fleet, which also included six Venetian galleasses, twenty Papal vessels and nine belonging to Genoa, Savoy and the Knights of St John.

The 105 Venetian galleys fell far below Spanish standards; they were in a thoroughly neglected condition, and so undermanned that Spanish and Italian infantry had to be put aboard to bring their crews up to strength. More than two weeks passed before all the problems were resolved and the fleet was able to sail. It was by then too late in the season for an attempt to be made to recover Cyprus, so it was decided instead to seek battle with the Turks in the eastern Mediterranean.

At that juncture, the fate of Christian Europe hung by the slenderest of threads, for the Turks had never yet been beaten at sea. The anxiety caused by the knowledge depressed even further the morale of Italians, who had lived in an atmosphere of terror throughout August. On the first of that month, Famagusta had fallen, and the Venetian commander, Bragadino, had been flayed alive before the eyes of his conquerors. The consequence of that disaster soon became apparent along the Adriatic coast of Italy, a coast left virtually unguarded by the absence of the Venetian fleet from their normal stations at Corfu and Crete. A fleet of Turkish galleys under Ali Pasha ravaged and pillaged at will to within three hundred miles of Venice itself and the city was saved only by the news that the fleet of the Holy League was gathering at Messina. Fearing he might be trapped in the Adriatic, Ali Pasha sailed his galleys away to the south.

The brutality Venice escaped did, however, fall on Corfu. On 27 September, the fleet of the Holy League sailed into harbour there, to find that Uluch Ali (or El Louck Ali), corsair king of Algiers, had preceded them, and had left Corfu an island of charred and ruined houses, desecrated churches and despairing people mourning over the mangled bodies of men, women and children. Uluch Ali, like Ali Pasha, had been recalled to prepare for battle. By the beginning of October, the Turks had concentrated about 250 galleys in the Bay of Lepanto, in the channel between the Gulf of Patras and the Gulf of Corinth.

On 3 October, while the Turks were making their preparations at Lepanto, the Christian fleet sailed out of Corfu; next day they sighted the rocky Ionian islands of Cephalonia and Ithaca. A strong westerly wind sprang up, halting the fleet in heavy seas at the end of the channel between the islands. Two days passed before the wind dropped and backed to the south-east. On the 6th, the Christian ships advanced across the Ithaca channel and anchored off the Greek coast, near the entrance to the Gulf of Corinth.

There, they spent the night, only twenty miles away from the Turkish fleet.

At dawn next day, the Turks left Lepanto and moved southwards into the Gulf of Corinth. Two miles from shore, they turned to face westwards and began to deploy into crescent-shaped formation. The ships of the Holy League were by that time nearing Cape Skropha, in the north-west corner of the Gulf of Corinth.

As the two fleets sighted each other, Don John gave orders for his ships to form up, with the six 44-gun galleasses in the van, and 150 galleys in line abreast behind them. Then, he embarked in a small frigate and sailed down the line, a striking youthful figure in a suit of light armour, holding a crucifix in his hand. 'He put galley after galley in battle array,' wrote an eyewitness, 'and exhorted them to fight valiantly against the hereditary enemy of the Christian faith ... Thereupon, the warriors shouted aloud for joy and formed for battle.'

Meanwhile, the Turkish reserve was taking up position. Then, with the wind filling their painted sails and the green flag of the Prophet streaming from the mastheads, the Turks swept down on the Christian fleet. It was a dangerous moment, for not all the Christian ships were in position. Even so, Don John ordered a gun to be fired as a signal to attack, and had the special purple-and-gold battle standard, given him by the Pope, broken from the mainmast of *Reale*. Then, suddenly, the wind died, giving the Christians precious time to deploy. Across the water, the Turks stepped up the rhythm of their oars and surged once more towards the enemy.

As they passed between the galleasses, the Turks were bombarded from above by cannon and pelted with musket fire and arrows. By the time they reached the main fleet, the Turkish front line had broken. In the centre, Ali Pasha, the Turkish commander, drove his galley straight for Don John's *Reale*. As the Turk approached, his cannon raked the length of the Christian ship. Under a great pall of smoke and flame, Ali Pasha crashed his prow into *Reale* and Turks and Spaniards poured arrows at each other from a range of two or three yards.

Then, Spanish knights and pikemen boarded the Moslem galley. They were driven back, but came on again. A rush of Turkish soldiers repulsed them, and swept in their turn on to *Reale*. The Papal admiral Colonna, whose galley was close by, rammed the stern of Ali Pasha's ship. As Colonna's arquebusiers fired straight into the mass of Turkish troops preparing to board *Reale*, his soldiers rushed the enemy. They fought until every Turk on board was killed. Ali Pasha died with his men; some reports say that his head was cut off and impaled on a spike on Don John's galley.

To the south, the flagship of the Knights of St John was locked in battle with ships of the Turkish centre. To their right, a gap opened up in the Christian ranks. The galleys of Geanandria (Giovanni Andrea) Doria, of Genoa, were running southwards, apparently to avoid being outflanked. Uluch Ali chased after them, but a mile away from the battle, his galleys turned and swept back the way they had come.

Soon, the Knights' flagship was surrounded, rammed and boarded. Only three Knights, so badly injured they were taken for dead, were left alive. The Turks rushed the Papal *Fiorenza*, captured the *Margarita di Savoia* and swept on to the next Christian ship, the Papal *San Giovanni*. The reserve, under the Spanish Marques de Santa Cruz, steered straight for the gap where Doria should have been. Don John came up with twelve ships and by the time a crestfallen Doria returned, Uluch Ali was fleeing westwards, his fast corsairs outpacing the slower Christian galleys.

By then, other Turks also were leaving the battle. Some fled back into the Gulf of Corinth, others ran their ships ashore and sought the safety of land. They left behind them 30,000 dead, 8,000 prisoners and, except for the thirty or forty galleys that had fled with Uluch Ali, virtually their entire fleet.

News of the victory prompted an outpouring of joy of a kind Europe had not experienced for over a century. Messages of congratulation reached King Philip from all over the Continent, including one from Elizabeth I, while in Rome, Pope Pius poured extravagant praise on the head of Don John. 'There was a man sent from God whose name was John,' he quoted from the Fourth Gospel. He went on to declare, 'the young chief has proved himself a Scipio in valour, a Pompey in heroic grace ... a new Samson, a new Saul, a new David ... and I hope in God to live long enough to reward him with a royal crown!'

Much the same idea had occurred to Don John himself, for his head was thoroughly turned by the universal adulation which had greeted his exploit at Lepanto. He became impatient to attack the remnants of the Turkish fleet, to storm Constantinople and, above all, to carve for himself a kingdom in the Levant, in the heart of infidel territory. He was brought sharply back to reality by an almost immediate waning of Christian unity. Spain and Venice began to argue

over the future activities of the Holy League, and in fact, their only point of agreement was that Don John should not be encouraged in his flamboyant schemes. The young man was bundled off to the Spanish Netherlands to cool his ambition in a less exotic atmosphere.

For the rest, Spain and Venice were irreconcilable. King Philip insisted that future campaigns by the League should concentrate on recovering his possessions in North Africa, and the Venetians, disliking war because it damaged trade, began to slide out of their obligations. Even worse was to come. Encouraged by the French, who feared Spanish domination of the Mediterranean, Venice concluded an astounding treaty with the Turks in March 1573. Its effect was to sink the Holy League for ever.

The Venetians agreed to hand over Cyprus to the Turks, with Albania and other territory, and to pay the Turks an enormous fine of 100,000 ducats a year for three years. It seemed to negate completely all that the Holy League had achieved; it was true that, as the Austrian noble Hans Khevenhuller put it, Lepanto failed to win for Christendom a single yard of land.

However, the real benefit of that victory was probably more valuable than any amount of territorial gain. For Lepanto removed the terror that had for so long pervaded Europe. The Turk, it appeared, was not invincible and Europe, it seemed, would not fall to the fanatics of Islam.

Below: A dramatic painting by an unknown artist of the Battle of Lepanto which is also remarkable for such details as permanent and temporary ships' castles; rams; ships of one, two and three masts; fighting men on platforms, and a variety of heraldic designs. NATIONAL MARITIME MUSEUM, LONDON

Overleaf: The painting of the 17th-century Venetian School depicts Francesco Morosini pursuing the Turks who had tried to gain possession of Crete some seventy years after Lepanto. M. PUCCIARELLI

FRAN:ᶜᵒ MOROˢⁱ CAP:ⁿ GⁿALE INSEGVISC
NVMEROSA ASSAI DELLA VENETA ARRI
PRENDE.

L'ARMATA TVRCA, CHE FVGGE. SEBENE PIV
DVE DELLE PIV GROSSE GALERE, E LE
APRILE. 1659.

Drake
Round the World

'DRAKE he was a Devon man and ruled the Devon Seas', wrote Newbolt, but Drake sailed further than the seas of Devon. He was eight years old when, to escape religious fanatics, his father took him in 1541 from his native Tavistock to live in an old hulk at Chatham, on the River Medway, in Kent. There, where the river flows into the Thames estuary, he spent his boyhood among boats and shipping.

Having Sir John Hawkins as his kinsman meant that young Francis Drake went to sea as a matter of course as soon as he was old enough. A description of him runs, 'Low in stature, of strong limbs, broad breast, round-heade, well-favoured face and of good countenance'. He was apprenticed to the skipper of an old coaster, a rough and hard school but one well qualified to teach seamanship.

When he was first in command of a ship, with Hawkins in 1568, he had his early brush with Spain. At San Juan de Ulua, in spite of binding promises to the contrary, the Spaniards suddenly attacked in overwhelming force. Three ships, one of them belonging to the queen, were lost and the knowledge of the treatment Spaniards meted out to the captured 'heretic' sailors gave Drake an undying hatred of Spain.

At Plymouth, he fitted out two small ships, with pinnaces on deck for inshore work, and sailed westward again. Aided by another

ship which came to join him, he took and sacked the chief Spanish port of Nombre de Dios, on the Isthmus of Panama, where the silver was brought from the mines for shipment to Spain. Then he crossed the isthmus, guided by friendly local Indians. He stopped on the way to climb a tall tree and looked out over the glittering sheet of the Pacific. There and then he made a vow to sail the first English ship on that ocean and went on to create havoc at Panama.

It took only three weeks for his ships to recross the Atlantic and they were back sailing up Plymouth Sound on a Sunday morning, giving the parsons barely time to preach their sermons. His ships, flamboyantly strung with streamers and flags, gave tongue with their guns. Sermons or no sermons, the people poured out of the churches as fast as people could run; it was not every day that Francis Drake came home to Devon, and with a bar or two of solid silver to show. The queen sent for him and made much of him and the Earl of Essex asked for his help in the Irish Sea.

However, five years passed before he was able to realise his ambition to sail the Pacific and by then he had reached the age of forty. He suffered at times with two wounds caused by Spaniards – a ball in his leg and an arrow-wound in his thigh – but they had not cost him his sense of humour. The preparations for his new voyage could not be kept secret, though whispers were spread of Alexandria being the intended destination in order to allay Spanish suspicions. Theoretically at least, all that Drake proposed to do was to sail through the Strait of Magellan into the South Sea. On that basis he was given support and encouragement by Queen Elizabeth and backed by her financial interest in the enterprise.

Five vessels were to take part, with a ship of about eighteen guns as his flagship. Her name was the *Pelican* at the start but it was changed to *Golden Hind* by Drake during the voyage. Accompanying her were a ship of two-thirds her size, the *Elizabeth*, two sloops, a pinnace too small to have a name, and other pinnaces on deck in sections. Presented by the queen with perfumed water and sweetmeats, Drake set sail from Plymouth half-way through November 1577.

Facing page above: Sir Francis Drake; a portrait by an unknown artist. NATIONAL PORTRAIT GALLERY, LONDON

Facing page below: A drawing of Drake's 'Golden Hind', formerly the 'Pelican'. NATIONAL MARITIME MUSEUM, LONDON

Below: Queen Elizabeth I; a portrait by an unknown artist. NATIONAL PORTRAIT GALLERY, LONDON

Off the Cape Verde Islands, more or less in mid-Atlantic, he had the good fortune to capture, probably illegally, the laden Portuguese ship *Maria*. She was a valuable prize, not only because of her stock of provisions but even more because of her pilot, Nuno da Silva, who was of great help to Drake and became his staunch friend.

After making a quick passage with the north-east trade winds, they sighted the Brazilian coast and sailed southward to Port St Julian in Patagonia. There Drake dealt with Doughty, the mystery-man of the fleet. Thomas Doughty, who had been a friend of Drake and captain of a ship, was loose of tongue, suspected of fomenting mutiny and of dealing in sorcery. Drake would have none of it; it was wrecking the voyage. He had Doughty tried by a jury of captains, who found him guilty, and he sentenced him to death. On the shore of the same little harbour where, strangely enough, Magellan had hanged his mutineer fifty years earlier, Doughty was beheaded after he and Drake had taken Holy Communion together. Afterwards, Drake mustered the ships' companies and made a speech. 'I will have the gentlemen to pull with the sailors', he said. It was to be the keynote of their life together.

At St Julian, he stripped and sank the two least seaworthy of the ships and the prize-ship *Maria*, spreading their crews among the other three vessels to fill the many gaps caused by illness and accidents. The ships were careened (turned on their sides) to have their bottoms scraped and cleansed of marine growths, thoroughly overhauled and refitted, before they sailed into Magellan's Strait. Drake had no chart of the strait, merely his skill and experience, but 'by guess and by God', as the old phrase goes, after a fortnight of effort, endurance and sheer determination, all three ships won through. They were in the Pacific, Drake's 'South Sea'.

A hurricane wind took charge and drove the *Pelican* under bare poles first to the north and then far to the southward. It whisked away the one little sloop, which was never seen again. The *Elizabeth*, after managing to anchor, was forced back into the strait and there she stayed for several weeks waiting in vain for Drake. Finally, she made her way back to England.

Drake gave her up and, with his single ship, followed the coasts of Chile and Peru, capturing Spanish ships, sacking towns and creating panic, until his mere name terrified Spanish ears. His richest prize, the *Nuestra Señora de la Concepcion*, caught after a long chase, was laden with gold and silver. In a generous mood, he gave the Portuguese captain valuable presents, and money and clothes to all the crew. Drake loved display and pomp. He had his gilded silver tableware, and a trumpeter and music, always at his meals. And his men adored it all as they adored his hearty wit and his occasional bellow.

At last he decided that it was time for the homeward voyage. In September of 1579, he careened his ship, then renamed *Golden Hind*, once more, and, after calling for water in the Philippines, sailed for the Moluccas, where he had a warm welcome from the Sultan. They made a treaty together while the crew packed the ship with spices.

Sailing on, they came to an uninhabited but pleasant island where, after building a fort, they spent an idle month. But as she was getting under way again, the *Golden Hind* ran hard on to a reef and Drake had to get her off by jettisoning eight of his guns and half the precious spices.

In mid-June he doubled the Cape of Good Hope, and at the end of nearly three years he arrived at Plymouth, the fifth navigator to have circumnavigated the globe. He brought back with him only fifty-seven men but plenty of gold and silver, certainly enough to please the eyes of Queen Elizabeth.

Her Majesty came down to Deptford to see the *Golden Hind* and there, defying Philip of Spain and all that he could do, on board his own ship and with his own sword, she knighted Sir Francis Drake. By the queen's order, the *Hind* was preserved in dry dock for posterity, though she lasted little longer than a century.

Waghenaer and Charting

THE earliest nautical maps, or charts, are things of mystery to the modern man. It is very difficult to make head or tail of them, especially the Arabic ones, and when the old cartographers have let their imaginations take charge, the task of reading them seems almost impossible. Even so, sailors apparently managed with them for a considerable time, until 1569, before the great advance of the Fleming Gerhard Mercator appeared. His new approach represented the earth's surface as if on a cylinder but spread out flat. Mercator's projection was later amended and perfected by an Englishman, Edward Wright, whose name is now nearly forgotten.

The great era of eager exploration of the sea, during the latter part of the sixteenth century, created the need for proper records of navigational hazards in strange waters. Soon the explorer and the pilot on their voyagings began to take written notes of shoals and tidal flows, of soundings and anchorages and the stars, instead of relying solely on experience and memory.

One can imagine them sitting over their schnapps or ale in harbour with their mates exchanging information that gradually grew into a stock of nautical lore. By 1550 a few small books, mainly Dutch or Flemish, appeared, giving sailing directions for stretches of the northern seas between Iceland and Cadiz, which usually were the limits of sailing for the ordinary mariner. The directions were almost entirely restricted to harbour and tidal information, illustrated with little sketches of churches and other landmarks along the coast.

The first to collect hydrographic material giving coastal navigation and sailing directions, known as 'rutters', was a Dutch pilot, Lucas Jabszoon Waghenaer, of Enkhuizen. In 1584-85 he published the first part of a book, *Der Spieghel Zeevaerdt*, containing an atlas of charts and directions charting a wide area east and west of the Zuider Zee, which he knew well. The book was a success with Dutch mariners and it was followed in the next year by a second and equally successful part. Each was at once popular and went through several editions and translations into many languages.

The English edition, entitled *The Mariners Mirrour*, was produced with re-engraved script in 1588 by Anthony Ashley, the Clerk to the Privy Council, who was commissioned to undertake it by Sir Christopher Hatton. It is indeed a sumptuous volume, large and heavy, with a splendidly coloured frontispiece surrounded with drawings of navigational instruments to introduce the wealth of tables in the following pages.

Starting with the declination of the sun, the phases of the moon and the tidal movements, it goes on to instructions in the handling of astrolabe and quadrant. There are lists of fixed stars and their uses, followed by an ingenious cut-out star compass. A table of distances by sea between the chief Continental ports leads to another for traversing degrees of latitude and different angles. Then come the charts, each with details of landmarks and depths of moorings in the various harbours shown and charted.

Originally the charts were uncoloured, but unknown hands tinted all of them some time in the seventeenth century and a few have been recoloured. Quite a number are magnificent. Between them, they extend from the north of Europe into part of the Mediterranean; Britain has been specially favoured, with a series of large-scale charts of sectors of the coastline. England has been well done but Scotland ends sadly decapitated and mangled in the northern counties.

Nearly every chart is decorated with fascinating pictures of spouting whales, here and there in tandem, and equally fascinating ships are scattered about the sea. The vessels

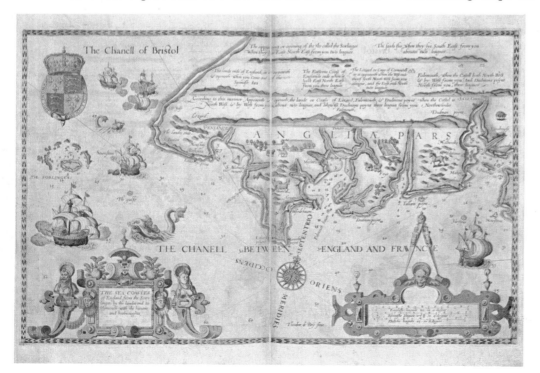

Left: 'The Chanell Between England and France', a map of England's southern coasts from 'The Mariners Mirrour'. BRITISH MUSEUM

Right: A chart of the Atlantic coasts of north Africa and Europe from the Catalan Atlas of 1339, one of the first world atlases. BRITISH MUSEUM

HONI SOIT QVI MAL Y PENSE

THE MARINERS MIRROVR

Wherin may playnly be seen the courses, heights, dis=
tances, depths, soundings, flouds and ebs, risings of
lands, rocks, sands and shoalds, with the marks for th'en=
trings of the Harbouroughs, Havens and Ports of the
greatest part of Europe: their seuerall traficks and
commodities: Together w.th the Rules and instrumēts
of NAVIGATION.

First made & set fourth in diuers exact Sea-Charts, by that famous
Nauigator LVKE WAGENAR of Enchuisen And now fitted with necessarie
additions for the use of Englishmen by
ANTHONY ASHLEY.

Heerin also may be understood the exploits lately atchiued by the right
Honorable the L. Admiral of Englād, with her Ma.tis Nauie and some
former seruices don by that worthy Knight
S.r FRA: DRAKE.

20 40 60 90

20 40 60

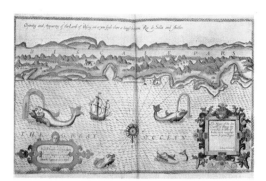

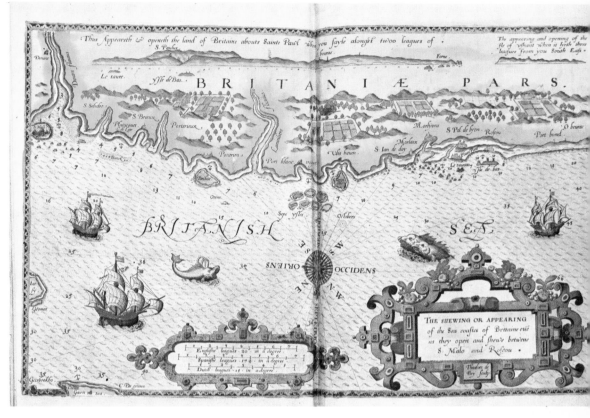

Left: Frontispiece of 'The Mariners Mirrour', commissioned by Sir Christopher Hatton and produced by Anthony Ashley.
BRITISH MUSEUM (D. RUDKIN)

Above: The Bay of Biscay between Rio de Sella and Auiles as a chart in 'The Mariners Mirrour'. BRITISH MUSEUM

Right: The sea coast of Brittany from St Malo to beyond the port of Roscoff, from 'The Mariners Mirrour'. BRITISH MUSEUM

are not mere copies and often differ in various ways in their size and rig.

In two separate charts of Portuguese waters ships are shown firing broadsides on both sides simultaneously, in mighty billows of smoke, one of them from her lower gun-deck with apparently five guns. Two Spanish ships have square sails and lateens in differing combinations. Then there is a fine carrack of Portugal with high ends, and several other large and small vessels with high poops.

Referring again to the British coast, a four-masted ship-of-war with two tiers of guns is shown heading down-Channel under a spread spritsail, foresail and mainsail, and a main topsail and a furled topgallant. She has lateen mizen and bonaventure mizen both drawing well.

More interesting still are the fishing-boats in English waters. The sea off Hartlepool is thronged with tiny en-quiring fishes breaking surface, while fishermen are over-hauling their nets. The tall mainmasts of their boats are un-shipped and lying out over the bows, although the mizen masts are still stepped and held by the stays.

In addition to the whales and a sea-serpent or two, with one solitary flying fish that has somehow found its way into the Bay of Biscay, Waghenaer has livened up his charts with appropriate animals here and there along the coastline. From wolves and a reindeer in Norway to farmstock and horses, they go south to pairs of parrots mounting sentinel over Spanish or Italian waters.

There is a German translation of *The Mariners Mirrour* in the British Museum with a facsimile of the text, but the quality of the colourings does not compare with the tinting in the original volume. In 1592 Waghenaer published another volume under the title of *Thresoor der Zeevaert*; it was similar to his first book, with the text rewritten and expanded and charts on a much smaller scale, but showing the coastline with greater accuracy.

During the following fourteen years, six Dutch and three French editions of *Thresoor der Zeevaert* were published but, although there was demand for them, the issues seem to have been rather scanty. Copies are now few and far between,

but one copy, in French, dated 1601, is in the British Museum. There are engravings in the book by an Englishman, Benjamin Wright. It appears to have been published in Amsterdam and the translation into French is not very good. However, it contains twenty-five double-page charts finely engraved in copper and a number of woodcuts in the text.

At the end of the volume there is a general statement of the growing interest being developed by the Dutch in the East Indies, thereby foreshadowing the formation of the Dutch East India Company in 1602. There are instructions for sailing round Africa, notes on the ports and trade in commodities of India, of the East Indies and even of China, together with a treatise on the five possible routes from England to the Far East. They are listed as:

1 By the Cape of Good Hope, sailing Eastwards;
2 By the Strait of Magellan sailing Westwards;
3 By Forbusscher's North-West Passage (which Waghenaer cheerfully admits had not then been explored);
4 By Barentzoon's North-East Passage (which also seems a non-starter since it had been explored only in part);
5 By going straight across over the North Pole.

There is no doubt, however, that the imaginative work of Waghenaer has been intensely valuable. His application of nautical science overtook the slow and tedious rule-of-thumb methods of many maritime adventurers.

Rule-of-thumb navigation nonetheless lingered on here and there almost into our present-day technical triumphs. In the 1940s, for instance, there flourished a hardbitten coaster skipper who more often than not worked his way down the east coast ports of England and Scotland. Not the most literate of men, just how he managed to pass his Master's examination was his own secret, but he knew how to handle his ship. When challenged, he would recite the names of every lighthouse and lightship between Aberdeen and Newhaven, with lightbuoys thrown in for good measure, giving their correct sequence and the class of light, whether occulting, fixed or flashing, and stating the colour of each. He never hesitated or made a slip. Lucas Waghenaer could have talked to that skipper.

Sixteenth-Century Prestige Ships

Top: James IV of Scotland, whose 'Great Michael' was a remarkable achievement.

Above: Henry VII who hired ships from Spain but also built the 'Sovereign' which was his flagship against James IV.

Right: Model of a late-18th-century Flemish carrack.

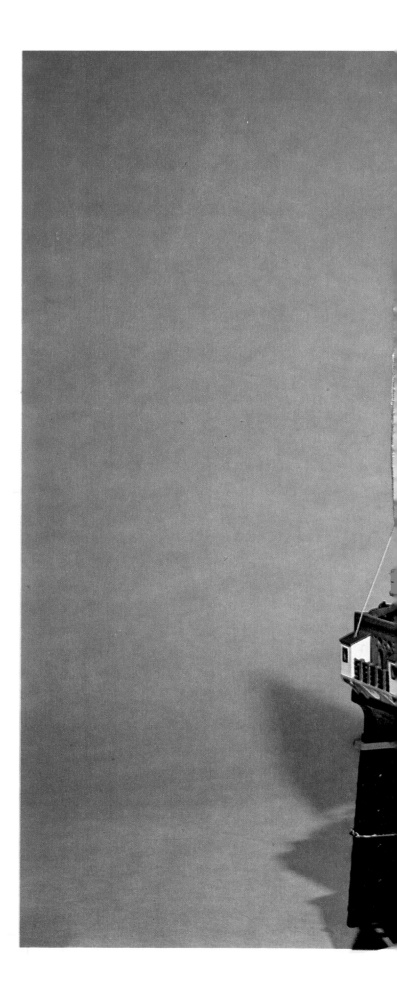

GENOA played a large part in the evolution during the sixteenth century of the type of big ship which became known as the carrack. At that time Genoese traders sailed regularly, year after year, from Italy to Southampton to market wines, fruit and oil in exchange for great bundles of English wool, and all the while their ships were gradually developing in size and shape. In time the term carrack came to be loosely applied to many large vessels, but the authentic carrack was unmistakable, with a well-rounded hull, square cargo hold amidships, and very high castled decks thrusting far out over bow and stern. The build and general appearance were adopted by Portugal and Spain, then spread northward until the fashion reached the Netherlands and, later, England and Scotland.

Those contacts between northerners and southerners brought about changes on both sides. The north Europeans were soon laying down big three-masted or four-masted carracks and making a break with the time-honoured method of clinker construction with overlapping planks. Instead they used edge-to-edge planking to enable the hull to support the weight of heavy cannon mounted on the open main deck. This explains why not one of the carracks of Henry VII was carvel-built, while those of his son, Henry VIII, were probably all carvel.

Henry VII hired carracks and other ships from Spain as well as from his own country during hostilities, because he apparently thought the English charges excessively high. He also tried to buy some Spanish vessels outright, but could not

persuade the Spaniards to sell. Perhaps it was as a result of this that he built two carracks of his own, starting work on both in the year 1487. One of them, the *Sovereign*, was armed with 141 small cannon of 1½-inch bore, known as serpentines. These little guns, some made of brass and some of iron, were probably effective only in attacking an enemy crew at close quarters, or in cutting the rigging. They could hardly have done any real damage to the stout sides of a carrack. To supplement them in a simpler kind of fight, the *Sovereign* carried 200 longbows with 800 sheaves of arrows. She saw some action as the flagship of Henry's fleet during his dispute with James IV of Scotland.

One difference between the carracks of Spain and Portugal and those of England lay in the huge pictures of saints, and other religious motifs, that covered most of the area of the Iberians' sails. In contrast, the decoration of English ships of the period seems to have been largely confined to bright paintwork about the decks and a little gilding with an array of streamers on the mast or from the tops.

In 1511 James IV was eager to avenge the murder of his friend and naval adviser Andrew Barton, whom he was supposed to have sent on an expedition against Flemish pirates. Barton had incurred the wrath of English merchants,

and King Henry VIII had encouraged the Earl of Surrey to fit out two ships and track him down. Following Barton's death in a heroic and desperate fight, his captured ships were brought back into the Thames.

Amongst other preparations, James ordered the laying down of a giant four-masted carrack, which was to be the largest and most powerful ship in the world. For her time James's *Great Michael* was a remarkable achievement. A Frenchman, Jacques Tarrat, was engaged to supervise her construction, and much of the timber had to be imported. Her dimensions as given by contemporaries seem incredible for the date. She was 240 feet long, thirty-six feet wide (internal beam), and to protect her against gunfire her sides were ten feet thick, thus giving her a total beam of fifty-six feet. She mounted 315 guns, mostly very light pieces for use against men, but she also had three basilisks, which fired two-hundred-pound shot. There were 120 master gunners, 300 seamen and a thousand soldiers in her crew.

Henry VII required a replacement for the *Regent*, destroyed in battle with France, and being at the same time jealous of the prestigious *Great Michael*, he decided to go one better than King James. His new ship was laid down by William Bond in September of 1512 to the design of Robert Brygandine. Named the *Henri Grâce à Dieu*, she was a carrack and similar to the *Great Michael* in appearance. She had four masts with topgallant sails on the fore, main and mizen masts and a topsail on the bonaventure mast. No other ship of the time is known to have had three tiers of canvas on more than one mast, but they were probably more for show than go.

The *Great Harry*, as she was generally called, had eight decks and originally carried 184 guns in all. Some were old-style breech-loaders and a few were the more powerful bronze muzzle-loaders then coming into use. She had 301 seamen, fifty gunners and 349 soldiers. All her men were assigned to stations and her quarter-bill is the earliest known.

Like the other giant carracks of her time, she was really a white elephant, better suited to displaying the wealth and pomp of her country in peaceful summer seas than engaging in serious warfare. This practice of building prestige-ships was so firmly established that it is true to say that the largest ships of the sixteenth century only went to sea on special occasions. In the course of her thirty-eight years of service, for instance, the *Great Harry* was only actually once involved in battle: at Spithead in 1545.

Left: A model of James IV's 'Great Michael' of 1511.
ROYAL SCOTTISH MUSEUM, EDINBURGH

Below: Painting by Norman Wilkinson of Henry VII's 'Henri Grâce à Dieu' of 1512. M. MUIR COLLECTION

The *Great Michael* also saw little service. She was in the Scottish fleet that was assembled when war broke out with England in 1513. James spent a few days on board to encourage his seamen before he marched off with his army towards his death in battle. James ordered the Earl of Arran to sail the *Great Michael* to France and join their allies, but Arran disobeyed and went instead to Ireland, sacking and burning Carrickfergus before returning to Ayr to sell the plunder. James was annoyed and ordered Sir Andrew Wood to take charge, but it was too late – the fleet had sailed to France before the message reached it.

James fell at Flodden, leaving his fleet in French waters. Purchased at a bargain price by King Francis I of France, the *Great Michael* was renamed the *Grande Nef d'Ecosse*, and remained on the French navy list until 1527 – although she took part in no operations, and might never have gone to sea. The other Scottish ships disappeared quickly, and are believed to have been broken up for timber.

Henry also very soon found that these giant ships were more of a nuisance than an asset, for the *Great Harry* was too big for most harbours, which although adequate for the normal ships of the time, were small and shallow. Indeed, the trouble with the *Great Harry*'s size began with her construc-

tion and led to the foundation of the first permanent English dockyard for the building and repair of ships of war. When Henry went to meet Francis in 1520 at the Field of Cloth of Gold, his prestige ship drew too much water for the harbours of Dover and Calais, so he had to use a smaller ship, the *Katherine Plesaunce*.

But if Henry was disillusioned with large ships, some foreign powers were not. In the second and third decades of the century the fashion begun by the *Great Michael* flourished and produced some interesting, though not very practical, monster men-of-war. In 1523 the Knights of Malta had the *Santa Anna* built at Nice. The Mediterranean shipwrights had more experience of building large ships than their north European counterparts, and the *Santa Anna* was an outstanding example of the culmination of the carrack type, which was soon to be replaced by the lower-built and more weatherly galleon. She had six decks; the two below the waterline were covered with lead and fastened by bronze nails, as was also the outside of her lower hull.

So strongly was she constructed that her sides could not be penetrated by shot and even a whole fleet would have been unable to sink her. A chapel on board was dedicated to Saint Anne, and her armoury had equipment for five hundred soldiers. The great cabin for the officers had butteries and serving-rooms, and she even had a garden of shrubs and flowers growing in boxes of soil in her stern galleries. Her company ate freshly-baked bread produced from her own windmill and ovens. There was a large forge for three blacksmiths, and she mounted fifty guns and numerous light pieces.

Gustavus Wasa of Sweden followed fashion with the *Elefant* (also called the *Stora Krafveln*) in 1532. She was 174 feet long and forty feet in beam, being referred to as the great carvel, since she was carvel-built, which was still a novelty in a Swedish ship at that time. Not to be outdone, Francis I decided to replace the *Grande Nef d'Ecosse* by an even bigger ship, a colossal five-masted carrack named the *Françoise*. She was built at his new port of Francisopolis (later Le Havre), but when they tried to put her to sea in 1533 she grounded on the bar and blocked the entrance. Refloated with much difficulty, she was towed back to her berth where she was capsized in a gale a few weeks later. Her wreck obstructed the harbour for a long time, until she was eventually broken up and her timber was used to build houses in the St François quarter of the town.

Portugal produced her own giant, the *São João* of 1534. She carried 336 guns, but was unlike the others in not being a carrack. She was something new, and an early example of the galleon type. Both the Maltese *Santa Anna* and the *São João* served in Charles V's successful Tunis expedition of 1535, and the former's sides were said never to have been penetrated by shot from the shore batteries during the fighting. Two artists went with the expedition and were responsible for the designs of the Madrid Tapestries which commemorate the event.

In this beautiful work of art, the *Santa Anna* is depicted (most probably with strict accuracy) as having four heavy guns on each side about half-way down the hull, three tiers of lighter guns in the very high somercastle, and two more tiers in the forecastle. She is full-bodied with a big tumble-home and a carrack head with a figurehead below it. Beneath this is a spur, evidently intended for use against galleys.

The *São João* is very different and plainly shows the influence of the galleasses then being developed by the Venetians. Her forecastle is low and there is no carrack-head, but a deadly-looking spur instead. With a long waist, she has a moderately high somercastle without the steep sheer found in carracks, and she shows five heavy guns on each side, situated very close to the waterline. Two tiers of lighter pieces are set in the somercastle and forecastle. The *São João* was truly the first ship to make the full break with the carrack tradition, and foreshadowed future developments along the lines of the galleon.

The Spanish Armada

E VER since David felled Goliath, the spectacle of the small audacious venturer, with all the odds against him, successfully challenging the proud and mighty mammoth has had unfailing appeal. It is this appeal which has firmly embedded in English folklore the dramatic and decisive humbling of the Spanish Armada in July and August 1588.

Superficially at least, the David-Goliath analogy seems apt. The force of about 130 galleons, galleases, merchantmen, carracks and pinnaces with which King Philip II of Spain sought to smash English seapower was certainly massive in size and armament and splendid as a show of strength.

In the face of that formidable fleet, the English initially had ready no more than sixty-four ships, only twenty-four

of them fighting vessels of any size, when the Armada was sighted off Dodman Point, Cornwall, on 30 July.

In the late sixteenth century, Spain was the dominant power in the world, with a gold- and silver-rich empire in America, from which she sought to exclude all foreigners, and possessions which stretched from the coast of California to the Philippines. It included much of Europe and, most dangerously for England, the Netherlands. It was there that an army under Philip's regent, the Duke of Parma, waited to join the Armada and invade England.

England, by contrast, was a small and overcrowded country, still reeling from years of vicious religious strife, poorly fortified, with limited resources, and materially far from rich. Yet, beneath the modest unpromising façade, there was a strength and power in England and the English which gave both an overwhelming potential. Similarly, the grandeur and glitter of Spain concealed inherent weakness.

Psychologically, the Spaniards were burdened with the stiff self-righteous attitude of those who were sure God backed their cause. Just as they assumed that the great Spanish Empire had been bestowed by God as a sign of their worth, they regarded the Armada as an instrument of 'God's obvious design'. Its purpose was to punish the heretic English, who had dared to raid Spanish colonies, seize Spanish treasure ships and so deny Spain's God-given right to

monopolise the New World.

The Spanish attitude was clear in the confident message emblazoned on the Armada's sails – 'Arise, Lord, and vindicate your cause,' and it also blinded Philip in his choice of commander. The hapless Duke of Medina Sidonia, on whom the king's choice fell, protested in vain that he was always sick at sea and in any case knew more about gardening than warfare.

The English were far more realistic. They had a hearty hatred of Spanish treachery, and an abhorrence of Spanish Catholicism, but they did not underestimate Spanish power. Lord Howard of Effingham, the English Lord Admiral, called the Armada the greatest fleet the world had ever seen,

and the terror which the thought of Spanish conquest inspired in England was very real. The English knew well that only their courage, their wits and their skill stood between them and disaster.

Fortunately, these very qualities had been thoroughly sharpened and tested in the years since 1561, when Queen Elizabeth first made it clear that England would not let Spain exclude her from the riches of America.

If this conflict of views and interests did not explode into war until 1588, the reason was that neither Elizabeth nor Philip had desired it. However, by the time the Spaniards at last lost patience and their long-threatened Armada transpired, a quarter-century of diligent English poaching in America, as well as vigorous experiments in shipbuilding, made the English far more suited than the Spaniards to the exigencies of naval warfare.

The Spaniards viewed war at sea as a floating version of war on land. That was why the Armada's main force of twenty galleons, with timbers four or five feet thick and up to fifty-two guns apiece, were so high in the stern, so wide in the beam and contained so many more soldiers than sailors; the ratio was three to one. The idea was to provide a broad lofty platform for deadly volleys of musket-fire and a springboard for grappling and boarding.

The English theory was to fight with sleek easily manoeuvrable ships that relied on longer-range gunpower to sink the enemy from a distance. In the late 1570s and early 1580s, John Hawkins had developed new revolutionary galleons based on that philosophy; when the Armada came, between fourteen and eighteen of them (the exact number is variously reported) were included in the English force, which totalled nearly 200 sail. Hawkins' ships cut down on the heavy bow and stern castles which made the traditional galleon so top-heavy and awkward to sail. They were slimmer in the waist, longer and more streamlined in shape and more level in the decks. The deep pit in the centre, which had formerly held contingents of reserve troops, was replaced by two decks of heavy guns. In addition, the new design allowed for lighter and more-numerous culverins that could send a 9-lb shot streaking over half a mile of water with an accuracy that was frightening by the standards of the time.

By contrast, the Spaniards' gunpower was as unwieldy as their galleons. Their heavy guns could lob a 30-lb or 50-lb cannon-ball over a distance of a quarter of a mile with only a questionable chance of hitting the target. The drastic difference between the ships of the Armada and the new English galleons was no secret to King Philip; neither was the difference in tactics which this implied. However, from his instructions to Medina Sidonia, it is clear that the fatal significance of it all did not occur to him.

'You are especially to take notice,' the king advised the duke, 'that the enemy's object will be to engage at a distance, on account of the advantage which they have from their artillery and (other) offensive fireworks ... On the other hand, the object of our side should be to close and grapple and engage hand to hand.'

The more level-headed captains who sailed for England when the Armada set out from Lisbon on 20 May 1588, doubted whether they would get the chance to carry out Philip's orders. They had already seen the audacity and daring of their foe in April 1587, when Francis Drake had swooped down on Cadiz, destroyed more than thirty of the Armada's ships, looted and burned his way along the Iberian coast and captured a treasure ship worth £114,000 on his way home.

'We are sailing against England,' one Spanish captain wrote 'in the confident hope of a miracle ...' that might yield 'some strange freak of weather' or strip 'the English of their wits.' The latter hope proved particularly vain, as the Spaniards discovered soon after sighting the Lizard, which they reached on 29 July, much battered and delayed by bad weather.

Medina Sidonia's instructions were to proceed along the

English Channel in strong defensive crescent-shaped formation towards the point off the Flanders coast where the Spanish army from the Netherlands was due to rendezvous with the Armada. To achieve that object, the duke needed to gain absolute control of the Channel, which was something the English had no intention of allowing him.

As the Armada made its stately and, for the moment, impregnable progress, the English ships shadowed it, pouncing in at intervals to snipe away out of Spanish range, irritating, pin-pricking the Spaniards as a picador does a bull. This particular bull was rattled, and refused to be provoked; Medina Sidonia was strict in obeying orders not to give battle and keep his formation tight and strong.

On the morning of 31 July, however, the Armada found itself in a very dangerous position. During the night, the flexible nimble English ships had sidled out of Plymouth on a contrary wind. Brilliant tacking had enabled them to cross the bows of the Armada, work their way westwards and take up a chosen stance well to the windward of the Spaniards, a feat of seamanship which proved the superiority of Hawkins' new design and gave the English the advantage of position.

The English never lost the advantage and, to the Spaniards' fury, they failed to be drawn by Medina Sidonia's next move. The duke ordered his ships to form the battle crescent, with his most powerful galleons at each tip. The English, however, refused to venture between the arms of the deadly trap. Instead, they came near, though not too near, and then swung away, bombarding the Spaniards with cannon shot as they did so.

Twice more, off Portland on 2 August, and off the Isle of Wight on 4 August, the English attacked at open range, harrying the Armada and peppering the thick Spanish hulls with round shot. But they were firing from a distance that kept them safe from the timber-splintering Spanish cannon, and the English were unable decisively to damage or even delay the Armada.

What damage did occur came about through sheer ill luck. The 46-gun *Rosario* provided pickings for Drake's galleons when she collided with her neighbour, smashed her own bowsprit, lost her foremast and lagged behind the rest of the fleet. Then, a massive and mysterious explosion ripped open the poop of *San Salvador*, hurling hundreds of Spaniards into the sea and littering the Channel with wreckage.

But the rest of the Armada sailed on towards Calais, where it anchored off the roads on 6 August, slightly scratched, rather ruffled, but intact. The English could do no more than emulate them, anchoring watchfully to windward.

It was at Calais Roads on 7 August that Medina Sidonia learned to his despair that bad luck had not only disposed of two of his ships, but of the whole 'enterprise of England'. Parma's invasion force was trapped in Dunkirk and Nieuwpoort by a double blockade; the English stood guard in the Downs (the Channel roadstead off Deal) and Dutch rebel 'sea beggars' stood off Flushing. Even if Medina Sidonia

Left: Close-up of action on board Lord Howard's flagship 'Ark Royal' as she engaged a Spanish ship.
ILLUSTRATED LONDON NEWS

Top: A British attack by fireships on the Spanish Armada.
NATIONAL MARITIME MUSEUM, LONDON

Above: A miniature portrait of Sir Francis Drake.
NATIONAL PORTRAIT GALLERY, LONDON

had been able to force his way to Parma's rescue, his enormous galleons had too deep a draught to get into harbour.

For the Armada, there was no alternative but an ignominious return home. It would be a hazardous one, for the way there had to be northwards, through the wild and treacherous North Sea and thence around the British Isles. The English and the unfavourable wind blocked escape back along the Channel, and to sail eastwards would mean suicide on the wicked Zeeland banks. That same night, the Spaniards discovered that they were not to be allowed to leave unscarred.

At midnight on 7-8 August, the Spaniards saw the flickerings of fireships glow, first dully, then more brightly, as eight flaming vessels drifted downwind towards them. The sight of those sinister silhouettes outlined in roaring fire, with cannon spiked and heating up to explosion point, snapped the Spaniards' nerve. They panicked, slashed their cables and swarmed away in a struggling formless mass. None was even scorched, for all the fireships missed their target. They had, however, served their purpose. The strong tight formation which English snipings had been unable to break was now irretrievably gone.

The English ships which charged the Spanish fleet off Gravelines on 8 August attacked a badly shaken enemy. For the first time, the English had numerical superiority, and for the first time they came in close – just far enough away for Spanish grappling irons to fall short, but near enough to thunder murderous broadsides into the Spanish hulls, now that the earlier error in range had been recognised and corrected. Another factor was that the Spaniards were running short of ammunition, whereas the English could replenish easily.

The English round shot tore through the high thick walls of the Spanish ships, spraying the Spaniards with splinters, smashing cannon to twisted heaps of metal and killing so many men that the Spanish decks were awash with blood and scuppers and hatches dripped with it.

As the air filled with the sounds, the screams and smells of battle, Lord Howard, Drake, Hawkins, Martin Frobisher and their fellow commanders veered off to hammer another victim to destruction or to impotence at point-blank range.

Soon, the once-proud Armada was a tattered bunch of limping leaking dismasted hulks. Here and there, Spaniards who had managed to survive the holocaust dotted the ships'

A portrayal of the defeated Armada retreating in confusion.
ILLUSTRATED LONDON NEWS

sides, taunting the English to come aboard and fight it out as men had long fought, hand to hand and to the death.

All the while, the crippled Armada was drifting towards shipwreck on the sandbars at Flushing. Then, at last, came a stroke of timely mercy. The English broke off the action as the wind became squally and shifted to south-west, allowing the Spaniards to struggle off the lee shore and steer northwards for deeper water.

Their path home to Spain was now inexorably set. Only sixty-six sail survived the long wind-lashed haul around Cape Wrath in north-west Scotland, out into the open Atlantic and back to home waters.

Ships that had escaped destruction by the English were pounded to a mess of debris on spiky rocks, rushed shorewards to disintegration by mighty Atlantic rollers or simply sank, as shot-torn timbers yielded to the sea and strained seams split apart.

Thousands of Spaniards drowned, succumbed to typhus, dysentery, hunger, exhaustion, melancholy, or died by English and Irish hands as they staggered despairing onto inhospitable shores. Of the 5,000 who reached home in mid-October with the mortified Medina Sidonia, two-thirds were dead within the month, and half of their ships never put to sea again.

The English, who had followed the fleeing Armada for four days, till 12 August, when they put into the Firth of Forth, were not at first aware of what they had achieved. September ended before English victory became acknowledged fact. Europe now realised to its amazement and, depending on Protestant or Catholic sympathies, its disgust or delight, that the might and pride of Spain had been soundly thrashed.

Defeat bit deep enough to make the Spaniards recast their navy in more modern mould, and copy English methods of shipbuilding. Future treasure fleets were defended from attack by slimmer more-supple vessels, and future treasure was transported in speedy frigates rather than lumbering carracks and galleons. The Spaniards learned, too, that their colonies abroad would be better preserved by fortified walls and batteries of guns than by arrogant injunctions to intruding foreigners.

By defeating the Armada, the most intrusive and insolent of those foreigners did not end the danger Spain posed to them. But the English certainly saved their country, their Protestant religion and their Protestant queen. The tactics that had trounced the Spaniards also proved to be the prototype for all naval engagements up to the battle of Trafalgar in 1805.

Above all, the week-long battle of the Channel in 1588 gave notice of England's coming stature as a first-class sea power and with that, of her dazzling imperial future. By one of the great ironies of history, the wealthy far-flung British Empire, which emerged three centuries later, was moving towards its zenith in those same years, the 1820s, that saw the Spanish Empire in America crumble and fade away.

Galleons

THE galleon, the ship which helped to mould history, was almost certainly born in Portugal. Well into the sixteenth century, it had become clear that some larger vessel was needed for the increasing number of Atlantic crossings to the New World. The caravel was really too lightly built and too small for long voyages and was very lively in a seaway, while the carrack, though not so top-heavy as it looked, can have been no joy to steer in heavy weather. When, for instance, the huge Portuguese carrack, the *Madre de Dios*, was captured in 1592 by an English squadron and taken into Dartmouth she required fourteen men to handle her steering-gear.

The mere mention of the word galleon, or *galeon*, as the Spaniards had it, somehow gives an impression of size, but for her period the average galleon was not enormous. Even the 'Grete Shippe', the *San Josef* of the seventeenth century, measured only 115 feet along the keel with 139 feet of gundeck, forty feet of beam and a hull nineteen feet deep.

Before the close of the sixteenth century, the early Spanish and Portuguese galleons were modified and improved a great deal. They became weatherly ships and quite fast. Their superstructures were not nearly so high, particularly at the bows, as were the carrack-built vessels although they were still noticeably higher than the galleons of other nations.

The fascinating model of a Royal galleon, dated 1593, which was presented to Philip II of Spain and which is now in the Naval Museum at Madrid gives an idea of the appearance of a ship of that period. The upperworks of the hull are carved, gilded and richly painted, with a long open gallery curved round the stern and running forward on each side as far as the mizen channels. The galleon is shown with four masts, with the foremast stepped in front of the forecastle.

The flood of bullion, with emeralds and minor cargoes such as hides, cochineal and cocoa, that was crossing the Atlantic from the New World, developed early into a regular routine. Each year there were two separate voyages to South America from Seville of 'flotas', merchant fleets of galleons sailing in company. On the outward voyage they carried chiefly humdrum cargoes of European manufacture and of no great importance. Each flota had its general to keep control and also an admiral who was the second in command. The first flota of the year left for Mexico in May and the second sailed in September or October for 'Carthagena of the Indies', nowadays known as Cartagena, in Colombia.

With the second flota, or soon afterwards, went their protectors, the Armada de Galeones, their escort of armed galleons for the homeward voyage. After making a landfall on the South American coast the Armada de Galeones sailed to Cartagena to start collecting the ships from their various ports.

Meanwhile the Viceroy of Peru had seen to it that silver from the mines at Potosi, far away to the southward, had been brought to Panama so that it could be carried across the Isthmus for loading into the galleons. Once the silver was in their holds the Armada de Galeones steered northward, picking up the last of the merchantmen on the way, until they reached western Cuba and Havana. There, the ships from the Mexican ports joined them and the two flotas, with the Armada de Galeones, all sailed homeward together in time to avoid the coming hurricane season. Their chosen

A model of an Elizabethan galleon with colourfully painted castles. SCIENCE MUSEUM, LONDON

course lay out through the Florida Strait and on, past the Azores and the Canary Islands, to Cadiz. When those islands had begun to rise above the horizon every ship cleared for action and kept on the alert until they had reached the comparative safety of Spanish waters; the Azores in particular were notorious for their lurking privateers and pirates.

The ships of the Armada de Galeones usually carried some

of the bullion, both for the king and for private merchants, but they could take only a third of the amount in the hold of any one of their ships in order to make room for the detachments of soldiers they had on board. However, they sailed at no expense to the royal purse, as their costs were covered by a royal levy of one-fifth of the value of all cargoes imported to Spain from the New World.

From time to time instead of the full flota with its Armada de Galeones a few armed galleons were sent on the voyages if there was a temporary shortage of silver from the mines or if there was some threat from pirates or privateers. Their captains were forbidden to carry any ordinary cargoes but gradually the orders were conveniently forgotten and the ships became merchantmen in all but name.

England, at the start of the Elizabethan era, was quick to copy the galleon build for her capital ships although there were marked differences in detail. Apart from the lower superstructure, the stern was far less prominent and cumbersome, making for a more shapely vessel. The smooth shape of the underwater hull has been described as being like that of a whale, in a curious repetition of the words used by the old Arab of a dhow three centuries earlier.

A good example of the well-designed Elizabethan galleon was the ship which was built for Sir Walter Raleigh at Deptford in 1587. She was bought for the Queen's Navy and had her name changed from the *Raleigh Royal* to *Ark Royal*. Like the Spanish galleons, she had forward a long protruding beakhead over a deck of grating. The forecastle was placed well back from the stem, adding to her trim appearance. A forward bulkhead was pierced for light guns only while her main armament was of about forty brass and cast-iron muzzle-loaders of various sizes firing cannon-balls ranging in weight from thirty-two to thirty-six pounds. Steering was by means of a whipstaff, a vertical lever working on a pivot in the deck with a not very efficient short tiller.

Ark Royal's measurements were one hundred feet length of keel, a beam of thirty-seven feet and a hold eighteen feet deep. As was customary in the sixteenth century, she had lateen sails on the two mizenmasts, but by 1618 all English warships had square topsails on their mizens though they ended in stepping a larger mizenmast and scrapping the bonaventure mizen. A novelty was the gallery projecting on each quarter and across the stern. The upperworks were gay with a colourful mixture of paints, although, except for an elaborate figurehead and the royal arms on the stern, there was very little decorative carving.

Although Drake succeeded in capturing his treasure ship off the Isthmus of Panama, neither Elizabethan adventurers, buccaneers nor French privateers were foolhardy enough to make a direct attack on a flota. That was left for a Dutchman to achieve. Admiral Piet Heijn, had once served as a galleyslave in a Spanish galley and so had a score to settle with Spain. In 1628, with a large number of ships, he captured the entire treasure-fleet off the coast of Mexico, a disaster of the first magnitude for Spain, particularly as the French admiral had handicapped his flagship by cramming her with trading goods; disobedience for which he was hanged.

Later, however, Spain had fallen into such straits that in 1700 her king had to ask Louis XIV for help in bringing the galleon home in safety. Louis had already planned to help himself to the treasure when the English Admiral, Sir George Rooke, forestalled him and swooped on the galleons at Vigo, only to find that the cargo had been landed and sent inland. This seems to have been much to the advantage of the carters and drivers, who made the most of their opportunity.

Eight years later Sir Charles Wagner, in command of three English men-of-war, caught three ships of the Armada de Galeones, of rather less gunpower, in the West Indies. One of them blew up, one managed to escape and the third was captured with her cargo of bullion.

Then in 1743 there came a much greater disaster for Spain. Long before, when one of the Spanish captains, Andres de Urdeneta, had gone as a leader to seize the Philippine Islands, he had discovered the phenomenon of the 'Japanese current' moving across the ocean. He left the Philippines to follow it all the way to Acapulco, in southern Mexico.

As a result of his discovery, for many years a vessel which, although at that date it could have borne little resemblance to the sixteenth-century galleon, was still known as the *Manila Galleon* or the *Acupulco Galleon*, sailed annually on a round voyage from Acapulco westward to Manila. She was without any escort though heavily laden with silver. At Manila she unloaded her cargo and took on board instead precious silks, spices and porcelain, the produce of the East Indies and China, that had been collected for her.

Her routine had become no secret and Commodore Anson on his famous voyage round the world after many misadventures determined to capture her in the Philippines. He hid his ship, HMS *Centurion*, among the islands and caught the galleon *Nuestra Señora de Cavadonga* completely by surprise, forcing her to surrender in one brief attack.

With her bullion in his hold, he worked his way homeward with a scratch crew, arriving at Spithead on 15 June 1744. Not long afterwards, the people of Portsmouth saw an astonishing parade. The treasure, packed into thirty-three wagons, guarded by *Centurion*'s crew and preceded by her officers with swords drawn, moved gaily out of the town. With music playing and colours flying they wound through the countryside and up to London. Through St James's Street, the Strand and Cheapside they went till they reached the Tower, the captured galleon's flags flying aloft.

That triumphal procession could well be used to illustrate the end of the story of the long-lived galleon.

Below: Portrait by A. Pond of Admiral Lord Anson.
NATIONAL TRUST, SHUGBOROUGH (JOHN RACKHAM)

Above right: Raleigh's well-designed galleon 'Raleigh Royal' which was bought for the Navy and renamed 'Ark Royal'; painting by M. J. Barton. M. BARTON

Below right: The 'Nuestra Señora de Cavadonga' is captured by 'Centurion' off the Philippines in 1743; a painting by John Clevely. NATIONAL TRUST, SHUGBOROUGH (JOHN RACKHAM)

Raleigh

SIR Walter Raleigh, that brilliant personality who stood out in any company, is perhaps most famous for the story of the sacrifice of his cloak to save Queen Elizabeth splashing through the mud of a gutter. He was born in 1552 of a West Country landed family and he went to France at the age of seventeen to join the Huguenot army, in which he saw service as a volunteer. It seems likely that he then developed the passion for ships and the sea which lasted through his life.

Raleigh was tall, handsome and always well dressed. In his youth he had spent his time in the company of 'boysterous blades' but later he became an ambitious man of business with clear-cut ideas of how to fashion his own future. His voice was small and had a broad Devonshire accent, but he had a formidable reputation as a wit. Surprisingly, his

contemporaries claimed that he had 'pig's eyes', and it is doubtful if his passion for the sea stemmed from love of adventure so much as from love of the challenge of organising adventures. He was above all a courtier and a negotiator, the driving force behind many enterprises.

After fighting as a colonel to subdue the rebellion in Ireland ably but ruthlessly, his personal charm won him a place at court, where he became one of the queen's favourites. He persuaded her, on the death at sea of Sir Humphrey Gilbert, in 1583, to transfer to him Gilbert's charter for colonisation in the New World, the more readily as the failure of Gilbert's attempt had cost him £2,000.

In reply to the petition Queen Elizabeth issued letters-patent on 25 March 1584 to plan a colony on terms similar to those given to Gilbert. But instead of Gilbert's plan to take a large number of settlers to the extreme north of America, Raleigh prudently decided to send only two ships to examine the coast further south, but not right down to Florida. With the co-operation of various gentlemen and merchants Raleigh was able to provide a ship and a pinnace, and he placed them under the command of two trustworthy captains, Philip Amidas and Arthur Barlow. They left the Thames on 27 April 1584 and reached the Canary Islands on 10 May. A month later they sighted the West Indies and by the beginning of July they were off Florida.

The two ships sailed north and reached Cape Hatteras, landing in Pamlico Sound to take possession 'for the Queenes most excellent Maiestie'. It was only ninety-two years after the discovery of the New World by Columbus.

Raleigh received favourable reports from Amidas and Barlow about the possibilities of colonising Windgandcon, a horrible name that was changed to Virginia. Preparations were started at once; the queen lent the ship *Tiger* and gave the expedition gunpowder worth £400. With the proceeds of the *Roebuck*'s spoils Raleigh was able to collect four other ships and three pinnaces. He dared not ask Elizabeth to allow him to sail with them, however, and he chose his cousin, Sir Richard Grenville, to be his General and Admiral. That was the Grenville who, a few years later, was to be immortalised by his fight in the *Revenge* against fifty-three Spanish ships.

The *Roebuck* still had as her captain John Clarke and with him as passengers Raleigh sent an artist, John White, and a man of scientific mind, Thomas Hariot, to sketch and note down unusual flora and fauna, thereby setting an example to future voyages of exploration. But the colonising attempt of an all-male society was doomed from the start and quarrels and misunderstandings with the Indians were leading to massacre when, in the nick of time, a large fleet hove in sight. There, all unexpected, were Sir Francis Drake and Sir Martin Frobisher fresh from their highly successful raid on the Spanish West Indies. They took off and brought home all the mightily relieved colonists.

Raleigh was surprised to see his colonists back in England, for he had just fitted out a ship to take supplies to them. In fact she arrived off Cape Hatteras just after Drake had taken the party home, and after her men had searched in vain, she returned to England.

In 1587 Raleigh made a second attempt but sent complete families. On that occasion there were only three vessels, a ship, the *Red Lion*, a flyboat and a pinnace for over a hundred men, women and children. They were packed tightly in makeshift cabins, and again all ended in failure and that time in unexplained tragedy. When a follow-up expedition was making ready to sail to Virginia, the news arrived of the coming of the Armada and the ships could not leave England. Raleigh was given the task of planning the country's defences against a Spanish invasion, and the colony, when visited at last, had vanished in an unsolved mystery.

The settlement was abandoned but had not been destroyed, but of the ninety-one men, seventeen women and nine boys there was no sign. Later efforts to find any proof of their fate were equally unsuccessful, but there was a persistent rumour that the colonists had gone inland. It is even claimed that an Indian tribe was speaking Elizabethan English as late as the nineteenth century, while another version has it that the survivors married into the Hatteras Indians.

It is hard today to appreciate the magnitude of the disaster. The loss of a few score of men and women and the failure of a business venture seem paltry by today's standards, but sixteenth-century England was still a poor country which had not gained the self-confidence that it had a hundred years later. Yet, paradoxically, Raleigh's vision implanted the colonising instinct in his countrymen, and within a generation merchants and navigators began to think of trade rather than piracy.

All the while Raleigh was active in other directions. In 1586 he led a daring attack on the Spaniards in the Azores,

after the failure of the 1587 expedition he backed expeditions to find the North-West Passage. But, however great his fame, he had few friends. His haughtiness denied him any popular following and he did not get on well with the queen's new favourite, the Earl of Essex. The dislike of the Cecils was ultimately to topple him from his pedestal.

For most of 1590 he was busy fitting out privateers; a year later he turned to collecting a large fleet to use against the Spaniards at his own cost of £34,000, although the queen lent him two of her ships. He sailed in command but was recalled to an irate Queen Bess. She had discovered his intrigue with one of her maids-of-honour, Elizabeth Throgmorton, and on his return she banished him at once to the Tower of London. The fleet, under Sir John Burgh, came back triumphantly with a bullion-laden prize, the *Madre de Dios*, known as the Great Carrack. Still a prisoner, Raleigh was sent to Dartmouth with Francis Drake and Lord Cecil to use his influence with the Devonians to refrain from helping themselves from the treasure under their eyes.

The Queen relented and Raleigh was freed. He sailed across the Atlantic to hunt for the mythical El Dorado but could find no more than a few scraps of gold. In 1596 he was given command of a squadron in an expedition against Spain under Howard of Effingham and the Earl of Essex. He suggested that they should start with an all-out attack

Engraving by C. J. Visscher of the 'Tiger', the ship loaned by Elizabeth to Raleigh.

on the Spanish fleet and he himself led the van into Cadiz harbour, where he was wounded. Cadiz was captured and the Spanish ships badly mauled.

He went as second-in-command to Essex in the following year for another attempt on Spain but one that was unsuccessful except that he took Fayal, one of the Azores. It was the last of his fights.

At the start of the reign of James I, Raleigh had the misfortune to fall foul of him personally and was sentenced to death but had the sentence commuted on the scaffold and was committed to the Tower. There for fifteen years he spent his days writing *History of the World*, or pacing up and down his narrow bridgeway, until, in 1616, James despatched him to the New World to find and bring him gold. He sailed with fourteen ships but they were scattered in a violent storm and theirs is a sorry tale of vessels lost or deserting, of mutinous crews, of men dying of scurvy and fever.

Raleigh returned empty-handed but also under suspicion of having intended to attack Spaniards. For that double crime, in James's eyes, he was executed by his unworthy monarch; a strange ending for one who was to become a great hero in English history. Raleigh could not face the threat of ruin, and tried to escape to France. On 29 October 1618, after being summarily charged with the 'treason' for which he had been convicted in 1603, he was beheaded at Westminster.

Evolution of the Square Rig

THE square rig derives its name not from the shape of its sails but from the fact that they can be set square to the centreline of the ship, as opposed to the fore-and-aft rig where the sails can be sheeted fore and aft along the centreline.

Medieval ships, such as cogs, had a single square sail. As ships increased in size, one and then two additional masts appeared (the mizen and the fore masts). The flagpole above the top (the fighting platform on top of the mast) was converted to carry a small upper square sail – the topsail, which first appeared on the late fifteenth-century carracks. The flagpole thus became the topmast; it was stepped on the lower mast trestle-trees because a single pole mast could not be made strong enough. Even so, the big lower masts had often to be made by assembling many baulks of timber, which were clamped together by rope bands, the wooldings. Each mast – the lower and top masts – had its own standing rigging of forestays, shrouds and backstays.

By a similar evolution, the topmast and topsail were surmounted by a topgallant (pronounced t'gal'nt) mast and sail. They first appeared on galleons during the first decade of the sixteenth century. Then came the royal mast and sail (first seen on the *Sovereign of the Seas* of 1637). The royal mast eventually became a single spar with the topgallant mast so that ships of the eighteenth century onwards usually had masts made up of three sections, despite the adding of yet another sail – the skysail – which came into use around 1812.

Above the skysail, a few freakish East Indiamen and extreme clippers would set flying handkerchieves known as skyscrapers, moonrakers (or moonsails) and stardusters (or star gazers). Those fancy kites were not worth their extra weight in rigging aloft as they were so small compared with the lower sail (the course) or the topsail. On the other hand, the lateral 'wings', or studding-sails (pronounced stuns'ls), set from booms run out from the yards, gave quite an improvement in speed in light winds from abaft the beam.

As the ships kept growing in size and as labour costs increased, the labour-saving device of splitting the topsail into two separate sails (the lower and upper topsail) appeared in the 1850s. Topgallants followed the same trend, with double topgallant above double topsails. Further labour-reducing trends included the disappearance of skysails and studding sails. The latter were rendered obsolete by the introduction of the much stronger steel yards and rigging so that the modern sails were proportionally much wider than the original pattern. Finally even the royals were dispensed with, and that rig is known as the stump-topgallant rig or the bald-headed rig. It was also nicknamed jubilee rig because it appeared the year of Queen Victoria's jubilee. The stump-topgallant rig carries in fact the same number of yards as the classical skysail rig but the staying arrangement is quite different.

Prior to the nineteenth century, sailing vessels were named mainly according to their trades and uses, to their hull types or to local practice. Thus we had the pink, the flyboat, the hulk, the cat-bark, the Baltimore clipper, the frigate, the sloop-of-war and many other types of vessel. The standardisation of rig nomenclature was a relatively late development. The square-riggers of the nineteenth and twentieth centuries are classified as follows:

'Sovereign of the Seas', the first ship to carry royals in 1637.
NATIONAL MARITIME MUSEUM, LONDON

The **ship** is a sailing vessel with three or more masts all completely square rigged. Because the ship rig was the standard rig, the name has almost become a synonym for vessel. The largest and only five-masted ship ever built was the German *Preussen* of 1902. One four-masted ship still afloat is the *Falls of Clyde;* she is in the process of restoration as a museum-ship in Honolulu.

The **barque** (or bark) has three or more masts, all fully square-rigged except for the sternmost one, which is fore-and-aft rigged. The rig appeared toward the beginning of the nineteenth century but it only became common after 1860. There were barques with up to five masts and several four-masters still survive, some in commission, such as the Russian *Kruzenstern*, which participated in the 1974 Tall Ships Race.

The **barquentine** (or barkentine) has three to six masts, all schooner rigged (fore-and-aft) except the foremast, which is square-rigged. Apart from an experimental model built in 1803, barquentine rig first appeared in the 1840s. It became popular towards the twilight of sail, as it involved smaller expenses than a barque, yet kept some of the running capabilities of the latter. Many barquentines were in fact ships or barques cut down for economy.

The **jackass barques** are square-riggers with three or more masts and any sail combination that falls somewhere between a barque and a barquentine. A three-masted jackass barque might have a fully rigged foremast, a main with a large gaff sail surmounted by square sails and a mizenmast like a barque's. A four-masted jackass barque usually has square-rigged fore and main masts and schooner-rigged mizen and jigger masts. Jackass rigs were never very common so that their different types never got a proper name beyond the deprecatory blanket name given by traditionally minded sailors. The Swedish *Meta av Bixelkrok* has a gaff sail on the lower main and fore masts and with those sails set, she is a jackass barque, although she can also set regular courses and assume the configuration of an ordinary barque.

The **brig** has only two masts (main and fore masts) both fully square-rigged, although brigs seldom set a main course in front of the gaff mainsail (which is comparable to the spanker of a ship). The brig was a successful coastal and deep-sea trader during the eighteenth and nineteenth centuries, as she could economically call at small ports offering too small a cargo to fill the holds of her larger sisters. The only two brigs sailing nowadays are Britain's Sea Cadet Corps *Royalist* launched in 1971 and the *Unicorn*, converted from a Baltic trader in 1973.

The **snow** is a brig on which the gaff mainsail is hooped on a small trysail mast stepped on deck just abaft the mainmast, its cap lodging in the main top. The arrangement allows a bigger hoist of the mainsail, above the crane holding the main yard. There are no snows in existence today.

The **brigantine** was an infrequent rig akin to the brig but with a much taller gaff mainsail surmounted by a square topsail and a topgallant carried on a pole mast (in one piece with the topmast). Also the main mast did not have a top (the decked platform) and was in effect identical to the main mast of a maintopsail schooner (see below).

The **hermaphrodite brig**, often also called brigantine, was much more common than the true brigantine. Her foremast was that of a brig and her main that of a schooner, hence the hermaphrodite. It is a handy and handsome rig for vessels in the 60- to 120-foot range. The largest hermaphrodite brig in commission is the 115-foot *Wilhelm Pieck* from East Germany.

The **bilander** was a coasting vessel (by-land-er) much in vogue from the seventeenth until the early nineteenth century. Bilanders were similar to the two types of brigantines, except that they had a lug mainsail and either a lug topsail or a square topsail and topgallant.

The **polacca** is a Mediterranean three-masted vessel in which at least the main mast is square-rigged, the others being either square-rigged or lateen rigged. The square-

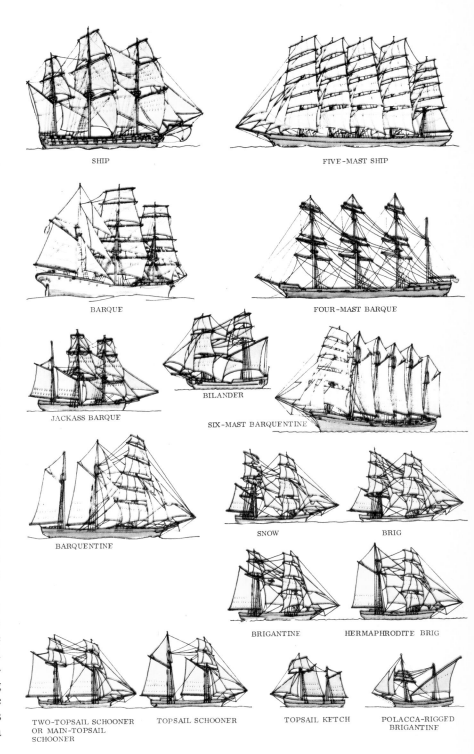

Drawings showing the general arrangement of various square rigs.
C. E. ABRANSON

rigged masts of such vessels are made of a single pole stayed only above the lower yard and at the truck. Thus the topsail, topgallant and royal yards can be lowered to just above the lower yard; such an arrangement is referred to as a polacca rig. There were also brigs and brigantines with such a rig, such as the British hermaphrodite polacca brig *Marquese*. The Sicilian **velocera** of the eighteenth and nineteenth centuries can be described as a barquentine with a foremast polacca rigged and the main and mizen masts each carrying a single large lateen sail.

To complete the list of ships with at least one mast purely square-rigged, we should mention the **Humber keel**, with a single mast fitted with a deep square mainsail and with a very short square topsail. Many of her rigging aspects are a direct legacy of the Norse ships and cogs.

Many fore-and-aft vessels also carried, and sometimes still carry, one or more running square sails. **The topsail schooner** is a schooner carrying one or more square sails on the foremast. The foretopmast usually carries one topsail (such as is the case with the French Navy's *Belle Poule* and *Etoile*) or a double topsail (such as the Sail Training Association's *Sir Winston Churchill* and *Malcolm Miller*).

If a fourth yard is also carried, extra stays are added making it a topgallant yard. An example of the **topgallant schooner** rig is the three-masted *Captain Scott*, launched in 1971. The lower yard of topsail schooners often carries a deep-running square sail which travels like a curtain along a rod fitted under the spar, and which brails against the mast. Some schooners only cross a single yard fitted with the sail just described, such as the brand new Dutch training vessel *Eendracht*, and it is sometimes topped with a triangular 'square' topsail (known as a raffee).

The two-topsail schooner is a schooner with one or more square topsails on two separate masts and not a schooner with double topsails. In that category are mainly two-masted schooners such as the Baltimore clippers, which are also referred to as **main-topsail schooners**, but the five-masted Vinnen sister-schooners (1,827 tons) also belong to the same group. They carried double topsails and a topgallant on the fore and mizen masts, while the main, jigger and spanker masts had gaff topsails. Every possible transition has been seen between topsail schooners and hermaphrodite brigs or barquentines.

The topsail ketch is a ketch carrying one or more yards on the mainmast. Because they remind us of topsail schooners, they are sometimes called schooner-ketches, which is barbarous, and it should be remembered that the original ketch was square-rigged on both masts.

There is not a single square-rigger left trading; all are either training ships, yachts, museum-ships or hulks. However, the new environmental awareness, the four-fold increase in bunker fuel and the depletion of oil reserves might provide the impetus necessary to build a prototype Dynaship. Designed by a German engineer, Herr Prölss, the Dynaship is a revolutionary square-rigger. The yards are aerofoil-shaped and are rigidly fixed to the mast column. There are no stays or braces; to trim the sails, the whole column is rotated. Wind tunnel experiments and computer simulations show that such a ship would be as fast on the average as a fast freighter and, although fully automatic, her power requirement would only be one-twentieth of a similar-displacement motor vessel.

Until the square dyna airfoils cross the seas, square sails will continue to be worked as they were a century ago. The standing rigging of stays and shrouds is quite similar on square-riggers to the ordinary fore-and-aft vessels and the modern yachtsman will understand it readily enough, but even he will feel like a meat ball in a spaghetti dish when confronted with the maze of running rigging to be found on a square-rigger in commission. Although there is not the space here to describe the leads and belaying points of the hundreds of running ropes, we can explain the use and function of the lines that control a square sail.

Since about 1800 the top or head of the sail is not attached or bent directly to the yard, but to a rod, the jackstay, which runs like a rail just above the yard to which it is screwed. The two lower corners of the sail or clews are brought down to a sheave in the yardarm, or extremity of the yard, below by means of a sheet. The rope then travels below that yard to its centre where it reeves through another sheave and leads down to the deck. The courses do not have a yard to stretch their feet and therefore the sheets lead directly to a block on the side of the deck abaft the sail.

It is desirable, for increased stability and for ease of working aloft, to lower the yards when the sails are not in use. There are two types of yards, those that can be lowered and those that cannot. Standing yards always remain at the same level on the mast. Course yards are left standing because they would clutter the deck if they were lowered and in the case of double topsail and double topgallant rigs, the lower topsail and lower topgallant yards are also standing because they are as low as they can go on their respective masts. Upper topsails, upper topgallants, or single topsail and single topgallant yards and all the higher yards are hoisting yards and when they are not in use they are lowered on their mast section as far as they will go.

The sails are trimmed by rotating the yards by means of braces which are ropes attached to the yardarms. The weather clew of a course is hauled forward by a tack which therefore works in the opposite direction to the sheet. Whereas the braces swing the yard in the horizontal plane, the vertical trim is achieved by way of lifts which lead from the yardarms to a block on the mast above, and hence down to the deck. The lifts always remain taut on standing yards and they help to relieve the weight on the crane hinging the latter against the mast. The hoisting-yard lifts are also taut when the yard is in the lowered position and they are left slack when the yard is hoisted for setting sail. In harbour the slings are often used to cant the yards to clear warehouses or other vessels alongside, or so that the yard can be used as a derrick. Canted yards (which are said to be a'cockbill) are also used as a sign of mourning.

The vertical sides of a square sail are called leeches and, as the head and foot sides, they are reinforced by a boltrope sewn on the canvas. The hemp boltropes of the leeches would stretch and the windward leech (the luff) would shake badly when working to windward. To improve the set of the sail a bridle fixed to the luff would be hauled forward by a rope known as a bowline. Bowlines disappeared when non-stretch wire boltropes came into use during the second half of the nineteenth century.

In order to furl a sail it is first necessary to draw it up against its yard to spill the wind. If the yard is of the hoisting type, it is lowered at the same time, so in effect the yard is drawn down to the folds of the canvas. The ropes used for gathering the sails are generically known as brails and on square sails there are three types of brails – the buntlines which haul up the foot of the sail, the leech lines which haul up and gather in the sides of the sail and the clewlines which bring up the lower corners of the sail to its yard.

Buntlines and leechlines are bent on the boltrope and lead up to the yard by passing in front of the sail, whereas the clewlines pass behind the sail. When dealing with the courses, clewlines are referred to as clew garnets. All the ropes mentioned lead to the pinrails on the deck but once the sail is clewed up (gathered), it is necessary to go aloft and walk along the yard, using the footrope that hangs beneath it, in order to roll the canvas in a tight bundle balanced on top of the yard and to lash it securely with gaskets.

Topgallants and higher sails never carried reefing gear; when it was blowing too hard for those sails, they were simply brought in. Topsails had up to three rows of reef points on merchantmen and four on men-of-war. Courses carry one or two rows. As for conventional reefing in sloops or ketches, a reefing tackle is used, but instead of drawing the leech down to the boom, it draws it up to the yardarm. The reef points can then be passed around the yard or the jackstay and when the row is all made fast the tackle is slacked and the reefed sail is trimmed.

The theory is simple but doing the job on an ice-sheathed topsail in a Cape Horn snorter called for real seamanship and many broken nails. Reefing is probably the most arduous work on a square-rigger and today the great majority of square-rigged school-ships either do not carry reef points at all or do not use them, preferring to hand the sail completely and to switch on if need be the 'iron topsail'.

Right: The French topsail schooner 'L'Etoile', wearing the square sail on the foremast, off Portsmouth during the Tall Ships Race in August 1972. A. GREENWAY

Following spread: Peter M. Wood's painting of the American ship 'Florence', an all-sail, square-rigged cargo ship built in 1877. P. M. WOOD

Who Discovered America?

JUST after dawn on 12 October 1492 a Genoese admiral waded ashore on a Caribbean island, sank to his knees in the soft sand of what he thought was an outlying part of Asia and claimed it in the name of his sponsors, the King and Queen of Spain. For Christopher Columbus, it was the triumphant culmination of sixteen years of hawking round the royal courts of Europe the idea that the riches of the East could be reached by sailing westward. For the great majority of people since, the scene signifies his discovery of America.

It is not surprising that the events of 1492 and after have overshadowed the fact that, long before Columbus, America was probably discovered not one, but many times. None of the other claimants to discovery – they include Arabs, French, Japanese, Romans, Turks – enjoyed Columbus's advantages. His voyage was meticulously documented; other accounts are incomplete, confused or fanciful. Some claimants rely only on a piece of evidence here, a piece there, some on historical detective work. No other discoverers saturated America with colonists as the Spaniards who followed Columbus did. There is therefore no living proof of settlement before 1492 to match that of the Spanish-speaking Americans of today. Most important of all, with the discovery in 1500-1 that America was a continent, the exact nature of the land Columbus reached was known and recorded for later ages to note.

The unbroken connection between America as Columbus discovered it and America as we know it now owed its existence to the fact that in 1492 Europe was emerging from the violence, ignorance and insecurity of the Middle Ages into the clearer, more curious and more venturesome light of the Renaissance. It was during the Renaissance that much of the knowledge and thought of the ancient Greeks and Romans were rediscovered, including their ideas of the geography of the world. Among the ideas lay an imperfect but unmistakable notion that something like the continent of America existed. In 380 BC Greek philosophers believed that there was 'an island of immense extent' beyond the ocean then thought to surround Europe, Asia and Africa; at about the same time the poet Plato was writing of the 'Island Continent of Atlantis'.

Such clues, and much else, became forgotten and precious writings and records became mislaid or lost during the long period of chaos that followed the fall of the Roman Empire in about AD 476. During that atavistic age, when barbarians ran wild across Europe, creating conditions in which physical survival was the prime aim in life, what learning and culture

Christopher Columbus, from an early portrait. Although Columbus is popularly accepted as the discoverer of America the probability is that the continent was known to a number of earlier travellers and navigators. ILLUSTRATED LONDON NEWS

managed to persist generally did so only when it was in the care of scholarly monks in remote monasteries.

Ireland, on the fringe of Europe, was one of the last places to feel the savage surge of the barbarian hordes, and this made it a crucible of culture long after the deep shadow of the so-called Dark Ages had blanketed the rest of Europe. Barbarian pressure could, however, be felt in Ireland in the sixth century AD and, with the possible approach of anarchy, the Irish began to look westwards for a place where they might in better safety preserve their civilisation, with its fine arts and devout religion.

Irish monk-sailors sought sanctuary in the Orkneys and Shetlands, the Hebrides and Iceland and, in about AD 570, one of them, it seems, crossed the Atlantic and found America. The evidence lies in *Navigatio Sancti Brendani*, which tells in fanciful fashion how St Brendan meandered all over the ocean, touching Greenland, the Canaries, the Bahamas and Chesapeake Bay. Yet, among tall stories of heavenly choirs and apocalyptic visions, there are descriptions which fit the American scene too closely to be entirely ignored.

There was, for example, the calm area into which the saintly seaman sailed where the sea resembled 'a thick curdled mass' – an apt description of the Sargasso Sea, that still seaweed-strewn tract of the Atlantic off the American coast. One port of call for St Brendan was an island with flat terrain, surrounded by water so calm and clear that he could see to the bottom of the sea-bed. The description might fit the Bahamas, the low-lying Caribbean islands set in the transparent lagoons of the only coral sea in the Atlantic.

According to *Navigatio*, one of St Brendan's crew stayed behind in the Bahamas to convert the natives to Christianity, and in that the Irish discovery claim is backed by circumstantial evidence. In 1519, when the Spaniards conquered Mexico, they discovered that the pagan Aztecs worshipped a white-skinned god called Quetzalcoatl, whose sign was a cross and whose mother was a virgin. Like Christ, Quetzalcoatl preached peace and charity, principles quite opposite to the rest of the Aztec creed, which normally required blood and violence to appease its gods.

Where could the obviously foreign idea of a Christ-like god have come from? If it did not travel west to Mexico from the Bahamas, it could have filtered southwards from Newfoundland where, according to one of the Norse sagas, the eleventh-century Viking Thorfinn Karlsefni learned of the presence of the Irish from a group of Skraelings, or Red

LANDING OF COLUMBUS AT GUANAHANI (BAHAMA ISLANDS) OCT. 12, 1492.

Indians. 'They said there was a land near by which was inhabited by people who wore white garments . . . and carried poles before them to which cloths were attached. People believed this must have been Hvitrammannaland, or Ireland the Great.'

If it was true, then America would have been the fourth new land, after the Faroes, Iceland and Greenland, where the Vikings arrived to find the Irish had preceded them.

The Norse Sagas, however, also propose the Vikings as discoverers of America, if only discoverers by accident. In AD 986, according to one Saga, Bjarne Hergulfsson set sail from Iceland for the new Viking colony in Greenland. After a few days, Bjarne and his crew were lost in unfamiliar waters, surrounded by fog and driven before strong winds. When the fog finally cleared, they had completely lost their bearings.

The Vikings had probably drifted southward well past the southern tip of Greenland, for when Bjarne eventually hoisted sail and pointed his prow westward, he reached a country not unlike Newfoundland. Where he should have seen mountains and glaciers, Bjarne saw instead the thick forests of the warmer south. Mystified, he sailed northward up the coast, only to find more forests fringing the coastline.

An illustration of Columbus landing at Guanahani that appeared in the 'Illustrated London News' in October 1892; four hundred years after the event. ILLUSTRATED LONDON NEWS

Still farther north, somewhere along the coast of Baffin Island, Bjarne turned eastward and sailed on until at last he sighted the great black mountains and glittering masses of ice he knew to be Greenland.

Nearly fifteen years passed before a second Viking voyage to America took place. In AD 1000 Leif Eriksson set sail with thirty-five men, reached Baffin Island and from there followed Bjarne's course in reverse, to land finally on the coast of Newfoundland. The Vikings were fascinated by the rich grassland, the plump salmon and trout of lake and river, the thousands of caribou and great forests with their birch trees reaching heights nearing a hundred feet. Greenland had nothing like it, nor did it have the abundance of wild grapes that led Leif to call the unknown country Vinland. The Vikings, who presumed it to be a westward extension of the continent of Europe, spent the winter in Vinland and returned to Greenland the following spring, their ship laden with timber and vines.

The obvious riches of Vinland led, naturally, to an attempt at colonisation. In the spring of AD 1003 a party of Vikings under Thorfinn Karlsefni left Greenland, crossed the narrow Davis Strait and sailed southward, to land on the northern tip of Newfoundland. Conditions in that second Vinland seemed ideal at first, but within two years the savage New-foundland winters and the hostility of the Skraelings put an end to the colony. In 1005 the Vikings returned to Greenland, taking with them a valuable cargo of vines, furs and timber.

It appears, however, that the Vinlanders left evidence behind them for, in the 1960s, excavations at Cape Bauld, the extreme northern point of Newfoundland, revealed the foundations of seven Viking-type turf buildings, as well as metalworking tools, anvils, spindles and whorls. Tests have shown them to date from the tenth century. In addition, certain cartographical evidence exists of a pre-Columbian, probably Viking, discovery of America. In 1300, 1424, 1434 and 1436, European maps and globes showed a land far west of the Atlantic called, variously, Antilia or Isola Nova Scoperta. The Vikings were not themselves cartographers. It was an art which flourished much farther south, particularly in Germany and Italy.

However, it is not difficult to see some of the ways in which the mapmakers' information could have spread southward from Viking Scandinavia. Soon after they returned from Vinland, Gudrid, wife of Thorfinn Karlsefni, went to Rome. She was, of course, well qualified to speak at first-hand of the Vikings' American discoveries and doubtless did so. The Vikings had by that time been converted to Christianity and for them, as for all Christians in western Europe, Rome was the cosmopolitan hub of the Continent, the city from which information was disseminated to all parts of the Christian world.

News of land to the west might also have travelled south with the reports of Tyrker, a German member of Leif Eriksson's party, who apparently returned home soon after the first Vinland expedition. Europeans in the Continent's northern ports also knew of the regular trading voyages the Vikings made to America until the fourteenth century and of the rich cargoes they brought back, cargoes which included turkey, a bird then peculiar to North America. So, in various ways, a large body of knowledge seems to have been created by the fifteenth century which, despite gross inaccuracies and serious misconceptions, contained the important fact that land lay across the Atlantic.

The Europeans who probably knew more about it than anyone else were the Portuguese, the finest and most experienced sailors of the time. In the course of wide-ranging expeditions west and south into the Atlantic, the Portuguese explored and colonised the west coast of Africa and, in 1427, discovered the Azores. Then, in 1452, they encountered the edge of the Sargasso Sea which, to their trained observant eyes, strongly indicated land to the west. On that voyage the Portuguese ranged as far east as the vicinity of Cape Clear, in south-west Ireland, and there they found another clue; though winds blew strongly in the area, the sea was found on that occasion to be calm, a feature which they considered to mean that it must be sheltered by a vast land mass to the west.

Intriguing as it was, Atlantic exploration westward was not a priority with the Portuguese at that time. Until about 1460, when it proved larger than they had expected, their main efforts were directed at reaching the East by sailing round Africa. Then, between 1460 and 1480, the Portuguese turned their attention westward once more, and in those two decades several navigators were sent to find 'Antilia and other islands in the Atlantic'. In the course of the new search one of them found something so important that, in 1480, the Portuguese imposed the death penalty for anyone who betrayed the secrets of their Atlantic expeditions.

The secret which the Portuguese were so ruthlessly intent upon keeping might well have been the existence of America, which their explorations by 1480 had indicated was of great size. That it appeared so great as completely to block the westward route to the East is perhaps corroborated by

Portuguese resumption of the round-Africa voyages in 1481, which consequently would seem the only way for them to reach Asia. Knowledge of America could explain, too, the cryptic refusal in 1484 of King John II of Portugal to sponsor Christopher Columbus. He had, he said, 'information regarding the western lands more positive than the visions of the Genoese'.

King John was, however, a realist. When the frustrated Columbus left Portugal in 1485 to try his luck in Spain, John knew he must act quickly to stop his Spanish rivals exploiting America. Accordingly, in 1486, John granted a charter to Fernão Dulmo, ordering him to colonise 'the islands and mainland in the West'. Dulmo, who had to bear the greater part of the cost himself, ran into financial difficulties and possibly his venture never materialised.

This is the last that is known of Portuguese intentions regarding America before 1492 and it leaves the unanswered question, which Portuguese navigator landed in what part of America and when? Favourites among some historians, not all of whom are Portuguese, are João Vaz Corte-Real and his sons Miguel and Caspar who, some time before 1472, are believed to have discovered Labrador, Newfoundland and the Hudson and St Lawrence rivers. Who were the Corte-Reals? Although his sons made minor names for themselves in the history of American exploration, the father, João, was the humblest of people – a porter in a duke's household. Yet, in 1474, this lowly servant was given the governorship of the richest province in the Azores. Surely only a truly remarkable feat could have raised such a man to such a position.

'About the time the governship of Terceyra became vacant,' Cordeiro's *History of the Azores* records, 'there landed two gentlemen who had recently returned from Stockfishland (Newfoundland), which they had gone to discover by order of the Portuguese king. One of these gentlemen was João Vaz Corte-Real . . . and he petitioned that he might have the governship in reward for his services'.

There is independent evidence that João might have been accompanied by three Danes, namely Johannes Sclovus, a pilot, Hans Porthorst and Diderik Pining. Co-operation between the Danes and Portuguese, whose royal houses were connected by marriage, might explain why the 1472 expedition made for Newfoundland and the area explored by the Danes' ancestors, the Vikings. In Newfoundland, of course, the Portuguese found the lucrative fisheries which they later exploited to the tune of £1 million a year.

Keeping the fisheries secret from their Spanish rivals was feasible, but America as an entity was far too huge to remain perpetually unknown, as the Portuguese might have hoped. After Columbus claimed it on behalf of Spain, the Spaniards built there a gold- and silver-rich empire that became the envy of sixteenth-century Europe. Envy was particularly strong in England, whose Welsh Tudor queen, Elizabeth I, longed to break the Spanish monopoly in America. Among the means she employed to do so was promotion of the story that in 1170 America was discovered by a Welsh prince called Madoc, who was, by inference, one of Elizabeth's ancestors.

The basic information came from innumerable old Welsh poems and ballads which made of Madoc a legendary hero who left his homeland for a life on the ocean because of quarrels among his royal relatives. Madoc, according to the Welsh bards, sailed south-westward from the north Welsh coast, turned west south of the Azores, touched the edge of the Sargasso Sea and the Bahamas, skirted the southernmost tip of Florida and landed at the spot where Mobile, Alabama, now stands. There is also a thirteenth-century narrative of Madoc's voyage which includes a description of what might well have been the Sargasso Sea. The author, Willem the Minstrel, called it 'a treacherous garden . . . which no storm could ever dissipate and which swallowed up ships'.

Evidence of Madoc's possible landfall in Alabama came to light 200 years after Elizabeth had tried to use it as a political pawn against Spain. In 1782 Governor Sievers of

Left: An early colour print of St Brendan and his monks at sea, from a manuscript in the Bodleian Library The 'Navigatio Sancti Brendani' tells how Brendan found America – an uncertain but possible fact that is believed by all patriotic Irishmen.
QUEEN'S COLLEGE, OXFORD

Below: John Cabot sails from Bristol in 1497. He made a landfall at Cape Breton Island (now part of Nova Scotia) which had been colonised by Norsemen 500 years earlier. Cabot has a good claim to being the first of the navigators of the middle ages to discover the mainland of America. CITY ART GALLERY, BRISTOL

Tennessee discovered some very ancient fortifications in Cherokee country. The aged Cherokee chief, Oconostota, told Sievers how he had heard his father and grandfather say they were built by people called Welsh, and that they had 'crossed the Great Water and landed near . . . Mobile'. Sievers also encountered a Frenchman who had lived with the Cherokee and had traded with a 'Welsh tribe'. The Frenchman found they spoke 'much of the Welsh dialect . . . many of them were very fair and white and frequently told him they had sprung from a nation of white people . . .'

These so-called Welsh Indians, the Mandans, aroused a great deal of interest and in 1792 a young Welshman, John Evans, set out for America to investigate. At that point the Spanish governor of New Orleans, seriously concerned, wrote 'It is in the interests of his Catholic Majesty that reports of British Indians in Mandan country be denied once and for all'. Such reports were not news to the Spaniards. In 1493, Columbus returned to Europe to report that 'the nations of Virginia and Guatemala celebrate the memory of an ancient hero whom they call Matec', a name not so different from that of the Welsh prince.

Also, in 1598, a history of Spain had been written which recorded that the inhabitants of Mexico believed 'a son of the Prince of Wales, called Madoc, in the year 1170 sailed into the West Indies and inhabited the country of Mexico'. A 1599 translation of the history was, perhaps, part of the evidence which prompted John Evans's trip to America. His activities were regarded by the Spaniards with deep suspicion, but he spent six months among the Mandans before they arrested him and charged him with being a British spy.

When Evans was eventually released, it was soon clear that he had been offered an irresistible bribe to stop his researches. He headed a party of Spaniards to a Mandan village, made speeches praising the Spanish king, tore down a Union Jack left there by British traders and ran up the Spanish flag in its place. Evans then received his reward – a large cash payment and a job as a land surveyor.

All this, one might argue, is hardly positive evidence on which to base a claim to the discovery of America, and with the possible exception of that of the Vikings, much the same could apply to the other claims. In any historical controversy spurious theories, ambiguous evidence and what has been called 'the silence of history' obscure the argument. The only certain thing is that historical habit dies hard. Widespread belief in Columbus's claim to have discovered America in 1492 will undoubtedly be transmitted to future generations, where, just as surely, dissidents will disagree and try as hard as they do now to substitute their own rival candidates.

First Rate to Sixth Rate

ENGLISH warships were first designated by the number of guns carried at the beginning of the seventeenth century, and from about 1630 the English fleet was divided into six classes known as Rates. First Rates were ships with more than ninety guns, Second Rates those between eighty and ninety guns, Third Rates fifty to eighty, Fourth Rates thirty-eight to fifty, Fifth Rates eighteen to thirty-eight and Sixth Rates those with fewer than eighteen guns.

From then until well into the nineteenth century every ship of the Navy was listed in one of the six classes according to her size and gunpower; each had a strict complement of officers and men. However, from time to time alterations occurred in the upper and lower limits of each division of Rate. Very similar classifications were adopted for most navies. In France the classes were known as the Premier to Sixième Range.

With the adoption, in the middle of the seventeenth century, of Formal Fighting Instructions and the enforcement of line ahead as the order of battle, it was necessary to ensure that a much smaller and less powerful warship was not opposed by a stronger vessel, therefore the smaller Rates of warships were excluded from the battle line, which was made up from vessels with more than fifty guns, that is, usually, the First, Second and Third Rates only, and the vessels of those Rates became known as ships-of-the-line.

The principal functions of the various Rates can be described as follows: First, Second and Third Rates – service as ships-of-the-line in general fleet actions; Fourth Rates – guard duties with convoys of merchant ships, service as cruising ships in foreign waters and on expeditions of great distance; Fifth Rates – acting as reconnaissance vessels when attached to fleets of larger warships, to repeat signals and for operating against privateers; Sixth Rates – coastal patrol duties. The above definitions are, of course, only a general indication, as the duties undertaken by individual warships of the different Rates varied considerably.

In the eighteenth century a large proportion of the warships with fewer than fifty guns were known by the various denominations of frigates. The name frigate was given to various types of warship at different periods, but the best known application was to the eighteenth-century vessel specially designed for scouting, convoy duties and attacks on enemy merchant ships, which carried its main armament on a single gundeck.

During the first half of the eighteenth century the largest vessels in the Royal Navy to carry their main armament in that manner were the Sixth Rates of twenty-four guns. In 1757 a new class was introduced, the 32-gun frigate and by the end of the century the navy had frigates of 40, 38, 36, 32, 28, 24 and 20 guns. In the nineteenth century the frigate continued to be a most important and useful unit of the sailing navies and at the beginning of the century the British Navy had over 200 frigates. The increase in size continued and frigates of fifty and sixty guns came into service.

The first attempt at standardisation for warships of the Royal Navy took place in 1677, when Admiralty officers and navy shipwrights prepared the first Shipbuilding Establishment which laid down the principal dimensions of warships of each class. After the first Establishment further official rules, laying down not only the standard dimensions of each class, but also the sizes of the timbers used in their construction, were issued.

A Dutch Second Rate (a ship of 80 to 90 guns) of 1670. The richness of the carvings and decoration of the stern is at least as impressive as the arrangement of firepower.
PARKER GALLERY (D. RUDKIN)

Although the successive regulations gradually increased the size of ships – for instance, a 100-gun ship built on the Establishment of 1745 was about two feet wider on the beam and about eleven feet longer on the gun-deck than a 100-gun ship of the 1677 Establishment – the rigid specifications of the rules retarded the progress of English naval architecture and constrained the initiative of the shipwrights as it gave little scope for experiment and new forms of construction.

During the period of the Establishments, British warships were often too small for the number of guns they were intended to carry and, therefore, lay low in the water so that lower-deck guns could not be used in rough seas, and the ships sailed and worked heavily. The ship designers and builders of other countries were free from the restrictions of standardisation and able to incorporate in their warships the result of experiments and investigations into the design of the underwater hull form of ships.

In particular, French warships were built with a greater space between each gunport in comparison with British vessels. That feature increased the length of the vessel in relation to the number of guns carried and the beam of the vessel was increased in proportion, making the ship more buoyant with the lower guns higher above the water and more space available around the weapon for the gun crew. After about 1750 British ship designers and shipwrights were allowed more freedom to experiment, to produce bigger and better warships and to copy the designs of captured vessels.

In the seventeenth century it was the practice to protect the underwater hull of a ship from damage by marine pests with wooden sheathing applied over a layer of tar, hair, sulphur and tallow. Experiments were also made with lead sheathing but it was unsuccessful because of corrosion caused by electrolytic action set up in salt water by the lead and iron fastenings of the hull.

In 1761 the British frigate was sheathed with sheets of copper below the waterline, but again corrosion occurred with the iron fastenings. After about 1780 copper was used instead of iron for underwater fastenings of the hull and copper sheathing was then found to be satisfactory. By the end of the century the underwater hulls of most warships were protected by copper sheathing applied in thin sheets, each about four feet long and fourteen inches wide. More than 3,000 such sheets were required to sheath a large warship.

Engraved for SPENCER'S New HISTORY of ENGLAND.

An ENGLISH FIRST RATE SHIP of WAR, with Rigging &c at Anchor.

A Ketch.   A Schooner.   A Sloop.

The SECTION of an ENGLISH FIRST RATE SHIP of WAR.

Facing page above: A study by N. Fielding of a new-class
First Rate line-of-battle ship of 110 guns. By this time ships were
becoming more functional and less decorative in their
appearance. R. N. FROST COLLECTION (D. RUDKIN)

Facing page below: Engravings showing a cutaway section and
the rigging of an English First Rate warship, and, in miniature,
the silhouettes of a ketch, schooner and sloop.
PARKER GALLERY (D. RUDKIN)

Top: A Virtue lithograph of a painting by W. F. Mitchell
depicting a 38-gun frigate (a Fifth Rate ship) of about 1770.
D. RUDKIN

Above left: Model of an 18th-century Fifth Rate warship
(18 to 38 guns). P. M. WOOD

Above: A new-class Second Rate line-of-battle ship of 92 guns
as portrayed by N. Fielding. D. RUDKIN

Overleaf: HMS 'Buckingham', a Third Rate warship of 70 guns.
Preparations for her launching at Deptford dockyard on the
Thames on 13 April 1751 are depicted here in a painting by
John Cleveley. NATIONAL MARITIME MUSEUM, LONDON

Sovereign
of the Seas

'H E understood navigation well but above all he knew the architecture of ships so perfectly that in that respect he was exact rather more than became a Prince'; thus Charles II was described by a contemporary of his, the Bishop of Salisbury.

Charles had inherited a consuming passion for ships from his father Charles I, who in his happier years had been a frequent visitor to Deptford and Woolwich to watch his men-of-war being built. One spring day in 1634 he was rowed down to Woolwich in his barge to inspect the half-

R.E GRANDIS ILLIVS ATQ CELEBERR NAVIS SVB AVSPICIS CAROLI MAGN: BRIT: FRA: ET HIB

built *Leopard* in company with Mr Commissioner Phineas Pett, the highly gifted creator of the *Royal Prince*. The *Prince* had set a new standard for warships in both size and design as the king knew, but he was not content. He took Phineas aside in the hold of the *Leopard* and told him that as the *Prince* had proved such a success, he had decided to build a new great ship. She would be no ordinary ship but the largest and most splendid vessel afloat. Her architect, it went without saying, would be Phineas Pett.

The project, it was agreed, was to be kept a secret for the time being. But somehow word of it reached the Brethren of Trinity House, with the surprising information that the ship would measure '124 foot by the keel in breadth 46 and for draught in water 22ft.' (Actually, her length turned out to be still greater, just under four times the beam; the conservative Brethren had been misled.) When they roundly declared that a ship of such 'strange and large proportions', as they had heard, could not be of any use, it made no difference whatever.

He did not intend to build the ship himself but kept

overall control while delegating the day-to-day supervision to Peter Pett, the fifth of his eight sons. At the age of twenty, Peter had stepped into his father's shoes as Master Shipwright at Woolwich when Phineas became Commissioner of the Navy and the two of them worked harmoniously together for twenty years.

The *Sovereign of the Seas*, as she was to be named, was laid down in 1636 and in September of 1637 the king gave peremptory orders for her to be launched on a certain date without troubling to ask if the tide would serve. On that date there was an exceptionally low tide, as Phineas knew, though nobody cared to argue with a king, especially when that king was Charles I. Down to Woolwich went the royal barge with King and Queen and their 'trains of lords and ladies', but only to see the great ship unable to move. King and Queen and lords and ladies had travelled in vain and they were not pleased.

The experts of Trinity House declared that they would examine the ship on Sunday, 14 October, to see where Phineas's design had gone astray. But on the evening of Saturday the 13th Phineas saw the water being piled up by a helpful breeze on top of a high spring tide and he at once set his men to work by the light of bonfires. In the morning the Trinity House bigwigs went down to make their inspection and saw the *Sovereign of the Seas* serenely at her moorings out in the river.

By 12 July 1638, the ship was fully rigged, had taken on board guns and stores at Greenwich and had completed trials. Then the King and Queen Henrietta Maria visited her and dined in the great cabin. After a second visit by Charles, who made a very thorough inspection, she sailed off down the Thames with a parting salute to him, and with Phineas as a passenger, to join the fleet in the Downs.

The *Sovereign* is sometimes thought to have been England's first three-decker but that distinction goes to the *Royal Prince*, also built by Phineas Pett, although in both size and gun-power the *Sovereign* was a long way ahead. While the *Prince* mounted fifty-five guns, the *Sovereign* mounted more than a hundred when she first put to sea. She was flush-decked (bow to stern without a break) with a forecastle and a quarterdeck. The lower gun-tier had thirty ports for cannon and demi-cannon, the middle tier had thirty culverins and demi-culverins, and there were twenty-six pieces of mixed ordnance in the upper tier. On the forecastle and quarterdeck there were twelve ports inboard for 'murdering pieces', to be fired at close range, and ten for chaser guns. In the cabins there were many loopholes for musketry fire.

The great ship could carry plenty of sail, although the fourth mast, a bonaventure mizen with a lateen sail, had gone out of fashion before her day. Above the foresail and foretopsail on the foremasts, she could set a topgallant sail and three similar sails on the mainmast, with a square topsail above the lateen on the mizen. Also, in addition to the sail below the bowsprit, was a spritsail topmast above, which could carry a second headsail. Royals, which could be set on the fore and main masts, were peculiar to the *Sovereign of the Seas*.

Although the tonnage of the *Sovereign of the Seas* was an increase of 400 over that of *Royal Prince* it does not by any means explain the difference in cost of the two vessels. Against the average cost of a 40-gun ship of between £5,500 and

£6,500, the *Sovereign*'s total was the staggering figure of £65,586-6s-9½d.

The disparity is largely accounted for by the extravagant decoration which covered her, from a huge figurehead and long beakhead to a riot of golden figures on the stern. At the bows, a mounted king charged over seven other monarchs in a wealth of detail, matched by the gilded carvings aft. In between were greyhounds and lions, cupids and satyrs, monograms and national emblems and laurel wreaths. They, and even the gods – Jupiter, Mars and Neptune – balanced by half a dozen larger-than-life-size damsels, apparently covered every available space including, not least, the gunport lids.

From early in the seventeenth century to the period of Queen Anne, it was the fashion in European navies to

ment the richest that ever spread cloth before the wind'.

As a warship, the *Sovereign* was a success. She took part in almost all the main engagements of her day and acquitted herself well. She fought against the Dutch in several battles and against the French at Barfleur. She had one or two defects; for example, in the early days while she still had three decks she rode rather too high in the water. She was always difficult to steer, but that was no different from most big ships of the time. The whipstaff – the vertical lever working on a pivot in the deck – in any case permitted only five degrees of helm each way; moreover, it was not powerful enough and had to be supplemented by men hauling on relieving tackles to take part of the strain off the tiller.

The best picture of the ship is the engraving by John

An oil painting by Peter Lely shows Peter Pett and the great ship built by himself and his father.
NATIONAL MARITIME MUSEUM, LONDON

embellish and ornament ships profusely but, as the recovered Swedish *Wasa* shows in the museum at Stockholm, the *Sovereign* went beyond all comparison. She had left far behind the bright contrasting colours of the Tudor ships and showed black and gold only and the gold was not stinted. Standing out among all the rest of the finery, itself gilded, was the great stern lantern in which, so it was said, ten men could stand upright.

The scheme of all the decoration was the responsibility, oddly enough, of a dramatist, Thomas Heywood, who was a friend of Inigo Jones, the King's Surveyor. Heywood had been chosen by Charles who, keenly interested, had his own suggestions to make on additions to the scheme. As one would expect, they were duly carried out. Heywood's lavish contributions included all the snatches of verse, the mottoes and classical tags that accompanied many of the carvings. John Evelyn, the diarist, was almost lyrical about the *Sovereign of the Seas* when he first saw her. He wrote of 'a glorious vessel of burden lately built for defence and arma-

Payne, which shows her under sail as she originally appeared. In the Civil War the name was whittled down by Cromwell or the sober gentry of Parliament to plain *Sovereign*, but at his restoration Charles replaced a touch of glamour by changing it to *Royal Sovereign*. She was rebuilt twice, in 1660 and again in 1688. During the first refit some of the guns were removed and she was cut down to two decks; in addition the opportunity was taken to remove some of the more cumbersome gilded figures. In 1696, however, the magnificent vessel shared the fate of many good ships in being set on fire by accident and burnt out in harbour.

Peter Pett had continued to work at Woolwich and Chatham throughout the period of the Commonwealth. In 1645, like his father before him, he was appointed a Commissioner of the Navy.

Tasman, Cook and Roggeveen

THE Dutch, as might be expected from their close association with the sea, have long produced fine navigators and they have been fortunate in their backers and overseas administrators. Prominent among them in the first half of the seventeenth century was Van Diemen, a merchant of Amsterdam who went out to Batavia and started a highly successful career in the Dutch East India Company, eventually becoming the governor-general. He gave much encouragement to his fellow countrymen in their maritime explorations, particularly in the Far East, where he established trading relations with the Chinese and Japanese, besides taking a hand in the capture of Malacca and the Portuguese settlements in Ceylon.

One of the navigators he chose to explore part of the western Pacific was Abel Janszoon Tasman, then aged thirty-seven, who was accompanied by Matthew Quast. They started their operations in June 1639 at Luzo, in the Philippines, and sailed north-westward to the Bonin Islands, south of Japan. After making several landings on the islands, which seem to have been hitherto unknown, they sailed still farther northward in a search for more exciting isles 'of gold and silver'. They reached a point about 600 miles east of Japan but alas found nothing, and certainly none of the fabled riches, though they continued along the same latitude for another 300 miles. At last deciding to give up the hunt, they sailed south-westward and after setting foot on Japanese soil they dropped anchor off Formosa.

Tasman then busied himself in various ways in the Indian Ocean until in 1642 he set out from Batavia with two ships to explore western Australia. He came upon a large island which he named Van Diemen's Land in honour of his governor-general, but which was later to bear his own name as Tasmania. Unaware that he was on an island, he hoisted a flag to claim the land for Holland and then steered eastward, expecting to find the Solomon Islands. Instead, on 13 December, he sighted mountainous country which he named Staatenland – now New Zealand. As he cruised along the coast of South Island several of his men, on landing, were set upon by the Maoris and killed.

He left New Zealand and, although from first to last he did not sight Australia during the voyage, he found himself among the Friendly Islands. Then steering north and west among the island groups he passed to the north of New Guinea and ultimately reached Batavia on 15 June after a voyage lasting ten months.

In 1644 Tasman set out again with three ships on a second and greater expedition, with explicit orders to survey the north and north-west coasts of Australia and also to bring back information on New Guinea. Unfortunately details of his discoveries are scanty but his chart gives clear evidence of his work; it is marked with the soundings he had taken for the whole of those two Australian coasts. It is an astonishing record and one that goes far to justify the claim that he was one of the greatest navigators of the seventeenth century. He died in Batavia in 1659.

Seldom have sons of farm-labourers commanded ships of the Royal Navy and fewer still have become members of the Royal Society or have made their names known across the oceans of the world. Captain James Cook achieved all that and more, far more. No maritime explorer of any period or nationality has ever approached the width of his discoveries and surveys in three voyages.

He was born in the Yorkshire village of Marton in 1728. At the age of thirteen he was apprenticed to a small shopkeeper but after a disagreement his indentures were cancelled and he became an apprentice instead to the skipper of a collier which worked on the east coast of Britain and at times into the Baltic. Life in a collier was no byword for luxury or softness and it taught seamanship and self-reliance to anyone strong enough to endure it. With young Cook, the result of a few voyages was that he quite early found himself the mate of the vessel.

In 1755, when war with France loomed imminent, he volunteered to join the Navy as an able seaman. His efficiency earned his promotion within a month to the rating of master's mate. Then his captain recommended him as sailing master in a sloop. In the *Mercury*, he was present at Wolfe's attack on Quebec in 1759. There, he played a notable part in helping to solve the problem of finding a passage for the warships and transports up through the shoals of the St Lawrence by exploring the river, at times sounding depths by a pole at night.

After the capitulation of Quebec he continued his surveying, aided by a military engineer who taught him mathematics as well as surveying, and he was able to publish a chart of the St Lawrence from Quebec to the sea.

When Newfoundland was retaken from the French he was appointed marine surveyor of both Newfoundland and Labrador. In addition he made time to write an article on a solar eclipse for a paper of the Royal Society. As a result he was chosen for the command of a projected expedition to the South Pacific to Tahiti to observe an impending transit of Venus. Not only was he promoted to commissioned rank as a lieutenant but he was also to be one of the two observers for the Royal Society. The Admiralty, in an enlightened mood, made a special purchase of £5,000 for the expedition of a Whitby collier as having the robust strength of hull and suitable size.

A number of men of science joined the ship, named the *Endeavour*, including the keen botanist, Sir Joseph Banks. There was little of importance for them to record until, on 3 April 1769, they reached Tahiti where they erected an observatory and made their observations. Cook's next object was to locate a mysterious large continent which was reputed to lie in the South Pacific. He failed to find anything of the kind in a great deal of searching and then, reaching New Zealand, attempted to explore inland. The Maoris however were so hostile that he had to content himself with making a survey of the coast, discovering in the process that New Zealand consists of two islands.

Sailing on, after six months he reached Australia and discovered Botany Bay, although he just missed seeing what became the great Sydney Harbour of future generations. He took possession of the country in the name of George III but, as in New Zealand, could do no more than keep close to the coast because of hostile natives. It was Cook who gave

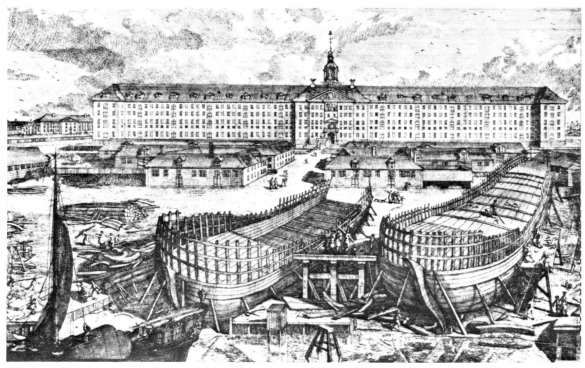

New South Wales its name, because the shoreline was reminiscent of the north coast of the Bristol Channel.

During his exploration inside the Great Barrier Reef off Queensland the *Endeavour*'s hull was pierced by a spike of coral, but fortunately the coral remained wedged in the planking and acted as a plug in the hole. Cook managed to sail the ship to New Guinea and Batavia for repairs.

He arrived safely in England in June 1771, after the voyage had lasted three years. The king promoted him to the rank of commander and in a little over a year he was starting off again on another expedition to Australia and the South Seas. He sailed from Plymouth in a larger ship, the *Resolution*, with the smaller vessel *Adventure* in company. The total complement of the two ships, 193, fared better than those in the little *Endeavour*. In the first voyage thirty men had died out of eighty-five and Cook was determined to prevent any similar casualty figures, common as they were in his day. With the aid of fresh fruit whenever obtainable and other measures he virtually eliminated fatalities.

After further fruitless searching for the missing continent, Cook sailed far southward into pack ice, becoming the first to enter the Antarctic Circle and to reach a latitude of seventy-one degrees. From there he sailed once more to New Zealand and after wintering in the Society Islands he cruised on a great arc eastward and northward. Steering southward again he made one landing in southern Japan.

At the end of the second three-year voyage he arrived back in England. He was at once promoted to full captain, appointed to a sinecure office in Greenwich Hospital and unanimously voted to membership of the Royal Society.

During his absence from England, the time-honoured question of the North-West Passage to the Far East had again come to the fore. Cook offered to lead a search and was given two ships, *Resolution* and again *Discovery*, by the

Admiralty. His orders were to sail through the maze of islands he had recently discovered, sailing north-westwards as far as latitude sixty-five and then to try to find the passage.

His expedition sailed from the Nore on 25 June 1776, and discovered more small islands in the spring of 1777; but the season was too advanced for exploring in the northern seas. After waiting in New Zealand until January 1778 he set course for the north and, finding the Sandwich Islands on the way, reached the coast of America. He followed the shoreline northward to the Bering Strait but the ice proved to be too thick and he returned to the Sandwich Islands. Then, still exploring, he came upon Hawaii. The natives there appeared to be peaceable enough and he anchored offshore. But unhappily, a native stole one of the *Discovery*'s boats and in the fracas that followed, Cook, the last to leave the shore, was struck down and killed. What made the tragedy all the more acute was that Cook had been the most humane of men and the last to use any form of violence.

Another Dutchman, one who also explored the South Pacific, made a notable voyage in 1721. Admiral Roggeveen sailed far to the south past Cape Horn, and came among icebergs. He then turned northward and reached Juan Fernandez before, steering westward, he discovered Easter Island and, long afterwards, Samoa.

Cook, Tasman and Roggeveen were only three of the great seventeenth- and eighteenth-century navigators who, as the result of lengthy tussles with the South Seas in all weathers, built up a store of information that has ever since held succeeding generations in their debt.

Overleaf: While the southern seas were being explored in the 18th century there was a revival of English whaling in northern waters. 'Whalers in Ice' is a painting by the contemporary artist Charles Brooking, who died in 1759 aged 36.
NATIONAL MARITIME MUSEUM, LONDON

The Sailing Frigate

AMONG the well-armed but slow and clumsy English men-of-war of the mid-seventeenth century, there appeared a three-masted 'light, nimble ship, built for the purpose of sailing swiftly' of 315 tons and thirty guns named *Constant Warwick*. Fast and powerful enough to capture merchantmen and elude heavier warships, she was called a frigate, a term derived from the earlier Italian *fregata*, a small galleas, through the French *frégate*. She inspired shipwrights during the time of the Commonwealth to experiment with finer underwater lines, reduced upperworks and longer keels.

The War of the Spanish Succession of 1701-1714 showed the lack of a fast, stable, well-armed and seaworthy small warship for reconnaissance. War with France and Spain in 1739-1748 produced the British 44-gun frigates of 678-914 tons, too slow for the job, which carried all their guns on two lower decks; the second deck was useless in heavy weather.

In 1756, the Seven Years War between England and France began. The English introduced a new class of vessel in the experimental 36-gun 718-ton frigates *Brilliant* and *Pallas*, launched in 1757; they were meant to counter the new French frigates of the *Aurore* class, launched in the same year, also with thirty-six guns, but larger (946 tons) and manned by better sailors. A year later the English captured the *Aurore*, renamed her HMS *Aurora*, and studied her fine lines.

By the time the American War of Independence broke out in 1775, the French were building new improved frigates, which the British Navy countered with a 32-gun class of 670-720 tons and thirty vessels of a 28-gun type of 600 tons. A good example of the latter was HMS *Ariel*, built to the design of Sir J. Williams at Dover in 1785, a model of which is in the Science Museum at South Kensington in London. She carried all her main armament (twenty-four 9-pounders) on one main gundeck, which became a basic feature of frigates, and a few light guns (four 3-pounders) on the long quarterdeck. The gangways joining foc'sle to quarterdeck were broader than in previous ships, but the waist, often called 'the shambles', was still wide open, exposing the ten guns and their crews located there.

American shipyards built thirteen frigates mounting from twenty-four to thirty-two guns. By 1778, all but four of them had been lost, but the American warships were active on both sides of the Atlantic, aided by their French and Spanish allies, and at times cut off all communication between the Old World and the New, capturing ships, ammunition and stores. In April 1778, the Scottish-born John Paul Jones sailed round the British Isles, spreading alarm everywhere, with a squadron composed of his flagship, the old converted French merchantman *Bonhomme Richard* of forty-two guns; the *Alliance*, an American frigate of thirty-six guns, well built but commanded by an incompetent Frenchman; the 20-gun *Pallas* and two smaller ships. Off Flamborough Head, they

met a large convoy from the Baltic protected by the frigates *Serapis*, and *Countess of Scarborough*. *Serapis* was a new fast 50-gun ship, but instead of using his superior speed and gun power, Captain Pearson overconfidently allowed the *Bonhomme Richard* to come to close quarters, where the desperate aggression of Jones beat him into surrender.

With the carronade, invented in the late 1700s, the armament of frigates advanced considerably. The carronade, or 'smasher', was a short thin-barrelled gun with a wide bore firing a ball with great penetrating power over a short range of about a hundred yards or less. It was a light gun, and could safely be fitted in effective numbers on a frigate's upper decks without endangering her stability. Filled with grape shot, the smasher could clear an enemy's decks and mangle his rigging. The large 956-ton Spanish frigate *Santa Monica*, captured in 1779 by HMS *Pearl*, carried twenty-eight long guns when taken, but was re-armed for British service with twenty-six 12-pounders on her gundeck, ten 6-pounders and eight 18-pounder carronades on her upper deck.

In 1793, Revolutionary France declared war on Britain. British frigates were immediately sent out to warn homeward-bound merchantmen, and to escort convoys across the Atlantic and North Sea.

Others cruised in the Channel, looking for the enemy's merchantmen and watching for signs of his fleet. Two young frigate captains eager to enhance reputations for skill and initiative were Edward Pellew of the *Nymphe* (thirty-six guns) and James Saumarez in *Crescent* (thirty-six). Pellew put out from Falmouth with a largely new and untrained crew which included eighty Cornish tinminers, and at daybreak on 18 June, off Prawle Point, encountered the crack French frigate *Cléopatre*. The two ships ran parallel before the wind, their broadsides crashing into one another. Skilful gunnery control by Edward's younger brother Israel cleared *Cléopatre*'s decks, shattered her wheel and brought down her mizenmast, and Captain Mullon surrendered. 'We dished her up in fifty minutes, boarded and struck her colours,' Pellew reported.

Saumarez was cruising off Cherbourg in October watching for a French frigate which had made repeated sorties at night to catch British merchantmen. In the small hours of the 20th, the *Réunion* came out, but the wind dropped and she could not get back before *Crescent* had cut her off. The Frenchman tacked with all sail but *Crescent*, with superior seamanship and a hull clean from the dockyard, closed her, and a two-hour battle began. The French gunners shot too high, and although *Crescent* lost her foretopsail yard and foretopmast, Saumarez manoeuvred her into the coveted raking position across the enemy's stern. 'Our guns were so well served', he reported, 'that the French ship soon became unmanageable, and enabled us to rake her fore and aft; in that situation she struck her colours.'

Repeated single-ship victories of this sort by British frigates revealed deficiencies in French seamanship and gunnery, discipline and morale, which went from bad to worse the more French ships stayed in harbour rather than risk action. But a hundred British frigates were insufficient to meet the heavy demands made upon them. At Christmas 1793, a French squadron of five ships of the line attacked a Newfoundland convoy escorted only by the frigate *Castor*, capturing the frigate and many merchantmen. On 16 June 1795, Cornwallis's five ships-of-the-line and three frigates almost went the same way when they fell in with a greatly superior French force that included twelve ships-of-the-line. With the enemy overtaking fast, the frigate *Phoenix* pretended to be signalling to an imaginary British fleet just over the horizon, and the French broke off the action.

The frigates did invaluable work as 'the eyes of the Fleet'. Patrolling frigates sighted Villaret-Joyeuse's elusive fleet and enabled Lord Howe to win the victory of The Glorious First of June in 1794. In September 1798, Captain Richard Keats in the frigate *Boadicea* sighted a French squadron of one ship-of-the-line and eight frigates slipping out of Brest. Keats crowded on all sail to inform the Admiral in Torbay, and the French were intercepted off the Irish coast. In a wild five-hour chase through high seas and a rising gale, in which the British frigate *Amazon*, in the van, carried away her mizenmast, the French flagship and six frigates surrendered. Captured aboard the French ships were 3,000 soldiers going to reinforce French troops in Ireland and the Irish rebel leader Wolfe Tone.

At Copenhagen in 1801, the *Amazon*, captained by Edward Riou, very efficiently piloted Nelson's division of the Fleet into the Sound and down the Outer Channel by the Swedish shore, to take the moored Danish ships by surprise from the south, having previously made a thorough check on the correct positioning of the buoys placed there to guide them. Unfortunately, she and the other four frigates present had later to be thrown in against the northern and stronger part of the enemy's line, and *Amazon* was so badly knocked about by the heavy guns of the Trekroner fort that she was forced to withdraw, and Riou was killed as she turned away.

In the evening of 1 September 1805, Captain Henry Blackwood's frigate *Euryalus*, with every scrap of sail on her, gusted into the Solent with the news that Villeneuve was in Cadiz. On 14 September Nelson sailed from Portsmouth, arriving off Cadiz a fortnight later. Withdrawing the main body of the Fleet fifty miles out into the Atlantic, he stationed the four frigates *Euryalus*, *Naiad*, *Phoebe*, and *Sirius*, under Blackwood, close in with orders to '. . . watch all points and all winds and weathers.'

With first light on 19 October, *Sirius*, the inshore frigate, signalled 'Enemy have their topsail yards hoisted.' By 09.30, Nelson had ordered 'general chase south-east.' For some hours on the 20th, the enemy ships were lost in bad visibility, but *Euryalus* picked them up again in the afternoon and held on to them. Through the night of the 20th-21st, Blackwood kept Nelson informed of Villeneuve's every movement,

Left: An unidentified English frigate, apparently caught in contrary winds, from a painting by F. Butterworth.
SCIENCE MUSEUM, LONDON

Above: HMS 'Little Belt', something the worse for shot, and the US frigate 'President' off Sandy Hook, New Jersey in May 1811; a painting by J. Cartwright.
BY COURTESY OF THE US NAVAL ACADEMY MUSEUM

using signal guns, blue lights and rockets. With the daylight, Nelson steered for the enemy, and the battle of Trafalgar was joined.

Trafalgar was won, but the war went on, with British frigates continuing the wearisome grind of blockade off the French coast. One of them was HMS *Shannon*, which was one of a new class of frigates, mounting thirty-eight 18-pounder guns and fourteen carronades, based on the design of the captured French frigate *Hebe*. She was constructed by Brindley's of Frinsbury, near Chatham, on the Medway, a firm which had not built frigates before, but specialised in seventy-fours and stout East Indiamen. *Shannon* had the familiar bluff bows, but fine underwater lines which gave her a good turn of speed, and a flush upper deck with waist decked in. In the spring of 1807, *Shannon*, with the frigate *Meleager*, gave protection to the British whaling fleet off Greenland, but in 1808, she was back cruising off Ushant and the Black Rocks of Brest, apprehending the occasional small brig or schooner.

She was still there two years later. 'Tough as I have been,' wrote her Captain, Philip Broke, 'I cannot last much longer. I have seen all the ships and men out two or three times . . . Many about me are yielding to the fatigue and confinement of a life which is not natural to man . . .' Broke was a captain of exceptional ability, a gunnery fanatic who had made of the *Shannon* a fighting ship of unsurpassed efficiency. His innovations included the fitting of 'dispart' sights to the guns for better aiming; scientifically graduated and notched

'quoins', or wedges, for the guns, to give a horizontal-fire reference in all attitudes of the ship, even at night; and a system of operating all the guns of a broadside in concert, involving common scales of elevation, and lines of bearing cut in the deck at each gun controlled by reference to a master compass rose on deck.

In the spring of 1811, *Shannon* sailed to join the British North American Squadron. She entered Halifax, Nova Scotia, on 24 September 1811, after a rough five-week passage, where she found the 60-gun *Africa*, the frigates *Guerrière* (thirty-eight guns), *Spartan* (thirty-eight), *Belvidera* (thirty-six) and *Aeolus* (thirty-two), and six sloops.

For ten months, *Shannon* cruised between Halifax and Bermuda in the protection of homeward-bound convoys. On the last day of June 1812, she was entering Halifax when Broke was hailed and told that the USA had declared war on Britain after the *Guerrière* had taken men out of an American ship. The American Commodore Rodgers had chased the *Belvidera* and fired on her. She lay in Halifax, her maintopmast and cross-jack yard fished with capstan bars where two 24-pound balls from the US frigate *President* had gone clean through them.

With seven frigates and ten smaller ships, the United States Navy was taking on only that part of the might of the Royal Navy's thousand active-service ships that were not engaging the prime enemy – France. The British North American Squadron was confident, but had not studied the opposition. When the Quaker shipbuilder Joshua Humphreys of Philadelphia had been asked by Congress in 1794 to design six warships, he had concluded, 'As our navy for a considerable time will be inferior in numbers, we are to consider what size ships will be most formidable and be an overmatch for those of an enemy . . . Frigates will be the first object, and none to be built less than 150 feet keel . . .'

Three very large frigates, *Constitution*, *President* and *United States*, were built, over 200 feet in length, with a displacement of 2,200 tons. Their long keels and especially fine lines, based on those of the speedy Baltimore clippers, made them fast and stable vessels, capable of carrying an exceptionally heavy battery, based mainly on 24-pounders, in contrast to the 18-pounder standard in British frigates. Their gundecks were higher than in British frigates and more efficient in bad weather. Their solidly planked upper decks were broken only by hatchways. *Constitution* carried fifty-four guns, comprising thirty long 24-pounders on the gun-deck, twenty-two 32-pounder carronades and two 12-pounder bow-chasers on the upper deck. Three smaller 38-gun frigates, *Chesapeake*, *Constellation* and *Congress*, were built on similar lines, with twenty-four 18-pounders on the gun-deck, twenty-one 24-pounder carronades and two 18-pounders on the upper deck.

The American crews contained no pressed men, and were captained by brilliant seamen. British seamen had grown over-confident, British captains, with the exception of men like Broke, put more value on spit and polish than on regular drill and practical seamanship.

Young Captain Dacres of the *Guerrière* was such a captain; his ship was an old French prize, smart in her new paint but slack from lack of drill. On the afternoon of 9 August she was idling her way to Halifax when Isaac Hull in *Constitution* overtook her from windward. Dacres opened the battle with a broadside at extreme range from his starboard 18-pounders, then wore and fired his port broadside. All his shots went high, except for two glancing blows. The two ships exchanged fire for nearly an hour, Dacres wearing to fire his broadside, Hull yawing to avoid being raked.

Then Dacres gave up his unsuccessful raking tactics. With the wind dead astern, he increased sail. But the swift *Constitution* overhauled him and brought up alongside *Guerrière* to deliver a series of coolly aimed broadsides. The Americans' heavier metal and more-accurate regular fire soon told. *Guerrière*'s mainmast crashed overboard to starboard and the slings of her main yard parted. Her speed dropped and the fallen mainmast in the water dragged her bow into the wind. Hull crossed her bows and raked her, wore round and raked her again. He shaved the *Guerrière*'s bows so close that her bowsprit stuck in *Constitution*'s mizen rigging. Both ships exchanged a murderous musket fire, then broke apart. *Guerrière*'s foremast and mainmast went overboard and she surrendered.

On 5 October, off the Canary Isles, Captain Stephen Decatur in the *United States* fell in with Captain John Carden in HMS *Macedonian*, a smaller but fast 38-gun frigate fresh from refit in England. Carden's notorious strictness did not extend to gun practice. Believing his opponent to be the 32-gun frigate *Essex*, which he knew to be armed chiefly with the short-range carronades, Carden kept his distance, only to suffer disastrously from Decatur's long 24-pounders. He lost his mizen topmast, and the *United States* was able to keep ahead of him, pouring in diagonal fire until *Macedonian* was forced to surrender.

In December, *Constitution* (Commodore Bainbridge) was at sea off Bahia when she sighted HMS *Java*. *Constitution* carried fifty-two guns that day, the British frigate forty-nine. Both were fast and light on the wheel, and it was a more even match than in the previous encounters between frigates.

At first both ships jockeyed for a raking position, exchanging fierce broadsides. *Constitution*'s wheel was shot away and she had to be steered by relieving tackles, two decks below. Bainbridge was wounded in the hip and thigh. Then *Java* lost some of her headsails and caught in stays,

so that *Constitution* was able to rake her. Captain Lambert rammed *Java*'s bow into *Constitution*'s quarter and led a boarding party, but murderous fire from carronades and muskets drove them back, and *Java* lost her foremast as the two ships separated. When she finally struck her colours, *Java* had lost all her spars except the lower mainmast, her crew was decimated and Captain Lambert lay mortally wounded.

On the afternoon of 1 June 1813, Captain James Lawrence brought the USS *Chesapeake*, with a crew new to the ship, out of Boston Harbour to fight the *Shannon*, a ship at peak efficiency, captained by the best gunnery officer in the Royal Navy. The American was trailed by small boats packed with Bostonians come to watch another *Guerrière*.

Lawrence, with undrilled gunners, wanted to come to close quarters. This suited Broke, who knew that the longer American 18-pounders outranged his own. As *Chesapeake* came up on *Shannon*'s starboard quarter, Lawrence, instead of crossing Broke's stern and raking *Shannon*, ranged alongside. At 17.50, *Shannon* opened fire and soon both ships were pouring grape and canister, bar shot, star and chain shot into each other. Superior training had its effect. *Chesapeake* had come up with too much way on her, and as she forged ahead she lost some of her forward sails, successive helmsmen were killed, and she swung into wind, away from *Shannon*. Lawrence was mortally wounded, his sailing master dead, his sailors and marines decimated. *Shannon* now poured in a raking fire, fatally wounding *Chesapeake*'s first lieutenant, captain of marines, fourth lieutenant and boatswain. *Chesapeake* gathered sternway, she ground into *Shannon*'s timbers, and the rigging of both ships became enmeshed. Broke's carronades and marine muskets reduced *Chesapeake*'s upper decks to a bloody shambles. There was great confusion among the now practically leaderless Americans.

Broke judged this the right time to lead a boarding party. *Shannon*'s men drove the desperately resisting American marines off the upper deck, and the ship was theirs. Then with a rending of rigging the ships broke apart. Resistance flared up again. Broke was hacked down by a cutlass, but as he lay bleeding he saw British colours hoisted above the American.

With that short bloody battle, the hey-day of the sailing frigate was really over. In Britain, the rush to design and build new frigates to match the great Humphreys vessels produced ships like HMS *Glasgow*, of fifty guns, built on the Thames in 1814, which took part in the bombardment of Algiers in 1816 and was at Navarino in 1827; and the *Liffey*, 1,269 tons, with forty guns, including twenty-eight 24-pounders, which served in the Burma war of 1824. That war saw the first use of a steamer on active service, and by mid-century sailing frigates were being modified with the addition of steam propulsion.

Until that time, sailing frigates did much useful work. HMS *Pique*, launched in Plymouth in 1834, operated against Carlist forces in northern Spain in 1837, and fought in the Syrian campaign of 1840. HMS *Arethusa*, 2,127 tons, launched in 1849, bombarded Odessa and Sevastopol in the Crimean War, and in 1861 was fitted with a screw. The USS *Constellation* ('The Yankee Race Horse'), bottled up in Hampton Roads for most of the War of 1812, fought Algerian pirates in 1815-1817, and served in the Mediterranean throughout the American Civil War of 1861-65. She is now preserved as a public monument in Baltimore, where she was built. *Constitution* also survives, preserved at her birthplace in Boston, the finest example of the sailing frigate ever built.

The Dutch and English at War

ENGLISH shipowners in the latter days of the seventeenth century were facing ruin. The Dutch had built up the largest fleet in Europe and had spread over a quarter of the globe. A constant irritation to British fishermen and seamen was the huge fishing fleet of two-masted herring-busses in their home waters, uncomfortably near to the coast, hauling their nets and protected by men-of-war. Stout allies as the Dutch had been, and would be again, monopoly bred arrogance.

On the Dutch side there was anger at the passing of the English Navigation Acts, which were intended to break the monopoly. Also, the captains saw no reason to honour the traditional salute of lowered topsails when their ships were passing up the Channel.

Feelings on both sides were such that it needed only an incident to provoke the First Dutch War. On 19 May 1652, Rear-Admiral Bourne was sheltering with eight ships in the Downs from a stiff breeze when the Dutch Admiral Martin Tromp, who was on his way to escort a convoy from the East, also appeared and took shelter with forty-two ships. Tromp had no love for the English. As an eight-year-old boy he had been captured by an English pirate and had spent two miserable years as a cabin-boy.

After the wind had dropped and he was sailing towards Calais, a Dutch captain overhauled him and brought news of trouble in the western Channel between English and Dutch over the question of the salute. Tromp at once altered course just as a British fleet was emerging from Rye harbour. In command was Robert Blake, General-at-Sea and a welcome opponent for the redoubtable Tromp. Short, thick-set and self-contained, Blake was a successful soldier in his fifties rapidly learning to be a successful admiral.

He was wearing his flag in the *James*, and Tromp was in the *Brederode*. The ships exchanged broadsides and the *James* took a battering. She had outsailed her consorts and had to fight the head of the Dutch line alone for some time until other ships of the fleet could come to her aid. Nearly surrounded by enemy ships, dismasted and damaged in the hull, with her sailing master dead and fifty other casualties, she was rescued just in time. Meanwhile Bourne had sailed from the Downs to the sound of guns. He attacked the rear ships, catching them unawares and cutting off two of them. His

A portrait by an unknown artist of Robert Blake, the English commander and opponent of Admiral Tromp.
NATIONAL MARITIME MUSEUM, LONDON

action decided the fight; after five fierce hours Tromp retired to his own coast, leaving the two ships in Bourne's hands (although one was later recovered by the Dutch) while the *James* was towed into Dover harbour.

Blake sailed north in September to deal with the warships protecting the Dutch herring fleet and had created havoc when Tromp, searching for him with a hundred sail, made contact near the Orkneys. But a sudden gale dispersed the Dutch while Blake found shelter in the Shetlands. Tromp's scattered vessels straggled home, having achieved nothing, and Tromp was in disgrace.

His command was taken over by Admiral Cornelius de Witt, who had junior to him Michael de Ruyter, one of the finest of all Dutch fighting admirals. But in the next battle, that of the Kentish Knock, Blake narrowly won the day. Two months later the old war-horse Tromp was in harness again. He escorted a big convoy, outward bound, into the Strait of Dover with eighty warships. Blake had half that number and a large proportion were only armed merchantmen. The battle, fought in November 1652, known as the Battle of the Ness, or Dungeness, left Tromp, so it was said, hoisting a broom at his masthead to announce that he had swept the Channel clear. As for Blake, he made it plain that he wanted no more armed merchantmen under his command.

The battle of the Ness was undeniably a defeat for Blake but when February 1653 came he had his revenge. In one action he met a new kind of engagement. It began when Blake caught an incoming Dutch convoy off Portland and developed into a running fight up the Channel, with Tromp striving manfully to screen the merchantmen from Blake's repeated attacks. It ended with over fifty Dutch merchant ships and men-of-war in English hands or sunk.

Blake had been wounded and when he was recovering, he took charge of eighteen ships refitting in the Thames while Deane and Monk, two other Generals-at-Sea, had joint command of the fleet. In June Tromp attacked them near the Gabbard shoal, east of Harwich, when a shot from the Dutch opening broadside cut General Deane in two. Monk flung his cloak over the body and, for all his lack of experience of sea warfare, carried on the fight until nightfall. On the following day the Dutch were so mauled that some ships,

Above: Admiral Blake defeating the Dutch fleet in 1652.
MARY EVANS PICTURE LIBRARY

Left: Detail from a painting by Peter M. Wood of a 17th-century warship in a squall.

Below: The Dutch Admiral Michael de Ruyter portrayed by H. Berckman.
NATIONAL MARITIME MUSEUM, LONDON

surprisingly for Dutchmen, broke away. Then Blake, hearing the gunfire as the fleets drifted southward, led out his eighteen ships for the finishing touch. Tromp himself had a narrow escape when the captains of two English ships with boarding parties actually succeeded in gaining the *Brederode*'s upper deck. A lesser man might have surrendered, but not Tromp. He set light to gunpowder and blew the upper deck, the boarders and probably some of his own men, overboard into the sea. He himself had severe burns. The English gained ten prizes.

There was still one final engagement to be fought, although the Dutch had by then lost heart. It was a July battle off Scheveningen, which Monk again won but which cost the Dutch still more. There, the great Admiral Martin Tromp

lost his life, fighting to the last at the age of fifty-six. The Dutch had lost the war but Cromwell treated them quite lightly. They had to agree to accept the Navigation Acts which broke their monopoly of trade, to give the salute in the Narrow Seas and to pay compensation for the atrocious massacre at Amboyna, but there was little else of importance.

Unfortunately, few Dutchmen appeared eager to carry out all their obligations, especially the awkward little matter of the salute. Then Charles II stirred up trouble by sending ships to create havoc with Dutch factors on the Guinea Coast, a curious step, which naturally brought out a Dutch fleet to take reprisals on British factors. In command of that fleet was Michael de Ruyter, who had taken the place of Tromp and was soon to make an undying name for himself.

King Charles had given Holland another cause for irritation by marrying Katherine of Braganza. She brought him a dowry that meant England owned not only Tangier, which would pose a threat to Dutch trade in the Mediterranean, but also Bombay, which gave England a foothold in what the Dutch considered to be their sphere. Already English merchants were nibbling at the seaborne trade.

The Second Dutch War, which was clearly inevitable, started in the early days of 1665. In June a major battle was fought off Lowestoft between two fleets, each of about 100 ships, with the Lord High Admiral proving his gift for command. He was now Monk, or rather the Duke of Albemarle, since he had been ennobled by Charles at the Restoration. Over a dozen enemy ships were taken in the fighting and as many more were sunk.

In the next big fight, in June 1666, the English fleet was divided between Albemarle and Prince Rupert, as the French were temporarily allied to the Dutch. Rupert, with the smaller detachment, was watching their ships. It was Albemarle who bore the brunt of the Four Days Battle, as it was called; one of the bloodiest and most hard-fought encounters in British history. Heavily outnumbered, on the third day, he was at last retiring towards the Thames estuary when Rupert's ships hove in sight to the south-west. Albemarle turned his shattered fleet and beat to windward through the enemy's line and saved the day.

He could hardly claim a victory when his losses were three times those of the Dutch, but he had lived to fight another day, and fight he did. Seven weeks afterwards he was at sea again and in the St James' Day Fight he more than squared the account by losing just one ship to the enemy's twenty. That was not all; he followed their retreat to the Texel and sent in Sir Robert Holmes to attack with fireships the shipping in the Vlie and the storesheds in the famous 'Holmes Bonfire', which burned long and most effectively.

But the war was not over even then. With peace negotiations dragging on, the king was persuaded, for the sake of economy, to leave the main fleet laid up in the Medway, at Chatham, instead of making it fit for sea with the coming of spring. The Duke of York gave specific instructions for the fleet's protection, including the stretching of a heavy chain across the river, but his orders, except for that referring to the chain, seem to have been ignored.

Albemarle did his best to alert Charles but his efforts came too late. News came that de Ruyter was off Harwich with a fleet of a hundred sail and making for the Thames. At once Albemarle rushed down to Chatham, to be appalled at what he saw: unmounted guns; cannon-balls of the wrong size; useless forts; and rotting gunpowder. Chatham was practically defenceless. While Albemarle struggled with the chaos, the Dutch entered the Thames, and de Ruyter detached three ships and some fireships from the main fleet to sail up the Medway. A landing party broke a bolt in the chain and, free to pass, the fireships burnt three of the finest ships in the Royal Navy. Still worse was the fate of the *Royal Charles*, flagship of Blake and the Duke of York, the very symbol of the restored monarchy. She was ignominiously towed across to Amsterdam, where part of her splendid decorated stern was set up as a permanent memento.

That astonishing feat of de Ruyter in 1667 marked the end of the Second Dutch War. However, in May 1672, the Third War erupted, with France an ally of England as the result of some dubious dealings between the French king and Charles. Four battles were fought, all of them drawn, with the French taking the part of interested spectators. In one of them, in Sole Bay, a ferocious old-style fight took place between Prince Rupert and de Ruyter, with another off the Texel matching it in courage and tenacity. Eventually, however, naval opinion, backed by the country at large, forced Charles to make peace. But the French continued and the effort of fighting two enemies proved too great even for the valiant Dutch. Exhausted, and with their dykes penetrated by the sea, they were unable to prevent their wealth of trade from falling into English hands, never to be fully regained.

Below: The opposing fleets of George Monk (Duke of Albemarle) and Michael de Ruyter in the English Channel; from an engraving published in Amsterdam in 1666.

Overleaf: The defeat of the English by the Dutch in the Strait of Dover during the Four Days' Battle of June 1666, as depicted in a painting by Abraham Storck.

The Seventy-four

IT is often said that there was little change in warship design between the Armada and Trafalgar. That statement is true in the sense that the fundamental basis of the design of the three-masted wooden man-of-war did not change. However, even if the development of the fighting ship between 1600 and 1800 appears small, viewed in context, the developments in detail introduced during those 200 years produced a great increase in fighting power and general performance. The *Revenge* (1577) and *Sovereign of the Seas* (1637) were both outstanding in their day, but would not have had a chance against the standard fighting ship of Nelson's period, the 74-gun line-of-battleship.

With the exception of minor specialised craft like bomb ketches, warships from the Armada to the introduction of steam were built to a common pattern. At any one time all but the smallest brigs, cutters and the like had a similar layout and a three-masted rig. The main variations were in size, gunpower and fineness of lines. Generally speaking, the larger the ship the more concentration there was on the guns, and less on fineness of lines, as the large ship needed more room in her hull for the bigger crew and their stores.

As the length of a wooden hull was severely limited, the whole length of the ship had to be used to carry an adequate broadside of guns, which meant 'full ends', or in other words bluff bows and sterns. However, a big ship could carry more sail and go faster in rough conditions than a smaller ship which was speedier in light winds. So size and gunpower were linked, and were the main distinguishing features of different types of warship. The bigger ships were for fighting battles, the smaller ones for subsidiary duties, such as scouting, carrying dispatches, escorting convoys and so on. Therefore, it was logical to classify ships by the number of guns they carried.

The English fleets that fought the Armada and later the Dutch included many merchantmen, for at that stage there was little difference between a well-armed merchant ship and all but the largest warships. However, warships were growing in size, and the differences grew greater until, by the end of the third Dutch war (1674), it was obvious that there was no longer any place for the ill-armed and poorly disciplined merchant ship in the increasingly rigid line of battle. Subsequently merchantmen might be hired for subsidiary naval purposes, but not to serve as ships of the line, although there were a few exceptions. In the American War of Independence, for example, an East Indiaman was converted on the stocks to become the 74-gun line-of-battleship *Bombay Castle*.

Just as the merchant ship was eliminated from the line of battle, so were the smaller types of warship as it became obvious that at least two decks of guns and thick sides were essential for a battleship. Any ship carrying fewer than fifty guns was too weak to take part in a major battle, but arming a ship with 100 guns or more pushed the art of building wooden ships to its limits, and was very expensive in terms of money, timber and men. Because of the difficulty of building a ship longer than about 200 feet from wood by conventional methods, any ship carrying more than eighty guns needed three complete decks of guns, with a deeper hull and more freeboard and, therefore, more windage and less handiness than a two-decker. The fact that the *Victory* was a popular flagship for half a century was due to the accident that although a three-decker, she sailed as well as a 74-gunner.

The *Victory* (and all other ships of 100 guns or more) was a First Rate; ships carrying ninety-eight to eighty-four guns were Second Rates, those with eighty to sixty-four guns Third Rates, and at the lower end of the battleship classes with fifty and sixty guns were Fourth Rates. The rating

system was in use long before the end of the seventeenth century but it was some time before the best compromise between size, power, economy and handiness was found. It took a long process of trial and error before the seventy-four was established as the standard battleship in the three largest eighteenth-century navies, those of France, Spain and Great Britain. The First and Second Rates were never completely supplanted as they were useful flagships and status symbols, and powerful adversaries in battle. The seventy-four had a smaller sister, the sixty-four, which was weaker but useful for outlying stations or convoy escort, and still capable of serving in the line of battle. The smaller Fourth Rates however gradually went out of use; by about 1756 50-gun ships no longer served as battleships.

Though there had been odd examples of ships carrying seventy-four guns being built earlier, the seventy-four as a type first appeared in the French and Spanish navies in the period between the Peace of Utrecht (1713) and the outbreak of war between Britain and Spain in 1739. At that period British major warships were notoriously smaller and weaker than their equivalents in the other major navies. The 70-gun ships, and even more the three-decked 80-gun ships, were both badly designed and too small for their armament. Even when the Royal Navy began to follow the example of the Spanish and the French in building seventy-fours (the first was built in 1747), they were still inferior to foreign vessels of the same nominal force. The early British seventy-fours had some difficulty in fighting their lower-deck guns (which were the heaviest) in a heavy sea or a fresh wind when their French contemporaries could still keep their gun ports open, precisely because the French ships had greater beam and were stiffer.

Although British ships improved later, throughout the eighteenth century the French and Spanish had the reputation of building better ships. Although their reputation was not wholly deserved, it was true that the French were much further advanced in the study of theoretical naval architecture, but their more scientific attitude did not necessarily mean that the British shipwrights, working more empirically, could not build equally good ships. Certainly British ships tended to be built with more of an eye to economy, and also usually carried more guns on a given tonnage. Undeniably the practical test of combat showed that the British ships were consistently superior as fighting machines, due almost entirely to the human factor. It meant that plenty of French and Spanish ships were captured by their supposedly inferior British contemporaries, and could then be used, and copied, by the Royal Navy.

As regards construction, the hull of a seventy-four was made of thick wood capable of resisting heavy punishment, and the most frequently used was oak. By the eighteenth century suitable trees, particularly for the great curved bow and stern timbers, were becoming rare, and many experiments were tried, the most successful being the building of a number of ships of teak at Bombay after 1800. The keel and frames of a seventy-four, which were so close together that the side was nearly solid before it was planked, took up an immense amount of timber even before planking and decking had been done. A ship of that size would require between 3,000 and 4,000 cartloads of timber.

Other requirements were tall straight pines to make the masts; by the time the seventy-four appeared most masts in the Royal Navy were made, that is, constructed of several pieces of timber carefully fitted together. All ships carried spare spars to replace those lost in action or through stress of weather. The complicated network of standing and running rigging could easily be replaced by a skilled crew.

The details of rigging did not change very much during the time when the seventy-four flourished, though the gaff spanker replaced the old lateen mizen sail, and staysails and jibs were adopted, as was the dolphin and chain rigging. The most important change affecting mobility was the general adoption of copper sheathing by the Royal Navy during the

Left: A 74-gun (Third Rate) ship of the line, circa 1794, from a painting by W. F. Mitchell. D. RUDKIN

American War of Independence. It meant that a ship could keep her speed for much longer when at sea for long periods, because the copper prevented the underwater growths that would otherwise slow her down. Coppering also stopped the depredations of the teredo worm and other marine borers which would otherwise weaken the hull, particularly in tropical waters.

The hull of a two-decker was divided by the gundeck; above it was the armament and accommodation space, below it the storerooms, magazines and bilges. Forward on the upper deck was the great stove which was used to cook for the entire ship's company. The only major pieces of machinery were the windlass used for raising the anchor, and the pumps (the chain pump was probably introduced about the same time as the seventy-four), and the ship's wheel; everything else was done by block and tackle and manpower. The crew was the most important part of a warship; they worked the sails and the guns, and because very few ships were sunk in action in that period, finished off an enemy by boarding. About 600 men lived sometimes for years on end within the hull of a seventy-four.

During the later eighteenth century there were important developments in ventilation, hygiene and diet, which meant that fewer men died, but still the death toll from disease and accident was far higher than from enemy action. The greatest dangers to a wooden sailing warship were fire and the weather; far more ships were lost by all navies to those causes than to enemy action.

Despite her primitiveness to our eyes, the seventy-four was the most complex artefact of her day. She was a complicated work of architecture in wood, capable of resisting the stress of storms, and carrying in her hold sufficient stores to support a large community over a long period. Her sails and rigging were a complicated and precise instrument for utilising the wind to provide propulsion. She carried more and heavier guns than an army would have in its train. Her navigating officers would use some of the most complicated instruments of their day.

The seventy-fours, and particularly those of the Royal Navy, also played an important part in the history of their time, in the eighteenth-century wars for overseas empire. For their last and greatest war a great naval historian put the matter in a nutshell; it was 'those far-distant storm-beaten ships upon which the Grand Army never looked' which 'stood between it and the dominion of the World'.

The main purpose of a ship of the line was to carry the largest possible broadside battery of guns. The smooth-bore muzzle-loader was not a very accurate or long-range weapon, so quantity had to replace quality. The earliest British seventy-fours carried twenty-eight 32-pounders on the gun (or main) deck, twenty-eight 18-pounders on the upper deck and fourteen 9-pounders on the quarterdeck and forecastle. There were, therefore, three separate deck levels for guns, but since the uppermost was not continuous, and the waist of the ship was open, the ship was called a two-decker.

The larger seventy-fours like the *Triumph* carried a slightly heavier battery, with thirty 24-pounders on the upper deck and only sixteen 9-pounders. During the American War of Independence a number of improvements in gunnery achieved widespread use in the Royal Navy. One of the most important was the use of a flintlock for firing the gun, much more reliable than the old slow-match, although that was kept as a standby. The other important innovation was a new type of gun, a light short-range piece called a carronade, which could fire a much heavier ball in relation to its own weight, and required a smaller crew than the conventional long guns. Carronades could be added to the armament of the poop and forecastle in the larger warship without much difficulty, and in 1779 the establishment of all seventy-fours was increased by the addition of two 12-pounder carronades to the forecastle and six 12-pounder carronades to the poop guns.

Although seventy-fours then carried eighty-two guns, they were still known under their original designation, because carronades were not carriage guns; they were mounted on slides, not on the usual truck carriage with its four little wheels, and so they did not count. By the end of the century heavier carronades were being carried – 32-pounders – but in 1806 it was decided to rationalise matters.

Instead of ships carrying a mixed battery of guns of different calibre, the order went out that all seventy-fours were to use only one size of shot. The new establishment was twenty-four long 24-pounders on the gundeck, twenty-eight medium 24-pounders on the upper deck, and four medium 24-pounders and fourteen 24-pounder carronades on quarterdeck and forecastle. The last four medium guns would be for use as chase guns, firing ahead and astern, and giving more range than the carronades. The change actually lightened the load the ship had to carry, as the guns weighed a total of 157cwt instead of 181cwt, and the weight of the broadside was only marginally less, 888lb instead of 928lb. After the Napoleonic Wars further improvements were made in ordnance, including the use of shell guns, but by then the seventy-four was on the way out.

While on the subject of weapons, it would not do to forget about the ship's boats of a Royal Navy seventy-four. During the long years of blockade the Royal Navy raised the

so-called cutting-out raid to a fine art; often the only way to strike at enemy coasters, warships in harbour, or small forts on shore was to send the boats in. The largest boats – the launch and the cutter – could carry small carronades, and they sometimes made quite extended voyages on their own. The boats greatly extended the offensive range of a warship, and it would not be unrealistic to think of a line-of-battleship as resembling a modern aircraft carrier, capable of launching strikes at otherwise inaccessible targets.

The gradual standardisation of the seventy-four can be seen by comparing the composition of the lines of battle in a number of famous actions. For example, in 1692 the British fleet at Barfleur consisted of a medley of types, typical of a seventeenth-century battle, although the high proportion of seventies can be seen from Table 1.

TABLE 1 (number of ships)

100 guns (4)	74 guns (1)	64 guns (2)	50 guns (6)
96 guns (3)	72 guns (1)	62 guns (1)	48 guns (3)
90 guns (8)	70 guns (21)	60 guns (4)	44 guns (1)
82 guns (1)	66 guns (2)	54 guns (3)	

Velez Malaga was fought in 1704 between the British and Dutch on one side and the French and Spanish on the other. The British fleet showed less variety than before, unlike the enemy fleets, while the Dutch squadron demonstrated the tendency of that navy to build smaller vessels of shallow draught because of the shallow seas around Holland. The disposition at Velez Malaga is shown in Table 2.

TABLE 2

BRITISH	DUTCH	FRANCO-SPANISH	
96 guns (3)	90 guns (1)	104 guns (1)	70 guns (3)
90 guns (2)	72 guns (3)	102 guns (1)	68 guns (2)
80 guns (9)	64 guns (6)	96 guns (1)	64 guns (2)
76 guns (1)	54 guns (1)	92 guns (4)	62 guns (2)
70 guns (16)	52 guns (1)	88 guns (4)	60 guns (6)
66 guns (1)		86 guns (2)	58 guns (9)
50 guns (2)		84 guns (2)	56 guns (5)
		80 guns (1)	54 guns (3)
		74 guns (3)	

Half a century later, at Quiberon Bay in 1759, the seventy-four was already established as the most common type on the British side, as shown in Table 3; at the Saintes in 1782 there were more seventy-fours than all other types put together in the British fleet (Table 4); and Trafalgar was fought mainly between seventy-fours (Table 5).

TABLE 3

BRITISH	FRENCH
100 guns (1)	80 guns (4)
90 guns (3)	74 guns (6)
74 guns (7)	70 guns (3)
70 guns (5)	64 guns (8)
64 guns (2)	
60 guns (5)	

(there were also four 50-gun ships).

TABLE 4

BRITISH
98 guns (4)
90 guns (1)
74 guns (20)
70 guns (1)
64 guns (11)

TABLE 5

BRITISH	SPANISH	FRENCH
100 guns (3)	140 guns (1)	84 guns (1)
98 guns (4)	112 guns (2)	80 guns (3)
80 guns (1)	100 guns (1)	74 guns (15)
74 guns (16)	80 guns (2)	
64 guns (3)	74 guns (7)	
	64 guns (1)	

Above left: Side view of the 1649 Second Rate 'Sophia Amalia'; a model showing the gunports.
ORLOGSMUSEET, COPENHAGEN

Above: Highly gilded stern on the model of 'Sophia Amalia'.
ORLOGSMUSEET, COPENHAGEN

Up to 1800 the Royal Navy operated a total of 139 seventy-fours (including ships building). Of those, fourteen were ex-French, ten ex-Spanish and one captured from the Dutch. An individual example of the copying of a foreign design was the first of a class of enlarged and improved seventy-fours, the *Triumph* laid down in 1758 and launched in 1764. She was for long considered the best of her type, and the inspiration for the design came from a ship wrecked in the same year as she was laid down. That was the French *Invincible* captured by Admiral Anson in 1747.

In that same year the first British-built seventy-four, the *Culloden*, had been built at Deptford. She was 161½ft long on her gun deck, 46½ft broad and her tonnage was 1,487. The *Triumph* was longer (171¼ft), broader (49¾ft) and of greater tonnage (1,825). A typical seventy-four of the Napoleonic period, the *Bulwark* of 1807, showed a further advance in dimensions (181ft 10in by 49¼ft and 1,940 tons).

The early years of the nineteenth century produced a number of structural innovations. The old-style 'square' bow with a bulkhead running across the width of the ship had always been a weak point, very few guns could be fired from it and, especially, it was much thinner than the massive sides. In 1804 Seppings put a 'round' bow, capable of taking more guns, on the *Namur* while she was being cut down from a ninety to a seventy-four at Chatham. It was only a matter of time before an even weaker area, the stern with its great cabin and its windows, was given similar treatment, but that was delayed because senior naval officers naturally preferred to keep their comparatively light and airy quarters.

In 1817, however, the first round stern appeared; it was uglier but much stronger than its predecessor. Another, and more important, innovation was made at Chatham in 1805, the use of diagonal framing in the seventy-four *Kent*. Later

the *Warspite* was entirely constructed using that system, and the *Tremendous*, when she was rebuilt, even had diagonal framing used for the deck beams. The new constructional method meant that less wood had to be used; instead of making the sides of the ship thick and solid with massive frames, greater strength could be obtained by laying the main timbers diagonally fore and aft. It was a change from a transverse system to a longitudinal one, but the real significance was that limitation on length had been lifted.

With longer ships possible the main reason for the seventy-four had gone. Not many ships were built in the long years of peace after 1815, and none of them was a seventy-four; the new ships were either larger or smaller. The number of seventy-fours on the Navy List diminished slowly, as wooden ships can have a long life, but most were in reserve or used as training ships or hulks of one kind or another. The last seventy-four to see action seems to have been the *Blenheim*, off Canton in 1841 during the First Opium War.

The *Implacable*, captured from the French as the *Duguay Trouin* in 1805, served off the coast of Syria in 1841 against Mehemet Ali. She survived for a long retirement until after the Second World War, when proposals were made to preserve her in dry dock at Greenwich (where the *Cutty Sark* now rests). She was badly infected with rot and, as enough money was not forthcoming, in 1949 she was towed out into the Channel, flying the white ensign and tricolour side by side, and was scuttled. Even then the last of the seventy-fours showed her toughness. Her bottom had been blown out, but she remained afloat, and more explosive had to be used to sink her.

Hudson's Bay Co Ships

ONE of the many ships belonging to the world's oldest shipping and trading concern, the Hudson's Bay Company, is the bark *Stork*. Hudson's Bay Co is the oldest active company with a royal charter, and one of the greatest merchant trading companies ever founded.

In the seventeenth century two French fur traders persuaded Prince Rupert of the Rhine and Charles II that a valuable trade in furs was waiting to be developed from the North American forests with direct access to the waters of Hudson's Bay, rather than by the southern river routes already commandeered by the Dutch and French. Two ships, the *Eaglet* and the *Nonsuch*, sailed for Canada but only the *Nonsuch* made the journey, as the *Eaglet* had to turn back. The cargo of beaver pelts that *Nonsuch* brought back assured the royal backers and King Charles granted a royal charter in 1670.

Side-by-side with trading went exploration and development of Canadian territories and for a time the quest for the North-West Passage to the Far East was still of importance to the HBC, although it became of less consequence as the company developed its foothold in Canada.

Ships employed by the Hudson's Bay Co to cross the Atlantic varied considerably throughout its long history. The successful ketch, an example of which was *Nonsuch*, was thought to be a useful type because of its size and manoeuvrability. In later years – the eighteenth century – the company operated brigs, barques and schooners in place of the earlier sloop. Many smaller craft were used for trade, communication and exploration on inland waters and in Hudson Bay itself, including shallops, York boats and canoes.

In 1888 the company acquired its first transatlantic steamer, the barque-rigged ex-whaler *Erik*. In that same year, the steam-paddler *Beaver*, which was built in 1834 and was of considerable use to the HBC, the Navy and general explorers, was wrecked at Vancouver harbour entrance. A famous ship acquired by the company in the early twentieth century was Captain Scott's *Discovery* which is now permanently moored on the Thames in London.

There were casualties and heroes among the long line of HBC ships, some fell victim to the severe ice of Arctic waters and were lost such as the *Lady Kindersley* in 1924 the *Baychimo* in 1931 and the *Fort James* in 1937. Two HBC ships the *Nascopie* and the *Pelican* claimed the distinction of sinking U-boats in wartime. The days of exploration are over and the ships of the Hudson's Bay Co no longer ply the Atlantic with animal pelts, although the company is still foremost in fur trading today, and memories of its illustrious past live on through the replica of the ketch *Nonsuch* built for the company at Appledore in Devon and Scott's *Discovery*.

Top right: Hudson's Bay Company pioneer ship 'Nonsuch', painted by Peter M. Wood.

Centre right: Some of the decorative carvings of 'Nonsuch'.
P. M. WOOD

Bottom right: Laurence Dunn's painting of the HBC ship 'Baychimo' – the 'will o' the wisp of the Arctic', which was lost in 1931 – adrift with the ice.

Overleaf: The Hudson's Bay Company's bark 'Stork'.
HUDSON'S BAY COMPANY

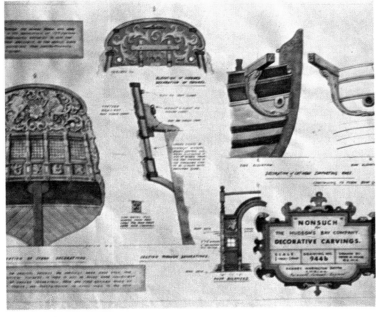

American Independence

THE Declaration of the American War of Independence in 1776 is often held to have been heralded by the 'Boston tea-party' of four years earlier. But even earlier than that there were outbreaks of force against the clumsy hand and blindness of the British Government, which was coupled with the imposition of taxes and the Colonists' disgust at not being allowed to handle their own affairs.

In 1769 the British armed sloop *Liberty*, which was busily suppressing smuggling, or evasion of taxes, so enraged the people of Newport that they seized and burnt her. Later, in 1772, the captain of the British sloop *Gaspee*, who is described as having an overbearing manner, had the ill luck when chasing a suspected smuggler, outward bound from Newport, to run aground. It was too good an opportunity to miss; boatloads of men rowed out to her, wounded the captain and set the *Gaspee* on fire.

The Boston tea-party came in 1773. A number of ships had brought cargoes of tea to Boston and some of their captains, finding them unwanted, had sailed back to England. Then the Governor asserted his authority and forbade the other ships to leave until all their tea had been unloaded. They were saved the trouble; about forty or fifty men dressed as Red Indians scrambled on board the ships and flung the boxes of tea into the sea.

As time went on minor affrays in different ports grew more and more violent and several English naval vessels, chiefly sloops with lieutenants or midshipmen in command, were captured after fights and their guns shared out.

George Washington's first step in nautical matters was to fit out a schooner, the *Hannah*, which sailed from Beverly, Massachusetts, in September 1775 and returned after two days with a couple of English prizes. By the end of the year several other vessels had been overhauled and manned by the army.

The chief asset at first lay in the wealth of privateers in the American States. Until the declaration of war there had normally been quite a large number cruising at sea in the hope of making prizes of French and Spanish ships; as official action against the British hardened their total was greatly augmented. They undoubtedly aided the States to win the war but they were prone to cause trouble with various abuses. All proceeds of their cruises were shared between the crews and the owners, not with the States. It is estimated that more than 2,000 men were engaged on privateering and that 550 letters of marque, which gave licences to make reprisals, were issued by Congress.

Since suitable ships for conversion into small warships were very few indeed, there was little difficulty in finding sufficient seamen to man possible vessels. In addition to the

John Paul Jones shooting a sailor who had attempted to strike the colours.
NATIONAL MARITIME MUSEUM, LONDON

fishermen of the Grand Banks and the whalers, there were the crews of merchantmen who had been trading with the West Indian islands.

The idea of what came to be known as the Continental Navy, meaning a combined navy of American States, was broached in 1775 (the same year that the American Marine Corps was brought into being). It led to the building and equipping of a joint American fleet instead of ships of individual States. The Naval Committee of Congress then set up formal prize-courts and ordered matters of discipline, rations and pay, all copied from the Royal Navy.

In November 1775 the committee authorised four merchant vessels for conversion as far as possible into men-of-war. They were visualised as the first of an armed fleet to be composed of five ships of thirty-two guns and five of twenty-eight guns, and three frigates of twenty-four guns up to 12-pounders. Also in November, manning was ordered 'with such officers as are proper to man and command'. In the subsequent list, the name appears of a senior lieutenant, the American national hero John Paul Jones. The list is a brief one; it has four first lieutenants, five second lieutenants and three third lieutenants. Surgeons, pursers, midshipmen and other warrant officers are not included.

The States were beginning to receive a great deal of nautical help from France, in spite of some disagreements. There were soon American agents in several French ports, besides a few in Spain and Holland. They actively discussed and dealt with a variety of topics such as prizes, privateers, stores and suppliers, docks and prisoners of war. For a while, however, France did not commit herself to sending material aid; she preferred to bide her time and watch events, always with an eye to England as the arch enemy.

During the course of the war the States themselves had no vessels of appreciable size; Massachusetts had fifteen seagoing ships and one galley, Pennsylvania had about ten ships, thirty boats and galleys, and Virginia from first to last had seventy-two ships including brigs and schooners, but they were small and weak. Other States had only small craft except Carolina with fifteen sea-going vessels. In short, the Continental Congress had practically nothing that could be considered a fleet. In 1777, when under a close blockade, only four frigates succeeded in cruising at sea.

Even so, during the war Britain lost a total of 625 vessels, thirty-eight of them privateers and the rest nearly all merchantmen. The captures were often of great value to the Americans as a source of arms and supplies.

An outstanding exception to the part played by the Colonial Navy was the foray of the redoubtable John Paul Jones. Perhaps because of his mixed seafaring experience he had been sent to France to take up an important command but instead he collected a small squadron with which to harry shipping on the British coasts. He obtained an old French East Indiaman, the *Bonhomme Richard*, overhauled her and mounted extra guns and manned her with a motley crew of Americans, some renegade British seamen who had been prisoners of war, French soldiers and marines and Portuguese sailors. The ships with him, two frigates and a small brig, all had French crews, although the whole squadron flew the flag of the Congress.

Before the end of 1781 Congress reached its lowest strength in ships. It then had only two frigates, the *Confederacy* and the *Trumball*, the sloop-of-war *Saratoga*, and the two schooners *Alliance* and *Deans* making up the whole

York, were making ready to move either on to New York or against Cornwallis in Virginia.

Another factor was that the gifted French Admiral de Grasse was crossing the Atlantic with his main fleet, at last, to aid the Americans. In anticipation, a British fleet under Admiral Lord Howe, the brother of General Howe on shore, had been dispatched to deal with him. Unfortunately, it was not to be an equal match, nor would it have been even had the two fleets been of exactly the same number. It was notorious that the French ships were larger, stronger and of better design than those that had come out of English shipyards.

Worse, the British Admiralty was passing through a shameful era of corruption and disarray. The First Lord,

of the navy. A 74-gun ship-of-the-line, the *America*, and a frigate, *Bourbon*, still lingered on the stocks, but at that period their navy list showed twenty-two captains, thirty-nine lieutenants, with twenty-two marine captains and twelve lieutenants. However, a change was looming. Washington and Rochambeau, having united their armies near New

An engraving from 'Penny Magazine' of the famous Boston Tea Party which was a direct challenge to the authority of the Governor. MARY EVANS PICTURE LIBRARY

Left: General Cornwallis's surrender at Yorktown.
MARY EVANS PICTURE LIBRARY

Below: HMS 'Serapis' and John Paul Jones' 'Bonhomme Richard' as painted by Dominic Serres.
BY COURTESY OF THE US NAVAL ACADEMY MUSEUM

the Earl of Sandwich, might have been held responsible but he was only one of many malefactors. At all events at least two, perhaps three, admirals of character would have nothing to do with him. There is a tale of how he at length persuaded Admiral Keppel to take command of the Channel fleet, which had, so he said, forty-two ships in all, thirty-five of them in commission and ready for sea. Keppel went down to Portsmouth and found just twenty ships and of them only six, to use his words, were 'fit for a seaman's eye'.

At that period morale in the fleet was not by any means high and it was under strain after years of almost continuous fighting, at first with the French and then with both Spain and Holland in addition. But when the French admiral appeared off the American coast with a fleet considerably larger than could be mustered under the British flag, Admiral Howe took it in hand without fuss. With involved tactical manoeuvres that bewildered the enemy he cleverly drove them clear of New York and Rhode Island. For the next few years comparative peace reigned at sea.

Then, in 1781, the French Admiral de Grasse appeared with his entire fleet. By that time General Cornwallis was on the shore of the Chesapeake, the great arm of the sea at Yorktown. Although Admiral Howe had gone home, an earlier attempt by a French squadron to enter the Chesapeake had been fought off without much difficulty by the British ships stationed there, but de Grasse was a very different proposition.

On hearing the news of his coming, the British Admiral Graves, at New York, reinforced by ships from the West Indies, sailed to the Chesapeake to protect Cornwallis. He had with him nineteen ships, a strong fleet, but to his astonishment he saw moving out of Chesapeake Bay no fewer than twenty-four enemy ships. In fact he had caught them in no sort of battle order but cluttered up in ragged disarray. However, instead of seizing the opportunity and dashing down upon them, he merely engaged them at long range and barely half his ships came into action at all. De Grasse, having cleared the Bay, remained in indecisive touch with the British for five days and then returned to his anchorage, while Graves tamely returned to New York.

In the following spring Admiral Rodney fought the Battle of the Saints, near Dominica. Fortune favoured him after the British and French fleets had fired their initial broadsides. While they were starting for each other on opposite tacks a sudden shift of wind set the French all aback. It was a golden opportunity, grasped by Rodney, who burst through their line and showed the way to his nearest ships; others ahead and astern saw and copied their admiral, and the French were caught. The Battle of the Saints cost them seven ships of the line and a number of frigates, but no less valuable was its calamitous effect on the French West Indies.

Some historians hold that de Grasse's Battle of the Chesapeake, while insignificant as a battle, was the one final factor in the result of the War of Independence. If that is the case, had it been fought by a Nelson, a Howe, a Rodney or a Hawke, and had both England and Congress been less rigid in their attitudes, the result might well have been different indeed. But General Cornwallis had surrendered at Yorktown and Rodney's victory arrived too late.

Opening up the China Trade

IN the late eighteenth century, when East met West in the form of the haughty isolationist Chinese versus the ruthless profit-seeking merchants of Europe, the encounter was the typically violent one of two cultures with not a scrap of mutual understanding between them. Many years later, when Rudyard Kipling wrote that 'East is East and West is West, and never the twain shall meet', he had that example before him to prove his point.

At the root of the conflict lay the complete inability of the Chinese to treat Europeans as anything but barbarian vassals of their Celestial Emperor, and their imposition on merchants who came to trade were of a weight of restriction and indignity that eventually proved unbearable. The foreigners were refused a fixed tariff, were bound by Chinese laws and Chinese law courts which could only be hostile to them, and after 1760 were allowed to trade only through Canton, and only through the officially designated group of middlemen named the Co-hong.

Under Co-hong rules, no foreign ship was allowed to enter Canton unless a Co-hong merchant agreed to serve as security and guarantee that the foreigners would pay all their dues and behave themselves. Conversely, the Co-hong merchants, who numbered between four and thirteen at various times, were the only merchants allowed to sell Chinese tea and silk to foreign traders.

For those dubious favours, the foreigners had to endure continual taunts and insults from the Cantonese who, like their emperor, regarded them as evil foreign devils, and they were forced also to keep the palms of venal officials liberally crossed with silver.

Nevertheless, where there were fortunes to be made, personal irritations and discomforts could be swallowed, at least for a while, and the China market was extremely lucrative, even under such severely limited conditions. By the end of the eighteenth century the British East India Company's strong well-armed East Indiamen, displacing up to 1,500 tons each, were bringing in over 220 tons of tea in their holds on each China-India run. In the other direction, there was a considerable rise in China's imports of British woollens and metals, which stood at a value of £99,113 in 1775 and grew to £590,775 in 1786 and £1,321,813 in 1803.

Pandering to the quirks of the supercilious Chinese could not, however, continue for very long once the foreigners became convinced that they were being excluded from tapping little more than the tip of what they were certain was a colossal commercial iceberg. One market upon which the British cast particularly interested eyes was the north of China, where it was believed that millions of customers awaited British woollens. Before long the Portuguese, the Dutch and the British decided that they wanted front door treatment; they were tired of doing business through the

Below: English East Indiaman leaving for the other side of the world; a painting by Adam Willaerts.
NATIONAL MARITIME MUSEUM, LONDON

tradesman's entrance and wanted a proper footing for their commerce, with free trading on the basis of equality and agreed trading ports.

The British also desired an officially acknowledged British ambassador in Peking; to press their suit they sent missions to the Chinese Emperor in 1793 and 1816. The Dutch and Portuguese did likewise, but all were refused in the same arrogant fashion. The answer received by Lord George Macartney, Britain's emissary in 1793, was typical.

'As your Ambassador can see for himself, we possess all things,' the Chinese Emperor Ch'ien-lung informed George III. 'The productions of our Empire are manifold and in great abundance; nor do we stand in the least need of the produce of other countries . . .' The Co-hong system, which the emperor had permitted 'as a signal mark of favour', was quite sufficient for the purchase of the Chinese tea, silks and porcelain which the 'foreign devils' appeared to crave so much, and to allow foreign trade anywhere apart from Canton would simply encourage 'other nations (to) imitate your evil example and beseech us to present them with a site for trading'.

George III was flabbergasted to discover that Ch'ien-lung regarded him as a lowly vassal, and saw the samples of British manufacture which Macartney had taken to show him as items of tribute. The foreign merchants were furious and frustrated, all the more so because Ch'ien-lung had been quite right to suppose that the Chinese economy was self-sufficient. Between 1792 and 1809, for instance, China exported twice as much as she imported.

However, despite their suppliant status, the British had one supreme advantage they could exploit – the fact that they could offer enormous quantities of opium grown on East India Company land in Bengal to a growing number of Chinese addicts. The idea was first mooted in 1767 at a meeting of the East India Company in Calcutta, but it was not until 1794 that Indian opium began to shift the balance of the China trade in favour of foreigners. In that year, an East India Company opium freighter anchored offshore at Whampoa, thirteen miles down river from Canton, and remained there for a year supplying opium to smugglers. That preliminary probe was an encouraging success and in the years that followed the illegal opium trade through Whampoa, and also through Portuguese-leased Macao on the other side of Canton, burgeoned into soaring profits for the traders and a matching rate of addiction among the Chinese.

As more and more Chinese fell under the soporific spell of opium, and more and more officials succumbed to foreign bribes and inducements, the Chinese authorities fumed and fulminated, issuing fierce decrees threatening to annihilate any foreign opium ship by means of 'dragons of war . . . with their fiery discharges'. No one took any notice, and the opium trade continued unabated. The Chinese war junks were toothless dragons, in any case, for their crews were well aware of the deadly firepower of foreign ships and kept their own craft a safe distance from the scene of opium-smuggling operations.

By 1821, when the opium trade moved from Whampoa and Macao to Lintin Island at the mouth of the Canton River, a well-tried procedure was already established for getting the contraband ashore. The opium ships unloaded their cargoes onto armed hulks which acted as floating depots, and from which the opium was handed on into the holds of the speedy 'scrambling dragons', the name given to galleys armed with cannon and grappling irons which ferried the opium ashore. Often, they took their cargoes to Canton, forty miles upriver, where British, French, Dutch and American trading stations were located on a quarter-mile stretch of waterfront to the north of the city. After 1829 the opium runs were refined still further, when speedy manoeuvrable clippers took over the trade and made better time with more certain success against the strong coastal headwinds that blew up the Chinese coast to Canton.

As time went on, the statistics of opium sales rocketed. In 1796, the number of 125lb-140lb opium chests leaving Calcutta, where the East India Company sold them by auction, stood at 1,070. By 1835, the year after the company lost its monopoly of the China trade, the number had increased to 12,977. Over roughly the same period, the Calcutta auctions brought the East India Company an average profit of 465 per cent and in 1831, the House of Commons was told that 'the monopoly of opium in Bengal supplies the Government with a revenue amounting to £981,293 per annum . . .' That was, of course, in addition to legal British imports into Canton, which in 1834 were valued at £1,345,523.

In terms of money the opium traffic, though officially illegal, was a splendid success. In human terms, opium was ravaging its victims at a horrifying rate; by the early 1840s

Right:
M. J. Barton's painting of 'Red Rover', an early opium clipper.

the number of addicts in China was nearing the twelve million mark. The Chinese Government, frantic to stop the spread of the pernicious habit which was doping and debilitating so many of the emperor's subjects, tried to fight it with propaganda, with executions of opium dealers and with the seizure of a few opium clippers. Such actions proved puny weapons and it was not until 1839 that the anxious authorities discovered the one means which gave them hope of success; it was that rarity among Chinese officials, an unbribable civil servant.

The official in question, the puritanical Lin Tse-hsu, set about his plan to exorcise the opium evil in high-handed forceful fashion. He arrived in Canton on 10 March 1839, and within three months had confiscated 20,283 chests of opium worth £2 million. During the first three weeks of June it was all destroyed by melting it down to a stinking black mass and tipping it into the Canton River. The foreigners in Canton, whom Lin had declared hostages for the opium, were then made hostages for British agreement to stop making opium and to withdraw from the opium trade.

It was at that point that the Chinese first began to realise the true nature of the foreigners they so disdained, for the upshot of Lin's arbitrary actions in Canton, and the outrage they caused in Britain, was war. On 21 June 1840, a force of twenty British warships, carrying 4,000 troops, arrived off Macao, sailed up the coast to Chusan Island and plastered the port of Ting-hai to a mass of rubble with broadsides from fifteen of its ships. Then, in January 1841, after six months of sporadic fighting during which the British occupied Chusan, the warships began to blast a way up the Canton River, landing raiding parties at intervals to occupy the forts

Above: The East India Company's steamship 'Nemesis' destroying Chinese junks in Anson's Bay in January 1841.
PARKER GALLERY

Left: Chinese officers hauling down the British flag on the 'Arrow' after she had been captured on the orders of Imperial Commissioner Yeh of Canton in October 1856.
CASSELL'S 'HISTORY OF ENGLAND'
(K. ROBINS COLLECTION)

that lined the river banks, and finally bringing Canton within reach of its guns in May. One of the British ships, a powerful paddle-steamer, appropriately *Nemesis*, caused near-panic among Chinese sailors whose archaic junks were in no state to challenge it.

Canton was saved from certain destruction when the British accepted a Chinese bribe of £600,000, but nothing could save the towns in the path of the British advance towards Peking that started in August. Chen-nai and Ningpo were looted; Chepai, south of Shanghai, was set on fire;

Shanghai itself fell in June 1842; and Chinkiang in July.

The Chinese were totally helpless before the inexorable advance of British armed force, and the grossly one-sided conflict ended with the Treaty of Nanking signed on 29 August 1842. It was the turn of the Chinese to be humiliated. At Nanking the emperor was forced to allow five 'treaty' ports to be opened at Canton, Amoy, Foochow, Swatow and Shanghai, to cede the island of Hong Kong to the British as a base for protecting their trade, to abolish the Co-hong system, to agree to pay an indemnity of £2 million, and to fix a tariff of five per cent *ad valorem*. Worse was to come, for other Europeans, perceiving that the British had at long last cracked the barrier of Chinese isolationism, scrambled for pickings. After 1844 the French, the Americans, the Belgians and the Swedes were all granted trading treaties, although a supplementary pact of 1843, the Treaty of the Bogue, reserved 'most favoured nation' treatment for Britain.

Nor did the long-dreaded foreign intrusion end there. By 1849 the British, Americans and French had all been granted consular courts and exclusive settlements for their nationals. By 1850 foreign merchants were operating the trade in tea and silks which, a century before, had been in the hands of little more than a dozen British East India Company supercargo passengers. The opium trade boomed again, soaring from 2,000 tons in 1843 towards the 5,000-ton mark it reached by 1866. Addiction soared with it, until by the mid-1860s it was reckoned that only one Cantonese out of ten, and only two inhabitants out of ten in Fukien Province had managed to remain unhooked.

The Chinese, rammed down into such depths of degradation, seethed with fury and resentment; what had formerly been plain straightforward hatred for the foreigner grew into a mood of malevolent loathing. Not unnaturally, it created an unhealthy atmosphere of tension and suspicion which made European merchants feel less and less secure in their gains, and more and more prone to demand greater concessions and further safeguards for their interests.

The camel's back broke over a very paltry straw. On 8 October 1856, Imperial Commissioner Yeh of Canton ordered the seizure of the lorcha – a European-shaped Chinese-rigged vessel – named *Arrow*; she was old and barely serviceable and had long since ceased to appear on Lloyd's Register. The British captain and Chinese crew were flung into prison, where several of them died. The incident was unremarkable in itself, but prodded on by the French, who were outraged over the recent murder of a French priest in Kwangsi, the pugnaciously patriotic British Prime Minister, Lord Palmerston, turned the *Arrow* affair into an insult to the flag and a clamour for vengeance.

When the resultant Anglo-French demands reached the Chinese emperor, it transpired that the British intended to gain far more than mere compensation for the loss of a near-hulk and the sufferings of its crew. What they wanted was the establishment of foreign legations at the imperial court, extra-territorial rights granting Europeans immunity throughout China, regulation of the opium trade and more treaty ports. It was too much. The emperor demurred, and the inevitably violent sequel was the Second Opium War, in which Anglo-French forces bombarded the Taku forts, which guarded the approaches to Peking, destroyed the emperor's Summer Palace and occupied his capital.

When the emperor finally yielded in 1860, it was on even harsher terms than the ones he had rejected. He was obliged to accept them, and also to agree that Tientsin, the harbour of Peking, should become a treaty port in order to safeguard access to the foreign legation quarter in the capital. Hong Kong was to be enlarged to include the mainland suburb of Kowloon and the treaty powers extracted a very large indemnity.

The long-term results were that Britons and other foreigners were able to transform China through commercial, moral, technical and religious influences exerted from a privileged protected position. That included, of course, a vigorous flowering of business enterprise in China, with merchants treating the country that was now prostrate before them as a milch cow, to be milked to the last drop. As a result, the value of opium imports into China rose from 20,946 Hong Kong taels (1,754lb of silver) in 1868, to 42,192 HK taels (3,533lb) in 1913. Cotton goods rose even more pronouncedly, from values of 18,351 HK taels (1,536lb) in 1868 to 110,041 HK taels (9,215lb) in 1913. Tea exports from China, worth 33,262 HK taels (2,785lb) in 1868, were much the same in 1913, but silk and silk goods rose from a value of 24,544 HK taels (2,055lb) to 102,036 HK taels (8,545lb).

As trade expanded, Shanghai and Hong Kong, the best of the treaty ports, blossomed as monuments to European effort, on the foundations laid after the First Opium War of 1839-42 as a stepping stone to great commercial lustre.

At Shanghai, where foreign trade opened on 17 November 1843, British imports stood at £500,000 in 1844 and £1,082,207 in 1845. Ten years later, the American firm of Russell & Co pioneered a steamship service between Shanghai and Hong Kong and, in 1862, Russell became managing agents for the newly constituted Shanghai Steam Navigation Company. The new venture helped promote the rise of Hankow to the status of an important inland tea market. Within a few years, Shanghai became the terminal port of the coasting trade and dominated the commerce of the entire 3,200-mile Yangtse basin, with the export market in tea and silks and the import market in opium and other European products passing in lucrative quantities through its fine deepwater harbour.

Hong Kong, which also possessed a superb harbour, was converted by its British lessees from a barren unproductive island wasteland into a thriving trading centre, with stone warehouses, jetties, wharves, hotels, a market and a town two miles long which in 1843 had a population of 15,000. Already, Hong Kong had emerged as a rich and busy centre of distribution. In 1844, twenty ships carried over 68,000 tons of British goods from Hong Kong to Shanghai, ninety-six lorchas totalling 5,774 tons took cotton and woollen goods to Canton, and sixty ships of a total of 26,937 tons arrived from Britain loaded with merchandise. After the Second Opium War of 1856-60 Hong Kong became a major ocean junction for steamships and an important focus for banking and the distribution of mail.

Europeans naturally claimed the cream of the Hong Kong and Shanghai trade, as well as that of Canton, Nanking and other Chinese ports, and a similar monopoly was established at Macao, which the Chinese reluctantly recognised as Portuguese territory in 1887. Towards the end of the century the rapacious Europeans were joined by a new and energetic force in the world, the recently westernised and industrialised Japan. Besides acquiring Western ways and Western methods, the Japanese had also acquired the Western taste for territorial conquest. In 1894 they cast covetous eyes on Korea, which was a semi-vassal State of China, and on 1 August declared war. The conflict was brief and, for the third time in fifty years, it ended in an overwhelming Chinese defeat. By the Treaty of Shimonoseki signed on 17 April 1895, Korea was declared independent – a temporary status as far as the Japanese were concerned – and Japan was awarded Formosa, the Pescadores Islands, the Liaotung peninsula in Manchuria, and the promise of a European-style trading treaty.

Japan's success promoted yet another scramble for yet more pickings among the other foreign powers already established in China, a scramble which approached very close to partition of the country. In 1900, when the maddened Chinese reacted with the hideous barbarities of the anti-foreign Boxer Rebellion, it was already far too late for Imperial China to reverse the irresistible foreign tide. The Boxers gave the foreign devils in Peking fifty-five days of terror and peril besieged in their legation quarter, but they totally failed to achieve the object which one of their slogans expressed as 'Protect the country! Destroy the foreigners!'

In the event, the foreigners remained, still sheltered by their special status, for more than forty years. On the other hand, the Imperial China the Boxers knew, disrupted by foreign exploitation and ruined by its own corrupt ineptitude, collapsed in 1912, in less than a quarter of that time. Nearly forty more years of unrest, anarchy and war ensued before it fell to the Communist People's Republic of China to begin, in 1949, to repair the damage, patch up Chinese pride, and help push East and West apart in ways Kipling never imagined.

Nelson: Man and Tactician

HORATIO Nelson, England's greatest sailor, was born in 1758 and started his nautical career in 1771. Although largely protected from rough usage by his uncle, Captain Suckling, in his first ship – after he had left his father's country parsonage – he soon developed a hatred of ships and the sea. Never robust and often ill, he was further handicapped by bouts of sea-sickness

Before long, Suckling was appointed to the Thames guardship and realising that life on board her would be too inactive for the boy, he arranged for him to go on a voyage in a merchantman. Young Nelson returned from the experience believing himself to have become a practical seaman, though still without enthusiasm for the sea. But he soon showed his natural gift for persuasion by gaining permission to practise navigation and pilotage in boats of the commander-in-chief.

Then, learning of an expedition in which two bomb-vessels, the *Carcass* and *Racehorse*, were to try to reach the North Pole, he succeeded again in having his own way. He persuaded Captain Ludwidge of HMS *Carcass* to take him as his coxswain in spite of the order that no boy was to go. His chief exploit when the vessels were caught in the ice was to try to kill a polar bear single-handed, merely explaining that he wanted to give the pelt to his father.

Shortly after the Arctic trip he found himself in the warmth of the South Seas and visited ports over a wide area, before a breakdown in health sent him home. In April 1777 Nelson passed the examination for lieutenant at the age of nineteen and was sent to the frigate *Lowestoft*. In the following year he joined the flagship *Bristol* in the West Indies and had quite speedily worked his way up to first lieutenant before he was given command of a brig; another year later he was promoted to captain.

After yet another illness he was appointed, in 1784, to the frigate *Boreas* and found himself in the thick of trouble on the Leeward Isles station. With the end of the American War of Independence, the colonists had assumed that they were free to resume trading with the British West Indies, conveniently forgetting that they had lost the rights of British subjects. Nelson did not tolerate such behaviour and defying British Governors and senior Custom-House Officials, he went to the length of seizing ships which were trading illicitly. He was much gratified, and perhaps surprised, to know

Above: A painting by R. Caton Woodville of action in the Battle of Trafalgar shortly before Nelson received his fatal wounds.
ILLUSTRATED LONDON NEWS

Facing page: Admiral Nelson; a portrait by William Beechey on loan to the National Portrait Gallery from the Leggatt trustees.

that he had the backing of the English Government. He discovered that in addition to that traffic, thieving contractors were fleecing the Crown of vast sums and he thought it safer not to leave his ship until action had been taken to deal with it.

He was fast becoming a notability, if only for his humanity. King William IV, when a midshipman under training at sea, described him as 'a boy captain with an enthusiasm that showed he was no common being'. Not the least feature of the *Boreas* was the state of the ship's company. During the three years Nelson spent on the station, which had a forbidding reputation, not a single officer or man of the ship had died. He never stayed long at any one of the islands but kept all hands in good heart by encouraging music, dancing and quarter-staff contests among the crew, and the officers took part in amateur theatricals.

It was also in the Leeward Isles, in 1787, that he met and married Frances Herbert Nisbet, the eighteen-year-old widow of a doctor who already had a child. They were back in England on the renewed declaration of war with France in 1793 and Nelson was given command of the old 64-gun *Agamemnon* with orders to join the Mediterranean fleet under Admiral Hood, one of his many admirers. He was soon in action. While returning from taking dispatches to Naples he sighted five enemy ships and although short-handed, having landed many of his crew at Toulon, he carried on a running fight, damaging the rearmost ship so severely that she had to fly distress signals.

One fight followed another so frequently that Nelson seemed to be almost continuously under fire. With a landing-party of his seamen who, so he said, 'minded shot as little as peas', he took a leading role in the siege of Bastia, in Corsica, and forced its capitulation. Then, still in Corsica, his men practically won the day for him at Calvia having 'fought the guns with only a single artilleryman'. It was there that a stray shot flung up sand into his face. Despite all that the surgeon could do, it blinded him in one eye for the rest of his life.

In the spring of 1795 the British fleet, under Admiral Hotham, exchanged broadsides with a much more powerful French fleet. One French eighty-four was dismasted and had to be taken in tow by a frigate with two French ships of the line standing by. Nelson in his sixty-four stood clear and then bore down and harried her with such cunning tactics, of the true Nelson type, that her consorts left the cripple to be picked up as a prize a little later.

In April 1796 he was promoted to commodore, and in June was appointed to HMS *Captain*. Then in mid-February 1797 Spanish and English fleets came in sight of one another off Cape St Vincent. The Spaniards had twenty-seven ships of the line as against the British fifteen but in their great vessels the Spanish gunners were not too well trained, which went some way towards evening the odds.

Admiral Jervis began the fight by cutting through the enemy line, isolating nine Spaniards. To meet the threat the Spanish admiral tried to link up with them by circling round his van. But away at the far end of the British line Nelson had been seized by an intuition. Sharply he put over his helm and in defiance of all tradition, sailed out of line to meet the on-coming Spaniards.

They made a fearsome sight. In addition to the *Santissima Trinidad* of four decks and 130 guns and the *San Josef* and *Salvador del Mundo* of 112, there were three Second Rates. For a quarter of an hour Nelson fought them alone, his ship in a sorry state. Then to his help came Troubridge, followed by Collingwood and Jervis himself in the *Victory*. The fight drove past and beyond Nelson in his splintered *Captain* but he had two big Spaniards alongside him, the *San Nicolas* and *San Josef*, which he proceeded to take as prizes, using one as a bridge to the other, with a boarding party he could not resist leading himself.

By 17.00 all fighting was over and Jervis sent for him. For good or ill, not knowing what to expect, the culprit who had so blatantly disobeyed orders was rowed over to the flagship. There Sir John Jervis, the cold disciplinarian, flung his arms round Nelson and embraced him.

It was later that a fellow captain remarked to him, 'You did just as you pleased in Lord Hood's time, the same with Admiral Hotham and now again with John Jervis; it makes no difference to you who is commander-in-chief'. Horatio Nelson, boy and man, seems to have been irresistible.

A Knight of the Bath and a rear-admiral as a result of the battle, he spent some months in operations against Spain, losing his arm in the attack on Vera Cruz but eventually carrying on. In May of 1798 Jervis, by then Lord St Vincent, ordered him to attack a large French fleet which was convoying Napoleon's army and equipment to Egypt. A gale scattered Nelson's ships and he could not locate the French until the army had landed. He found their fleet lying at anchor in front of Aboukir Roads with its rear protected by shore batteries.

The stage was thus set for the Battle of the Nile. The French admiral was confident that his ships would be safe from any attack, but Nelson saw farther. His skill in pilotage coupled with his special instinct told him that if there was room for a ship to swing round her anchor then there would be room for another ship to force a passage. He began his attack, both inside and outside the line of ships, at nightfall and soon the great French flagship had blown up in terrifying scenes of explosion and flame. By daybreak only two French ships out of thirteen had managed to escape.

After the Battle of the Nile, Nelson's most thorough-going victory, he became involved in the dealings of the Court of Naples. There he became re-acquainted with Emma, Lady Hamilton. Whatever has been said or written about that association, Lady Hamilton was able to give him some quality of renewal which he needed.

On the resumption of the war with France, Nelson was given the Mediterranean command. Napoleon was mustering an army for the invasion of England with flotillas of flat-bottomed craft and a large war fleet in the Channel. However, in March 1805 Villeneuve, the French admiral, led Nelson on a wild-goose chase to the West Indies and back. Eventually Villeneuve sailed southward into Cadiz, but an emphatic order from Napoleon drove him out again.

At dawn the two fleets were in sight of one another, off an

Above: Cuthbert, Lord Collingwood, second-in-command at Trafalgar, painted by H. Howard
NATIONAL PORTRAIT GALLERY, LONDON

Top right: Aboukir Bay, 1798; a painting of the line-up of French ships.   NATIONAL MARITIME MUSEUM, LONDON

Right: Nelson lies mortally wounded on the deck of 'Victory'; from a mid-19th-century print.   J. SANDILANDS COLLECTION

Following spread: A painting by P. J. de Loutherbourg showing scenes of destruction at the height of the Battle of the Nile.
TATE GALLERY, LONDON

obscure cape named Trafalgar, in a light breeze that barely gave steerageway. The English were in a state of eager excitement; their beloved admiral had circulated a memorandum to all captains as a guide to the tactics he had evolved for the coming battle. The memorandum seems to have set minds alight; it was itself the Nelson touch, and what could be more inspiring than that?

The battle opened with the British in two columns and with Admiral Collingwood leading the southernmost one and breaking the enemy's line. The *Victory*, flying Nelson's flag, came up at the head of his column, her broadsides making havoc of Villeneuve's flagship and exchanging fire with two of the biggest ships afloat – the *Redoubtable* and the *Santissima Trinidad*. But one small musket-ball fired from a top in the *Redoubtable* found its mark and Nelson fell mortally wounded. In spite of protests from his officers he had dressed for the battle in his full ceremonial uniform, with sash and stars and all decorations, so that he stood out conspicuously on the *Victory*'s deck. It was strange of him, as mystifying as was his motive in writing out his own prayer the previous night and leaving it open on his desk to be read.

The Beginnings of Steam

THE idea of a vessel propelled by steam is of quite a respectable age. As far back as 1736 a gifted Englishman, Jonathan Hulls of Gloucestershire, wrote a book on the subject. The title he gave it was *A Description and Draught of a New-invented Machine for carrying vessels or ships out of or into any Harbour, Port or River, against Wind or Tide or in a calm.*

His book had an illustration of a large open boat with a squat funnel amidships and with twin paddles at the stern towing a two-deck man-of-war. Hulls built a tug to demonstrate his invention but when he came to do so on the River Avon it came to grief, among the jeers of onlookers. He had, however, foretold the steamship well ahead of his time.

In 1775 a small boat was driven by steam power on the river Seine, but it was not until the 1780s that boats were to be seen steaming successfully along rivers. In France on the River Saône, a tributary of the Rhône, the Marquis de Jouffroy's *Pyroscaphe* was, in 1783, propelled by paddle-wheels driven by a steam engine, and in America James Rumsey and John Fitch were engaged in experiments with marine steam propulsion. In 1785 Rumsey used hydraulic jet propulsion for a boat; a steam-driven pump was employed to draw water in at the bow of the boat and force it out at the stern. Fitch initiated a service on the river Delaware in 1790 with a boat with a steam engine driving three 'duck-leg' paddle-boards at the stern.

In Scotland, Patrick Miller experimented with a double-hulled vessel propelled by paddle-wheels driven by manual power. In 1788 Miller fitted a steam engine, specially designed by William Symington, to one hull of a double-hulled vessel and the boiler on the other. The engine drove paddle-wheels placed one in front of the other, in the space between the hulls, and the boat achieved a speed of five miles per hour.

Three years later Symington built the engine for a steam tug, the *Charlotte Dundas*, commissioned by Lord Dundas for experiments on the Forth and Clyde Canal. In March 1802 the *Charlotte Dundas* towed two loaded barges on the canal for a distance of nineteen and a half miles in six hours. The performance was regarded as remarkable but fears that the wash from the paddle-wheels would damage the canal bank brought the experiments to an end.

An American, Robert Fulton, had been a keen spectator of the Scottish experiments. On his return to New York

Fulton built a vessel, the famous *Clermont*, and had her equipped with engines and boilers supplied by the Birmingham firm of Boulton and Watt. The *Clermont*, in 1807, started the first regular passenger or pleasure-craft service between Albany and New York. She was driven by her paddles worked with an engine of twenty horse-power and covered 150 miles at a speed averaging five knots. Her name and reputation spread far and wide through the States.

In Europe, the earliest steam vessel to travel regularly for passengers on any river or in the open sea was the *Comet*. Built at Port Glasgow to the design of Henry Bell, who had also seen the *Charlotte Dundas*, she was forty-two feet long and eleven feet in beam. With her engine of about four horse-power and with a single vertical cylinder standing five feet high on deck, she plied regularly between Glasgow and Greenock at what would seem to be the fashionable speed of five knots.

She made her maiden voyage from the Broomielaw in Glasgow during August 1812 and Bell, who clearly had something of a flair for the uses of advertisement, did not stint himself over her 'elegant furnishings: the handsome carpeting and sofa; the tassels, fringes and velvet cornices ornamented with gilt'. The *Comet* may not have proved to be a commercial success in spite of his decorative efforts, but at least she had begun genuine steam navigation in British waters.

The paddle-steamer *Margery*, built by Denny of Dumbarton in 1814, was the first steamship to cross the English Channel. First employed on regular passenger service between London and Margate, the *Margery* passed into French ownership, was renamed *Elise*, and in March 1816 sailed from Newhaven to Le Havre.

In 1818 a sailing-vessel, the American *Savannah*, was fitted with a steam engine with a single cylinder. The engine drove paddles which could be collapsed and hoisted up on deck to be out of the way when not in use and the ship was sailing under canvas. The *Savannah* left New York on 24 May

Below: A reprint of Jonathan Hulls' pamphlet of 1737 concerning his proposed paddle steamer.
SCIENCE MUSEUM, LONDON

Right: A model of the American ship 'Savannah' which made a crossing of the Atlantic (much of it only under sail) in 1818.
SCIENCE MUSEUM, LONDON

Right: Model of the 1801 steam tug 'Charlotte Dundas', commissioned by Lord Dundas and successfully employed on the Forth and Clyde Canal. SCIENCE MUSEUM, VICTORIA

Below: Another, more complete, model of 'Charlotte Dundas' whose engine was designed by William Symington.
SCIENCE MUSEUM, LONDON
(D. RUDKIN)

1818, and arrived off the coast of Ireland on 17 June, but the greater part of the voyage had been made under sail alone.

The first vessel to cross the Atlantic under continuous steam power was the paddle-steamer *Sirius*. She left Cork Harbour on 4 April 1838, and reached New York in eighteen days ten hours.

Nearly all the early steamers were driven by paddles but realising that there should be a more efficient method, a number of experimenters set out to find one. As far back as 1770 James Watt had suggested that an improvement on the paddle form of propulsion might well be a 'spiral oar' and several attempts to produce one had been made at intervals ever since. Joseph Bramah, in 1785, had taken out a patent for a system of propelling ships by 'a wheel with inclined fans or wings' which would be set on a spindle at a ship's stern. Seventeen years later John Shorter, of Doncaster, displayed a means of propulsion by screws which could be driven by hand, or at least by manpower, when sailing vessels were becalmed. In England and in the United States many eager minds were busy with the problem.

Perhaps the saddest yet most ironic story is that of the Frenchman, Frederick Sauvage, who might have won the race. After ten years of effort he succeeded in evolving a satisfactory screw propeller but unfortunately in doing so he bankrupted himself and was imprisoned for debt in Boulogne. During his absence thieves broke into his house and stole his notes and drawings, which they sold. In 1839 Sauvage was set free, only to see a vessel of the French Government being driven by one of his own screws.

An English farmer, Francis Pettit Smith, more or less as a hobby, began experimenting with ship models driven by clockwork on the Hampstead ponds and discovered how to arrive at an effective screw propeller. He patented the result and formed a company to develop it. One of his propellers was fitted to a small Thames steamer, the *Archimedes*, and happened to catch the eye of the engineering genius, Isambard Kingdom Brunel. It so impressed him that he went to the length of persuading the Great Western Railway Board to alter the enormous ship, the *Great Britain*, being built at Bristol 1839-1843, so that she became the first screw-driven Atlantic liner.

The British Admiralty, in its traditional conservatism, could raise little enthusiasm over this new-fangled screw propeller when it was first discussed by their lordships. In the end, however, they rather grudgingly agreed that a screw propeller should be fitted to the *Ardent*, a sailing sloop being built at Sheerness. Renamed HMS *Rattler*, the sloop was launched in 1843 and used for a series of tests and trials which showed the superiority of the screw, in comparison with the paddle-wheel, for most purposes.

Yet with it all some degree of ancient conservatism still lingered round Whitehall. It took some time before the Royal Navy had spread its last canvas aloft and for the last time a boatswain's mate had piped to the order of 'Up funnel, down screw' for the ship's funnel to be hoisted up from the deck on its hinge while the propeller was lowered back into the sea, for the ship never again to be content with the power of the wind alone.

Paddle
versus Screw

A PART from the application of muscular power to oars or paddles, the first mechanical means of propelling a ship was the paddle-wheel. Representations from the sixth and fifteenth centuries show ships with paddle-wheels turned by men or animals. As early as 1817 Londoners could claim that there were actually as many as five paddle boats all driven by steam to be seen puffing along the Thames. But the Scots were well ahead of that by the following year; they had eighteen steamers trailing their smoke on the Clyde, there were six others on the Forth and four more on the Tay.

That was not all; in 1814 the *Marjorie* (or *Margery*) steamed south from Scotland to find work on the Thames and in 1816 became the first steam vessel to cross the English Channel. In 1815 the first steam ferry on the Mersey was the *Elizabeth*, which had braved the Irish Sea from the Clyde to start her ferrying between Liverpool and Runcorn.

One and all, those early boats were paddlers, though with more than a little variety. A few had their paddles splashing away at the stern in the style of the later sternwheelers of the Mississippi. Still fewer had twin hulls, linked together in modern catamaran fashion with the engine between them, following the early example of Patrick Miller's boat of 1788.

The type that was more generally in use in Britain, however, had a paddle-wheel on each side of the hull. In spite of the usual nautical distaste for new ideas, engines soon began to find their way into quite large ships.

Three vessels using paddles each made a lasting name for themselves within a short period. The *Savannah*, to start with, in 1818 became the first steamship to cross the Atlantic although, truth to tell, she sailed most of the way and used her engine for no more than eighty hours in the course of the twenty-five days of the voyage. The paddle wheels could be disconnected and hoisted up on deck when not needed.

Next on the list of firsts was the *Aaron Manby*, which in 1822 became the first iron steamship to cross the Channel from London to Le Havre. Third, in 1825, the *Enterprise* of 470 tons was the first steamship to voyage from London to Calcutta. Her paddles were described as 'collapsible', pre-

155

Top: The paddle frigate HMS 'Terrible' as painted in 1847 by W. Knell.   SCIENCE MUSEUM, LONDON (D. RUDKIN)

Above: The steamer 'Archimedes' which was fitted with a screw-propeller, off the Nore in May 1839.
SCIENCE MUSEUM, LONDON (D. RUDKIN)

Below: Brunel's famous 'Great Britain' with details of the engine and stern propeller.   SCIENCE MUSEUM, LONDON

sumably because they could readily be stowed in heavy weather.

Another steamer that made a long ocean voyage from Canada to England in 1833 was the ps *Royal William*. Strangely, she made the trip for the sole purpose of finding a buyer. She had been built in Quebec in 1831 with the object of running a packet service between Quebec and Halifax; when the project fell through her owners considered that they would find a surer market for her in Britain.

Outdoing all other vessels in size and completeness, the earliest of Isambard Brunel's trio of mammoth ships, the *Great Western*, began her career in 1838. She just missed the honour of being the first transatlantic steam passenger ship when the much smaller *Sirius* fought her way through stormy seas to reach New York ahead of the *Great Western* on the same day. The *Sirius* had burnt every scrap of coal and practically everything else that could be used as fuel.

An early steam-propelled vessel in the Royal Navy was HMS *Diana*, a steam paddler that served in the first Burmese war of 1825 but little else seems to be known about her. There was also a naval paddler laden with the unfortunate name of *Rhadamanthus*, of 813 tons, which sailed from Plymouth to Barbados in 1832, but the first orthodox paddle-steamer warship appears to have been HMS *Penelope*, launched in 1829 as a 46-gun sailing frigate. She was cut in two in 1843 and lengthened to take an engine of 650 horse-power. The *Terrible* of 1845, a paddle frigate of twenty-one guns, was designed as a steamship and constructed to carry the heavy armament and machinery.

The screw propeller had been introduced a few years earlier by F. P. Smith, of Hendon, followed by the Swedish engineer John Ericsson, who had already made his name in England by building a steam locomotive for the Liverpool & Manchester Railway. In order to awaken the Admiralty's interest in the screw, Ericsson in 1837 arranged a demonstration for their lordships by towing the Admiralty barge with them as passengers from Somerset House to Blackwall and back at a speed of ten knots with a screw-propelled boat.

Soon afterwards Ericsson left England for the United States, where he became an American citizen of renown. He

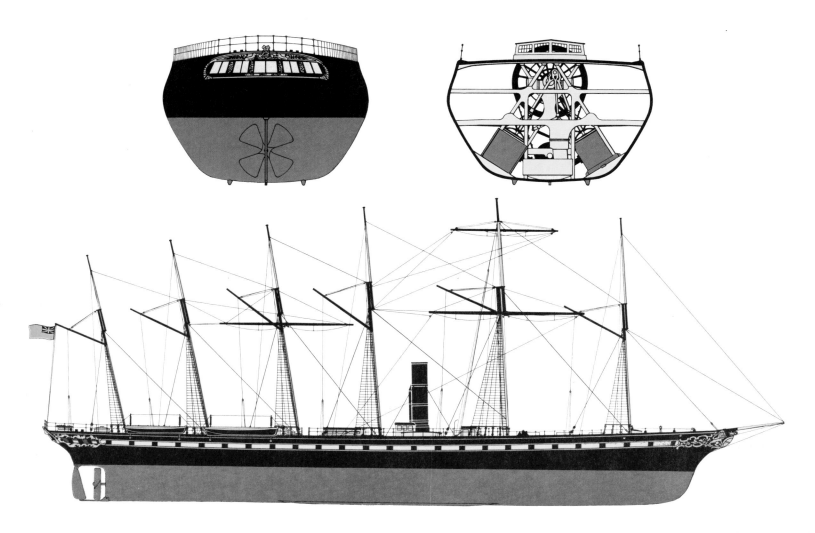

received from the Admiralty only one-fifth of the £20,000 that had been intended as a reward for the invention of the screw propeller as there was some dispute over patent rights.

By 1843 the propeller had been satisfactorily developed. One caught the eye of Brunel, who had chanced to see it driving a small steamer, the *Archimedes*. He promptly bought the vessel in order to make a series of tests for himself and as a result he altered the partly built hull of the *Great Britain* so that screw propellers could be installed instead of the paddle-wheels he had originally planned to use.

Whether or not Ericsson's towing party had influenced matters, the Royal Navy embarked on an extensive programme of trials and experiments to assess the relative effectiveness of paddle and screw, culminating in 1845 in the famous tug-of-war that ended with HM screw-steamer *Rattler* triumphantly running away with the paddler *Alecto*. Struggling hard in a welter of foam and smoke, the *Alecto* was hauled backwards at a speed of three knots, paddles vainly beating the sea.

Yet even ten years or so later, from 1853-6, the large British fleet supporting the Allied armies in the Black Sea was an astonishing medley. It included wooden ships entirely dependent on sails, other wooden ships with sails and paddles or screw propellers, and iron ships. Only here and there in stark contrast among the forest of masts, yards and rigging were seen the tall thin funnels of the early steamship.

The British force used in the campaign totalled ten sailing ships, four paddlers and six screw-propelled vessels, not counting those of six or fewer guns. Among the sailing ships were the *Britannia* of 120 guns, the *Albion* of ninety-one guns and the *Vengeance* of eighty-four guns. The 91-gun *Agamemnon*, the flagship of Rear-Admiral Sir E. Lyons, was screw-propelled but the *Trafalgar* of 120 guns and the *Bellerophon* and the *London* of ninety guns had sail only.

The French fleet was much smaller but there were a number of very large ships among those with sails only, two of them flagships. In addition there were four paddlers and six vessels with screw propellers.

With such an assortment on its hands, the Admiralty, only two years after the end of the Crimean War, announced that 'sailing ships are unfit for active service'. Surprising and a little premature though the statement might have been, it had become obvious that not only the pure sailer but also the paddler, with or without sails, had been made obsolescent by the screw propeller. The paddle-steamer, quite apart from the question of efficiency, was very vulnerable and the paddles were bound to obstruct the view to some extent.

Improvements in the design of both engine and screw were continually coming forward. In 1874, for instance, triple-expansion engines designed by A. C. Kirk were first fitted in a sea-going vessel, and high-pressure steam soon followed. The 'battle of the boilers' in Parliament over the adoption of the water-tube boiler was fought and won. Finally, in the 1890s came a major triumph – the steam turbine. Its practical achievement was largely the work of Sir Charles Parsons, who displayed his invention by driving a vessel he named *Turbinia* at a speed of thirty-four knots in the Naval Review at Spithead in 1897.

Today, the originator of it all, the steam paddler, has practically vanished. In British waters only one ship, the pleasure steamer *Waverley*, can still be seen puffing along the Clyde and she continues only by grace of the preservation society. It seems almost a touch of ancient history to recall that in 1940 three paddlers were patrolling the Bristol Channel by day and night armed and flying the White Ensign.

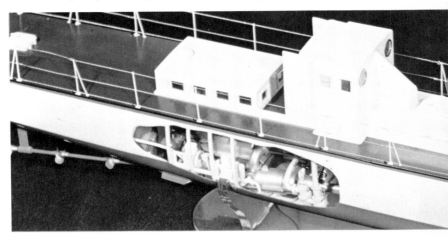

Left: Model of double-reduction gearing giving reductions of about 32 to 1 and 21 to 1 from high-pressure and low-pressure turbines to a single propeller shaft.
SCIENCE MUSEUM, LONDON (D. RUDKIN)

Above: A model of the 'Turbinia' which shows the engine-room arrangement and one of the three propeller shafts.
SCIENCE MUSEUM, LONDON

Overleaf: Painting by J. Walter of SS 'Great Britain', the auxiliary steam clipper built by the Great Western Steamship Co of Bristol to the design of Isambard Kingdom Brunel who also designed the earlier 'Great Western'.
NATIONAL MARITIME MUSEUM, LONDON

The Anglo-American War

IN 1812, when the United States declared war on Great Britain, it seemed as if a midget had challenged a mammoth.

A loose-knit, often quarrelsome, federation of States, barely forty years old as a nation, was pitting itself against a power of imperial proportions, and one which possessed the largest and most successful navy in the world. In 1812, Great Britain had over 200 fighting ships in commission, of which a dozen 74-gun ships-of-the-line and thirty-four frigates were on the Atlantic station alone. Against that, all the Americans had to offer were twenty frigates and about sixty one- and two-cannon gunboats.

Not surprisingly, the ludicrous disparity of the two navies inspired much contemptuous quipping in Britain; yet within six months, the joke had turned sour and the wits were silenced. The British had been jerked out of complacency and into the startled realisation that their former colony could no longer be regarded as a recalcitrant child, nor its

'few fir-built frigates', as one London journalist laughingly called the American ships, viewed as mere toys.

The reversal of attitude was the work of a handful of American naval commanders whose audacity and skill exploded the myth of British invincibility at sea, particularly in duels between individual ships, and added a whole new generation of heroes to American folklore.

In many ways, men like Oliver Hazard Perry, Stephen Decatur and Isaac Hull, were the equivalents of the English sea-dogs who shocked the world by trouncing the Spanish Armada in 1588. Like Francis Drake and John Hawkins, the Americans achieved brilliant unexpected success, producing profound embarrassment and gloom in the heart of their enemy, and creating soaring elation at home. But however lustrous the individual exploits, the early part of the War of 1812, like the fight against the Armada, was a sideshow in global terms.

The main preoccupation of the world, and of Britain in particular, was the Napoleonic Wars which, by 1812, had enmeshed Europe for nearly twenty years. Initially, Napoleon's dream of creating a continental empire had been a matter of straightforward conquest. After 1806, however, it took on a new dimension. The British were proving much tougher than other Europeans, whose defeat Napoleon had accomplished with comparative ease. France's own defeat at Trafalgar in 1805 had destroyed Napoleon's hopes of invading England and, in the following year, he began instead to try to blockade the 'nation of shopkeepers' into surrender.

In 1806 and 1807, Napoleon issued decrees closing Continental ports to British commerce, and giving notice that any neutral vessel trading with Britain would be regarded as an enemy. When Britain replied with a blockade of her own, through orders in council which, in 1807, banned all European trade except through British ports, the lively overseas commerce of the United States faced virtual extinction; it was clearly impossible for the Americans to observe both sets of conditions.

In practice, neither blockade was watertight. However, the system of evasions and special licences which enabled international trade to resume after 1809 did not satisfy the Americans, with their attachment to free open trade and their sense of outrage at the way international law had been infringed.

In any case, the blockade of Europe was not the only source of American grievance. There was strong disagreement with Britain over the principle of naturalisation; the British maintained that British birth conferred indelible British nationality, while the Americans supported the right of any foreign national to assume American citizenship. The dispute had been inflamed by the British practice of stopping American merchantmen at sea, and forcibly removing members of the crews, often for impressment into the Royal Navy. The human haul had its quota of deserters and men with false naturalisation certificates, but large numbers of 'genuine' Americans were also taken, on the grounds that they were British-born.

Dispute also existed in North America itself. There, land-hungry southerners and westerners were casting acquisitive eyes on the broad acres of the Indian hunting grounds. At the same time, these Americans nursed the resentful conviction that the British in Canada were arming the Indians to help them check any expansion westwards of United States territory.

In 1810, Napoleon deliberately dropped a fuse into the potentially explosive situation. His cue for action was the move, announced by Congress on 1 March, that trade would cease with Britain or France if one of them lifted their blockade and the other failed to follow suit. When Napoleon appeared to exempt American shipping from his blockade decrees, the British realised it was a pretence, and refused to waive their orders in council.

President James Madison of the United States was more ingenuous. More-realistic Congressmen warned him that Napoleon was simply trying 'to catch us into war with

England', but Madison ignored them, accepted Napoleon's move as genuine and banned trade with Britain. This opened the door for the young 'war hawks' in Congress, led by Henry Clay of Kentucky and John Calhoun of South Carolina, who thirsted for war as a means of avenging the insults and subversions of the British, and perhaps wresting Canada from them.

The conflict they so passionately advocated materialised on 18 June 1812, the day President Madison signed a declaration of war. Two days before, the British had at last ended their blockade; they had done so less to placate the United States than to try to relieve the cripplingly high prices, the distress and unemployment, and the stagnation in British trade which the years of blockade had produced.

Because of the slowness of trans-atlantic communication, neither government became aware of the other's actions for several weeks. By the time they did so, around the end of July, the Americans had already embarked on the invasion of Canada by land and, at sea, the main American naval force had already spent five weeks marauding in the Atlantic. There, it chased a British frigate, and harried a British convoy to within a day's sail of the English Channel.

The initial foray, though audacious and determined, did nothing to shake British convictions that the war would end as soon as news of the lifting of the blockade reached the United States. Nor did it diminish British amusement at the idea of the Americans taking on the mighty British Navy, even though that navy was taxed to the limit by the demands of the struggle against Napoleon.

One British captain, James Dacres of the 49-gun frigate *Guerrière*, had such a cocksure view of his chances that he issued a general invitation to battle to any American frigate of comparable size. Ironically, and perhaps aptly, Dacres was the first among many Britons to have his illusions rudely shattered and his pride badly damaged.

At two o'clock in the afternoon of 19 August 1812, the look-out on Isaac Hull's 55-gun frigate *Constitution*, recently out from Boston, sighted *Guerrière*'s sail in the distance. Hull set out in swift pursuit, and closed with his adversary an hour later. *Guerrière* sidled out of the way, let loose a broadside that sent just over 550lb of metal screaming in the direction of the *Constitution*, then came about and fired another broadside on the opposite tack. Both broadsides missed.

An hour of manoeuvre and counter-manoeuvre followed. Then, Hull brought *Constitution* into a position only fifty or sixty yards from *Guerrière*. A holocaust of fire and shot leapt across the gap, smashing the British mizenmast, and sending it splintering down over the starboard quarter. The barrage sliced into *Guerrière*'s sails, rigging and hull, and ceased, after fifteen minutes, only to allow Hull to take up a new position on the starboard bow.

Then the pounding began again, with *Constitution*'s 700-lb broadsides battering Dacres' ship into a listing hulk, stripped of her foremast and mainmast and with all main deck guns under water. At 19.00, a chagrined Dacres ordered *Guerrière*'s colours to be struck.

According to *The Times*, the shock caused in Britain by the loss of *Guerrière* 'spread a degree of gloom . . . which it was painful to observe'. It even eclipsed the gladder news of British success in the land war, where the capture of Detroit in August proved the prelude to a run of fiascos for the American army.

Amid the agonising over *Guerrière*, much was made of the fact that she had encountered the enemy grossly undermanned – with 270 men against *Constitution*'s 460 – with sprung masts, and after long weeks at sea. *Constitution*, on the other hand, was a newer, larger, faster ship, fresh from port and operating close to home waters. They were genuine considerations, but no amount of rationalising could conceal the mortifying fact that American gunnery and seamanship had been far superior to the British. Even the rabidly anti-American *Times* conceded as much when, in October, it

squeezed out the admission that American sailors were at least the second best in the world, and American frigates 'finer and better-built' than anything the British possessed.

The one spark of consolation was that the *Guerrière* disaster might prove an isolated mishap. However, those who tried to patch their pride with that notion were soon stripped of it. Two more disasters in October confirmed that *Constitution* had not scored a piece of beginner's luck.

On 18 October, the American sloop *Wasp* encountered the British brig *Frolic*, which was escorting a convoy home from Honduras. The convoy escaped, but the *Frolic*, battered to a virtual hulk by *Wasp*'s blazing gunnery, was boarded and captured. Exactly a week later, on 25 October, a confrontation occurred off Madeira between Stephen Decatur's 44-gun 1,630-ton frigate *United States* and a British frigate of roughly equal gunpower, the 1,100-ton *Macedonian*, commanded by John Surman Carden.

Carden made an irreversible error at the very start. With the advantage of the wind, he failed to close at once, so laying

Macedonian open to withering long-range gunfire which shredded her rigging and toppled the mizen topmast. Three hours later, after a belated attempt by Carden to close, and board *United States*, *Macedonian* was, in Carden's own words, 'a perfect wreck and unmanageable log'. More than 100 British seamen, (about a third of the crew) had been killed, while the Americans sustained only twelve casualties and their ship only nominal damage.

A survivor from *Macedonian*, who afterwards joined the Americans, later pointed out one very vital ingredient in the *United States*' success; vastly superior morale among the crew, of whom the greater number were volunteers. 'They understood what they fought for,' he wrote. 'They were better used in the service.'

In *Macedonian*, as in too many British ships at the time, morale was often sapped by conditions of the utmost squalor and hardship, and by commanders who, like Carden, were overly devoted to 'whip discipline'. British ships, in fact, were habitually undermanned as a result, and experienced seamen comprised only about one quarter of their crews.

The percentage on American ships was a good deal higher, and this was so not only because the United States navy had fewer vessels to man. Conditions were better, provisions and pay more generous, and the spirit on board was permeated with concepts of individual liberty and human dignity totally alien to the retributive and grossly unequal society that existed in Britain.

In such circumstances, desertions from the Royal Navy and the British merchant marine had been so common that the ranks of American petty officers were dominated by Britons, who also formed the majority of the crews on American ships. In that sense, the War of 1812 was a form of civil war, but that fact did nothing to detract from its

Below: An aquatint of the fight between the 'Chesapeake' (in the foreground) and the 'Shannon' which was shattered in thirteen minutes of destructive action.
BY COURTESY OF THE NEW BRUNSWICK MUSEUM

ferocity. If anything, it added to it, spicing with extra zeal the American war effort at sea, and helping to produce statistics of shocking proportions for the British.

By the end of 1812, a third British frigate, the 39-gun *Java*, had been pounded into submission by the *Constitution* off the coast of Brazil, and American privateers had captured about 500 British merchantmen. By the time the war ended two years later, the privateers had seized 800 more and, with the arrogance of success, some had felt free to venture as far as the English Channel to claim their prizes.

The alarm provoked among British merchants, whose trade faced ruination, was matched across the Atlantic by desperation and despondency. The mood was evident in the actions of Admiral John Borlase Warren, who had assumed command of the North American station in August 1812, and almost immediately began pestering London for more and more reinforcements. Within five months, the strains of his task had driven Warren to ask that the Jamaica and Leeward Islands commands be detached from his area of responsibility.

It was an unusual request, but Warren was being required to do the impossible. With a force that was far less than he required, but soon became almost more than the Admiralty could spare, he was expected to blockade the creek- and inlet-ridden American coast, control the privateers, keep on the alert for the American Navy and protect British convoys.

Something of Admiral Warren's plight was reflected in the comment of Charles Napier, a young British soldier who wrote from Bermuda in January 1813: 'Two pacquets are due, and we fear they may have been taken. For the Yankees swarm here; and when a frigate goes out to drive them off, by Jove! they take her! Yankees fight well and are gentlemen in their mode of warfare . . . though so much abused, (they) are really fine fellows!'

The British public, however, could not be expected to share the admiration fighting men like Napier have often felt for particularly courageous and enterprising enemies. What concerned them was the sullied image of their Royal Navy, and the disgraceful loss of three frigates and several smaller vessels to those upstart 'colonials' who one newspaper had recently assured them were only 'a handful of bastards and outlaws'.

Retrieving the public image of the Senior Service became a matter of emergency in government circles. 'It is of the highest importance to the character and interests of the country,' Secretary of the Admiralty John Wilson Croker warned Warren in January 1813, 'that the Naval force of the Enemy should be quickly and completely disposed of.' To accomplish it, Warren's forces were to be increased to thirty frigates and fifty sloops, but to make quite sure the public did not receive any more unpalatable shocks Croker added, 'It is highly desirable that ships should not, by being detached

singly, be exposed to the risk of meeting a superior force of the Enemy.' More clearly than anything else, the order showed just how severely rattled the Admiralty was.

Nevertheless, there was a wait of another four months before the dazzling exploit ardently longed for to boost flagging public confidence materialised. On 1 June 1813, in thirteen destructive minutes outside Boston, the British frigate *Shannon*, under Philip Broke, shattered the American frigate *Chesapeake* with broadsides that raked her quarterdeck, splintered her hull, wrecked her rigging and littered her decks with dead.

Broke ordered the two ships to be tied together and stormed across the bulwarks at the head of a boarding party. The British surged into the forecastle, killing the defenders, or flinging them down the hatchway. British success was swift, bloody and complete. Broke and his men were in command of *Chesapeake* even before her dying captain, James Lawrence, had finished gasping out his last command: 'Don't give up the ship!'

The exultation with which news of Broke's exploit was received in Britain had a quality of hysterical relief about it, and the usually drily worded official reports verged on melodrama with their references to 'the irresistible fury' of 'our gallant bands'. However, the palm for propaganda in the *Shannon-Chesapeake* affair went to the Americans. Just over three months later, on 10 September, Oliver Hazard Perry inscribed Lawrence's dying words on a blue flag which fluttered above the scene of his own victory that day over a British squadron on Lake Erie.

By then, the Americans were beginning to need inspiration of that somewhat jingoistic sort far more than the British did. As 1813 progressed and blended into 1814, the really decisive factor in the war – the overwhelming power and numbers at the disposal of Britain – began irresistibly to assert itself. Not without significance was the taking of the US frigate *Essex* off Valparaiso in March 1814 by HMS *Phoebe*. The action demonstrated the vulnerability of a ship armed primarily with carronades when involved in a fight at long range. Also, as a stop-gap answer to the big American frigate, a new ship-type was evolved by the British; several were produced by razing the upper decks from existing 74s. The resulting bastard vessels were called Razees.

The pressure increased after April 1814, when Napoleon abdicated and the war in Europe was over. The British were then able to turn more single-minded attention upon the enemy and slowly, relentlessly, American resistance was throttled.

There was far more headline potential in the burning of Washington by British troops in August 1814, or the ravaging of the shores of Chesapeake Bay by British landing parties, but what really brought the war to an end was the patient diligent blockade of the coast, the holing up in port of most of the privateers and US naval vessels, and the stranglehold imposed upon American trade.

Neither side gained anything really concrete from the peace treaty signed at Ghent, in Belgium, on 24 December 1814. Both planned to make demands, but all that happened was that the pre-war situation was restored. On paper, it certainly was, but, in less tangible ways, the situation was by no means the same.

The United States had won for itself a distinct respect in British eyes, and a position as a power worthy of serious consideration. The Anglo-American habit of amicable arrangements over matters in dispute became firmly established, and if complacency re-entered the general British attitude, it never again marked British dealings with America.

Chastened and more circumspect as a result of the war, Britain proceeded after 1814 towards her destiny as the world's greatest political and commercial, as well as naval, power. The Americans, their own sense of national unity greatly bolstered, turned towards consolidating their own continent, gathering their own riches and awaiting their own turn at the top.

Below: An early stage in the action between 'Chesapeake' (again in the foreground) and 'Shannon' from a coloured engraving. BY COURTESY OF THE NEW BRUNSWICK MUSEUM

The Early
Ironclads

THE glory of the British Navy, the finest and largest in
the world, had been built on sailing wooden warships.
'Heart of oak are our ships' was the start of the refrain of a
popular song, and it was also the truth. Oak forests had disappeared to build the fleet of so-called wooden walls. However, in early Victorian days, changes were looming up;
steam power was increasingly challenging sail and iron was
beginning to be used for shipbuilding. Tradition has always
been very dear to the Royal Navy, as it is today, and there
was considerable resistance to change.

Iron was already being used to build commercial craft
and the Navy had some iron ships, but they were not fighting
ships. Britain was not at war with anyone and many ships
of the fleet were laid up. There were large stocks of timber
and this was the material the shipwrights were skilled in
using. With the normal feelings of the need for economy
while in a state of peace, there was little urge to build in new
materials.

Some of the early iron was very brittle and when the Navy
did firing tests on the light iron-built *Ruby* in 1840, damage
was worse than on a similar-sized wooden vessel. The Navy
built some iron craft, but they were not completed as warships. One of them was the *Birkenhead*, which was launched
in 1845 and became the subject of the famous heroic tragedy
in 1852, when she foundered as a troopship off the coast of
Africa. Of course, later iron, largely as a result of the process
invented by Bessemer, was of much better quality and less
brittle.

It was left to the French to make the first moves in the
use of iron as armour. They built what were floating batteries
of guns, rather than boats, for use in the Crimean War. The
batteries were wooden platforms, protected by iron, so as to
resist the effect of Russian shells. For their purpose they were

very successful, and Britain followed France by building
similar batteries; two were of wood with iron armour and
three were entirely of iron. However, it was 1855 before the
British batteries were ready and they were too late to prove
themselves in the Crimea.

As the batteries had to get from where they were built
and fitted out to the scene of action in the Crimea, they were
made boat-shaped. The lower portion was in the form of a
flat-bottomed pointed box, equipped with sail and screw-
driven. They must have been most odd-looking craft, and
indeed were found to be inefficient and unwieldy under their
own power, so they had to be towed most of the way. They
were not all the same, but all had armour four inches thick
taken to three feet below the waterline, which must have
been a considerable weight on a platform such as one
described as 186ft long and mounting sixteen 68-pounder
muzzle-loading guns. One of the British batteries, the *Terror*,
completed too late for the Crimean war, spent her days as a
commissioning base at Hamilton, Bermuda, until 1903.

France was then second to Britain as a world sea power.
As a result of her experience with the armoured batteries, she
went ahead building armoured ironclad warships. Britain
stuck to wood, of which she had plenty, and the skill to
fashion it into ships. The French had a half-built warship,
intended to be an all-wood two-decker. The design was
altered by M. Dupoy de Lôme in 1858 and cut down a deck
so that it could be armoured all round with iron. The vessel
was launched as *La Gloire*, to become the first ironclad and
to mark the start of competition between the maritime
nations to build better, and usually bigger, warships armoured with iron, and later steel. Britain was forced to join
in.

The mid-Victorian period was the time of great engineers

and inventors, as well as the industrial revolution. British facilities and technical knowledge were ahead of France and the rest of the world, so Britain was in a good position to go ahead with iron shipbuilding, despite the reluctance of the Navy to move away from wood. The *Warrior* was launched on 30 December 1860; the world's first iron-built and armoured warship. She was a very different ship from any that had gone before and started a new era of warships.

At that time the naval dockyards could not cope with the construction of an iron ship of such a size and a commercial yard received the contract; the builder was the Thames Ironworks and Shipbuilding Co, at Blackwall, on the tidal Thames down-river of London, from the design prepared by Sir Isaac Watts and John Scott Russell. The *Warrior* is in use today, more than a century later, as part of an oil pipeline pier at Pembroke in Wales.

The size of the *Warrior* was arrived at by the intention that there should be a battery of fifteen 68-pounder guns with 15ft between the guns. To the resultant dimension of the gun platform were added a fine bow and a good run aft, to provide a fast hull. Main dimensions were length 380ft, beam 58½ft and draught 26ft, and the displacement was 9,210 tons. The ship was described as a frigate, because all the guns were on one deck, although she was very different from any frigate that had preceded her.

At that time there was a distrust of steam engines and even ships fitted with engines were fully rigged for sailing, partly as a reserve source of power and as a means of economising in the consumption of coal, which needed considerable space for stowage. The *Warrior* was fully rigged, but she was given the most powerful engines fitted to a warship up to that date. The coal-fired steam engines were of the horizontal trunk-type with cylinders 104.6in in diameter and of 48-in stroke. Indicated output on trials was 5,470hp, giving a speed with the single propeller of 14.35 knots. Best speed under sail was about ten knots.

At that time armour was used to protect the fighting area and not the whole ship. One reason for having all the guns on one deck was to reduce the amount of armouring needed. The only protection given to the ends of the ship was an arrangement of subdivisions to make watertight compartments. The armour plating was iron 4½in thick, backed by 18in of teak. The plates extended for 213ft along both sides and were 22ft deep, stretching from the upper deck to 6ft below the waterline.

Although originally designed for existing guns, better guns became available while the *Warrior* was building. The new main armament was of 110-pounder breech-loading rifled guns to fire conical shells. Eight of them were installed in the armoured area, with one each at bow and stern. They were supplemented by twenty-six of the 68-pounders originally intended, eight of which had to go outside the armoured area. Additionally, there were four 40-pounders on the quarterdeck, but they were mainly for saluting.

When launched, the *Warrior* was the most powerful warship in the world, with guns and armour superior to all other ships; perhaps with justification, she was regarded as invincible. However, although rifled breech-loading guns eventually became accepted, those originally fitted to *Warrior* gave some trouble and were removed in 1867. They were replaced by four 8-in and twenty-eight 7-in rifled muzzle-loaders, which became standard in the Navy until the 1880s.

Up to that time, warships had been rated according to the numbers of guns. Although *Warrior* was the most powerful warship afloat, according to the rules she was a third-rater, giving her captain a lower status (and pay) and making her complement 670 instead of the 1,000 she could have carried. It was not until the 1880s that the word battleship came into use, to give a more reasonable recognition of ships of the new form.

It was a transitional period between sail and power, so even such a new conception as *Warrior* showed the influence of earlier sailing warships. She was flush-decked and had three masts, with their attendant rigging. The two funnels were between the two forward masts and each mast carried square sails and a gaff-headed fore-and-aft-sail. There could be up to three headsails on the bowsprit.

The boilers and engines were low and occupied much of the centre of the vessel. Coal bunkers were below the waterline. Accommodation for the crew came above the waterline, with the men sleeping in hammocks in every available space. The captain's cabin aft had the galleried windows around the quarter, reminiscent of the more gentlemanly and less violent days of sail.

In March 1862, in Hampton Roads, Virginia, two ironclads fought an inconclusive battle in the American Civil War. The Confederates had raised the sunken *Merrimac* and armoured it with sloping iron sides; it played havoc with Union shipping. The Union's answer was the *Monitor*, also iron-cased. Both ships finished intact. Even if they had little effect on the progress of the war, they proved the ability of iron to resist the gunfire of the day.

The success of *Warrior* brought an end to the building of large wooden ships for the Royal Navy. *Victoria* was one of the last of the three-decker wooden warships. She was completed after the supremacy of ironclads had been established, yet she was sent to Malta as flagship to the Mediterranean fleet in 1864. Expert opinion was hostile and both Parliament and the press condemned the action. The official reasoning was that a roomy well-ventilated ship was needed as a headquarters. It was believed that the crowded ironclads would be unhealthy in hot climates. Conditions were not as bad as expected and the *Caledonia* took over as the first ironclad flagship of the Mediterranean Fleet in 1867.

Ironclads had their comfort improved by forced-draught ventilation, which was introduced in 1873. Newer ships were given greater weights of armour, and the ability of sails to drive them became less, so that steam became increasingly important, but it was a long time before sails disappeared.

Left: A Le Breton representation of the world's first ironclad, 'La Gloire'. NATIONAL MARITIME MUSEUM, LONDON (D. RUDKIN)

Below: T. Buttersworth's painting of an earlier HMS 'Warrior'. NATIONAL MARITIME MUSEUM, LONDON

After *Warrior*, the Admiralty began to catch up on the production of ironclads, with eleven iron-built and nine wooden-hulled ironclads built during the 1860s. The *Black Prince* came first, in 1861, as a sister ship to *Warrior*: she was also built by a commercial yard. The *Achilles* was built at Chatham in 1863, as the first iron ship to be built in a naval dockyard. She was also the only British warship to be built with four masts, and had the largest sail area of any warship (44,000sq ft). At 9,820 tons, she was heavier than *Warrior* and her dimensions were 380ft long, 58¼ft beam and 27½ft draught. Her engines produced 5,720hp and drove the ship at fourteen knots, and she was claimed to make almost as much under sail. Later, she was reduced to three masts, but she still carried the largest sail area in the British Fleet.

The next three ships were given armour the full length of their hulls. They were the *Minotaur*, *Agincourt* and *Northumberland* and were all alike, with displacement of 10,700 tons, length of 400ft, beam of 59½ft and draught of 27¾ft. They were given ram-bows and were the only five-masters in any battle fleet. The 400ft of armour each side was 5¾in thick at the centre, tapering to 4½in at the edges, on a backing of 10in of wood. Not surprisingly, the performance under sail with such a great weight to drive was poor,

but speed under power was quite good, at fourteen knots. All three ships became flagships.

Up to the time of *Minotaur* and her sisters, steering was still manual, that is, the rudder was turned by the steering wheel directly through cables and linkage. Despite the introduction of gearing, the effort needed to move the rudder became too much at times. Soon after the *Agincourt* came into commission, during heavy weather in the English Channel, the effort of fifteen men fighting to hold her four-tier wheel was insufficient to keep her under control. As a result, the *Northumberland* was given power-assisted steering, the first ship so to be equipped; it was then fitted to the other two of the class. Increasing trust in steam propulsion was implicit in the removal of the second and fourth masts from all three ships.

Britain still had plenty of good shipbuilding timber and small craft continued to be built of wood. Some smaller warships were built as iron-cased wooden hulls, both to use up good timber and economically to maintain British supremacy at sea over the French.

The *Lord Clyde* and the *Lord Warden*, both built to use up large amounts of wood still in the dockyards at Chatham and Pembroke, were built as iron-cased frigates. They were the heaviest wooden-hulled ships, of 7,750 tons and 7,940 tons respectively, and were launched in 1864 and 1865 and given rigs almost the same as *Warrior*. The wooden construction was massive. The 2-ft oak ribs were filled between with oak which was covered by a skin of $1\frac{1}{2}$-in iron plates, followed by a further 6-in layer of more oak and a belt of armour tapering from $5\frac{1}{2}$in at the centre to $4\frac{1}{2}$in towards the ends. There was a further sheath of 5-in oak covered with a layer of Muntz metal (as a protection against fouling and marine borers) below the waterline.

The *Lord Warden* had a comparatively uneventful honourable service of eighteen years, the last six as flagship of the Mediterranean fleet. The *Lord Clyde* was a sister ship, but she had a short life full of trouble. She was given new trunk-type engines, which were the most powerful at that time, but they wore out in two years. She was given new engines, but after six months' service she ran aground. When docked

to have the damage inspected, a serious fungus attack was found on the green wood from which she had been built, so she was sold out of the Service in 1875 for a small sum.

With the realisation that sail was no longer needed there came a gunnery change. Because of the masts and rigging, guns could only be conveniently arranged to fire broadside. Any sort of swivelling gun would have only a small arc of fire, without the risk of shooting away masts or rigging. With steam engines as the only means of propulsion, a different deck layout became possible.

Turret guns with restricted movement had, however, already been tried on sailing ships. The armoured warship *Monarch* served forty-five years on the effective list and can claim to have given the longest service in the armoured battle fleet. She was built in 1868 and was 8,300 tons and 330ft long. She was given two turrets with restricted arcs of movement between her three masts. After a modernisation refit lasting seven years, she emerged in 1897, still with three short masts, but without sails. Engine power of 8,126hp gave a maximum speed of $14\frac{3}{4}$ knots, and coal bunkerage was sufficient for a range of up to 6,000 miles.

Monarch had a freeboard of fifteen feet and, judging from her long active service, was stable. *Captain* was a generally similar vessel, built in 1869, but had only nine feet of freeboard. While sailing with Captain Cowper Coles, her designer, on board, she heeled so far under the press of sail in a beam wind, that she did not recover but turned over completely and sank, taking with her all but eighteen men.

After a fairly lengthy period of transition, in 1872 there came *Devastation*. She became the prototype sail-less battleship. She had new compound engines and a central island carrying funnels, derricks, boats and controls. The design enabled turrets to be arranged, one forward and one aft, each having a clear swing of more than 180 degrees. With the passing of sail, the term ironclad was also on the wane and steel completely replaced iron in the hulls of British warships from 1881 onwards.

Below: An artist's impression of the battle in 1862 between the two ironclads 'Monitor' and 'Merrimac'.
NATIONAL MARITIME MUSEUM, LONDON

Clippers on the Tea Routes

TEA had been imported into Britain from China since the days of Charles II, and for a century and a half the lordly East Indiamen carried it around the Cape of Good Hope to England. In times of war the ships sailed in convoy but a year's reserve of tea was held in London in case the ships should be captured. Thus the tea drunk was always about twelve months old. The Chinese restricted trade to the port of Canton, but after the Anglo-Chinese War of 1839-42, additional ports such as Hong Kong, Foochow, Shanghai and Hankow were opened to trade, the volume of which increased rapidly. The Honourable East India Company had meanwhile lost its trade monopoly, and smaller ships were by then carrying tea.

To increase sales, dealers in England advertised that 'new teas' had arrived by a certain ship and it was said that they had a better flavour than that kept in stock for a year. Thus a demand grew for fresh tea. The tea was gathered in May and was ready for shipment in June and July but the problem was that the south-west monsoon was at that season blowing strongly straight up the China Sea and the ships had to beat down against it before they could pass through Sunda Straits between Java and Sumatra and out into the Indian Ocean. To overcome the difficulty, ships capable of sailing at faster speeds and of beating to windward were attracted to the trade.

But in 1849, the British Navigation Acts were repealed, thus permitting ships of any nationality to bring cargoes to Britain, including tea from China. The change coincided with the discovery of gold in California, to supply the needs of which vast numbers of large clippers were built on the east coast of America, and when they had delivered their gold-hungry passengers at San Francisco, they found the

tea trade to England was conveniently ready for them. Indeed, their fame had already preceded them, and they were quickly engaged to load tea for London at rates of £6 and £7 per ton, much to the annoyance of the British shipowners, who received about £2 or £3 per ton less.

So began a rivalry which lasted some years, until the fever of the Californian gold rush cooled by 1855. Five years later, the American Civil War removed all competition from that quarter, but competition between British owners continued throughout the next decade.

The principal difference between the British and American ships was size. For instance the *Oriental*, which was the first American ship to enter the Thames with China tea, was of 1,003 tons, double that of the British clippers. But many American clippers that carried tea were much larger such as the *Challenge* of 2,006 tons, *Comet* of 1,836 tons, *Sovereign of the Seas* of 2,420 tons. They were all built of wood with very few iron structural members in the hull, with the result that the construction became massive to support the strains encountered in such a large vessel. Unfortunately, the ports in China were not accustomed to such big ships and the arrangements for collecting the cargo were only geared to loading small vessels, with the result that delays occurred in filling the big clippers with tea.

Large ships were not necessarily faster than the smaller

British ones, especially among the hazards of the China Sea, and there was some consolation to be gained in England from news of the *Oriental's* arrival in December 1850, which showed that the Aberdeen-built ship *John Bunyan* had earlier that same year made a passage of 101 days between Shanghai and London, or only four days longer than the American ship.

It was to Aberdeen shipyards that British owners turned for clippers in the early 1850s, and it was the yard of Alexander Hall & Sons that turned out some of the fastest ships for the tea trade during that decade. Examination of surviving builder's models shows that *Reindeer* (1848), *Stornoway* (1850), *Chrysolite* (1851), *Cairngorm* (1853), *Vision* (1854) and *Robin Hood* (1856) were undoubted clippers. All these ships had the Aberdeen clipper bow, which was plainer and less ornate than conventional British practice, but resulted in far greater overhang forward. All were full-rigged ships carrying four or five yards on each mast, and the sails were further extended on each side by the use of studding-sails.

The *Cairngorm's* design was not dictated by an owner's requirements but embodied her builder's convictions of what a large clipper should be. It was a bold decision for a builder to construct such a specialised ship on speculation, without first obtaining a firm order, but Alexander Hall & Sons were proved right because, after she was bought by the eminent firm of Jardine, Matheson & Co, she turned out to be one of the fastest British clippers in the tea trade during the 1850s. She cost £15,434, which works out at about £700 less than the original cost of the *Cutty Sark*. *Cairngorm* registered 939 tons new measurement, which meant that she cost £16.43 for every ton. By today's standards, it is an incredibly cheap price for a first-class ship.

Acknowledged as 'Cock of the Walk', the *Cairngorm* made many fast passages, such as her maiden trip of seventy-two days from Lisbon to Hong Kong in 1853. (She had been obliged to put into Lisbon after being dismasted.) Her fastest homeward passage from China was in 1858-9, when she raced home from Macao to Deal in ninety-one days.

The American clipper *Comet*, in 1854, sailed from Liverpool to Hong Kong in only eighty-four days, between dropping one pilot and picking up the other one, and a year later another American ship, the *Eagle Wing*, took half a day less between her pilots, from Deal to Hong Kong. The design, launching, and sailing of the American clippers were attended with great enthusiasm at their home ports, and the descriptions in the local papers far exceeded anything that the British could read about their own ships. For instance, the *Boston Daily Atlas* ended its description of the *Challenge* in the following manner: 'She is owned by Messrs N. L. & G. Griswold of New York, was built by Wm. H. Webb, and is commanded by Captain Robert H. Waterman. Like the knights of old, who threw their gauntlets down to all comers, her owners send her forth, to challenge the world afloat!'

In the past, the term 'Clipper' was used quite loosely to cover any ship that had made a fast passage, but research today bestows the term only on ships for which plans or models can prove a clipper rating. Such ships had the lines of a yacht and little attention was given to the amount of cargo to be carried, the attainment of high speed at all times being the chief factor. Some of the American clippers had comparatively flat bottoms, to provide the required stability for rounding Cape Horn en route to California, but they made up for that by having extremely sharp ends.

British clippers in the tea trade, not having to encounter the big seas of the Roaring Forties, were designed with sharper V-shaped bottoms. American clippers sometimes achieved speeds of twenty and twenty-one knots, and on several occasions, sailed over 400 miles in the course of twenty-four hours. The smaller British clippers, with their shorter hulls, did not possess the same potential for speed, yet ships such as *Thermopylae* and *Cutty Sark* could sail at speeds of seventeen knots and cover 360 miles in twenty-four hours.

Other British shipbuilders who specialised in building tea clippers during the 1850s were John Pile of Sunderland, who built the barques *Spirit of the Age* and *Spirit of the North*, and his brother William, who built *Crest of the Wave*, *Spray of the Ocean*, *Kelso* and *Lammermuir*; Benjamin Nicholson of Annan, on the Solway Firth, who built *Annandale*, *Queensberry* and *Shakspere*; and Bilbe and Perry of Rotherhithe, who built *Celestial*, *Lauderdale* and *Wynaud*. It was becoming increasingly rare for deep-water ships of over 500 tons to be built in the south of England after 1850.

A number of extremely sharp clippers were constructed entirely of iron for the Australian trade, after gold was found there in 1851; some of those ships later participated in the tea trade, but they were always regarded with suspicion as it was claimed that the tea was damaged in their holds through lack of adequate ventilation. Two such ships, built in 1853, were the *Gauntlet* and *Lord of the Isles* from shipyards on the River Clyde. An engraving of the former published in the *Illustrated London News* described her as 'the most perfect clipper ship ever launched on the Clyde, and she appears more like a yacht of large tonnage than a private merchant ship.' A similar description was given of *Lord of the Isles*, whose fastest passage from China was one of ninety days made in 1858-9 between Shanghai and London or eighty-seven days to passing the Lizard. Many passages were calculated as the elapsed time between losing sight of land and catching sight of it again, or between dropping the pilot and picking up another on arrival.

Although the tea clippers built during the 1860s consistently made shorter passages than those of the previous decade, the majority did not possess any sharper form of hull, and the faster passages must be attributed to the greater experience of the captains and of the shipbuilders. The design of the earlier ships was somewhat experimental in nature, as the building of large clippers was in its infancy. After 1863, design of tea clippers became more stylised as the success of ships built by Robert Steele & Sons asserted itself.

In 1860, there appeared the *Fiery Cross*, designed by the celebrated naval architect William Rennie, and constructed in Liverpool. This ship had a length of 185 feet, a maximum breadth of 31.7 feet and a depth of hold of 19.2 feet and registered 695 tons. She was a beautiful ship and, more important, a fast and successful one, both of which attributes she certainly owed to her first two captains, John Dallas and Richard Robinson. In those days, the first ship to dock in London with the new teas received an extra premium of up to £1 per ton of tea carried, to be divided pro rata among the crew, and *Fiery Cross* won the premium in the years 1861, 1862, 1863 and 1865. No doubt her success influenced ships built in other yards.

The long-established firm of Robert Steele & Sons of Greenock had already produced *Kate Carnie* and *Ellen Rodger*, but it was probably with the *Falcon* launched in 1859 that they first achieved fame with a tea clipper. As a result of the success, they were later able to build such crack ships as *Taeping* (1863), *Ariel* and *Sir Lancelot* (1865), *Titania* (1866), *Lahloo* (1867), and *Kaisow* (1868). Those ships accomplished some of the fastest passages ever made under sail to and from China. In 1866-7, *Ariel* took only eighty days (between pilots) from London to Hong Kong; in 1869, *Sir Lancelot* was a mere eighty-four days from Foochow to the Lizard, bound for London; and in 1871, *Titania* took ninety-three days between the same ports. The ships possessed the advantages found in all fast clippers – a comparatively high speed in light winds and the ability to beat dead to windward in a stiff breeze.

But although so much care and devotion was lavished on the great ships, they still had to produce a satisfactory income for their owners, and the builders were obliged to quote in competition with each other to get orders. The ships built by Steele probably cost no more than £17 or £18 per ton. That would have been for a composite hull, that is to

say, an iron framework with external wooden planking – a form of construction that gave extremely long life. Several vessels so constructed still survive. For example, there are the incomparable *Cutty Sark* in dry dock at Greenwich; the *Carrick*, ex-*City of Adelaide* (1864), used as an RNVR club in Glasgow; and the *Ambassador* (1869), now a hulk at Punta Arenas in the Straits of Magellan, with her iron frame intact but most of her planking stripped off by the locals.

Needless to say, there were many races between the 'full bloods', as the crack clippers were called, but the most celebrated occurred in 1866 between *Fiery Cross*, *Ariel*, *Serica*, *Taeping* and *Taitsing*, which left Foochow in that order at the end of May. Beating down the China Sea, *Fiery Cross* reached Anjer in twenty days, beating the field by one day. *Taitsing*, which had left a day behind the others, gradually closed the gap as they caught the favourable trades in the run down the Indian Ocean to the Cape of Good Hope. The first four all passed Flores in the Azores on the same day, but somehow *Fiery Cross* dropped back in the rush for the English Channel. *Ariel* and *Taeping* logged fourteen knots as they ran up the Channel within sight of each other for most of 5 September while *Serica* was out of sight near the French coast. *Ariel* signalled her number off Deal at eight o'clock in the morning of 6 September ninety-eight days twenty-two and a half hours after dropping her pilot, and *Taeping* did likewise ten minutes later. The two ships docked later the same day and *Serica* also just managed to get in before the lock gates closed. All England was thrilled with the news, except the dealers who were faced with a sudden glut of tea. In later years, the premium for the first ship home was abandoned.

But there were other splendid clippers which fiercely competed with Robert Steele's ships for the accolade of supremacy. Chief amongst them were the *Maitland* and *Undine*, designed and built at Sunderland by William Pile; the *Taitsing*, *Spindrift* and *Windhover* produced by Charles Connell at Glasgow; *Norman Court* and *Black Prince* designed by William Rennie; *The Caliph* built by Alexander Hall & Sons at Aberdeen; *Leander* and *Thermopylae* designed by Bernard Waymouth; and the *Cutty Sark* built by Scott & Linton at Dumbarton. The ships themselves were mostly in the 750- to 950-tons range, and so were fairly evenly matched in many cases. All were sailed by skilful captains and hand-picked crews of about thirty men.

Many seamen have rated the *Thermopylae* as the fastest all-round British clipper. She was launched in 1868, a year before the Suez Canal was opened, from the Aberdeen yard of Walter Hood & Co, and was of very similar form to *Leander*, which was built the previous year. She registered

'We were running our easting down ... when we sighted a vessel astern. It was blowing hard from the nor'west, and the next time I looked, a couple of hours later, there was the ship close on our quarter, and we were doing twelve knots. "Holy jiggers," says I to the mate, "there's the Flying Dutchman." "Naw", says he, "it's the *Thermopylae*." But when she was abeam a little later, she hoisted her name, the *Lothair*, and it's been my opinion ever since that she was making mighty close to seventeen knots.'

The *Lothair* was built on the Thames by Walker for Killick, Martin & Co in 1870, and was one of the last composite clippers to be built. After steamers forced the clippers out of the tea trade to London, she made some exceptionally fast passages with tea to New York. In the same year that she was launched, two other tea clippers were built on the Thames. They were the *Blackadder* and *Hallowe'en*, both built of iron at Greenwich by Maudslay, Sons & Field. The latter's first three homeward passages from Shanghai were made in ninety-two, ninety-one and ninety-two days to London, a most remarkable performance.

John Willis, who owned the two iron ships, had had the *Cutty Sark* built the previous year by a small yard at Dumbarton on the Clyde, and with her he hoped to beat the *Thermopylae*. The two ships had a close race of it in 1872, but *Cutty Sark* had the misfortune to carry away her rudder off the Cape of Good Hope. Nevertheless, she managed to reach London only a week behind. She never made a passage with tea in less than a hundred days from China, yet she was capable of high speeds and was given a large spread of canvas with a sharp-bodied hull. It was often the captain who gave a clipper that extra turn of speed, and sometimes he required nerve and daring to keep a thoroughbred clipper

An impression of the famous race between the two 1866 China clippers 'Taeping' and 'Ariel' as they passed the Lizard and ran up the Channel at 14 knots well within sight of each other.

948 tons. How lovely she must have looked when making sail in the Downs at the beginning of her maiden passage in November 1868, with her green-painted hull and white masts, her crew sheeting home the snow-white canvas of her new sails as she heeled to the wind. It was the beginning of a momentous voyage, because on each of the three legs she broke the record. From leaving the Lizard to sighting Cape Otway, near Melbourne, it was only sixty days, and the Australian papers marvelled at her speed. Thence, she sailed to Newcastle, New South Wales, to load coal, from where she took only twenty-eight days between pilots, bound for Shanghai. In China, she loaded tea at Foochow, left on 3 July 1869, and was off the Lizard eighty-nine days later. How disappointing for Captain Kemball that his record stood for only twelve days, until *Sir Lancelot* passed the Lizard eighty-four days from Foochow.

Paul Stevenson records a yarn told by the captain in his book, *By Way of Cape Horn*:

under a press of sail day after day.

The clipper captains were a varied bunch; there were the bully-boys, the hell-fire preachers, the pious ones and the strong silent types. To survive, however, they had to have one thing in common – they had to drive ships.

The opening of the Suez Canal in 1869 brought the days of the tea clippers to an end, because steamers could make a much quicker passage home with tea through the canal and earn the highest freight rates. The clippers continued racing home until about 1875, but could not afford to load at £1.50 to £2 per ton and so were switched into other trades.

The *Cutty Sark* was one such ship. She was really built too late for the tea trade, but in the Australian wool trade, under the redoubtable Captain Woodget, she proved fast and almost unbeatable. Her survival and preservation at Greenwich today form a fitting epitaph to the glorious days of the tea clippers.

Sinope and Explosive Shot

GUNPOWDER, Shakespeare's 'villainous saltpetre', has been known for two thousand years or more in China. There, mixed from the right proportions of sulphur, saltpetre and charcoal, it has long played a great part in festivals or devil-scaring in firecrackers and ingenious fireworks. The Chinese merchant fleets brought the components, or knowledge of them, quite early to India and Arabian traders carried them on until they reached the Mediterranean. It was left to the Western world to use them for destruction.

The Arabs are known to have used gunpowder in the year 690 at the siege of Mecca, but at sea they naturally preferred the closely related fierce incendiary material known as Greek fire with which it is often confused. Some kind of explosive rockets are believed to have made history during the reign of the Greek Emperor in 880 though gunpowder

Below left: Czar Nicholas I; a lithograph by I. Fridrits from a painting by G. Dau. NOVOSTI PRESS AGENCY

Below: A plan of the destruction of the Turkish squadron at Sinope. ILLUSTRATED LONDON NEWS

Bottom: An engraving of the port of Sinope as it appeared in 1854. MARY EVANS PICTURE LIBRARY

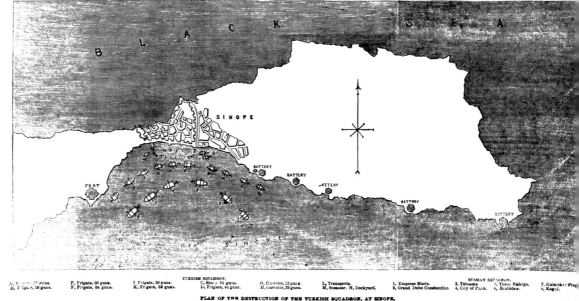

PLAN OF THE DESTRUCTION OF THE TURKISH SQUADRON, AT SINOPE.

seems to have been slow in reaching western Europe. It was not until 1325 that the Moorish King of Grenada, Ismail Ben Feraz, 'had among his machines some that cast globes of fire with resounding thunders and lightning causing fearful injuries to the towers and walls of the city'.

In England in 1345 Edward III, who had some primitive cannon, has left records of accounts of the purchase of gunpowder and a hundred years later Henry V when preparing for his invasion of France gave orders that no gunpowder should be taken out of the kingdom without a special licence.

As the years and the centuries went by and the guns on land and sea were being steadily improved, the solid roundshot gave place to shells, rifled and shaped for maximum effect, which caused much damage. But the Russians were the first to fire a naval gun with an explosive shell.

That was in 1853. With Britain, France, Turkey and Egypt on one side and Russia alone, on the other, there was a diplomatic tangle over the question of the future of the weakening Turkey. The Czar Nicholas I was anxious to protect the Christian Slavs of the Balkans and to win free access to the Mediterranean by occupying Constantinople. He suggested to the British Ambassador a partition of Turkish territory between England and Russia. It was not a policy to please Turkey, still less Britain, nor was it welcome to France, who had Napoleon III thirsting for glory.

When in May 1853 it was learnt through the Turkish Sultan that Russia was intending to occupy the Danube, a British fleet of seven ships-of-the-line under the command of Vice-Admiral Dundas and a French fleet of nine large ships sailed to Besika Bay, near the entrance to the Dardanelles, and anchored to await events. Then the Czar proposed to take under his protection the Greek Church in Palestine which had been caring for the Holy Places while France, nominally in charge of them, had latterly been apathetic.

Unfortunately, at that juncture the British Ambassador does not appear to have been the soul of tact. The Sultan refused the Czar's demand and although neither side declared war, war it was. At once the British and French fleets entered the Dardanelles by Turkish invitation and moved up to Constantinople to protect the Turks, not yet as full allies but much more than sympathetic friends.

With the main Turkish fleet was a captain of the Royal Navy, Captain Adolphus Slade, who later became Rear-Admiral Sir Augustus Slade. He bore the name of Mushraver Pasha, with temporary rank of rear-admiral while he was on loan to the Sultan. His opinion of the Turks as seamen was not high. In 1853 he found them to be half-trained or hardly trained at all and their senior captain objected to their practising reefing and handling sails while at anchor, to spare the feelings of the Sultan should a man fall from aloft. Allah, he said, was expected to make sailors.

On one occasion at sea when Slade looked round in a squall for the men presumed to be stationed at the topgallant sheets and halyards he saw them on their knees in prayer. On the other hand they were generally lively and alert and quick to obey orders.

The Russians were reported to be at sea with a squadron of three battleships, two frigates and a steamship. Consequently it was decided to send the large frigate *Nusretie* to strengthen the Turkish squadron which had been ordered to sail to the Black Sea port of Sinope. Slade himself sailed in the *Nusretie* to Sinope and suggested that at least two battleships should be sent to Sinope as a reinforcement. Instead it was agreed that the next squadron, which was to winter at Sinope, should be composed of battleships and frigates instead of frigates and corvettes as had been originally proposed. Yet when Slade returned with the first squadron to Constantinople he found that his advice had been ignored and the decision to send a more powerful fleet had been reversed 'by the desire of the British Ambassador'. The unfortunate Vice-Admiral Osman Pasha had sailed for Sinope with no ship larger than a frigate.

The small Black Sea port of Sinope had long enjoyed a life of peaceful trading and fishing. Once it had been a colony of Greeks until it had fallen into the hands of the Tiurk, the Byzantine Turks. Ships had come and gone with their cargoes, with seldom anything to disrupt the port's placid routine. But now came ships of war, none of them very large it was true, but still quite exciting to see, although their crews were not in good shape and were practically without winter clothing in bitter weather.

The excitement became rather doubtful when Russian ships, big ships some of them, came over the horizon. They gradually showed themselves to number three battleships, a frigate and one of the new-fangled steamers, but they sailed away again to the relief of everyone watching. Then four more steamships hove in sight but to everybody's relief they turned out to be flying the Turkish flag as they entered the bay of Sinope and moored alongside. After a day or two, three of them steamed away but the fourth one stayed.

The Russian ships appeared again and then began sailing to and fro, plainly waiting until, nearly a week later, more vessels joined them. In command of the united fleet was the Vice-Admiral Nakhimov, who had the reputation of being an upright and courageous sailor. He saw that the weather was too rough for his ships to try to enter the bay and kept them to seaward for three more days. He had under his command a total of eleven ships. There were three ships-of-the-line with 120 guns, three others of eighty-four guns; two of fifty-four guns; and two little steam vessels, not including the small steamship which had earlier arrived in the bay.

The Turks had a good deal less than half the Russian gunpowder, at least in numbers. Reports vary widely but at least the flagship of the Turkish admiral, Vice-Admiral Osman Pasha, can fairly safely be listed as armed with sixty-four guns. Five frigates probably had between forty-two and forty-five each, the two corvettes twenty-two each and perhaps ten or twelve on the small steamers.

On 30 November the weather moderated and the Russians moved into the bay and anchored on a curve before the town and near the Turkish squadron, with the three-deckers opposite the two Turkish frigates. The Turks held their fire for a while, except for a single old-fashioned five-gun battery perched and nearly hidden on a low cliff, which was causing some damage to the enemy. When a signalled request to open fire from the second-in-command of the squadron was disregarded the other vessels waited no longer, hopelessly outnumbered and outgunned as they were. For half an hour or so the Russians' guns were fired with too much elevation, their shells passing over the frigates' bulwarks; but the aim was corrected and soon it was all at an end except for the burning Turkish wrecks.

Sinope was not the kind of battle that is bright with glory in the history books. The Turks had only out-of-date guns firing old solid roundshot against the Russians, who were firing shells filled with gunpowder. Explosive shells had, of course, been used for years by mortars or bomb-ketches, but conventional ships had rarely used them previously since the first recorded use by the French at the bombardment of San Juan d'Ulua in November 1838.

The fighting (some called it a massacre) lasted for not much longer than an hour before the Turkish squadron ceased to exist; it had been smashed into wreckage. One of the little steamers escaped, although chased by the three Russian steamships. Most of the other ships had been sunk or set on fire and burnt out during the battle and the rest were burnt by the Russians afterwards. Vice-Admiral Osman Pasha and three of his captains had been taken prisoner and the loss of life was estimated to have totalled 3,000 or more, which might be an exaggeration. The Russians lost thirty-eight killed and 240 wounded.

The Battle of Sinope was a lesson in the effect of high-explosive on wooden ships. But that was not all; shells falling in the town were said to have destroyed two-thirds of the

buildings. The effect on the bewildered townsfolk of the sudden murderous bombardment must have been stupefying, as terrible as a modern bombing raid with no aircraft to be heard or seen. The story of Sinope, with additions, spread all over Europe in shock and horror, particularly in France. Russia became a fearsome bully, an inhuman monster, and in less than two years France and Britain were to do battle with the ogre in the curious and bloody conflict that was the Crimean War – and their ships would have high-explosive shells.

Apart from the common shell, various new types of explosive shell were soon to make their debut in actual warfare. Among them was the one invented and developed at his own expense in 1784, by Major Henry Shrapnel, who eventually became a lieutenant-general and commander of

Top: Sinope harbour after the battle.
NATIONAL MARITIME MUSEUM, LONDON (D. RUDKIN)

Above: An artist's portrayal of the Turkish fleet being destroyed at Sinope.
NATIONAL MARITIME MUSEUM, LONDON (D. RUDKIN)

artillery. Others included case-shot, designed to burst inside the gun barrel and discharge a rush of leaden or iron balls; and grape-shot, which differed from case-shot only in the size of the balls. But the most lethal of breech-loading explosive shells was Shrapnel's; it was exploded by a small charge set off by a time-fuse and flung its spread of bullets over a wide arc, and immortalised the name of its inventor.

Devastation to Inflexible

I N November 1869 the warship of a new era was laid down in the Royal Dockyard at Portsmouth. Not only was she to be the first battleship to do without sails and the first large iron ship to be built at Portsmouth, but the massive main armament of four 35-ton muzzle-loading guns intended for her also had novel features. They were to be mounted in forward and aft turrets, with two guns in each, which would give direct fire ahead and astern and clear arcs on the beam.

The *Devastation*, as the new ship was named, was equipped to train the turrets by steam power, but the guns would still be loaded laboriously by hand. Even the training round would be far from swift; from full elevation to full depression, for instance, was an operation taking at least thirteen minutes. In contrast to their size, the secondary armament was far behind,

with a total of half-a-dozen 6-pounders and fourteen smaller guns.

The *Devastation* was well provided with armour. Along the sides it varied in thickness from twelve down to eight and a half inches and the turrets were thicker still at fourteen down to ten inches, with a backing of eighteen to sixteen inches; the conning-tower had armour between nine and six inches thick. The full weight of the armour was 2,540 tons and to keep it down to that weight the bow and stern were left practically unprotected, a point that gave rise to controversy but was later accepted.

The ship was square in section, with the maximum beam running for two-thirds of the length, and the bottom was almost flat. The flat forecastle had no sheer and only nine feet of freeboard, the straight bow terminating under water in a ram.

Since steam was her sole motive power it was necessary to provide considerable capacity in her coal bunkers in the days before coaling stations existed. Having two propellers, she had an even chance of retaining mobility in the event of a major mechanical breakdown.

Although she was in several ways a big advance in naval architecture, the design advances had in fact been foreshadowed in the so-called breastwork monitors, of which the *Devastation* and her sisters were enlarged repeats. The two funnels and lack of a mast and yard, and the all-round low freeboard and great turrets roused a good deal of comment. In fact she was roundly condemned on nearly every side. Even so, when she was rammed by HMS *Resistance* in 1874, although some side plating was displaced, she did not spring

Facing page top: HMS 'Devastation' which was equipped to train the gun turrets by steam power.
NATIONAL MARITIME MUSEUM, LONDON

Facing page below: HMS 'Inflexible' whose two turrets were arranged in echelon between the funnels.
NATIONAL MARITIME MUSEUM, LONDON

Above: Detail of a painting by de Simone of the bombardment of Alexandria in July 1882. PARKER GALLERY

a leak or incur serious damage, which says much for her stout build.

The record of the new guns was not so favourable. There was certainly one incident with the Devastation class, and possibly another, of a gun exploding during practice and killing some of its crew. It was possible, apparently, to reload a gun even when the previous round had failed to fire. If that happened the double-charged gun could burst at the next firing.

The *Thunderer* was built at Pembroke in 1872 as a sister ship of the *Devastation*, but there were some improvements and modifications incorporated. Her big turret guns were of two different sizes, with one pair of thirty-five tons and the other of thirty-eight tons. She was of rather greater displacement than the *Devastation*'s total of 9,330 tons and was fitted with hydraulic gun-loading gear. Soon after being commissioned she took on board 16-inch Whitehead torpedoes for tests and experiments, an unusual employment in a battleship at that date. The *Thunderer* also had her troubles. In 1876 off Portsmouth a safety-valve failure led to

a boiler explosion, causing forty-five deaths and fifty injured in the ship's company. A double-charged gun explosion in 1879 resulted in eleven men killed and thirty injured.

Accidents notwithstanding, turrets and big guns had come to stay and the next step in development was in 1876, with the *Inflexible*. She was of about 11,880 tons and was something of a phenomenon in the British fleet, probably inspired by the Italian turret ship *Duilio*. *Inflexible*'s armour on the waterline was restricted to a central citadel and she had thick protected iron decks fore and aft. Her looks were strange indeed when she started life rigged as a brig and with two funnels. She had a full set of sails, amounting to 18,500 square feet of canvas, in the rather optimistic idea that she could take her place and keep station in the manoeuvres and exercises of the wooden ships of the Channel Fleet. The original rig did not last for very long. In her first refit the masts and yards were taken out and replaced by pole masts with signal yards.

The two turrets were arranged in echelon between the funnels under a 'flying bridge' and both were integral with the central citadel, a major item which measured 110 feet by 75 feet and rose $9\frac{1}{2}$ feet above water. The turrets held the heaviest guns of the British Navy – muzzle-loading giants of eighty tons. With high bulky funnels spaced widely between the masts, low freeboard and apparently no bulwarks, and with a great beam and narrow superstructure, she was certainly no beauty. But she did have one unique feature that was eventually adopted in all navies; her ends, otherwise unprotected, incorporated an armoured deck along the waterline with very full subdivision above that line in order to localise flooding.

In general, *Inflexible*'s armour was thicker than in any other ships of her era, or indeed since. Besides that, she carried two 60-foot torpedo-boats and some newly developed torpedo equipment, including submerged tubes and a grid for launching torpedoes over the bow. In addition she had electric lighting, watertight compartments for engines and boiler, and even anti-rolling tanks.

Both the *Devastation* and the *Inflexible* were among the nine big ships that sailed to Egypt under the command of Admiral Sir Beauchamp Seymour in a time of crisis. In 1882 a notable Egyptian character and wayward rebel, Arabi Pasha, was threatening to seize the Suez Canal, which was vital to Britain, and diplomacy proved useless. Arabi, in spite of all efforts to dissuade him, persisted in building or strengthening the line of forts guarding Alexandria. When an ultimatum sent by Seymour was ignored, he ordered a bombardment of the forts.

The majority of the ships engaged were broadside ironclads, which meant that only about half their guns could be used. Although their fire was impressive and accurate, the damage it did to the forts was a good deal less than had been expected. After enduring nearly four hours of shelling, the defenders of the main fort decided that they had had enough and abandoned it, whereupon a landing-party from the *Inflexible* spiked or blew up its guns. During the afternoon one fort after another stopped firing and it was all over. The casualty-list in the fleet at the end amounted to a total of six killed and twenty-seven wounded; a very light list considering that seventy-five projectiles had hit the ships.

The engagement had at the least served to show the effectiveness of the iron plating of all the ships that were under continuous shelling and cannon-ball fire. It provided a realistic proving ground, fortuitous or not, in those days of change, experiment and discovery, which covered the general replacement of the muzzle-loading gun by the breech-loader. The timber-built ships, those 'Wooden Walls of Old England', were fast vanishing and the torpedo had made its ominous appearance. There was the coming of the twin screw-propellers, and improvements in engines and boilers. Last and certainly not least, there was the reign of the all-big-gun ship that was to endure until the era of the aircraft carrier after the Pacific battles of the Second World War.

The Great Barques

THE opening of the Suez Canal – that 'dirty ditch', as a sailing ship apprentice disdainfully called it – virtually ended the clipper ship era, although the clippers continued to race each other home with tea from China or wool from Australia. In the 1870s the trend was to build much larger ships constructed of iron and later of steel. The greater strength given by metal allowed much longer ships to be constructed than was ever possible with wooden ships, with a few exceptions, which permitted much larger cargoes to be carried.

With big wooden ships, vast areas in the hold were occupied with enormous baulks of timber to give sufficient longitudinal strength, and the huge beams were supported by a forest of pillars, all of which occupied valuable cargo space. In metal ships, the space occupied by the structural members was negligible, to the infinite delight of stevedores and dockers. With the increased capacity, shipowners could afford to give their ships moderately sharp ends, even if the bottom was pretty flat.

To drive the large hulls through the water, very lofty masts were required to set a great spread of canvas, and many ships had as many as seven yards on each mast, allowing them to set twenty-one square sails altogether. But lack of experience in both building and handling such ships led to an unnecessarily large number of dismastings. When masts were of iron or steel, rigging of steel wire and sails of extra stout canvas, then a vessel under a great press of sail could go over on her beam ends in a squall, and if none of the gear gave way, capsize. Such a fate befell the *Stuart Hahnemann* in 1875. She was a large ship, of 1,997 tons with a length of 274 feet, and her spars were of immense length; the fore and main lower yards were each ten feet long, and the truck of her mainmast was about 175 feet above the deck. Many of the huge ships were also given full suits of stunsails on both fore and main masts.

Before 1870, sailing ships of over 1,500 tons were considered exceptionally large, but by 1875 there were many afloat, and the number increased every year. The largest three-masted full-rigged ship ever built was the *Ditton* of 2,901 gross tons, launched in 1891, with a length of over 310 feet. But the gear was immensely heavy and clumsy. Many thought that 2,000 tons was the maximum size for a three-masted ship.

An important change occurred in 1875 with the introduction of a fourth square-rigged mast, which first appeared in the *County of Peebles*. The ship was built on the Clyde by Barclay, Curle & Co and had a tonnage of 1,614 and a length of 266 feet. The four masts were named, beginning at the bow, fore, main, mizen, jigger. The result was to make all the yards slightly shorter and the total height of the masts less than in a three-masted ship. Compared with the *Mermerus* from the same yard, which had a hull of practically similar size, the *County of Peebles* set slightly less canvas. The actual figures were 30,610 linear yards as against 34,997 linear yards. About fifty such ships were built, but none of them outside Great Britain.

The *Falls of Clyde*, recently rerigged in Honolulu, was a four-masted ship. She was built in 1878 and it has been a mammoth task to restore her as nearly as possible to her original condition, and not only to make all her spars again, but also to find the men who could actually do the rigging. Owing to the fact that American ships were mostly built of wood, all the preserved ships in that country are of British or Continental build, with iron or steel hulls. The New York South Street Seaport has resuscitated the 2,118-ton iron full-rigged ship *Wavertree*, built as the *Southgate* back in 1885, which was found in South America. In the summer of 1973 the same establishment towed the hull of the four-masted barque *Moshulu* across the Atlantic from Amsterdam.

It was soon found that a fore-and-aft rig on the jigger mast was equally effective as square rig and cost the ship much less in wear and tear, so the yards were dispensed with and there appeared the four-masted barque. The first was the *Tweedsdale* built in 1877, of 1,403 tons. She also came from Barclay, Curle's yard, so they must have had some very inventive geniuses at work in the 1870s to think up so many new rig variations. In passing, it might be worth observing that there had been four earlier four-masted barques, although all were built in America or Canada. They were the two log rafts *Columbus* (1824) and *Baron Renfrew* (1825), Donald McKay's monster clipper *Great Republic* (1853), and the *Ocean King* (1874) built in Maine.

The four-masted barque rig became increasingly popular as the nineteenth century advanced, and the majority were in the 2,000 to 3,000 tons range, which allowed them to shift between 3,500 and 5,000 tons of cargo in a single load. Although economy had become the watchword, some barques were as graceful as ever, such as the white-hulled *Queen Margaret*, which carried skysails on her square-rigged masts. The single topgallants gave her six yards on each of the three masts, which produced a very dainty appearance aloft. There were other barques with three skysail yards, such as the *Primrose Hill*, built in 1886 of 2,436 tons, and the lofty *North Star* launched in 1892, of 2,761 tons. The seven square sails, starting from the deck, were called course, lower topsail, upper topsail, lower topgallant, upper topgallant, royal and skysail.

During the last dozen years of the nineteenth century, some large four-masted ships and barques were built. There was the full-rigged ship *Liverpool* of 3,330 tons and 333 feet in length which could stow 26,000 bales of jute. Like many of them, she was fast and powerful in strong winds, but she ran ashore on the rocky coast of Alderney in a fog in 1902 and broke her back. Also built in 1889 was the *Peter Rickmers*, built for the Rickmer firm of Bremen. Slightly smaller than the *Liverpool*, she was more lofty and crossed skysails on each of her four masts, giving her seven yards on each mast. She was very attractive to the eye and carried many cargoes of coal and of paraffin oil in tins, or 'case oil', to the East, bringing back rice from Burma or wheat from California. Such cargoes were the principal ones in which sailing ships could still earn a good living.

In 1891, two four-masted barques were built in Stockton of more than ordinary speed for Nova Scotian owners. They were the *Oweenee* and *Muskoka*. When commanded by

Right: A three-masted Danish timber barque getting under way; detail from a painting by Samuel Scott.
NATIONAL MARITIME MUSEUM, LONDON

Captain Albert Crowe, many considered the latter the fastest sailing ship afloat. She made three passages from California to the English Channel in under 100 days, and in 1898 she made the extraordinarily fast run of only eighty-five days from Cardiff to Hong Kong with steam coal. This was up to the best clipper ship performance. Also launched in 1891 was another big barque, the *Wanderer*, which the poet John Masefield described as a 'clipper, outward bound, the loveliest ship my eyes have ever seen'. But she was unlucky, with men being killed, yards falling from aloft, and sails being blown to ribbons. Yet her figurehead was so beautiful that sailors are said to have fallen in love with the white maiden.

In America, the building of ships entirely constructed of wood continued until the late 1890s, and many of them were of more than 2,000 tons. With vast forests to call on, wood had been a cheap commodity, but as the century advanced the iron and steel ships from European yards became more economical to run. Being built in the Down East states of Maine, New Hampshire, Massachusetts and Connecticut, the big wooden ships were called Down Easters. It was common for them to set skysails on each mast, and many ships were launched with all the masts and yards in position.

The majority were three-masted full-rigged ships, but in 1885 came the four-masted barque *Frederick Billings*, of 2,628 tons. In 1892, six of the crew were washed overboard in a gale off Cape Horn, and the captain made no effort to rescue them. Life aboard many ships was extremely hard and although good food was served in American ships, compared with British ones, the men were driven to the limit by 'bucko' mates. 'Belaying pin soup' was a popular dish handed out by those tough officers.

Beginning with the *Rappahannock* of 3,054 tons, the Bath firm of Arthur Sewall & Co began to build some huge wooden four-masted barques. Built a year later, in 1890, the *Shenandoah* of 3,154 tons spread two acres of canvas and the truck of her mainmast was 217 feet above the deck. She could load 5,300 tons of grain. In 1898 Captain Murphy armed his ship with two 4-inch guns, because of the Spanish-American War, and when logging fifteen knots off the Irish Coast, he fired at a Spanish gunboat which was unable to keep up with him.

Other big four-masted barques followed, of which the gigantic *Roanoke* was the largest wooden vessel, with the exception of the *Great Republic*, ever built in America. She had a gross tonnage of 3,539 and measured 350 feet overall. In the first three years of this century, the Sewall company built three four-masted barques of steel, each of over 3,000 tons, to carry oil in drums.

In the matter of sheer size, there was of course nothing to touch the five-masted square-rigger, but only seven of them were ever built. One was a full-rigged ship, the *Preussen*, and the others were barques, although four of the latter were fitted with auxiliary engines. The first five-master was the *France*, built in 1890 on the River Clyde for the French firm of A. D. Bordes, and she measured 3,784 gross tons. With her imitation gun ports painted on the hull – a style widely adopted by European ships after about 1870 – she is sometimes considered the most attractive of the five-masters.

The second five-master was the auxiliary barque *Maria Rickmers*, built in the same year, of 3,813 tons and also built on the Clyde. Her owners were the Bremen firm of Rickmers. She had skysails on fore, main and mizen masts, making seven yards on each mast; on the jigger there was no skysail and the mast was shorter; the fifth mast was shorter still with a spanker. The funnel was placed between the fourth and fifth masts.

Third came the *Potosi* in 1895, built at Geestemunde in Germany for Frederick Laeisz of Hamburg, with a gross tonnage of 4,025 and a length of 366 feet. She was a fast ship specialising in carrying nitrate from Chile to Germany. Her fastest outward passage was fifty-nine days from the

Isle of Wight to Valparaiso in 1905; homeward, her fastest was fifty-seven days between Iquique and Prawle Point in the English Channel in 1903. She had logged sixteen and a half knots in strong winds on her maiden passage and there is an impressive story of how she beat a 12-knot steamer up the Channel to Hamburg by six or eight hours. In the first ten years, her average speed was over seven knots, an incredible feat.

In 1902 came the unique *Preussen* square-rigged on every mast and again owned by Laeisz. She was huge with a gross tonnage of 5,081 and a length of 408 feet. The lower yards

on her first four masts were each 102 feet long and she crossed six yards on each mast. It has been calculated that she had no less than twenty-six miles of rigging. Just think of all that! Robert Hilgendorf had been master of the *Potosi* since she was launched, but rather than take the *Preussen*, he retired ashore. The sail driver Frömcke was driven mad by the *Potosi*, but the problems of handling the *Preussen* were much worse. It took almost half an hour to tack or wear the *Potosi*, and the yards on the second, third and fourth masts had to swing together. This was a great responsibility and the mass of sails and spars had to be patiently watched.

Below: A Captain's painting of the three-masted, fully-rigged barque 'Oleander' (1861) leaving Marseilles.
COLIN DENNY COLLECTION

'My ships can and shall make fast passages', read the sailing instructions from Laeisz to his captains, who drove the ships so fast in the strong winds around Cape Horn that they averaged shorter times than many tramp steamers. *Preussen* once ran 368 miles in twenty-four hours, although some American clippers had done more than 400.

The next five-master appeared in 1906, namely, the auxiliary barque *R. C. Rickmers* of 5,548 gross tons. Her first four masts were of equal height and her funnel was located between the third and fourth masts. All the Rickmer ships had green-painted hulls with red boot topping. Under power alone she could make only about eight knots, and could load 7,500 tons of coal or 7,180 tons of grain, which were enormous amounts for a sailing ship.

The sixth five-master was the second *France*, built in 1911 at Bordeaux. Her gross tonnage of 5,806 makes her the largest sailing vessel ever built. Even the American seven-masted schooner *Thomas W. Lawson* was smaller, at 5,218 tons. The dimensions of *France* were 418.8 feet by 55.8 feet by 24.9 feet. She was given twin screws and every labour-saving device. She had a big sheer but as she was 'bald-headed' she only crossed five yards on each mast. (A bald-

barques were meant to shift bulk cargoes and be safe, economical vessels. They were never designed to be exceptionally good at going to windward. Anyone who has ever tried to sail a dinghy against wind and tide may think he knows something of the problems involved, but imagine waves thirty feet high with a great hulk of a ship 300 feet long, and try to imagine what the masters had to contend with. Many of them were old men, because the younger ones had given up sailing ships and gone into steamers.

In 1905, the big steel-hulled three-masted full-rigged ship *British Isles* took seventy-two days to beat around Cape Horn from east to west, and five men lost their lives. The same year the German ship *Susanna* took ninety-four days. Some ships received such a severe battering that they had to run to the Falkland Islands to carry out repairs, and then return to the fight. Yet in 1938, the German four-masted barque *Priwall* beat around the Horn, from east to west, in only five days fourteen hours. What a phenomenal difference. But wind and weather conditions can vary enormously. Finding favourable winds at any season of the year, in any part of the world, was part of the art of being a successful sailing ship captain, and the Germans practised the

headed rig meant that a ship carried courses, double topsails and double topgallants but no royals.) The topgallants in such a rig were larger than usual so that sufficient sail area was preserved, but the amount of wear and tear on gear was reduced. Many three- and four-masted barques were also similarly rigged, such as the *Lawhill*.

Last of the five-masters was the auxiliary barque *Köbenhavn*, which was built in 1921 at Leith as a cargo-carrying training ship for the Danish East Asiatic Co. She was of 3,901 tons and had 27½ miles of rigging weighing a total of 50 tons. Each suit of sails weighed four tons and there were 1,200 blocks in the rigging. She mysteriously went missing in December 1928 in the South Atlantic.

By 1900, more and more of the surviving sailing ships regularly rounded Cape Horn on their passages, bound for Europe with grain from Australia or California, or with nitrate from South America. Such destinations took them around 'Cape Stiff', as it was sometimes called, with the wind behind them; but many others had to beat their way round in the teeth of one gale after another, and the big four-masted

art to a high degree. Oceanographers over the years had recorded what courses to sail to find the best winds, depending on the time of year. It was not always the shortest distance between two points that produced the shortest passage, as many inept captains knew to their cost.

Many of the German captains were skilled at being just in the right place to get the best wind, such as Captain Robert Miethe, when in the four-masted barque *Pitlochry* – owned by Laeisz but built in Dundee – he beat the mighty *Preussen* by twenty days in a passage from Tocopilla, Chile, to Hamburg. With great love for his ship, Captain Miethe once said that 'she listened to the wind better than any ship I ever had'. What an expressive remark.

French shipping was encouraged by the existence of a bounty system between 1881 and 1913, in which a sum was paid to the shipbuilder on the gross tonnage of every iron or steel ship, and an operating subsidy was paid on the number of miles sailed. The operating grant subsidised French ships to go seeking cargoes while ships of other nationalities were laid up for lack of money. The result was a fleet of fine big

Facing page:
'Hougomont' built in 1897
by Scott & Co of Greenock
and painted by Peter N.
Wood. D. RUDKIN

Left: The 2,799-ton barque
'Pamir' a painting by
Peter M. Wood.
D. RUDKIN

Below: A model of the last
British square-rigger
'Garthpool'.
SCIENCE MUSEUM, VICTORIA

Overleaf: HMS 'Discovery'.
A painting by T. G. Purvis
of one of Britain's famous
exploration ships, which was
bought by the Hudson's Bay
Co and operated by them for
the French government
during the First World War.
BY COURTESY OF THE
HUDSON'S BAY COMPANY
(D. RUDKIN)

three- and four-masted barques, in which due attention was paid to the safety of the seamen, principally by extending the length of the fo'c'sle and poop, and in very long ships by placing a long raised deck amidships. The effect was to prevent water continually pouring over the ship's side in gales, and rushing the full length of the deck, carrying men and gear overboard.

By the first decade of this century, British owners of sailing ships had either sold their fleets to foreign owners or were considering it. The term Sold Foreign suggests that the ship's life was finished, yet the new owners ran the former British ships quite as well as their previous owners, and frequently at greater profit. Thus many of the sailing ships survived, with changes of name, until after the Second World War.

Between the wars, sailing ships were able to make a reasonable living carrying timber from Europe and bringing back nitrate from South America or grain from Australia. The so-called Grain Races were eagerly followed every year by a growing number of admirers, although the last British square-rigger, the *Garthpool*, was wrecked in 1929. Many will remember the *Herzogin Cecilie* which drove ashore on the south Devon coast in 1936, loaded with grain. Gustav Erikson, who lived in the Baltic Aland Islands, owned the biggest fleet of such ships, and his crews were largely composed of young men who sailed for love rather than money. With expenses pared to the bone, the ships could earn their living. Even as recently as the year 1939, thirteen big square-riggers sailed from Australian ports with grain for Europe.

The Second World War decimated the surviving square-riggers, although *Pamir* and *Lawhill* continued trading in the Indian Ocean and the Pacific. The four-masted barques *Pamir*, *Passat* and *Viking* all visited London again, and the *Pamir* once more hit the headlines when she was lost in a hurricane in 1957. The commercial days of sail were over, but the square-rigged training ships make the memory linger on as, heavily subsidised, and with their decks high above the water, they cruise about the world. Perhaps a more nostalgic note is struck by the new role of ship preservation in which every year sees a growing number of iron- and steel-hulled square-riggers lovingly restored to their former glory.

Controlling the Ship

I N basic terms there are only two important factors affecting any voyage at sea. Firstly, the ship must move in the water, and secondly it needs to proceed in the required direction. The development of sophisticated power systems over the centuries called for many improved methods of navigation and communication, but the first obstacle to efficient propulsion was the problem of how to harness engine-power and make it work reliably.

For many years after the fully rotative engine had been perfected, transmission was simple and direct, but the crankshafts used in those early days were something of a problem in themselves. At first they were made from a single forging with bearing surfaces finished by hand, and the situation was improved when this gave way to the practice of building up crankshafts from separate forged-steel parts. Even after the introduction of the screw propeller, direct mechanical drive remained quite common, the engine being simply turned through ninety degrees so that its shaft rotated on the required alignment. But changes soon came to increase the efficiency of propeller systems, and accommodate new ideas in engineering design. Non-reversible engines became more practical through the adoption of these advances in power transmission.

There are three fundamental types of power transmission: mechanical, hydraulic and electric. Mechanical transmission is by far the most widely used in vessels of every size, but there are advantages with the other methods. Hydraulic transmission is effected either by a hydrodynamic drive used in place of a gearbox, or by a clutch in a basic mechanical transmission layout, and, in a few small vessels in recent years, by a hydrostatic system. Here the engine drives a hydraulic pump and the fluid pressure is piped to a hydraulic motor operating the propeller shaft. With electric drive, the engine drives an electric generator, producing the current to power a motor driving a propeller shaft. This method has been most favoured for big ships powered by steam turbines.

One early problem with screw-driven ships was that of providing a durable bearing for the tailshaft – and one that would not admit too great a quantity of water. Early screw ships had a cast-iron sterntube with a stuffing-box fitted to the inboard end to prevent the ingress of water. The tailshaft ran directly on the cast-iron bearing surface: an arrangement that caused rapid wear of both tailshaft and sterntube and necessitated frequent and expensive renewals. This rate of wear was cut down by the introduction of bushes.

Lubrication and cooling of sternbushes is generally the result of a natural flow of seawater from outboard through passages in the bushes, controlled by a stuffing-box on the inboard end of the sterntube. The arrangement has the advantage of simplicity, but sandy or gritty water can cause considerable wear of the bearings and tailshaft. In some ships, particularly deep-diving submarines subject to high external water pressures, wear presents a problem. Rather than lubricate the tailshafts of submarines with gritty water, designers have devised a system whereby seawater is filtered and pumped through the bearing from inboard.

The early timber boats presented their builders with the problem of boring the sterntube. The keel was usually bored out to take the shafting after the completion of the hull.

Boring would begin from the outside and a hole would eventually appear inside the boat. It is likely that the whereabouts of the hole and the angle of the shafting depended more on craftsmanship than on engineering design. In fact, before the introduction of iron ships, engineers as we know them today did not exist. The men of vision who designed the early steamships had to rely upon the skills of shipwrights, carpenters and blacksmiths to solve their practical problems.

One of the first significant innovations was an engine bedplate, which at least kept parts of the engine in their correct positions. Previously, the engine's component parts had been simply bolted onto convenient parts of the ship. The flexing of a ship at sea and the resultant movement of both engine and shaft bearings did little to promote any reliability or confidence in marine engineering. The first types of gear fitted to screw steamers consisted of toothed wooden cogs and a cast-iron pinion on the screw's shaft. Although they were noisy and dangerous and had exposed gears, they seemed not to have been particularly unreliable.

When steam engines operating at higher pressures and higher speeds came into operation in the second half of the nineteenth century, transmission became much simpler, and it was often possible to connect the propeller shaft directly to the engine. Possibly the first diesel engine to be fitted to a ship as a commercial proposition was that of the tanker *Wandal* of 1904. Built in old St Petersburg, now Leningrad, she was propelled by three screws, utilising an electrical transmission system which enabled her engine to run in one direction at a constant speed, driving a generator, while the screw motion was produced by an electrical motor.

In 1910, the *Vulcanus* was built as an ocean-going tanker, with a reversible slow-speed diesel engine directly connected to the propeller shaft. Reversal of the engine was achieved by first stopping it and then restarting it in the opposite direction: starting was by means of a system using compressed air. The *Vulcanus* concept set the scene for approximately a decade until the arrival of medium-speed diesel engines. These ran at between 400 and 700rpm, and therefore had to have a step-down gear to drive the screw shaft at an acceptable speed. They were usually connected to a reduction gearbox incorporating a reverse gear, either through a fluid or electromagnetic clutch.

Vespasian, reduction gearboxes became generally accepted. However, turbine speeds were increased as power output and efficiency improved. To maintain sufficiently low shaft speed, greater reduction ratios were necessary, which meant reducing the size of the pinion or shaft wheel, or both. In practice it was found that there were limits to which that solution could be taken, and double-reduction gearing was adopted.

This system was a lot noisier than the single-reduction gearboxes in common use, and the separate gear and turbine casings had to be very accurately aligned to avoid operating problems; even with the most careful preparation, mis-

Most of the early screw ships were basically sailing ships, equipped with engines rather as a luxury. To some extent, it was a matter of steaming through calms and sailing through the engine repairs. To reduce the drag caused by the screw when under sail, the propeller shaft could be disengaged by means of a clutch to allow the screw to rotate, or the screw-blades could be feathered or lifted clear out of the water. This latter method was popular at the time, the screw being connected to the shafting through a form of dog clutch, and raised or lowered by pulleys and tackle.

A major advance in propulsion occurred when Sir Charles Parsons fitted a steam turbine to a ship named *Turbinia*, and quite literally ran rings round the fleet at Spithead in 1897. One of the biggest problems with the steam turbine was its extremely high speed of rotation, which required a very big gear reduction to drive a propeller efficiently. The *Turbinia* herself had three propellers fitted to each of her three shafts. Naturally, only the forward propeller of each trio contributed any appreciable thrust, because the other two were working in already moving water.

The Cunard passenger steamer *Carmania* is a good example of the compromise effected in the turbines. She was powered by two low-pressure turbines, each developing 20,000 shaft horsepower. The *Lusitania* and the *Mauretania* were also designed with directly coupled turbines, each ship developing a total of 68,000shp. They were the largest ships ever to use direct-drive steam turbines. The first reduction gearing used in conjunction with a marine steam turbine was designed by Sir Charles Parsons in 1897. He fitted a ten-horsepower turbine with a 14-to-1 reduction gearbox and ran successful trials. As a result of further experiments involving the

alignment was always possible in a ship working in heavy weather.

In the meantime, the Americans were still experimenting with turbo-electric drives. The *Frieda* was built in 1911 with a three-phase fifty-cycle alternator driven at 3,000rpm by a turbine, and an electric motor developing 1,900shp driving a single shaft. The system was successful, and in 1918, the *Wulstey Castle* was built in Britain with similar machinery. Subsequently, turbo-electric equipment gained widespread popularity, and is to be found in many modern vessels, notably the liner *Canberra*, which develops 45,000 horsepower per shaft.

Both turbo-electric and diesel-electric propulsion systems are now widely used throughout the world. Both systems mean that the prime source of power can be situated anywhere in the ship, shafts are kept short, and it is easy to establish control on the bridge, although the high initial cost of the switchgear is a drawback. Turbo-electric machinery is usually fitted to larger vessels, while diesel-electric systems are usually fitted to small ships such as tugs.

Gas turbines have been used to propel ships since the end of the Second World War. They are high-speed machines and will often utilise a double-reduction gearing similar to that fitted to steam turbines, although there is no reason why they should not be coupled through a suitable electric transmission. The hydrodynamic or hydrokinetic transmission takes two basic forms. The hydraulic coupling transmits power between two shafts with virtually the same output as input speed, and replaces a dog clutch or other direct-drive coupling. As with the other options to the dog clutch – friction or magnetic couplings – the hydraulic coupling has

the advantage of smooth gradual application of power and some ability to absorb transmission shocks.

The hydrodynamic torque converter is similar in basic principle to the coupling and can additionally provide for differential input and output speeds. Thus, it can be used in place of a mechanical step-up or step-down gearbox, but, unlike electric transmission, it does not reduce the shafting required.

Right from the very early low-pressure reciprocating steam engines, builders of screw-driven ships have had to ensure that the thrust developed by the ship's propeller was suitably transferred to the structure of the ship. Some early directly connected engines absorbed the screw-shaft thrust on their

Left: The bridge of the liner 'Canberra' showing the chartroom with a situation display radar screen positioned vertically.   KELVIN HUGHES DIVISION OF SMITHS INDUSTRIES LTD

Below left: An engine telegraph developed by Chadburn in the 1870s.   SCIENCE MUSEUM, LONDON (D. RUDKIN)

Below right: The experimental marine gas turbine built in 1947 by Metropolitan-Vickers Electrical Co Ltd of Manchester and fitted to MGB 2009, a triple-screw motor gun boat which was the first sea-going gas turbine vessel.   SCIENCE MUSEUM, LONDON

Bottom right: A model of hydraulic steering gear which was patented in 1877 and thereafter adopted on the Thames.
SCIENCE MUSEUM, LONDON (D. RUDKIN)

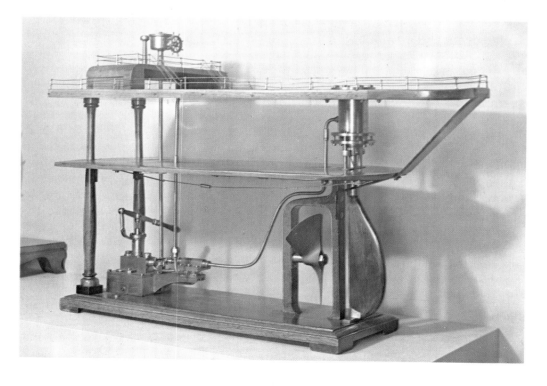

crankshafts. Some ships with gearboxes had the thrust transmitted by the gear casing, an arrangement that made little contribution to the accuracy of their alignment, but a more efficient method of absorbing propeller thrust is to fit a large flange to the end of the shaft arranged to bear against another flange fitted to a thrust-post on the keelson. This is a device which has evolved into the present-day thrust-block, which is rigidly secured to the ship's structure. Modern ships are also fitted with a means of locking the shafting to prevent it from rotating.

· All of these dramatic changes in the field of marine engineering would have been valueless if it had not been possible to evolve systems of navigation and communication to keep pace with them. From the earliest days of ships, one of the crew – sometimes several – has had to con and steer from a position which gave the best view of which way the ship was heading, and which was close to the steering device. In the large ships of the seventeenth century there was no discernible bridge as we know it, because the master usually moved about the quarterdeck and, if necessary, mounted the poop in order to get a better view. Of course, the helmsman, whose task also included watching the set of the sails, had to keep to the end of the tiller, to the upper end of the whipstaff and, after about 1700, to the wheel.

At the time of the Napoleonic wars and the great Franco-Britannic sea battles, the principal control position in a ship-of-the-line was on the quarterdeck abaft of the mizenmast. During the first half of the Victorian era, warships lost the massive superimposed decks astern, and the main deck, quarter deck and poop were contiguous, with only the main- and mizenmasts to show where one ended and the next started. The primary steering position, however, was still on the quarterdeck.

Even after steam power had started to replace sails, the primary con remained close to the wheel. Eventually captains complained about the cinders and smoke which drifted down when they were steaming into the wind, and they took station further forward. With the paddle-wheel boxes on each side making convenient platforms from which to con the ship, it was not long before they were joined by a bridge.

Since then the bridge has seldom been moved from a position close amidships. Changes only came with the advent of the bulk carrier and the roll-on–roll-off ferry: in the former it was placed close to the stern above the machinery spaces, and in the latter, close to the bow.

In both merchant ship and warship the bridge evolved, in the later nineteenth century, into a nearly standard arrangement of houses and platforms. The navigating bridge extended athwartships the full width of the hull. The central part of the bridge was usually enlarged in area to give room for wheel, binnacle and engine telegraphs. The charthouse in the larger vessels was often an integral part of the navigating bridge, but the wheel and binnacle and the helmsman were not necessarily given any protection from wind and spray. By the end of the century, the navigating bridge carried both a wheelhouse and a charthouse.

In the last two decades of the nineteenth century, the warship began to take on a form very different from that of most merchant ships, and the primary or forward steering and conning positions were arranged and constructed so as to resist the effects of shellfire.

By the start of the First World War, the British Navy had adopted the arrangement of steering and conning positions which has been used up to the present day, and which is unique among the major naval powers. The primary or forward steering position, along with the engine-order telegraphs, was either in the wheelhouse or, in heavily armoured ships, in the conning tower. This was separate from the primary con, which was on and around the compass platform, and which in turn had evolved from the mercantile ship with its 'monkey-island' above the bridge. In British naval vessels of cruiser size and above, the helmsman could not see out, and in many ships the wheelhouse was below the armoured belt low down in the hull.

The ship's wheel had not come onto the maritime scene until the start of the eighteenth century, but once a method ,was devised of joining the tiller cables to a windlass, and the problems caused by moving the tiller from amidships were overcome, the wheel soon came to replace the tiller in nearly all medium and large vessels. From the mid-nineteenth century until more recent times, the wheel retained its 'sail' form with traditional spokes and handles. However, once muscular effort gave way to steam steering engines, small tillers, joy-sticks or push-buttons came into operation. Miniature wheels first came into use on the pedestals of the automatic pilot, which was usually positioned alongside the conventional wheel and binnacle.

The log is an interesting example of the evolution of an originally crude instrument to the speed indicators in the modern bridge, chartroom or tactical plot. It started with timing how long a piece of wood, dropped from the bow, took to reach the stern. Next, there evolved the technique, which lasted until the mid-nineteenth century, of the log-line: the end of the line was dropped over the stern, and as the knots in the line passed over the counter the rate at which they moved gave the speed in knots.

Eventually the log-line method was superseded by the patent taffrail log, which was fixed to the stern with a trailing rotating cable turning a spinning float in the water. The rotating cable entered the speed-indicator mechanism and was converted by a chronometric movement into a reading on a dial. There were further minor adaptations of this general principle until the more recent hull-mounted propeller and pitometric logs.

Verbal communications aboard ship have always played a major role in the efficient handling of vessels, and great strides were made in this connection when Chadburn developed his engine telegraph in the 1870s. This was the precursor of all systems for signalling orders to the engines from the navigating bridge, and, just as importantly, for receiving confirmation that the orders had been understood and carried out. Originally dependant on steel cables, the telegraph progressed to hydraulics and then almost universally to electrical operation.

Today, the unmanned ship's engine-room is a reality: it has small remote-control levers on a bridge console and engine-control consoles on each wing of the navigating bridge for direct control of thrust when docking.

No review of control and communication would be complete without mention of radar. From its beginnings as an electronic method of detecting and ranging hostile targets, both by sea and by air, radar developed rapidly after the Second World War in the fields of pilotage and navigation. Within limitations, radar could present an accurate picture of a situation, with the ship in the centre. Coastline features, buoys and other vessels could be discerned, and the navigator was no longer made blind by fog or limited night vision. By continuously and simultaneously measuring the bearing of, and hence the distance from, two or more transmitters, the modern navigator has been able to fix his position through radar without reference to landmarks or heavenly bodies.

Today, the bridge is the nerve-centre of the ship, with all controls and means of communication close to the eyes and hands of the watchkeeper. Most importantly, the safety of the ship is monitored by sensors, including closed-circuit television. The watchkeeper does not have to rely on other watchkeepers or patrols to guard against fire or dangerous conditions of cargo, or the other hazards that accompany technological progress.

Even in smaller craft, such as tugs, workboats and fishing-vessels, with narrow bridges, the controls and indicators can be closely grouped around the skipper's chair. From there, seated, he can con, navigate, steer, control both ship and cargo, and communicate, without having to walk from one vantage-point to another.

Blue Riband Liners

THE occasion when the expression 'Blue Riband of the North Atlantic' was first coined appears not to have been recorded; certainly it seems to have come into common use only after the First World War. The term Blue Riband is particularly apt, however, and the Oxford Dictionary quotes in that context a definition, in use since 1848, which reads, 'The greatest distinction, the first place or prize'. It qualifies the honour in so far as the North Atlantic ferry is concerned although, in fact, the Blue Riband carried no prize or material recognition other than the attendant publicity.

It is a matter of history, however, that in 1935 an American citizen, Mr H. K. Hales, did present an imposing trophy, but the idea of such tangible recognition was not welcomed by certain leading shipping companies. In August 1936, when the Cunard-White Star liner *Queen Mary* took the record from the French *Normandie*, her owners refused to accept the award. In July 1952 the record passed finally to the 53,329-ton liner *United States* of the United States Lines with an average speed of 35.39 knots eastbound and 34.51 knots for the homeward passage. Now, the regular North Atlantic ocean ferry has itself passed into history and the likelihood of there being another contender for the honour is indeed remote.

The first crossing of the North Atlantic by a steamship whose owners intended anything by way of a regular service was that of the 703-ton wooden paddle steamer *Sirius*, which arrived in New York from London via Cork on 23 April 1838, after a passage of eighteen days ten hours from Cork

(2,961 miles). Within a few hours, however, the performance was eclipsed by Brunel's steamship *Great Western*, which secured alongside Pike Street Wharf later that same day having covered the 3,223 miles from Avonmouth in fifteen days ten and a half hours.

In November 1838, the British Admiralty, then responsible for the carriage of British mails overseas, invited tenders for a mail steamship service between an English port and Halifax with a through connection to New York. Proposals were submitted by the British & American Steam Navigation Co, operators of the diminutive *Sirius*, and the Great Western Steamship Co, but in the event a contract, valued at £50,000 per annum, was awarded to the British & North American Royal Mail Steam Packet Co (later to become the Cunard Steamship Co Ltd) as the result of an agreement dated 4 May 1839. Cunard undertook to provide a regular service, fortnightly during eight months of the year and otherwise monthly, between Liverpool, Halifax and Boston (rather than New York) employing three 800-ton wooden paddle steamers. Later, it was decided to build four considerably larger

Above: The Cunard Line's RMS 'Queen Mary' at Spithead in July 1967. A. GREENWAY

Right: The 'Baltic' of 1871 and her master, Captain Charles W. Kennedy, became the subjects of a waltz by D. M. Levett which was published as sheet music.
J. SANDILANDS COLLECTION (RICHARD SHARPE STUDIOS)

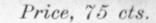

BALTIC WALTZ

Respectfully dedicated to

Capt. Chas. W. Kennedy,

OF THE STEAMSHIP

Baltic.

Composed by

D. M. LEVETT,

NEW YORK.

NEW YORK:

JAMES SUTTON & COMPANY.

1872

The S.S. GREAT BRITAIN

vessels to ensure maximum availability, and the annual subvention was increased to £60,000.

The first of the quartet in service on the Boston route was the 1,135-ton paddler *Britannia* which left Liverpool with sixty-three passengers on 4 July 1840, but not until 1847 did Cunard appear on the premier New York route. By that time, rival (unsubsidised) concerns having dropped out one by one, Cunard was in a position to command the bulk of the first-class traffic; in 1848, the company's reputation was enhanced when the 1,834-ton *Europa* recorded a time of eleven days three hours for the 3,047 miles separating Liverpool from New York. Like her several consorts, the *Europa*

was a wooden paddle steamer with twin simple side-lever engines of 1,400 ihp and a speed of about ten knots. Of course, steamers of the day were usually barque or barquentine-rigged with a full outfit of sails, which would account partly for the *Europa*'s record passage at an average speed of 11.52 knots.

In October 1845, the US Government invited tenders for the carriage of mails between the United States and Europe and eventually a contract was awarded to the New York & Liverpool United States Mail Steamship Co, usually known as the Collins Line, which undertook to provide a fortnightly steamer service between those ports during eight months of

194

TWIN-SCREW R.M.S. "ADRIATIC."
24,541 TONS.

Far left: Model of the 'Great Western' paddle steamer of 1837, the first steamer built specially for Atlantic ferry service.
SCIENCE MUSEUM, LONDON

Left: The White Star liner RMS 'Adriatic' of 24,541 tons, from a souvenir postcard.
A. DEAYTON COLLECTION

Below: 'Great Britain', Brunel's great ship of 1845, set the pattern for big ships built entirely of iron.
PARKER GALLERY

Overleaf: The French passenger 'Normandie', operated by the Compagnie Générale Transatlantique, as she appeared in the Hudson River at New York in 1936.
L. DUNN COLLECTION

...ed by Isambard Kingdom Brunel, Launched on 19th July 1843

the year, and monthly during winter. The subsidy of $385,000 per annum was to run for ten years and eventually, after several changes of plan, orders were placed for the construction of four wooden paddle steamers to be named *Arctic*, *Atlantic*, *Baltic* and *Pacific*.

At 2,860 tons each, the vessels were the largest afloat, except for Brunel's iron steamship *Great Britain*. Their accommodation, originally for 200 first-class passengers only, was far more luxurious than that of the Cunard ships. Among the amenities provided there were steam heating, fitted bathrooms, a smoking-room and a barber's shop. Like most other early ocean paddle steamers, they were driven by simple twin-cylinder side-lever machinery, in their case of 2,000ihp. In the event, additional government money had to be injected before the quartet could be completed but in April 1850, the *Atlantic* took the first sailing from New York to Liverpool and, despite damage to a paddle caused by ice, completed the passage in thirteen days.

The advent of the Collins Line marked the beginning of the first real struggle for steam supremacy on the North Atlantic and in July 1850, the *Atlantic* took the eastbound record with a time of ten days eight and a half hours. By that time, the value of the attendant publicity was acknowledged and, in the following October, Cunard fought back

with an eastbound passage of ten days seven hours by the 2,226 ton paddler *Asia*. Westbound, however, Collins took all the honours and the *Baltic*'s passage in August 1851 of nine days eighteen hours was to stand untouched for a full ten years.

Despite the apparent success of the Collins Line, which in 1851 carried three passengers for every two travelling by Cunard, the company failed to generate a profit and, notwithstanding further injections of government capital, the line foundered finally in 1858, a demise helped no doubt by the adverse publicity stemming from the loss of the *Pacific* without trace in January 1856.

In May 1856, the eastbound record was taken by Cunard's iron paddle steamer *Persia*, a handsome clipper-stemmed brig-rigged vessel of 3,300 tons with a service speed of thirteen knots. During later passages, the *Persia* improved on her own time but in the absence of any sustained competition there was little incentive for any radical change in the pattern of the service. The last of the great mail paddle steamers, the 3,871-ton *Scotia*, established records in both directions, in December 1863 (eastbound) and July 1866 (westbound) but her success marked the end of an era.

The early mail contracts had insisted upon the use of paddle steamers but that requirement apart, Cunard had not paid sufficient attention to the several unsubsidised fleets of screw steamships by then making a name for themselves on the North Atlantic. Operators such as the Inman, Guion and Hamburg American Lines had come to the North Atlantic primarily in the migrant trade, but their ships were well found and usually provided for a number of first- and second-class, in addition to steerage passengers. In course of time, such companies put emphasis more on the first-class traffic and to the construction of ships fully equal to the best of the subsidised mail steamers. Thus it came about that on her second eastbound crossing in December 1869, the 3,081-ton Inman liner *City of Brussels* broke all previous records and destroyed Cunard supremacy with a passage between New York and Queenstown at an average speed of 14.66 knots.

The credit attaching to a record run led to a tacit agreement between the companies concerned that the recognised departure points should be Sandy Hook off New York and Queenstown (now Cobh) in Ireland. In later years, however, with the increasing use of south coast and European ports, vessels headed for the Channel were timed to either Eddystone or Cherbourg until finally, in the 1930s, the American Ambrose light and English Bishop's Rock lighthouse became the accepted departure points.

A new challenger appeared in 1870 in the guise of the White Star Line, which set out to achieve new standards of comfort and reliability on the North Atlantic. Orders were placed with Harland & Wolff of Belfast for four iron compound-engined screw steamers with a designed service speed of fourteen knots. Speed and superior passenger accommodation were the prime aims and, despite early teething troubles in the *Oceanic* (1871), the quartet quickly settled down. In the meantime, two somewhat larger vessels had been laid down and it was the first of the later pair, the 3,888-ton *Adriatic*, which secured the westbound record for the White Star Line in May 1872 at an average speed of 14.52 knots. Eight months later, the *Baltic* crossed eastbound from New York at 15.09 knots.

The battle then began in real earnest. The Inman Line was determined to regain the premier position and ordered from Caird's on the Clyde a 5,500-ton 15-knot express liner to be named *City of Berlin*. The ship had the greatest length/beam ratio of any Atlantic liner ever built at 11 to 1. She was commissioned in April 1875 and in September/October of that year regained the record for Inman in both directions with average speeds of 15.21 knots westbound and 15.37 knots eastbound.

Despite the fact that five of the White Star's six ships were sufficient to maintain a weekly service between Liverpool

and New York, pride and a desire to regain first place prompted the company to order two 5,000-ton 15-knot improved versions of the *Oceanic*, which were completed in 1874-75 as the *Britannic* and *Germanic*. They were two-funnelled barquentine-rigged steamships of the build that even then was becoming recognised as typical of Harland & Wolff. So, the *City of Berlin*'s record was short lived, for after a mere four months the *Germanic* retrieved the eastbound record for the White Star Line by a comfortable margin with an average speed of 15.79 knots. The *Britannic* followed with the westbound record in November 1876 with a passage from Queenstown in seven days thirteen hours (15.43 knots).

The Inman and White Star Lines were not the only North Atlantic operators to seek fame in the early 1870s. In 1871, the Liverpool & Great Western Steamship Co (Guion Line) placed orders with Palmer's of Hebburn for the construction of a pair of 4,300-ton compound-engine steamships with the avowed intention of securing the record. The *Montana* and *Dakota* were given 100psi water-tube boilers which proved utter disasters; they had to be fitted with boilers of lower pressure before their long-delayed entry into service. Undeterred by the experience, Guion went ahead with new plans and ordered a 5,150-ton vessel to be named *Arizona* from John Elder & Co on the Clyde. That time, the outcome was left in no doubt and in July 1879 the *Arizona* wrested the eastbound record from the White Star liner *Britannia* with an average of 15.96 knots.

The success of the *Arizona* encouraged the Guion Line to build a consort, the 6,900-ton *Alaska*, which entered service in November 1881 and soon proved herself equally satis-

Sinking of the "KAISER WILHELM DER GROSSE" by the "HIGHFLYER"

factory by taking the record in both directions, for the first time at average speeds of more than sixteen knots. Both the *Arizona* and the *Alaska* proved expensive to run and it was decided that the only way to ensure profitability was to build a third comparable vessel to make possible regular weekly express sailings from Liverpool. Surprisingly, the 7,400-ton *Oregon*, completed for service in October 1883, was built of iron rather than the by then readily available steel, but the new liner proved a flier, taking the record outwards and homewards at speeds in excess of eighteen knots. By that time, however, the Guion Line was overstretched financially and within a few months the record-breaking *Oregon* was sold to Cunard, which thus fortuitously regained the North Atlantic prize after a lapse of fifteen years.

In the meantime, yet another contender for the record flourished briefly, encouraged no doubt by the Guion Line's ephemeral success. The National Line's 5,528-ton single-screw steamship *America*, an impressive looking schooner-rigged vessel with two tall elliptical funnels and a clipper stem, entered service in May 1884 and achieved immediate fame by breaking the record in both directions – only to be overshadowed within two months by the *Oregon*!

The *Oregon* was purchased by Cunard as a consort for the 7,718-ton sisters *Umbria* and *Etruria*, completed in 1884-85, but her career under her new flag was brief, for within two years she was lost in collision near Fire Island off New York. The *Umbria* and *Etruria* shared the record for a couple of years but in 1889 the Inman Line, which had become the Inman & International Steamship Co and American controlled, reappeared to take the honours in both directions with the elegant three-funnelled clipper-stemmed sisters *City*

of New York and *City of Paris*. The White Star Line also made a brief comeback with the 9,950-ton sisters *Majestic* and *Teutonic* in 1889, but, thereafter, the company abandoned the construction of record breakers in favour of medium-powered vessels of extreme size and solid comfort.

With the completion of the 12,950-ton steel twin-screw sisters *Campania* and *Lucania* in 1893, the Cunard Line returned to the top. Equally magnificent in appearance and in the opulence of their appointments, they were driven at twenty-one knots by five-cylinder triple-expansion engines of 31,000ihp and proved reliable and consistent performers. The *Lucania* retained an edge over her sister in the matter of speed, but each took the record in turn and, with age, the performance of both improved, occasional crossings being made at more than twenty-two knots.

Apart from the short-lived supremacy of the Collins Line, the Blue Riband had been a completely British affair, although in fact the Inman & International record breakers of 1889 were American inspired and financed. The passage time between Queenstown and New York had been reduced to five and a half days and, once again, Cunard held the coveted honour with a weekly service by the *Campania*, *Lucania*, *Umbria* and *Etruria*.

Towards the end of the century, the Bremen-based Norddeutscher Lloyd company determined to secure for itself a greater proportion of the lucrative North Atlantic ferry traffic and in particular to attract more custom from among the American and British public. To that end, an order was placed for a 14,350-ton twin-screw steamship which entered service in November 1897 as the *Kaiser Wilhelm der Grosse*. Capable of twenty-two knots, she was of strikingly individual

CAMPANIA

R. H. Neville-Cumming
1894

appearance, with four funnels arranged in separate pairs and two pole masts. The new ship took the eastbound record at an average of 22.35 knots between Sandy Hook and the Needles on her third voyage and quickly followed that success with the westbound record in March of the following year.

The other great German North Atlantic company, the Hamburg American Line, followed with an order to Vulkan of Stettin for the 16,600-ton *Deutschland*, a vessel of somewhat similar appearance to the *Kaiser Wilhelm der Grosse* with four funnels in two separate pairs. Completed in 1900, the *Deutschland* fulfilled her owners' expectations by wresting the record from the NDL, but she proved expensive to maintain and suffered from severe vibration. So, after one brief and none-too-satisfactory experience, Hamburg American withdrew from the race and, like the White Star Line, sought public custom through size and comfort.

The Norddeutscher Lloyd built two further ships, the *Kronprinz Wilhelm* (1901) and the 19,350-ton *Kaiser Wilhelm II* (1903), both of which took westbound and eastbound records in turn. The machinery arrangement in the latter vessel was of particular interest in that she had four sets of quadruple-expansion engines, two to each shaft, sited in separate engine rooms.

In 1902, the British Government appointed a committee to look into the question of building two large fast vessels suitable for rapid conversion into armed merchant cruisers. In due course, agreement was reached with the Cunard Company and in the light of the report of a technical committee it was decided that the vessels should be powered by Parsons direct-drive turbine machinery. Orders were placed in May 1905 for the construction of the two express steamships the first of which, the 31,550-ton *Lusitania*, was delivered by John Brown & Co in September 1907. A graceful vessel, with four evenly spaced funnels and two pole masts, she marked the beginning of a new era in design for the Atlantic ferry and on her second voyage recaptured the Blue Riband for Cunard with record passages in both directions. Her sister, the famed *Mauretania*, built on the Tyne, entered service in November 1907 and after a certain amount of give and take between the two, the *Mauretania* settled down as slightly the faster, averaging over twenty-five knots.

Passage times were then under five days and it was apparent that any further reduction could only be bought at considerable expense. Thus the *Mauretania*, which first gained the eastbound record in November 1907 with a crossing at 23.69 knots, retained the honour for the following twenty-two years! In point of fact, the *Mauretania* matured with age and continually bettered her own times until August 1929, when, in a magnificent attempt to better the time of the NDL *Bremen*, she crossed from the Ambrose light to Eddystone at an average of 27.22 knots.

National pride brought Germany back to the competition with the construction of the Norddeutscher Lloyd quadruple-screw geared-turbine steamers *Bremen* (1929-51) and *Europa* (1930-49), which were, in fact, the first vessels to challenge the *Mauretania*'s long tenure. Completion of the *Europa* was delayed by fire but the *Bremen* took her maiden sailing in July 1929 and crossed in record time from Cherbourg at an average of 27.83 knots. Eastbound, she made sure of her claim to the Blue Riband by crossing at 27.92 knots. The Norddeutscher Lloyd hold on the record was threatened briefly in August 1933, when the 51,062-ton Italian liner *Rex* crossed from Gibraltar at 28.92 knots, but that fast one-way passage on a fair weather route was not repeated. Hence, the achievement did not qualify for the Blue Riband, which needed record double crossings.

In May 1930, Cunard announced plans for an 80,000-ton 29-knot geared-turbine liner, the first of two for the weekly service from Southampton as replacements for the company's ageing trio, *Mauretania*, *Berengaria* and *Aquitania*. Yard No 534 was ordered from John Brown & Co on the Clyde and her keel was laid in December 1930, but a year later work was suspended in the wake of the world-wide depression. In the meantime, the French Line (Compagnie Generale Transatlantique), with similar plans in mind, had ordered an 80,000-ton quadruple-screw turbo-electric vessel, which was launched as *Normandie* in October 1932. Work on No 534 was resumed with government assistance in April 1934 after agreement to a merger of Cunard and White Star interests and the vessel was launched as *Queen Mary* on 26 September following.

Delivered to the French Line in May 1935, the *Normandie* left Le Havre on the 29th of the month and, during her first round voyage to New York, broke all existing records with an average of 29.98 knots outwards and 30.35 knots in the homeward direction. The *Queen Mary* followed a year later and although Cunard stated that it was not their intention to indulge in record-breaking attempts, she did, in due course, bring the honour back to the house-flag under which the diminutive *Britannia* had first crossed the Atlantic nearly a century before. The *Queen Mary* consolidated her position in August 1938 with crossings at 30.99 knots eastbound and 31.69 knots westbound, but in fact the two vessels were very evenly matched and the French Line made no further attempt to regain the Blue Riband before war began in September 1939.

To all intents and purposes, the race was over, since there was no longer any commercial benefit to be gained by higher speed which could be bought only at prohibitive cost, and which might reduce passage times at the most by a few hours. Commercial considerations notwithstanding, however, there was one record breaker still to come, namely the *United States* (1952-53), designed as a fast transport to meet US Navy Department requirements and sold on completion to United States Lines for the sum of £32 million, having cost an estimated £77 million to build. The *United States* took her first sailing from New York on 3 July 1952, and covered the 2,942 miles from the Ambrose light to Bishop's Rock in three days ten hours forty minutes at an average speed of 35.59 knots. She returned at 34.51 knots and thus made sure of the record for the foreseeable future.

Today, even the *United States* has been taken out of service and the North Atlantic ferry passenger is whisked by jet to New York without sight or sound of the sea. Occasional summer seasonal sailings are offered by Cunard, the French Line and Hapag-Lloyd (the Norddeutscher Lloyd and the Hamburg American Line having merged their interests) but few today can connect those names with the aura and public interest once generated by any reference to the Blue Riband of the North Atlantic.

Left: The 'Campania', a steel twin-screw vessel of 12,950 tons completed for the Cunard Line in 1893 and painted by R. H. Neville-Cumming in 1894. COLIN DENNY COLLECTION

The United States Navy

ON 16 November 1776, the United States brigantine-of-war *Andrew Doria* anchored off Fort Oranje, St Eustatius, in the Dutch West Indies, and for the first time a salute was fired to honour the American flag. At that time, early in the history of the independent United States, the flag was the Grand Union, which took the form of thirteen red and white horizontal stripes, with the British pre-1801 Union flag in the upper hoist.

The *Andrew Doria* herself was one of the first vessels of the Continental Navy, which was to prove itself such a thorn in Britain's side through the activities of such commanders as the redoubtable John Paul Jones. After the Peace of Versailles in September 1783, however, financial considerations led to the dispersal of the small US fleet; the last ship, the frigate *Alliance*, was sold out of service in 1785.

The United States remained neutral throughout the French Revolutionary War, but experience soon demonstrated that some naval force was a requirement for national safety. Consequently, in the 1790s, a programme was approved for the construction of a class of powerful frigates. Designed by Joshua Humphrey of Philadelphia, the first three vessels, the *United States*, *Constellation* and *Constitution*, mounted forty-four guns and were much more heavily built than their contemporaries in other navies.

In 1812 the United States went to war with Britain over the issues of impressment and the right of search by the British of American ships. Already overstretched, however, by the primary requirement to maintain a close blockade of continental Europe, the British Navy was able to spare few ships to meet new commitments and those vessels which did come up against the well-found American frigates were quickly overwhelmed. The British were not helped, either, by a general attitude of complacency, not only on the part of the public but also by commanders, who for many years had not experienced the kind of determined opposition mounted by the all-volunteer crews of US vessels. Two years of weary and sometimes bloody conflict, with both sides suffering inevitable reverses, showed that there could be no decisive victor. So, in December 1814, the two English-speaking nations thankfully accepted the honourable settlement worked out at Ghent.

The earlier post-war run-down of the US fleet was not repeated; throughout the following half-century, US warships were actively employed in operations against the Barbary States and Mexico, in the suppression of piracy in South American and Chinese waters, and in the suppression of the slave trade. Much police duty was shared with the Royal Navy and on many other occasions unofficial co-operation helped the work of both fleets.

The United States Navy was early in the adoption of steam propulsion. Its first steam warship was laid down in 1814 during the course of the war with Britain. Designed and built by Robert Fulton, the *Demologos* was intended for coastal defence and, with a single-cylinder engine driving a single paddle-wheel mounted centrally in a well, was good for a speed of five to six knots. Her paddle-wheel being thus effectively protected and with an armament of twenty 32-pounder guns, she would have been a formidable opponent for anyone attempting to mount an attack against New York by sea.

No other steam men-of-war were built until the 1830s and 1840s, when a number of paddle frigates and sloops joined the fleet, and, such vessels apart, the United States Navy, like its contemporaries under other flags, remained primarily a sailing navy. By 1859, however, the technological revolution was making itself felt to the extent that in addition to six ships of the line, eleven frigates and about twenty-five lesser sailing warships, there were seven screw frigates, eight screw sloops and eleven armed paddle steamers. By way of weapons, the ships were armed with shell guns of from eight to eleven inches calibre, with 68-pounder pivot-mounted guns firing solid shot or the older well-tried truck-mounted 32-pounders.

Apart from the protection of American overseas interests, the navy played an important part in the coastal defence of the United States. It was with the latter role in mind that the government was persuaded in 1861 to build a low-freeboard armoured turret ship to the designs of John Ericsson, a Swedish engineer. By that time, however, the Federal north was at war with the dissident Confederate States of the south, who had themselves ordered already the conversion of a cut-down wooden frigate into the armoured screw battery *Merrimac* mounting a mixed armament of smooth-bore 9-in and rifled 6-in and 7-in guns. The Federal turret ship *Monitor*, mounting a pair of 11-in Dahlgren guns in a revolving turret, was completed in February 1862. A few weeks later the two vessels met in Hampton Roads in an indecisive action which proved only that contemporary projectiles were of little use against iron armour.

The experience was sufficient, however, to convince the Federal Government that the monitor-type had a future, and orders were being placed for a number of coastal-defence turret ships during the Civil War. In 1864 that concept was taken a stage farther by John Ericsson in the design of the 6,000-ton sea-going monitors *Dictator* and *Puritan*. The single turret carried a pair of 15-in smooth-bore guns and was protected by fifteen inches of laminated iron armour. Unfortunately, the design was not as successful as it might have been because a draught greater than predicted resulted in reduced freeboard and speed.

Ericsson's seagoing monitor type was developed further after the Civil War, when the four vessels of the Miantonomoh class were built. Of composite wood and iron construction, the vessels proved successful within the design limitations of the monitor concept. In fact, the *Miantonomoh*, in the summer months of 1866, successfully undertook the double crossing of the Atlantic to test her sea-keeping qualities.

The monitors apart, the US Navy at the close of the Civil War comprised a number of wooden-hulled screw frigates and corvettes, various gunboats and a variety of mercantile auxiliaries. Funds for the maintenance of the navy were not forthcoming, however, for having settled its internal differences, the nation looked to westward expansion across the North American continent rather than to the sea. Such was the state of affairs in 1881 that the US Navy ranked twelfth among the world's maritime powers; it consisted of only one wooden screw frigate, a number of wooden screw sloops and four iron gunboats! There were about fourteen monitors, all laid up in various states of disrepair.

A committee appointed to enquire into the affairs of the navy came to the conclusion that orders should be placed immediately for thirty-eight unarmoured cruisers, and twenty-five torpedo boats of the Herreshoff type for harbour defence. Once again funds were not made available and the navy had to be content with a modest three protected cruisers, named *Chicago*, *Atalanta* and *Boston*, and the dispatch vessel *Dolphin*. In addition work was restarted on five monitors, nominal rebuilds of post-Civil War vessels, but it was to be ten years and more before all were commissioned.

The first battleship for the new Navy, the 6,300-ton *Texas*, was authorised in 1886. By that time, US resources were able to supply the necessary armour plate, although a design prepared by the Barrow Shipbuilding Co, of Barrow in Furness in England, was selected as being best suited to the requirement for a coastal defence ship. The *Texas* mounted a pair of 12-in guns, placed in echelon arrangement in single turrets; in service, the arrangement proved unsatisfactory and it was not repeated in later vessels.

The building of three seagoing coastline battleships, to be named *Indiana*, *Oregon* and *Massachusetts*, was authorised in 1890, and they were designed around a main armament of four 13-in guns arranged in twin mountings forward and aft. With a secondary battery of eight 8-in guns in twin turrets, in addition to four 6-in case-mate guns, the ships were considerably overgunned for their displacement of 10,250 tons, and their low freeboard made them very wet in all but the lightest weather.

Contemporary cruisers, as in other navies, were of the armoured and protected types; the former had a narrow belt of armour to shield their vitals and an arched armoured deck extending the length of the ship, while the protected cruiser was given only a light protective deck.

Like the battleships of the Indiana class, the armoured cruiser *New York* of 1891 suffered through her low freeboard making her very wet forward, but this defect in design was overcome in the *Brooklyn*, which followed in 1895, by the addition of a forecastle. The 22-knot vessel mounted eight 8-in guns on a displacement of 9,200 tons and possessed many features in common with French ships of her date. It was in the *Brooklyn* that the comparative merits of steam and electric turret machinery were evaluated, with the result that electric power was adopted generally in new construction for heavy-gun-mountings throughout the US Navy.

The make-up of the late nineteenth century war fleet was completed by the smaller torpedo craft and gunboats, though in the matter of torpedo boat design, the US Navy lagged far behind the navies of western Europe, Russia and Japan. The first such vessel, the 116-ton *Cushing*, had been completed as late as 1890. Thereafter, several boats of the type were built and when the United States went to war with Spain in 1898 the nation had available a small but modern balanced fleet which was to prove more than a match for the scattered Spanish maritime forces.

The fleet then included six coastal defence battleships, of which one, the 6,682-ton *Maine*, was destroyed in the incident in Havana Harbour which precipitated the war, two armoured cruisers, twelve smaller protected cruisers and ten torpedo boats. The half-dozen surviving monitors proved of little value and it was amply demonstrated during the course of the war that the heavily armed coastal defence battleship was no real substitute for the true ocean-going type. As a result, the United States turned to a blue-water naval policy in keeping with its post-war overseas commitments, which had been magnified by the newly acquired ex-Spanish territories.

The first battleships authorised as a result of the new policy were the five vessels of the 15,000-ton Virginia class, completed in 1906-07, which brought the US fleet into line with the pre-dreadnought navies of other nations. Like many of their contemporaries, they were given a main battery of four 12-in guns, but once again overgunning with a secondary battery of eight 8-in guns, in addition to twelve 6-in guns, impaired their stability and made them rather tender. In the Connecticut class which followed, however, the worst of such faults were overcome and the ships compared very favourably with those under other flags.

The United States Navy acquired its first submarine, USS *Holland* (SS1), from the builder J. P. Holland in 1900; it was thus early in the field with a relatively successful submersible. Thereafter, the Holland type was developed progressively until, in 1917, the US Navy became responsible for its own submarine design.

A feature which came to distinguish American heavy warships for several years first appeared in 1908-09, when the cage mast was substituted for the heavy military style, in the belief that such a structure would be more resistant to disabling action damage. In practice, however, the cage type of mast proved liable to whip, but it remained in use until the older battleships then in service were taken in hand for reconstruction in the 1920s and 1930s.

Meanwhile, battleship development in the US Navy kept pace with that in the Royal Navy and the construction of two vessels of the Dreadnought-type was authorised in 1905.

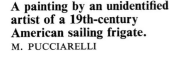

A painting by an unidentified artist of a 19th-century American sailing frigate.
M. PUCCIARELLI

Although smaller and considerably slower than the *Dreadnought* herself, the *South Carolina* and *Michigan* were significant in that they were the first to mount an all-big-gun main armament on the centreline, with the second and third turrets at sufficient height to enable their guns to fire over the first and fourth turrets. This layout of eight 12-in guns in four twin mountings permitted an eight-gun broadside, the same as that of HMS *Dreadnought*, and within a few years the so-called super-firing arrangement was adopted for all heavy warships.

The *North Dakota*, launched in 1908, was the first US battleship with steam turbines, but early difficulties in getting engine builders to meet the required specification for that type of machinery resulted in the retention of the reciprocating engine (two shafts) for a number of new ships. At a later date, problems associated with the manufacture of reduction gearing for the high powers involved led to the adoption of a turbo-electric drive on four shafts for the battleship *New Mexico* of 1919, and for the subsequent California and Colorado classes.

In the early years of the present century, the small cruiser force was greatly expanded by the construction of the ten armoured cruisers of the Pennsylvania and Tennessee classes, nine protected cruisers (Denver and St Louis classes) and three small unarmoured scout cruisers (Chester class). It was from one of the Chester class, USS *Birmingham*, that in 1910 the first successful shipboard aircraft launch was accomplished.

Unlike the British, German and Japanese navies, the US Navy for many years showed little interest in the battlecruiser concept of a lightly armoured fast battleship and not until 1916 were designs prepared for vessels of this type. In the event, the six ships of the Lexington class were not laid down until 1920-21 and construction was not very far advanced when work was suspended in 1922 as a result of the limitations imposed by the Washington Naval Treaty. The United States was permitted, however, to retain the hulls of the *Lexington* and *Saratoga* for subsequent completion as aircraft carriers.

The massive programme of naval and mercantile construction mounted by the United States after her declaration of war against the central powers in 1917 included no fewer than 272 destroyers, mostly of a four-funnel flush-deck design, and a large number of smaller anti-submarine vessels. Few were completed in time to see service in the war for which they had been intended, but a considerable number survived to play their part in a later war, including fifty of the destroyers which in 1940 were to be transferred to Britain for service with the Royal Navy.

Between the wars, the US fleet was cut back to the strength permitted by the Washington Naval Treaty of 1922, which allowed for parity in numbers of battleships with Britain. During the course of the conference, however, the United States had pressed for and secured an upper limit of 10,000 tons on the size of cruisers and agreement that the maximum calibre of their guns should be eight inches. The first two ships in that category were authorised by Congress in December 1924 and were launched about four years later as *Pensacola* and *Salt Lake City*. Armed with ten 8-in guns, they were better protected than the early vessels of the British County class, although they suffered from lack of freeboard in heavy weather.

Most other navies turned from the Washington Treaty heavy cruiser to the construction of smaller 6-in-gunned vessels in the late 1920s, but the US Navy continued to favour the 8-in-gunned type until the mid 1930s, when the Brooklyn class, armed with fifteen 6-in guns, was laid down in reply to the Japanese 6-in cruisers of the Mogami class. Thereafter, the delivery of both 8-in- and 6-in-gunned cruisers continued in parallel until after the end of the Second World War, when cruiser construction came to an end.

Destroyer construction was restarted in 1932 with the Farragut class mounting five 5-in guns and eight 21-in torpedo-tubes. By 7 December 1941, when Pearl Harbour was attacked by the Japanese, the US Navy had in commis-

Below: An American submarine in the Grand Harbour at Valetta, Malta. TOURIST PHOTO LIBRARY

Right: The aircraft carrier USS 'Constellation', one of America's great ships and the most recent in a long line of famous and proud 'Constellations'. DAILY TELEGRAPH COLOUR LIBRARY

sion 171 destroyers, of which all but seventy-one were of post-1914-18 design.

It was realised that any future war would probably involve the United States Navy in long-range operations in the Pacific; consequently, efforts were directed to the build-up of a fleet capable of operating well away from fixed forward bases. Techniques for refuelling at sea were perfected, the uses of carrier-borne air power in strike and defensive roles were exploited and practised, and the concept of a fleet train was developed to provide the combatant fleet with the necessary logistic support.

The assault on Pearl Harbour crippled the US Pacific Fleet, but by then, once again, a vast emergency war construction programme was under way and the losses were soon made good by the commissioning of new and rebuilt ships. By virtue of the nation-wide shipbuilding effort, the US Navy had in commission in 1945 the largest fleet the world had ever seen, in addition to which a considerable number of ships had been made available under Lend-Lease arrangements for service with the British and Russian navies.

The United States fleet today retains its premier position among the world's navies, but the battleships have gone. Or almost, for USS *New Jersey* of 1943 (59,000 tons) was recommissioned in April 1968 for a brief tour of duty off the coast of Vietnam, during which she provided the army with gunfire support. The striking power of the fleet is now centred upon fourteen attack carriers, including the nuclear-powered *Enterprise* of 1961 (89,600 tons), while the strategic deterrent is deployed by about forty-one fleet ballistic-missile submarines. Many ships of Second World War design still feature in the US Navy List, but with the war in Vietnam at an end it is only to be expected that the majority will be relegated to the reserve fleet.

By 1980, the active combatant surface fleet will be reduced to about 110 ships but, on the other hand, the majority will be of new advanced design. In the absence of any further commitment to an intervention of the scale of the involvement in Vietnam, such a fleet should be fully capable of looking after the interests of the United States when and wherever the occasion demands.

Pearl Harbour

THE self-congratulation with which the Japanese greeted their notorious strike of 7 December 1941 at the American fleet in Pearl Harbour was soured in the mind of its architect, Admiral Isoroku Yamamoto. His comment on the 110-minute attack which pitchforked the United States into the Second World War was a gloomily prophetic one; 'I fear all we have done is to awaken a sleeping giant and fill him with a terrible resolve', he said.

About ninety years before, in far less obvious circumstances, the Americans had done much the same for the Japanese. In July 1853, when Commodore Matthew Galbraith Perry steamed into Sagami Bay with a demand from the American President Fillmore that Japan open her ports to world trade, he was intruding on a society that had been petrified in ancient ways for over two hundred years. Ever since 1638, when an imperial decree isolated Japan from the outside world, the country had remained aloof from foreign books, foreign science, foreign religion and foreign ideas. While the world outside advanced into the industrial and imperialistic age, the Japanese were perpetuating a feudal state in which divinity belonged to the emperor and power and privilege to the shogun (warlord) and the samurai

warrior caste; unquestioning instant obedience was the lot of peasantry. Educated Japanese, however, realised that unless the shogun could be persuaded to accede to the American request, Japan might face the same humiliating fate that had recently overtaken neighbouring China.

China had been dragged out of isolation by the British and the French after the Opium War of 1839-1842, whereby the Chinese emperor had been obliged to open ports for trade, cede territory and grant to foreign nationals privileges that placed them beyond imperial control. Fortunately for Japan, the shogun proved susceptible to reason; rather than give Westerners a similar chance for exploitation, he concluded trading treaties with the United States, Britain, Russia and Holland between 1854 and 1856.

However, the conversion that began in this rather negative fashion soon acquired a driving zeal. During the forty-five-year reign of the progressive Emperor Meiji (1867-1912), a wholesale graft of Western ways transformed Japan from a medieval to a modern state, and did so in a tenth of the time the same process had taken in Europe. By 1899, railways, factories, electric power, telephones and the cinema had been introduced into a land which, half a century before,

Complete MARKETS

THE CHICAGO DAILY NEWS

66TH YEAR—288. MONDAY. DECEMBER 8, 1941—THIRTY-FOUR PAGES. Telephone DEArborn 1111 ★ THREE CENTS

JAP PLANES RAID MANILA!
CONGRESS DECLARES WAR

Left: A painting by Norman Wilkinson of the action at Pearl Harbour. NATIONAL MARITIME MUSEUM, LONDON

Above: Headlines from 'The Chicago Daily News' which confirmed Admiral Yamamoto's 'I fear all we have done is to awaken a sleeping giant and fill him with a terrible resolve'. JOHN FROST HISTORICAL NEWSPAPER SERVICE

had no steam engine, no industry and no telegraph.

By 1890, local government elections, a modern system of education, a cabinet of ministers and a parliament had been given to people who for generations had known nothing but the rule of feudal samurai overlords. By 1896, the Japanese were operating steamships on international routes, and possessed a navy of disciplined efficiency trained by the British. Yet, until 1853, Japan had been forbidden to build ocean-going vessels, and few of its people had ever seen a craft larger than a fifty-foot junk.

The enthusiasm with which the Japanese accepted the great revolution was as remarkable as the quickness they displayed in grasping so much that was so strange in so short a time. However, the very speed of the change was its weakness. What Japan acquired was not modernity, but the gloss of modernity; beneath it, all the despotism, innate violence, mindless obedience and impenetrable arrogance of old samurai ways were still dangerously alive.

Under the influence of such ways, it soon became all too obvious that the Japanese wanted to emulate the West in more than its outward trappings. They had cast their country in a Western-type role as a world power, a role they intended to play in violent style. By 1915, through war, forcible annexation, doubtful diplomacy and barefaced bullying, the Japanese had acquired Korea, Formosa, the Pescadores Islands and a decisive influence in the Chinese province of Manchuria. During that period, the Japanese set a precedent for Pearl Harbour by the attack on Port Arthur in 1904 before a declaration of war.

The significance of all those events was not lost on the United States. The nation Commodore Perry had roused from medieval slumber was turning out to be a marauding tiger, and, in response, the Americans, with the British, attempted after the First World War to confine the upstart beast to its own part of the forest.

Conveniently for Anglo-American plans, Japan was ruled during the 1920s by liberally minded men. It was they who agreed to a ratio of three ships for Japan to five each for the USA and Britain, and also signed treaties binding themselves to respect the integrity of China and the status quo in the Pacific.

However, not all Westerners were blinded by the naive post-war belief that aggression could be signed out of existence, or exorcised with good intentions. The possibility of warlike moves by Japan in the Pacific was acknowledged as early as 1924, when the Americans formulated the Orange Plan as a counter-measure, and Brigadier-General William

Mitchell, of the US Army Air Corps, spread the portentous notion that Oahu, the Hawaiian island on which Pearl Harbour stands, was 'an easy, compact and convenient object for air attack'. Mitchell's views were endorsed in the 1930s by several American service chiefs who, by that time, had dire proof that liberalism in Japan was a frail and ephemeral flower.

In Japan, as in Nazi Germany, the poverty, despair and anger that resulted from the Great Depression snuffed out moderate democratic politics and replaced them with ferocious militarism. The samurai spirit which surged once more to the surface led the Japanese into what they now call *kurai tanima* (the dark valley). Its way to war was marked by bombing and slaughter in China, by Japanese withdrawal in 1933 from the League of Nations, by their pacts of 1936 and 1940 with Nazi Germany and Fascist Italy and, most dangerously of all, by the grand ambitious concept of the Great South-East Asia Co-Prosperity Sphere.

The establishment of the co-prosperity sphere, which entailed virtual domination by Japan of the Pacific area and its resources, received a sharp setback in mid-1941, when the United States, Britain and Holland responded to the Japanese occupation of Indo-China by freezing Japanese assets. The Americans, who had opposed Japan's aggression in China from the first, also cut off oil supplies and banned the export of war materials. Of all the sanctions, the ban on oil was the most serious, for Japan's own stocks were limited.

Prince Konoye, the Japanese Prime Minister, was willing to withdraw from China and Indo-China in order to get the ban lifted, but he was stopped and, in October 1941, forced to resign, by his War Minister, General Hideki Tojo. Concession, even for the sake of short-term expediency, was utterly foreign to Tojo. For him, the co-prosperity sphere was as much a sacred mission as a military objective.

Tojo was, in any case, determined on war. Although he sent two negotiators to Washington in mid-November, it was with the private proviso that unless agreement was reached by 29 November hostilities would be started. Preparations for offensive action began even before ambassadors Kichisaburo Nomura and Saburo Kurusu left Japan. A war fleet was already massing in the Kurile Islands to the north of Japan before the two of them walked through the front door of the State Department.

Admiral Isoroku Yamamoto, Commander-in-Chief of the Japanese Combined Fleet, placed neither faith nor hope in their negotiations. He was convinced that, despite their current isolationist mood, the Americans were bound to enter the war sooner or later. Accordingly, since January 1941, Yamamoto had been working on a plan to prevent the American fleet based at Pearl Harbour from hampering Japanese conquest of the Pacific. The prime virtue of the plan was that it made possible a surprise blow as well as a decisive one, and dispensed with a formal declaration of war and the risks delay might involve.

Pearl Harbour, situated on the south coast of Oahu, was

the perfect site for punching the Americans out of the Pacific. The fleet they had stationed there since April 1940 consisted of nearly a hundred vessels, including eight battleships, two aircraft carriers, and over sixty cruisers and destroyers. Equally tempting targets were Oahu's well-stocked Army, Navy and Marine airfields.

Apart from the fact that this treasure-house of naval power was so conveniently concentrated in one place, the Japanese possessed an advantage that was unknown even to them. It was a widespread sense of euphoria among Pearl Harbour personnel, which bred what an American admiral later called 'an unwarranted feeling of immunity from attack'. The mood even pervaded the thinking of naval and military chiefs at Pearl Harbour – Admiral Husband E. Kimmel, Commander-in-Chief of the US Pacific Fleet, and Lieutenant-General Walter C. Short, Commanding General of the Hawaiian Department.

The mood persisted despite a regular flow of warnings from Washington since the spring of 1941. As time progressed, the tone of the warnings rose in urgency from advice in April to be wary at weekends, to information in August that an attacking force of Japanese carriers could approach

Pacific. On 26 November, a Japanese task force of thirty vessels, including six aircraft carriers, had left the remote fog-wrapped Kurile Islands. Blacked out, observing strict radio silence and keeping well away from the regular shipping lanes, the task force sailed towards its attack position off Oahu, 3,000 miles away.

On 2 December, the task force commander, Vice-Admiral Chiuchi Nagumo, received from Yamamoto the signal 'Niitaka Yama Nobore' (Climb Mount Niitaka); it told Nagumo that negotiations had broken down in Washington, and that the Pearl Harbour strike was to proceed. Nagumo's carriers and their escorts reached the attack position, two hundred miles north of Pearl Harbour, on the dark stormy night of 6-7 December.

There they lurked while five midget submarines were launched by Japanese submarines scouting the entrance to Pearl Harbour. Between 03.42 and 06.30, an American minesweeper, a destroyer and a naval Catalina flying-boat detected between them two of the midgets as they tried to slip into the harbour. The first midget escaped, and its presence was not reported to the authorities ashore. The second was attacked with guns, depth charges and bombs, but by the

Hawaii from the north-west, to clear statements in October and November that war could be imminent. The statements, formulated in the light of growing suspicions that Nomura and Kurusu were merely playing at negotiations in Washington, evoked only a low-key response from Kimmel and Short.

On 28 November, Kimmel ordered the Pacific Fleet into a state of Number Three readiness, the Navy's lowest. It meant in practice that one in every three machine-guns was manned, with the key to the locked ammunition boxes retained by the officer of the deck. No move was made to man the main batteries, or the ammunition supplies, or the plotting rooms.

On the Army side, Short ordered six mobile radar sets to scan round Oahu between 04.00 and 07.00, the most likely period for an attack by carrier-borne aircraft. However, he failed to man or supply the anti-aircraft guns, despite the fact that defence of the naval base was an army responsibility. Both Kimmel and Short arranged for their aircraft to be placed in parade-ground rows on the airfields, virtually wing-tip to wing-tip, on the premise that it was the best way to preserve them from sabotage.

It was also, of course, the best way to ensure their mass destruction from the air and, by that time, the instrument of that destruction was already on its furtive way across the

time reports of the incident had struggled through the decoding and relaying processes, it was already 07.30 before Admiral Kimmel learned of it. No one thought to inform Lieutenant-General Short and the Army.

Short's ignorance was just as complete – and in this case, so was Kimmel's – about an urgent message dispatched from Washington at 06.30. 'The Japanese are presenting at 01.00 Eastern Standard time (07.30 in Hawaii) what amounts to an ultimatum,' signalled General George C. Marshall, Chief of Staff of the US Army. 'Just what significance the hour set may have, we do not know, but be on the alert accordingly.'

Marshall's message, which went undelivered for seven hours, arrived in Hawaii at 07.30, at almost the precise moment when an Army lieutenant was throwing away the Americans' very last chance to realise that something sinister was about to happen at Pearl Harbour.

At 07.02, an Army private on practice duty had spotted on radar a massive plot of aircraft about 137 miles north of Oahu. The Army lieutenant, the only officer available at the time, dismissed the sighting as a flight of American B-17s due to arrive from California that morning. The private followed the progress of the aircraft until they disappeared behind some hills at a distance of twenty-two miles and the radar screen blacked out.

The aircraft – 185 Japanese torpedo-bombers, dive-bombers and fighters launched at dawn from the decks of Nagumo's carriers – swept across those twenty-two miles in a few minutes and at 07.55 roared in over a sleepy Sunday morning scene of almost total unpreparedness. Lieutenant-Commander Mitsuo Fuchida, leader of the squadrons, radioed back to Nagumo the triumphant message: *Tora! Tora! Tora!* (Tiger! Tiger! Tiger!). It signified that complete surprise had been accomplished.

The Japanese Val dive-bombers were at that time poised at attack height, and within seconds, they were tearing down through the sunlit sky towards the neat rows of aircraft lined up on the ground. Explosions shuddered through the earth, spiced with the screams of dying and injured men, and the sinister crackle of leaping fire. As more and more bombs plunged down among the American aircraft, survivors pelted for shelter, coughing and choking in the clouds of acrid smoke that funnelled up into the sky. The dive-bombers banked away, leaving the stage momentarily free for the Japanese Zeke fighters to rake over the scene of burning ruin with round after round of machine-gun fire.

While the attack on the airfields continued, Kate torpedo-

For the loss of twenty-nine aircraft, a hundred airmen and five midget submarines, the Japanese had sunk four American battleships and a minelayer, badly damaged four more battleships, three light cruisers, three destroyers and a repair ship, destroyed ninety-two Navy and ninety-six Army aircraft, practically laid waste the airfields and shore installations and killed or injured more than 3,500 people.

The humiliation for the Americans was real and very painful. But elation among the Japanese was not justified, for they had made serious errors and miscalculations. Amid the wild orgy of destruction, their attack had left untouched Pearl Harbour's superlative ship repair and maintenance yards, as well as its copious stores of oil. Also, the Japanese had attacked at a time when the aircraft carriers of the Pacific Fleet were absent, as were eleven cruisers and eleven destroyers. With the five cruisers and twenty-nine destroyers which escaped serious damage in the raid, it still added up to a formidable fleet, and one equipped to evolve into the sort of force required by the naval warfare of the immediate future – warfare no longer fought by battleships but by carrier-borne aircraft. If the Japanese had failed to administer the knock-out blow they had planned, they had also failed

Far left: A direct hit at Pearl Harbour from the film 'Tora! Tora! Tora!' BY COURTESY OF FOX RANK

Left: Fire aboard ship in the film 'Tora! Tora! Tora!' BY COURTESY OF FOX RANK

Above: The protected remnants of USS 'Arizona', part of the memorial at Pearl Harbour. D. J. KINGSTON

bombers swooped in shallow dives towards the long sweep of American vessels moored in 'Battleship Row'. Their torpedoes, specially equipped with stabilisers to make sure they did not sink harmlessly in the shallow water, splashed below the surface and began slicing their way towards their targets.

Five battleships split open with an awesome rending of tortured metal as torpedoes slammed into them. One, the 32,000-ton *Arizona*, blew up in a mass of searing fragments when a Japanese armour-piercing shell penetrated her forward magazine; *Arizona* sank, with over one thousand men sealed inescapably below her decks. Two more Japanese shells ignited ammunition inside another battleship, the 32,300-ton *California*, and tore apart her bow plates. A third battleship, the 31,500-ton *West Virginia*, swallowed in raging fire, sank and settled on the harbour bottom.

The Japanese attack was by then half an hour old, and the Navy's anti-aircraft and other guns were pounding back in fierce defence. Five torpedo-bombers and several dive-bombers plummeted into the harbour, and more were shot out of the sky when the second wave of Japanese aircraft began their attack at 08.40. For another sixty-five minutes, the Japanese bombed and strafed the docks, the harbour and the airfields, finally leaving the scene of mangled vessels, smashed aircraft, wrecked buildings, fire, smoke and slaughter at 09.45.

correctly to interpret the reaction to it. In the arrogant manner of autocrats, they had concluded that the freedom and tolerance of democracy denoted weakness in those who lived under that particular form of government. American reaction to Japanese perfidy soon showed how wrong they were, and General Tojo's ambassadors in Washington were among the first to have their ears blistered with the lesson.

At 14.22 on 7 December, eighteen minutes before the Pearl Harbour attack ended, Nomura and Kurusu delivered their peace negotiation reply to Cordell Hull, the American Secretary of State. Hull, well aware of what had happened, unleashed on them a tirade of fury and bitterness. 'In all my fifty years of public service,' he declared, 'I have never seen a document more crowded with infamous falsehoods and distortions – on a scale so high that I never imagined until today that any government on this planet was capable of uttering them.'

They were not the fulminations of a diplomat embarrassed and enraged to find out he had been fooled. Hull's sentiments became those of the American nation as a whole. The attack on Pearl Harbour not only catapulted the United States out of the smug belief that the war was none of their business. As Isoruku Yamamoto had feared, it filled Americans with an irresistible resolve to avenge the day which President Roosevelt had declared would 'live in infamy'.

The Standard Ship

AFTER the outbreak of war in 1914, apart from the completion of those vessels already fitting out afloat, merchant ship construction came practically to a halt for a time, so that shipbuilding capacity could be concentrated upon essential naval work. But by the end of 1915 more than one and a half million gross tons of British-flag shipping had gone to the bottom or had been otherwise lost. Early in the following year the Board of Trade, aware that the situation was rapidly becoming critical, advised the government of the pressing need for increased replacement tonnage.

However, not until the very steep rise in losses to more than a quarter of a million tons in the third quarter of 1916 were any positive steps taken. Losses in that fateful three months totalled 617,563 gross tons and in December provision was made for the appointment of a shipping controller with wide powers to expedite the supply of merchant ship tonnage. It was decided that a programme should be put in hand to build ships of a simple standard type which would take priority over all construction work then in hand to meet the piecemeal requirements for replacement tonnage under contracts placed by individual shipowners.

The first designs prepared were for 5,030grt 11-knot general cargo carriers of the single-decked A type and the two-decked B type. The lead shipbuilder for both types was D. & W. Henderson of Glasgow; in all, more than 200 were built in British yards, about two-thirds of them going to commercial buyers after hostilities had rumbled to a halt in November 1918. All were allocated *War——* names, although in many cases the vessels were launched after the Armistice under names chosen by their purchasers. The first to be completed for sea was the A-type tramp *War Shamrock* which entered service in August 1917, about seven months after being laid down at Belfast by Harland & Wolff. Like other wartime deliveries, the *War Shamrock* was given a low silhouette in order to present the minimum target to lurking submarines, but that apart she was a conventional single-screw three-island tramp with a 2,500ihp triple-expansion engine.

In addition to those built in United Kingdom shipyards, nine B-type steamers were built in Hong Kong for British Government account. At the same time, in view of the acute shortage of tanker tonnage and the increasing demand for liquid fuel, a number of hulls of A and B types were fitted with cylindrical tanks in their holds and completed as 6,500-ton (deadweight) tankers. In all, twenty-five of the AO and BO conversions were completed before the war ended.

After the A and B types, a smaller version called the C type was introduced. It was a single-decker of 3,000 gross tons intended primarily for the shipment of coal or iron ore; more than eighty such vessels were built. Other designs were tailored to suit building berths of restricted dimensions and included the D type, a 2,300-ton (gross) collier sponsored by S. P. Austin of Sunderland. A different approach was adopted in the design of the N (National) type, which was a single-screw geared turbine vessel of 6,500 tons erected from prefabricated parts prepared by inland constructional engineering firms. The frames were straight and the shell plating was flat wherever possible in order to simplify fabrication, and turbines were chosen because they could be easily transported from inland engine builders where

capacity was currently under-employed. Mention should be made also of the fast (13-knot) vessels of the 8,000-ton (gross) G type, intended to make good losses of refrigerated meat carriers, but only one, the *War Icarus*, was complete at the time of the armistice.

The AO and BO conversions were followed by the Z-type tanker, which was of similar dimensions but designed as a tanker from the outset, with conventional cargo tanks and a central expansion trunk above the weather deck. In all, thirty-four of the type were built, of which a dozen were taken up by the Royal Fleet Auxiliary for service as fleet oilers. Others were transferred to the Admiralty in 1921 and the last surviving units, the *War Hindoo* and *War Afridi*, were not sold for breaking up until 1958, having served for some years as storage hulks at Malta and Hong Kong respectively.

Excluding coasters, about 550 standard steamers of British design were ordered for government account from ship-yards in Britain, Hong Kong and China (Shanghai); of the 500 or so actually completed for service, about 430 were still afloat in 1939. Of those vessels, serving under many flags, nearly 300 were to become the victims of another war in which once again the desperate need for replacement tonnage was to be met by a far-ranging programme of standard ship construction.

Despite the fact that construction during the First World War was only just into full stride when hostilities came to an end, certain shipbuilders achieved notable records in building times. In particular, Harland & Wolff completed the B-type *War Snake* at Belfast in twenty-three weeks from laying down, while Workman Clark & Co engined and fitted out the *War Beetle* in three and three-quarter days from her launch! It was not only in Britain that extensive programmes of standard ship construction were mounted during the earlier war; in Canada, Japan and the United States government-sponsored shipbuilding schemes were put in hand in support of the allied cause. Of particular interest were the American-designed Hog Islanders – 5,000-ton two-decked cargo vessels built by the American International Shipbuilding Co in a shipyard laid out for the purpose at Hog Island, Pennsylvania.

As with the British N type, it was intended that frame sections and plating should be produced by inland firms and, in order to simplify fabrication and assembly, curves were eliminated wherever possible. In keeping with American industrial practice, the principle of mass production was utilised to the maximum extent, with plates, frames and beams cut and jig-drilled in batches. Completely devoid of sheer and lacking grace, the vessels appeared 'hogged', so the choice of the building site seems to have been peculiarly apt. Nevertheless, for their task they were completely satisfactory and with double-reduction geared turbines of 2,500-shp, they were capable of about twelve knots.

Once again, the war was over before the construction programme could make any impact, the first vessel not being launched until well into 1919. Of a total of 110 Hog Islanders built, about thirty were lost during the Second World War, three of them under the British flag as the *Empire Hawk*, *Empire Mahseer* and *Empire Barracuda*. Like the War-class ships, the Hog Islanders made their main contribution to Allied victory in a later war than that for which they had been designed.

When the Second World War began, the British Government assumed control of all United Kingdom shipbuilding activity. In the early days, orders for new construction called for ships based, albeit somewhat austerely, upon individual shipbuilders' available designs. In the case of some specialist vessels, such as refrigerated meat carriers, that policy was maintained throughout the war. However, in the matter of the design for a standard 7,000-ton (gross) tramp, ideas soon crystallised into a requirement for two versions, both about 432 feet between perpendiculars and of eleven knots service speed, with different propelling machinery. The X type had diesel engines and the Y type was fitted with Scotch boilers and a conventional triple-expansion engine.

The X- and Y-type ships were built in various yards and, once again, a standard form of nomenclature was adopted, with the word Empire in every name. It was a style which was to be employed for the majority of merchant vessels built in the United Kingdom or otherwise acquired for British Government account, and to ex-enemy craft, throughout the war and for several years thereafter.

In 1940 a design was drawn up for a standard cargo ship of prefabricated construction, 431 feet long between perpendiculars and of about 7,050 tons gross. Called the PF(A) type, the design was modified before any had been built by breaking down the units in order to facilitate handling in smaller shipyards. It then became the PF(B) type, of which the first keel was laid in 1941. Once again the machinery was triple-expansion steam and forty-one vessels of the type were completed.

Of greater historical importance, however, was the 7,157-ton standard emergency tramp *Empire Liberty* designed, and completed in October 1941, by J. L. Thompson & Sons of Sunderland. It was intended to be a simplified version of the 11-knot cargo ship *Dorrington Court* built by Thompson's for the Court Line in 1939. In September 1940 copies of the plans were taken to the United States by a British Merchant Shipbuilding Mission in the full knowledge that ships were being sunk faster than they could be built in Britain, and that in America, with its capacity for expansion, lay the only possible answer.

Although the then limited facilities in the United States were found to be fully bought up, successful negotiations with a syndicate formed by the Todd Shipbuilding Corporation and Henry J. Kaiser led to the construction of new shipyards. They were near Richmond, California (later Todd-California) and at Portland, Maine (later Todd-Bath) and orders for the construction of thirty vessels were placed at each site. Lack of the appropriate skills for riveted construction necessitated a welded hull but in the event work went ahead so fast that the first keel was laid at Richmond on 14 April 1941. The vessel was launched as *Ocean Vanguard* on 16 August and was delivered in October 1941.

As in the British prototype, the single screw was driven by a 2,500ihp triple-expansion engine designed by the North Eastern Marine Engineering Co of Wallsend-on-Tyne. Once again the Scotch boilers were coal fired, since UK supplies of coal were more readily assured than supplies of imported fuel oil. The *Ocean Liberty* followed from the Portland shipyard a few months later and by November 1942 all sixty Oceans had been delivered.

After satisfactory conclusion of the American negotiations, the British Mission visited Canada where, as in the United States, the inter-war shipbuilding capacity had been extremely limited. Once again the mission achieved its aim and in January 1941 contracts were signed for the construction of twenty vessels (increased shortly afterwards to twenty-six) of the same Empire Liberty (North Sands) type from which the Oceans had been evolved. In that case, however, the hulls were ninety per cent riveted, resulting in a somewhat longer construction time than had been the case with the US-built vessels. The first ship, the *Fort St James*, was laid down by the Burrard Dry Dock Co of Vancouver on 23 April 1941,

Top: A Liberty ship in a North Atlantic gale; a painting by L. Dunn.

Above centre: The 1944 Liberty ship 'Aurora', formerly 'Eldy Alfaro', at London in 1965.   L. DUNN

Above: A Liberty ship of the Second World War in New York Harbour.   L. DUNN

nine days after her counterpart *Ocean Vanguard*, and was completed in January 1942.

In April 1941 an agreement was signed leading to the construction of a further ninety North Sands tramps in Canada on behalf of the United States Maritime Commission,

by whom they were transferred to Britain on bareboat charter as part of the wartime Lend-Lease arrangements. Those vessels were all given names beginning *Fort*. Still more Forts were ordered on behalf of the Canadian Government, some to a modified Victory design with two oil-fired water-tube boilers instead of the three coal-fired Scotch boilers of the North Sands ships. Difficulties over the supply of fuel oil in the United Kingdom led, however, to the building of a third version, called the Canadian type, which were equipped with Scotch boilers arranged for alternative coal or oil firing.

In 1942 the Canadian Government formed the Park Steamship Co to operate war-built tonnage on its behalf. The ships concerned all bore —— *Park* names and of the 176 built for Canadian-flag operation, 114 dry-cargo vessels were of the North Sands, Victory and Canadian types. In all, about 331 Forts and Parks of those three types were built, including twelve adapted for service as stores-issuing ships for the British Pacific Fleet Train. Like the Oceans, all were driven by the standard 2,500ihp three-cylinder triple-expansion engine, which was manufactured in Canada and the United States by seventeen engine builders.

All parts were made to jigs so as to be fully interchangeable, as indeed were the engines themselves. At one stage, Canadian engine production so outstripped hull construction that twenty-three engines were turned over to the US Maritime Commission for fitting into US-built hulls. They were replaced in due course for installation in Canadian hulls by engines of American manufacture.

The United States Maritime Commission had been established in 1936 as one of a series of measures aimed at arresting the decline of the ageing US-flag merchant fleet. Plans were drawn up for a range of standard 16-knot turbine-engined cargo ships of rather sophisticated design which could be adapted to the needs of individual operators. However, in spite of the fact that in August 1940 the rate of construction was boosted to 200 hulls a year, it was obvious that that number was going to make little impact if and when the United States became involved in the European war. In September 1940, however, the British Merchant Shipbuilding Mission put its case to the United States and from that time on, the American nation was more or less committed to the Allied cause, short of a declaration of war.

A change in shipbuilding policy followed in January 1941, when an emergency construction programme was first proposed, but much argument ensued before a decision was taken to adopt the slow but well-proven British Empire Liberty design. Thus, in February, President Roosevelt announced an initial 200-ship order as part of an emergency programme which was eventually to make a major contribution to the defeat of the Berlin-Rome-Tokyo axis. The Liberty ship, as the type became known, was a simplified version of the British vessel, adapted to permit the maximum use of welding and prefabrication techniques.

One change was the rearrangement of the crew accommodation in a single amidships deckhouse, which could be built as a unit and shipped complete with all plumbing, wiring and steam heating ready for connection to the ship's systems. Thus the basic hull shell was simplified, and formed of the forward and after cargo spaces separated by the machinery spaces, fuel bunkers and store rooms. The same 2,500ihp triple-expansion engine was retained but, as in the Canadian-built Victory type, steam was generated in a pair of oil-fired water-tube boilers.

The Liberty ships were of a standard 7,176 gross tons and, like their forebears, were capable of a steady eleven knots at sea. Admittedly, the extensive use of welding brought difficulties, particularly in the application of such techniques to a design that had originally involved a riveted structure. The use of inexperienced labour and a lack of understanding of the stresses induced in the fabric by welding only served to aggravate the resultant problems. They were highlighted by a series of structural failures, particularly among vessels serving in the sub-zero temperatures of the Arctic winter. There were indeed instances of ships breaking in two and propellers lost through fractured tailshafts. However, the overall design was sound and many Libertys stood up to tremendous punishment from mine, torpedo and aerial bombing, or became marine casualties, yet survived.

The first keel was laid by Bethlehem-Fairfield at Baltimore in April 1941 and the vessel was launched as *Patrick Henry* on 27 September, the day nominated subsequently by Admiral Emory Land, chairman of the US Maritime Commission, as Liberty Fleet Day. The *Patrick Henry* was completed for sea in 245 days but fifty ships later the same shipyard was able to complete a Liberty ship in fifty-eight days, fifty-one on the slip and seven fitting out afloat. In September 1942 the *Joseph N. Teal* was launched after only ten days on the slip and was completed for sea five days later. In November of that year the *Robert E. Peary* was launched at Richmond, California, only four days fifteen and a half hours after the first section had been placed in position on the slipway!

The grand total of Liberty ships completed reached more than 2,700 and today, thirty years later, some are still trading as tramps under Eastern-bloc and other flags.

Supplementing the Liberty, to meet the need for a faster (15½-knot) vessel, the 7,650-ton turbine-engined Victory ship

was developed and no fewer than 531 were completed in 1944 and 1945.

After the war, the Empires, Oceans, Forts, Parks and the bulk of the Liberty and Victory ships were sold out to help make good losses among the world's shipping lines. For the next twenty-five years they served their various owners well, being transferred as the years went by to convenience-flag fleets, until finally they made their way to breakers in Spain, Hong Kong or Taiwan. Thus, in the 1960s the need grew for a Liberty ship replacement, relatively low in initial cost and economical in operation. Several shipbuilders marketed designs for general traders in the 10,000- to 15,000-ton (deadweight) class.

Of the wide choice offered, only the British SD14 (shelterdeck 14,000dwt) designed by Austin & Pickersgill Ltd of Sunderland, and the joint G. T. Campbell/Ishikawajima-Harima Heavy Industries venture – the Freedom ship – have achieved sales running into three figures. The 14-15 knot Sulzer oil-engined SD14 cargo vessel first appeared in 1966. It has since been built not only on the Wear but also by Hellenic Shipyards at Skaramanga in Greece and by the Companhia Comercio e Navegacao of Rio de Janiero. Currently the last-named shipyard has orders booked for twenty-one SD14s and one is being launched every seven weeks.

Like the SD14, the Canadian-designed Japanese Freedom type first appeared in 1966 and is offered with various powers of engine for speeds of fourteen to fifteen knots to suit the requirements of individual owners. In addition to the vessels built by IHI in Japan, the Freedom type has been constructed by Astilleros de Cadiz in Spain. To date, however, the SD14 retains a slight edge in numbers sold around the world.

It was estimated that a potential market existed for about 500 relatively inexpensive standard cargo vessels in that class. To date nearly 300 SD14s and Freedoms have been built or are on order to help satisfy the demand for replacement tonnage. In the foreseeable future, ships of that size and speed will be required to serve the smaller ports away from the main ocean traffic routes and it is to be expected that only the economical standard vessel will be capable of fulfilling such a need with any prospect of profitable operation.

Left: An American Liberty ship unloads a P38 Lightning fighter aircraft for use by the US Army.
IMPERIAL WAR MUSEUM, LONDON

Below: The 'City of Colchester', built in 1944 as the Liberty ship 'Samlea', under the Ellerman flag in 1950.
L. DUNN COLLECTION

The Submarine

IN 1888, a Spanish naval officer, Isaac Peral, built the first electrically powered submarine. France quickly developed this idea too, and in the same year launched *Gymnote*, a 60-foot cigar-shaped submarine driven by an electric motor supplied with a current from 564 lead-acid accumulators. The submarine proved sufficiently successful for a much larger submarine, named *Gustav Zédé* in honour of its designer, to be ordered in 1890. Design followed design, and by the beginning of the twentieth century, the French had an unchallenged lead in submarine development.

The United States was the only other country to show anything like the same enthusiasm and in 1893 organised a submarine design competition. The winner of this competition was an Irish-American, John P. Holland. Holland's ideas survived a disastrous attempt by the Americans to alter his design, and he eventually built a second boat at his own expense. This one was bought immediately, and in 1901 the British Government bought the rights to build Holland-designed submarines.

With three of the world's major navies now firmly committed to the submarine, progress was rapid. The Holland designs proved that their idea of separate propulsion for working above and below water was preferable to the French idea of all-electric propulsion. This led to an improvement in engine design, first with the heavy oil engine using paraffin, and finally with the diesel motor, which was the most economical. The first diesel-engined submarine was the French *Aigrette*, launched in 1904, followed by the Russian *Minoga*, but the British, Americans and Germans were more conservative, the latter not introducing diesel-engined submarines until 1912.

By August 1914, there were over 270 submarines in service with various navies, as shown in the table.

Distribution of submarines in navies in August 1914

	Boats in service	Boats building
Austria	6	6
France	45	25
Germany	29	—
Britain	77	—
Italy	18	2
Denmark	7	2
Greece	2	—
Holland	7	4
Japan	13	13
Norway	4	—
Peru	2	—
Portugal	1	—
Russia	28	2
Sweden	5	—
USA	35	6

Between 1914 and 1918 the submarine not only developed into a reliable and efficient type of warship, but also became a deadly weapon which caused millions of pounds' worth of damage and almost brought Great Britain to starvation and collapse. In the early stages of the war, warships proved easy targets for German U-boats but later they became less vulnerable when protected by an escort of destroyers. The declaration of a war zone around the British Isles in February 1915 allowed U-boats freedom to sink any merchantman on sight, and their power was quickly demonstrated. Losses rose from a total of 48,000 tons in January 1915 to a peak of 185,000 tons in August.

At this point the U-boats were ordered to restrict their attacks to transport and cargo-carrying vessels, and unrestricted warfare was not resumed until April 1917, when shipping losses rose to new levels (888,000 tons). On 5 April, the United States declared war on Germany and put her entire resources at the disposal of the Allies. Convoy was put into effect and this caused the U-boats to expose themselves to attack by warships surrounding groups of merchantmen. A giant programme of shipbuilding was begun and by 1918 the offensive had passed to the Allies. When the Armistice came in November 1918 the U-boat arm had lost 178 submarines and forty per cent of its personnel. U-boats had sunk over eleven million tons of shipping, or a total of 6,520 ships of all nationalities.

Between the wars there were a number of experiments in all navies, based chiefly on wartime designs produced by Britain or Germany. The chief German idea developed was that of the cruiser submarine, with long endurance and heavy gun-armament, while the principal British contribution was the concept of submarine-borne aircraft. Neither had much influence on submarines during the Second World War or on tactics, and when Germany began to build U-boats in 1934 she chose the medium-sized designs which had proved themselves sixteen years earlier. The Americans and the Japanese, on the other hand, developed large boats for the immense distances of the Pacific, and the American boats proved particularly well designed for the job.

When war broke out in September 1939 there was no doubt on either side about how submarines would be used, and the sinking of the liner *Athenia* on the first day, although against orders, set the pattern. The British put convoy into immediate effect, but lacked the number of escort vessels that had been available in 1917, and the losses in 1940-41 were grievous. The entry of the United States into the war in December 1941 did little at first except to offer the U-boats a vast number of new targets. But the major contribution of the United States was its enormous shipbuilding capacity, and in 1942 mass-produced mercantile hulls and warships began to appear.

In the Pacific, American submarines soon demonstrated the superiority of their design and tactics by making large inroads into Japanese shipping. By comparison, Japanese submarines scored few successes, and the American camapign in the Pacific showed what catastrophic damage could be inflicted on an island nation by the destruction of its commerce. The enormous losses of oil tankers immobilised Japan's air force, and those surface ships which escaped destruction were unable to put to sea for lack of fuel. The reluctance of the Japanese to adopt convoy, under the

called SONAR), which had actually been under development in 1918, a sonic underwater ranging device which had not only been perfected by the British but was also a closely guarded secret until 1940. Then radar allowed escorts to detect submarines operating on the surface, and refined forms of the device could even detect periscopes. The third important device was High-Frequency Direction-Finding, known as 'Huff-Duff' for short, which enabled escorts to pinpoint U-boats which were transmitting to base. The three devices can be said to have made a victory over the U-boats possible, but they were accompanied by a whole range of weaponry and tactics used by ships and aircraft.

Aircraft proved a tremendous help to convoys, for their presence made it even harder for U-boats to stalk convoys, but in the early years of the war aircraft lacked the range to fly across the Atlantic. Finally a judicious blend of long-range aircraft flying from advanced bases, and small extemporised aircraft carriers known as escort carriers and merchant aircraft carriers, gave convoys air cover all the way across the Atlantic. New ideas on convoy dispositions, particularly raising the number of ships in each convoy, also enabled the escorts to match each new development by the U-boats. The crisis came in 1943, when new countermeasures were tested against the new tactics and equipment introduced by Dönitz. The Battle of the Atlantic was decided in 1943, although it did not end until 1945, for it marked the last time that Germany had any hope of sinking sufficient merchant ships to cut communication between America and the British Isles.

Dönitz continued to develop the U-boats' weaponry, and two innovations stand out. The first, a Dutch idea, was the schnorkel, an air mast to enable submarines to recharge their

Facing page: **A modern German submarine in surface trim.**
GERMAN EMBASSY, LONDON

Above: **The US missile submarine 'John C. Calhoun', is given a firefloat welcome at the base in Holy Loch, Scotland.**
US NAVAL PHOTOGRAPHIC CENTER

illusion that it was merely a defensive measure, was paid for in blood.

The U-Boats, organised by Admiral Dönitz, himself a submariner in the First World War, improved their techniques, and Dönitz introduced the 'wolf pack', which was a co-ordinated mass attack. The first U-boat to make contact with a convoy merely shadowed it and broadcast details to U-Boat HQ which then guided other U-boats to the target. When all were in position the pack attacked on every side, and theoretically a convoy and its escorts could be swamped.

Several convoys were badly mauled in 1942-3, but no convoy was ever annihilated by U-boats, thanks to the heroic efforts of escorts and the tireless devotion and discipline of civilian crews. The first counter-measure was ASDIC (now

batteries while running at periscope depth, and thus reduce the time spent on the surface. The second was the fast underwater submarine with large battery capacity and a streamlined hull to give higher submerged speed and endurance. From the second idea came a third, the hydrogen peroxide submarine designed by Professor Walther, with a steam turbine using oxygen released from the peroxide fuel, and thus needing no outside air. A drawback was the extreme instability of the fuel.

Fortunately for the Allies very few of the new submarines were finished by 1945, and the Germans' ideas were mainly of use to the victors. One such idea was the missile submarine.

The origins of the missile submarine date back to the early 1940s with the German invention of the V1 flying bomb and the V2 ballistic missile. As far back as 1942, rockets were launched at Peenemünde, on the German Baltic coast, from underwater launchers. The German submarine U-511 had launching ramps fitted for solid-fuel Dornberger missiles of 8.4-in calibre. At about periscope depth – between thirty and fifty feet – the rockets were successfully launched from the submarine. Only the success of the Allies' anti-submarine measures in the North Atlantic prevented submarines so equipped from bombarding targets in North America.

Even more startling was a German plan to put V2 rockets in 500-ton tanks which would be towed by a U-boat. The U-boat would use the tanks to supply its own diesel fuel and could tow as many as three. When off the target area the tanks would be partially flooded by a technical party sent across from the U-boat. The missiles would then swing upwards through ninety degrees so that the tops of the tanks showed above water. Once the V2s had been fuelled (liquid fuel was used), the tank bow doors would open and launching would be initiated from the U-boat. Only the ending of the war prevented the development reaching the prototype stage.

After the war, the United States led research into missile submarine development and looked initially at the V1. By 1947 an American version, known as Loon, had been developed and went to sea in the diesel-electric submarine *Cusk*. It was not until Russia's increasing superiority in land-launched long-range ballistic missiles with nuclear warheads was seriously worrying Washington, that the idea of using large ballistic missiles from a submarine was looked at closely.

Initially, it was intended to use the liquid-fuelled Jupiter intermediate-range ballistic missile (IRBM) for this purpose. Developing Jupiter for submarines was the responsibility of (then) Rear-Admiral W. F. 'Red' Raborn, who headed a new organisation known as the Special Projects office inside the Navy Department in Washington.

It was soon found that the liquid-fuelled Jupiter was far too dangerous for use at sea because of the fuel's instability. Special Projects office therefore looked at a solid-fuel version, but that was found to be too bulky to be fitted in a submarine.

However, in summer 1956, there were indications that progress was being made by the Atomic Energy Commission in developing a nuclear warhead small enough to be fitted in the compact missile needed for use in submarines. Admiral Raborn at once set up a Steering Task Group composed of some of the best brains from the Navy, the Atomic Energy Commission, the Massachusetts Institute of Technology and several major industrial concerns, such as the Lockheed Missiles and Space Division who would build the missile. So great were the talents and resources Raborn was able to harness that only three months after the Task Group had been formed it came back with the solution, in April 1957. Basically, it was that the new missile's size and the components used should stride across several years of missile development and employ techniques then only in the embryo stage. The missile, which Raborn had called Polaris, was to be as modern as possible.

When Polaris left the drawing board it was only twenty-eight feet long, compared to a minimum sixty feet for Jupiter; it weighed 28,000lb and was to have had a range of 1,500 miles. But such was Russia's missile progress that instead of having the first American missile submarine ready in five years as had been planned, it had to be ready in two years. Certain penalties resulted. The range of the A1 Polaris, as it was known, would be only 1,200 miles and, if the target date was to be met, an existing nuclear submarine would have to be used. Accordingly, the nuclear attack submarine *Scorpion*, then building at Groton, Connecticut, was cut in two and a new 130-ft midships section was added to her 250ft-long hull. This raised her tonnage from 2,861 to 6,700 submerged. Into the new section went the sixteen vertical tubes in which the missiles were to be housed.

On 9 June 1959, *Scorpion*, renamed *George Washington*, was launched and she was completed six months later. Her missiles had already been tested at sea from special launch tubes fitted in the converted mercantile hull of the USS *Observation Island*. To test the system of ejecting the missile from the tube underwater, a prototype tube was placed on the sea-bed off San Clemente Island and wooden telegraph poles were 'launched' as well as dummy missiles. On 20 July 1960, off Cape Canaveral (since renamed Cape Kennedy), Florida, the *George Washington* launched her first missile down the Atlantic testing range to a point more than 1,000 miles away.

In the course of the next seven years, another forty Polaris submarines were to be added to the American fleet. New depot ships were built to join the modernised *Proteus*, the first missile submarine depot ship which was based at Holy Loch, off the Clyde in Scotland. Polaris submarine squadrons were eventually also based at Rota in south-west Spain, at two ports on the eastern coast of the United States and at Guam in the Pacific.

The A1 version of the missile was replaced by the 1,500-mile-range A2, which in turn was succeeded by the 2,500-mile-range A3. The ten earliest Polaris submarines will retain the A3, but later ones have been converted to carry Poseidon which, while having the same range as the A3 Polaris, has several warheads able to hit separate targets, thus greatly adding to the problems of defence.

But these submarines represent a technological achievement that goes far beyond the ability simply to launch missiles underwater against virtually any point on earth. They are true submarines in that, throughout each two-month patrol, no part of the submarine ever shows above water. Using very-low-frequency (VLF) radio transmissions, it is possible to send messages to a submerged submarine lying not too far below the surface. While on patrol, Polaris submarines maintain radio silence except in the event of a life or death emergency.

To provide air, each boat has CO_2 'scrubbers' which remove the carbon dioxide and other impurities from the atmosphere whose oxygen is recharged by a method of electrolysis of sea water.

For navigation, the submarines use a method called SINS (ships inertial navigation system). Basically, the system consists of three gyroscopes and a computer into which is fed every change of course, depth and speed. The computer is programmed to take account of tidal and current variations and thus a constant plot of the submarine's position on the earth's surface can be obtained. Clearly, highly accurate navigation is essential, since only a small error in a submarine's position could mean the missiles falling many miles from their targets.

From time to time it has been suggested that if, for example, a missile submarine captain became insane he could plunge the world into a nuclear holocaust. But no one man can launch a missile; a minimum of three officers is needed. In addition, certain numerical co-ordinates must be supplied in the signal from the government authorising the submarine to launch its missiles. Such is the level of security on board that only very few of the crew who need to know are aware of the submarine's position at any given time.

In order to keep as many submarines on patrol as possible each has two crews, known in the US Navy as Blue and Gold, and as Port and Starboard in the Royal Navy. The earlier American Polaris submarines have a crew of 112 but the later vessels have 140.

In many respects the British and American Polaris submarines are very similar in design. The four British boats, *Resolution*, *Renown*, *Repulse* and *Revenge*, have their origins in the 1962 agreement signed at Nassau, Bahamas, between Britain's then Prime Minister, Harold Macmillan, and America's late President, John F. Kennedy. In the late 1950s, Britain agreed to share development with America of the bomber-launched nuclear missile Skybolt. However, increasing problems caused the American Air Force to cancel its order and Britain, unable to shoulder the huge continuing development cost, sought American agreement to buy Polaris.

It was decided that the Polaris programme would take a little under six years and would be a completely British one, except that the missile bodies (but not the warheads) would be built and supplied by America. The first of the British submarines, *Resolution*, was completed in 1967 and set out on her first patrol in June 1968, almost on the exact day planned back in 1963.

But by that time, Britain and America were not alone in having nuclear ballistic missile submarines. Like America, Russia benefited from German technology and the brains of a number of German missile experts in the early years after the war. One of the earliest Russian air-breathing missiles, code-named Golem by NATO, was a development of the German V1 flying bomb.

America also developed air-breathing tactical missiles, which culminated in the 500-mile-range Regulus I fitted in five submarines, one of them nuclear powered, in the mid-1950s. In due course, Regulus II, which was nearly supersonic and had a range of 1,000 miles, was developed, but it never became operational and was cancelled in favour of Polaris. That decision was a mistake by the Americans, since Polaris is a strategic weapon which could never be employed tactically against ships, for example.

The Russians, having no aircraft carriers, wanted some credible defence against such ships and consequently continued the development of tactical missiles. The first really effective missile was the Shaddock which appears to have been completed in the late 1950s. Initially it was fitted in eleven reconstructed diesel-powered W-class patrol submarines, whose curious appearance excited considerable Western interest when they were first seen in the early 1960s. Shaddock cannot be launched under water and has a maximum range, it is now believed, of about 200 miles, although at one time it was credited with a range of as much as 450

In the field of strategic nuclear missiles, Moscow clearly could not go on accepting a range of only 650 miles for its submarines' principal weapon. So, in 1968, the first Y-class submarine made its not entirely unexpected appearance. Like the British and American Polaris boats, which it closely resembles in appearance, it has sixteen launching tubes and each missile is credited with a range of 1,500 miles. A more advanced version might now be in service with a range of 3,000 miles. There are thirty-five known Y-class submarines in service or building and a further seven are planned. If the earlier G and H classes are included, the Russians have sixty-six strategic missile submarines to America's forty-one and Britain's four.

France has five strategic submarines, and their missiles, sixteen of which are carried in each boat, have a range of 1,900 miles.

The only other nuclear power, Communist China, has one missile submarine built to the Russian G-class design, but China's efforts seem concentrated on producing land-based nuclear missiles.

Looking to the future, unless disarmament talks prevail, the American Polaris-Poseidon missile submarine force will probably be replaced by ten of the new Trident missile submarines. The new missiles will have a range of about 5,000 miles, making unnecessary the basing overseas of American missile submarine forces. The new submarines might displace as much as 15,000 to 16,000 tons, or roughly double the size of the Polaris submarines.

Whether Britain will remain content with the A3 Polaris or will opt for Poseidon cannot at this time be forecast,

miles. Its biggest disadvantage is that if launched at a target beyond the launching ship's radar horizon, about twenty-five miles, it must be guided in flight by another submarine, surface ship, long-range maritime patrol aircraft or helicopter. The guidance vehicle therefore becomes very vulnerable to enemy counter-attack.

Simultaneously with the introduction of Shaddock, a 350-mile-range nuclear ballistic missile made its appearance in G-class diesel-electric submarines. It also suffers from the disadvantage that it cannot be launched under water. This missile was also fitted in H1-class nuclear-powered submarines, but subsequently H1s were converted to carry an underwater-launched missile with a range of 650 miles, although also having a nuclear warhead. Shaddock continued to prove its reliability and today is fitted in about sixty nuclear and diesel-electric submarines as well as surface vessels. But the principal offensive capability against surface ships possessed by the Soviet Navy is the SS-N-7 missile fitted in the eight C-class nuclear submarines. Since it does not employ mid-course guidance like Shaddock, its range is only twenty-five miles, but it can be launched from a submarine which is completely submerged.

although the Americans have no doubt that the former will remain a credible weapon into the 1980s. Certainly there is nothing to indicate that any startling new breakthrough is in the offing which would allow submerged submarines to be detected at long range. Attempts have been made to use space satellites for the purpose, but effective detection is possible only if the submarine is very close to the surface and the atmosphere is not obscured by cloud. Biggest enemy of the submarine at present is the helicopter, against which it has little so far to defend itself. However, in Britain, a Vickers Army missile has been modified and developed into SLAM (submarine launched anti-aircraft missile). It can operate at periscope depth and is under trial in the old submarine *Aeneas*.

Above: HMS 'Resolution' in August 1967.   HMSO (MOD NAVY)

Overleaf: A painting by Frank H. Mason of the Royal Navy submarine M1 (whose 12-inch gun is notable) off the coast of Sedd-el-Bahr in the Dardanelles in 1918.
IMPERIAL WAR MUSEUM, LONDON (RICHARD SHARPE STUDIOS)

The Destroyer

F EW people remember today that the destroyer was originally the torpedo-boat destroyer; it was brought into being for the specific purpose of protecting the major units of a fleet from the small fast craft evolved to operate the newly invented automobile torpedo. The name, shortened to destroyer, continued to be applied long after the initial purpose had become but one of a number of tasks allotted to that type of ship. Nevertheless, a historical survey must begin with a brief account of the torpedo-boat.

The first of the type were steam launches towing the explosive device known, after its inventor, as the Harvey torpedo; or they were fitted with a spar torpedo – a long pole projecting forward and downward from the boat with an explosive charge on the end, detonated by ramming against the target's side below the waterline. The latter were successfully used by both sides in the American Civil War. Between 1873 and 1875, the British firms of Thornycroft and Yarrow specialised in torpedo-boats and built a large number for many nations. They were craft of about seven or eight tons displacement and a speed of fifteen knots.

Then, the Whitehead locomotive torpedo came on the scene. First in the field to construct a sea-going craft designed to operate locomotive torpedoes were the French, in 1877, whose Torpedo Boat No 1, of 101 tons, had two axial torpedo-tubes, one forward and one aft between the twin screws. Although the concept was ahead of its time, its speed of only just over fourteen knots made it of little value. Meanwhile, Thornycroft had produced the *Lightning*, a little craft of nineteen tons, but with a speed of eighteen knots. When *Lightning* was adapted to mount a Whitehead torpedo-launching gear in the bows, she became the first of a large number of such boats which were built by Thornycroft and Yarrow for several governments.

Next in the process of evolution came larger boats, the first of which was the *Batoum*, a 40-ton craft built for the Russians by Yarrow, which achieved a speed of twenty-two

Left: HMS 'Fife' leading other guided-missile destroyers in August 1973. R. ADSHEAD

Below: The US destroyer 'Maddox' which was attacked by North Vietnamese vessels in the Gulf of Tonkin in 1964. CENTRAL PRESS PHOTOS LTD

knots. She and her successors were designated 1st Class Torpedo Boats, the smaller craft being 2nd Class. Russia and France were the chief advocates of the torpedo-boat, acquiring respectively 115 and fifty of the first-class boats by 1884, compared with Britain's modest nineteen. The French in particular, under the influence of Admiral Aube, believed that the era of the battleship had passed. In its place should be a swarm of fast light craft for coastal defence and light cruisers for attack on an enemy's sea-borne trade, the classic *guerre-de-course* so often resorted to by them in the past. In 1886 Aube, then Minister of Marine, ordered thirty-four new torpedo-boats and established a Torpedo School.

By that time the British Admiralty had woken up to the threat being posed by the Royal Navy's traditional rival across the Channel. Between 1886 and 1892, they built a series of classes of ships known as torpedo-gunboats, or catchers, the last of which, the Jason class, were ships of 700 to 800 tons although with a speed still less than twenty knots. Similar ships were being built by the French. They were all too slow and unmanoeuvrable to catch torpedo-boats.

The first to perceive the required design were the Spanish, who had had a ship built for them in 1884 by Thompson of Clydebank (later the John Brown shipyard). She was the aptly named *Destructor* (destroyer), of 386 tons and the first warship to be driven by twin triple-expansion engines, which gave her a speed of twenty-two and a half knots. As the speed of torpedo-boats rose, however, she was soon outmoded. Therefore, a breakthrough was necessary; at last, in 1893, it came about when Yarrow produced HMS *Havock*, the first true torpedo-boat destroyer.

Displacing only 240 tons, and with a low silhouette, she was still able to house twin reciprocating engines and the water-tube boilers to supply them with steam for a speed of twenty-seven knots; on her upper deck she mounted one 3-inch (12-pounder) gun and three six-pounders, and she had three torpedo-tubes altogether.

The *Havock*, her sister-ship *Hornet*, and the *Daring* and *Decoy* built by Thornycroft, were so successful that thirty-six more similar boats were ordered by the Admiralty. The class became known as the 27-knotters (later A class). From that time onward, TBDs formed a substantial element of the British Navy, new classes following almost annually, with

efforts made to improve the performance of each. Consequently, when the French produced a torpedo-boat, the *Forban* in 1895, and Yarrow built the TBD *Sokol* for Russia, each of which achieved thirty-one knots, the British ordered the large class of TBDs known as 30-knotters.

They were still quite small ships – 300 to 400 tons – extremely wet and uncomfortable in a seaway, when their low turtle-back forecastles were constantly awash. To drive them at thirty knots, their reciprocating engines had to develop very high piston speeds and, apart from numerous breakages, few actually achieved that speed in loaded condition. Two of them, however, the *Viper* and *Cobra*, in 1899 became the first warships to make use of the marine steam turbine invented by Charles Parsons, the *Viper* achieving thirty-six to thirty-eight knots and the *Cobra* a knot less.

Unfortunately for the progress of turbine drive in British destroyers, in pursuit of spectacular speeds *Viper* and *Cobra* were built with very light scantlings and only a quarter-inch side plating. When the *Cobra* broke her back and foundered in rough seas, a reaction against turbines and high speeds arose. The Royal Navy, between 1903 and 1905, preferred to have instead larger (550 tons) ships, powered by reciprocating engines; they were the more seaworthy River class, slower (twenty-five and a half knots) and sturdier and with a high flared forecastle (which became standard for British destroyers). At the same time they were able to mount the increased gun armament of up to four 3-inch guns compared with the single 3-inch and five six-pounders of the 30-knotters.

Turbine technique was nevertheless preserved in one of them, the *Eden*, and in 1907 turbine drive as well as boiler firing with oil fuel became standard practice with the Tribal class. Although the Tribals varied in size and armament, their performance was similar, with speeds between thirty-three and thirty-five knots, and their armament was two 18-inch torpedo tubes and either five 3-inch or two 4-inch guns.

The French, under the influence of the *Jeune Ecole*, were at first content with their large number of basically defensive torpedo-boats. Not until 1899 did they acquire their first destroyer, the *Durandal*, a 300-ton vessel built by the firm of Normand. It might be that they profited by the delay to iron out some of the problems of high-speed reciprocating engines, as the *Durandal* and her successors, some of which achieved thirty-one knots, attained a reliability which their British contemporaries lacked. Certainly, the French experimented exhaustively before finally adopting oil firing or turbine

drive, the first class to incorporate both concepts as well as a raised forecastle being the 700-ton Casque class, laid down in 1909; they mounted two 3.9-inch and four 9-pounder guns and four 18-inch torpedoes. The designation *contre-torpilleur* (torpedo-boat destroyer) was temporarily abandoned by the French Navy, in favour of *torpilleur d'escadre* (fleet torpedo-boat).

The Germans, when they began to develop an Imperial Navy, built a number of torpedo-boats annually from 1887 onwards, increasing successively in size, engine power and armament until 1906, when they built the G137, the first boat to incorporate turbine drive, giving her a speed of 33.9 knots, and an armament of one 3.5-inch gun and three 6-pounders. Favouring a large number of torpedo-tubes (five in this case) at the expense of gun power and, therefore, the concept of attack rather than defence, the Germans designated their boats High Seas Torpedo-Boats rather than Destroyers. By 1913, whereas the standard British destroyer, with a displacement of 1,200 tons and a speed of twenty-seven to twenty-nine knots, mounted three 4-inch guns and four 21-inch torpedo tubes, the contemporary German craft of 700 tons mounted only two or three 3.5-inch guns, but up to six 19.7-inch torpedo tubes and had a speed of thirty-two to thirty-four knots. In other words, the Germans operated basically torpedo-boats (hunters) and the British torpedo-boat destroyers (hunter-killers).

By that time, all navies incorporated a force of destroyers or torpedo-boats, mostly capable of thirty knots. Their task, whether called by one name or the other, was the dual one of attacking an enemy's battle fleet with their torpedoes and driving off enemy torpedo craft attempting to do the same. In the United States, where a naval renaissance was taking place, about twenty-six new destroyers of 700-740 tons, thirty knots and mounting five 3-inch guns and six 18-inch torpedoes, joined the fleet between 1909 and 1912.

The Japanese had been the first to operate destroyers in war; they were British-built vessels of the 30-knotter type with which they had opened hostilities against Russia in 1904 by a night attack on the fleet in the Roads outside Port Arthur. They also played an active part in the three major sea battles of the Russo-Japanese War. On each occasion their achievements were less than impressive. Even at Port Arthur, where the Russian fleet was taken completely by surprise, out of eighteen torpedoes fired at the anchored enemy ships only three hit, damaging, but not sinking, two

battleships and a cruiser. Only in the Battle of Tsushima did they achieve anything further. They gave the *coup de grâce* to the shattered and stationary battleships *Suvarov* and *Navarin*, fatally torpedoed the battleship *Sissoi Veliki* and damaged the *Admiral Nakhimoff* and the old cruiser *Vladimir Monomakh*. To gain that achievement during the annihilation of an incomparably less effective enemy fleet, well over 100 torpedoes were fired.

That disappointing performance in one of the two main roles expected of the destroyer, the torpedoing of enemy heavy units, was to repeat itself during the First World War. During the night phase of the Battle of Jutland, more than seventy British destroyers opposed the passage of the German Battle Fleet across the wake of the British Grand Fleet. In a series of encounters at point-blank range they succeeded in sinking only one battleship, the pre-dreadnought *Pommern*. On the other hand, the threat of the torpedo fired *en masse* had earlier probably done more to rob the British of a decisive victory than any other factor. Twenty-eight torpedoes fired by the German flotillas to cover the escape of their battleships from the trap sprung on them by the Grand Fleet had caused the latter to turn forty-five degrees away and lose touch with its prey for the remaining period of daylight.

By the end of the war, the standard British destroyer was one of the very numerous V and W classes, about 1,500 tons at deep displacement, mounting, after later modifications, four 4.7-inch guns and two triple clusters of 21-inch torpedo-tubes, with a shaft horsepower of 27,000 driving them at thirty-five knots. Not until 1924 were new destroyers laid down for the Royal Navy. They could be said to be only improvements of the W class, as were all the flotillas, each of eight boats and a leader, added annually, the A to I classes, the last of which was laid down in 1936.

By that time, though destroyers were still given a powerful torpedo armament and a gun armament calculated to put them on equality with others of their type in foreign navies, their principal function had become that of screening major units – battleships, aircraft carriers and cruisers – as well as troop convoys, against submarine attack. British and American destroyers were, therefore, equipped with sonar submarine-detecting devices – called **ASDIC** by the British – and mortars and launching rails for a 'pattern' of depth-charges.

Other navies took similar building 'holidays' before beginning modernisation programmes. The French Navy then added the larger Tigre-class *contre-torpilleurs* of about 2,126

Far left: HMS 'Fife', a County-class guided-missile destroyer. R. ADSHEAD

Above centre: Destroyer D183, in the background, with other Federal German Navy ships at NATO Spithead Review in June 1970. A. GREENWAY

Below centre: HMS 'Somali', one of the Tribal-class destroyers of the Second World War. J. G. STEEL

Above: The guided-missile destroyer HMS 'Hampshire' in the Pacific Ocean in 1969. A. GREENWAY

tons and with an armament of five 5.1-inch guns. They were followed, between 1928 and 1934, by a further eighteen ships of 2,400 tons and a similar armament, but an increased speed of between thirty-seven and forty knots. Six later ships of the Fantasque class achieved forty-three to forty-five knots.

The US Navy began its modernisation programme, so far as destroyers were concerned, by laying down in 1932 the eight ships of the Farragut class, great improvements upon the flush-decked four-funnelled destroyers of their earlier war and post-war programmes. With an armament of five of the new 5-inch 38-calibre dual-purpose guns which were to become the standard US destroyer guns, and twelve 21-inch torpedo tubes in quadruple mountings, geared turbines of 42,900 horse-power and a speed of thirty-six and a half knots, they can be said to have been prototypes of the huge number of destroyers built for the Second World War.

For all the major navies, including then a reborn German navy, the lapsing of the Washington and London Naval Armament Limitation Treaties in 1936, the signing of the Anglo-German Naval Agreement and the looming of the clouds of war, led to a feverish programme of building. Included were the British J, K, L and M classes and the Tribal class. The J to M class, with a displacement of 1,610 guns, generally mounted six 4.7-inch guns and two quintuple torpedo-tube mountings. One of the torpedo mounts was later removed to allow an increased anti-aircraft armament. The Tribal design, with a displacement of 1,870 tons, accepted a decreasing role for the torpedo in fleet operations and, to mount eight 4.7-inch guns, the torpedo armament was from the start limited to a single quadruple mounting.

Had the British persevered with their experiment with liquid-oxygen-driven torpedoes in the 1930s to produce such weapons as the Japanese Long Lance torpedoes, which could carry a 1,000lb warhead at thirty-six knots for twenty-two miles or half that distance at forty-nine knots, their destroyer

Above: 'Rostam', a Mk 5 destroyer built for the Iranian Navy by Vickers of Birkenhead, in dry dock at Southampton in March 1973. J. EASTLAND

Below: HMS 'Cavalier', one of the Royal Navy's C-class destroyers in 1973. A. GREENWAY

armaments might perhaps have been different. The average Japanese destroyer from 1933 onwards, when the Long Lances were perfected, was a ship of about 2,000 tons displacement, six 5-inch guns and nine 24-inch torpedo-tubes, with nine reload torpedoes in upper-deck housings, and had a speed of thirty-four knots.

Such ships were to achieve spectacular successes in night surface actions with American forces during the Solomon Islands campaign. American destroyers of the Fletcher class, built in great numbers during the war, were of about the same size and armament, with the exception of their 21-inch torpedoes. They proved to have numerous defects, which had not been rectified when, late in 1944, they were replaced by new electric torpedoes of a type copied from the German.

The primary importance of the role of convoy escort for all but the most up-to-date destroyers during the Second World War led to the readoption of the classification, derived from the days of sail, of frigate for the older destroyers modified for that role. For a time, indeed, after the war, it seemed as though the anomaly of retaining the title destroyer long after it had ceased to have a contemporary meaning would cause it to disappear from the navy lists of the world. Many ships that would have otherwise been classified as destroyers became frigates in the Royal Navy, *escorteurs* or *frégates* in the French (where the term *contre-torpilleur* has again been abandoned) and *uniti scorta* in the Italian.

In the British and Italian navies, however, the name has lingered on, applied to ships immediately below the cruiser in size, such as the 5,650-ton County-class guided missile destroyers of the British and the 3,900-ton Impavido class of the Italians. In the United States Navy the classification of similar ships does not follow any simple or clear-cut rules; some frigates are larger than destroyers and even larger than war-time cruisers.

Ignoring the anomalies, however, it is perhaps fitting to close this historical outline of the destroyer's story by saying that today, where the name occurs, it indicates a warship of moderate size whose main weapons are missiles, either surface-to-air, ship-to-ship, or a combination of both, with the addition of a rocket-transported anti-submarine homing torpedo.

The Battleship

AT the beginning of the twentieth century the battleship reigned supreme among warships. She had evolved from the eighteenth century 'ship of the line' or line-of-battle-ship into the ungainly steam-and-sail ironclads of the 1870s, but after twenty-five years of experiments and freaks the broad outlines of the modern battleship had been decided. Battleships were built to fight for supremacy on the high seas, armoured to protect their vital machinery, guns and magazines from enemy shellfire and proof against hits from lighter shells. They were armed with heavy gun-mountings and protected by armoured sides and decks.

In 1905 two important events upset all previous theories of battleship design: the battleship *Dreadnought* was laid down and the Russians and Japanese fought the Battle of Tsushima. This battle was the first major action at sea in over forty years, and it was taken to show that battle ranges should be opened out to 7,000 or even 10,000 yards, and that medium-calibre guns were of little use. This *Dreadnought*, with her massive increase of main armament to ten 12-inch guns in five twin turrets and virtual elimination of all but the very lightest guns, expressed the new philosophy very well, but her most important contribution was to introduce the Parsons' steam turbine. She had no trouble in making twenty-one knots, with none of the problems associated with high speed triple-expansion engines.

The introduction of the *Dreadnought* coincided with an important quickening of pace in the arms race between Great Britain and Germany and politicians and navalists on both sides seized on 'dreadnoughts' as units of naval supremacy. Suddenly naval strength was divided into 'dreadnoughts' and 'pre-dreadnoughts'. Although the interpretation differed from navy to navy, the broad lines of the *Dreadnought* were followed, and steam turbines soon became standard.

Following on this upheaval the British built what they called a 'dreadnought' armoured cruiser. If the battleship can be defined as a warship with emphasis on armour, gunpower and speed in that order, the new ship-type reversed those priorities, by leaving out one twin 12-inch turret and thinning the armour to increase speed to $25\frac{1}{2}$ knots. The original purpose of these ships was merely to replace the unwieldy armoured cruiser and to scout for the battlefleet, secure in the knowledge that they could outrun battleships and sink anything smaller. But such a role was impossible to fulfil if an enemy fleet had its own dreadnought armoured cruisers, and in the absence of any other role there was an inevitable temptation to think of them as fast battleships. The coining of the term 'battlecruiser' in 1912 reinforced this pernicious idea, and when the latest examples proved to be larger than contemporary battleships the two types came to be referred to under the heading of 'capital ships'.

The decade 1904-1914 was the hey-day of the battleship. With the submarine still only a toy with great potential but little else, and the destroyer holding the balance against the surface torpedo threat, naval supremacy could truly be gauged by the huge fleets of dreadnoughts which were being built. By 1914 the British had built twenty-two dreadnoughts and ten battlecruisers, while Germany had built seventeen dreadnoughts and five battlecruisers. The United States, Japan, France, Austria and Italy had all followed their example, and even South American countries caught the battleship fever. Guns grew bigger, 13.5-inch, 14-inch and 15-inch in an effort to produce greater range and destructive power, and armour had to keep pace.

The opening months of the First World War seemed to vindicate the battlecruiser as a more valuable type than the battleship. The main British battlefleet was sent to Scapa Flow in the Orkneys, where it was well placed to block the exit from the North Sea into the Atlantic. The German High Seas Fleet made no attempt to dispute the Grand Fleet's control, for its policy was to try to lure a part of it, perhaps only a division of four ships, into a trap. To do this the German battlecruisers were sent across the North Sea on diversionary raids, to bombard east coast towns in the hope that British units would be sent south to deal with them. The British public, which had been led to expect a new Trafalgar in the North Sea in a matter of days, was very critical of the Navy, for British heavy units always arrived too late. As a concession the Admiralty stationed the battlecruisers at Rosyth, nearer to the Germans' escape route, and in January 1915 this finally resulted in action. The Battle of the Dogger Bank was, however, a disappointment to the British, for their staffwork was poor. Despite being faster and more heavily gunned they were only able to sink the armoured cruiser *Blücher*, while their own flagship HMS *Lion* was damaged.

Meanwhile the battlecruisers *Invincible* and *Inflexible* had been sent out to the Falkland Islands to hunt down the German cruiser squadron under Admiral von Spee which had sunk two British cruisers at Coronel on 1 November. Little over a month later the two battlecruisers overwhelmed Spee's ships at the Battle of the Falklands, performing the task for which they had been designed. After this the battlecruiser was hailed by many as the only suitable type of capital ship, and it was not until the Battle of Jutland in May 1916 that its shortcomings were to be exposed.

Jutland was the only fleet action of the war, and indeed the last full battleship versus battleship action in history. The British had twenty-eight dreadnoughts and nine battlecruisers, the Germans sixteen dreadnoughts, six pre-dreadnoughts and five battlecruisers. Once again the battlecruisers lived up to their reputation for dash and *élan* by making first contact. Admiral Hipper and Admiral Beatty were each trying to lure the other into the arms of his Commander-in-Chief, but first the British battlecruisers were subjected to an ordeal which showed up alarming weaknesses in their design. First the *Indefatigable* and then the *Queen Mary* blew up suddenly, with the loss of nearly all hands. The flagship *Lion* was also on fire, but she survived almost by a miracle.

The British battle line, nine miles long, inflicted serious damage on the Germans, but poor visibility prevented any decisive moves by either side before nightfall. The British wisely declined to fight at night, and hoped to finish off the High Seas Fleet in the morning, but the Germans managed to brush aside the destroyers which barred their way and returned safely to harbour. Having lost a third battlecruiser, HMS *Invincible*, the British could be said to have come off worse than the Germans, who had lost only one and the pre-dreadnought *Pommern*. Although the light armour of the battlecruisers' protection was blamed the chief culprit appears to have been unstable propellant in the British ships,

Admiral Sir David Beatty (later Earl Beatty and First Sea Lord) watching the surrender of the German Fleet in November 1918.
ILLUSTRATED LONDON NEWS

combined with poor precautions against cordite flash, but what finally robbed the Grand Fleet of victory was poor-quality armour-piercing shell.

The fleets did not engage again, but the British took the lessons to heart and overhauled their organisation; had another Jutland occurred in 1918 the results would have been very different. Paradoxically it was the older ships which saw much more action, as they were sent abroad on subsidiary duties. The Dardanelles expedition in 1915 was supported by a large force of British and French pre-dreadnoughts which proved their worth in shore bombardment. Some old ships went as far afield as Murmansk and the East Indies, while others performed useful but humdrum tasks at home. In all thirty-seven battleships of all nations were lost, six in action, twenty-two by mine or torpedo, eight by ammunition explosion and one by scuttling. By 1918 the mine and the submarine had come to dominate naval warfare, and the battleship could no longer roam the seas at will. The war-weary nations were only too happy to see big reductions in the world's battlefleets after the Armistice. The High Seas Fleet was scuttled in Scapa Flow to prevent its use by the Allies against Germany, and when the President of the United States convened a naval disarmament conference in Washington in 1921 the chance to limit expenditure was seized.

In 1922 the United States, Great Britain, Japan, France and Italy signed the Washington Treaty to limit their strength in capital ships, both in numbers and in quality. The new limit was to be 35,000 tons with guns no bigger than 16-inch. The Royal Navy was allowed to build two new ships, however, and retain the *Hood*, which exceeded the 35,000-ton

limit, but the Americans and Japanese had to scrap virtually all their incomplete ships. There was also to be a ten-year 'holiday' in battleship construction and no ship could be replaced until she was twenty years old.

Rebuilding was allowed under the Treaty and so vast sums were lavished on modernising the ships which had only recently been considered the best in the world. The British were in the best position for their ships had spent four years at war, with frequent damage from mines, torpedoes and shells. A new defence was found against torpedoes, the 'bulge' or 'blister' – an air-space outside the hull in which a torpedo head could explode and dissipate its force. Deck armour was strengthened to keep out aircraft bombs and anti-aircraft guns were added. To compensate for the extra armour engineers worked on new types of boilers and lighter machinery, and in little more than fifteen years machinery weights dropped by as much as fifteen per cent.

Under the Versailles Treaty the Germans could only build coast defence ships, and they set about designing a vessel of 10,000 tons armed with 11-inch guns, as allowed. The *Deutschland* astounded the world, for she was a powerful commerce-raiding cruiser with a welded hull and diesel propulsion. Christened a 'pocket battleship' by an hysterical world press, the *Deutschland* was really nothing more than an overgunned armoured cruiser of modest speed, but it was claimed at the time that she could only be brought to action by the three surviving British battlecruisers, *Hood*, *Renown* and *Repulse*. What was important was that she and two near-sisters triggered off a Mediterranean naval race, with France insisting on her right to build two battlecruisers as a counter. This in turn provoked Italy to begin building battleships, and when Germany finally threw off the shackles of the Versailles Treaty it was impossible to stop her building her own capital ships as well.

In the Pacific the apparent calm of the 1920s was also giving way to a new round of battleship building, but not openly. The Japanese had modernised their older ships as far as they could, and had reluctantly come to the conclusion that there was no way of achieving a decisive margin of superiority in a 35,000-ton battleship. Being careful to give warning of her intention not to renew the limitation treaties, Japan planned to have two or three battleships ready by 1940, of such overwhelming power that no rival could be built to match them. These battleships were to be the largest and most powerful ever built, 64,000-tons and armed with nine 18-inch guns.

Faced with German re-armament and French and Italian rivalry the Royal Navy began a programme of battleship construction in 1937, as did the United States. Although the growing importance of the aircraft carrier was admitted, the crude state of development of aerial bombing against ships meant that a battleship was the only reliable counter to another battleship. The new generation of ships solved the dilemma of speed, for improvements in machinery meant that all battleships could now be as fast as the old battlecruisers. Now triple and even quadruple gun-mountings were the fashion, and fire-control was about to be improved beyond recognition by the advent of radar.

The wisdom of building battleships was demonstrated in the Mediterranean, where the British were able to dominate the Italians, and in the Atlantic, where the older British ships were enough to deter attacks by German capital ships. In May 1941 only battleships could finish off the *Bismark*, but, even with all the improvements in anti-aircraft armament and fire-control, battleships could not face heavy air attack unsupported by friendly aircraft. In December 1941 the US Pacific Fleet was knocked out by a Japanese aircraft carrier strike at Pearl Harbour and three days later land-based bombers sank the British *Prince of Wales* and *Repulse* off Malaya. Despite their bulk and power, these ships had all been sunk with what seemed ridiculous ease.

Pearl Harbour forced the US Navy to change its tactics from reliance on the battlefleet to the use of fast carrier task

Above: HMS 'Hood', the battle cruiser which survived the Treaty of Washington and was blown up by 'Bismarck' in 1941.
ILLUSTRATED LONDON NEWS

Below: The 70,000-ton Japanese battleship 'Yamato' on trial in October 1941. She was to be sunk early in 1945.
IMPERIAL WAR MUSEUM, LONDON

forces, but, even so, the battleship had an important role to play. Not only did its guns defend the carriers against enemy attack, but as the American amphibious strategy developed into the 'island-hopping' campaign across the Pacific, battleship gunfire was needed to soften the defences. It is often said that the battleship became too expensive and too vulnerable, but the new capital ship, the aircraft carrier, was just as costly and just as vulnerable to hits from torpedoes and bombs. The real reason was simply that the 16-inch shell with its range of twenty to twenty-five miles was not as destructive as a torpedo or bomb delivered by an aircraft 300 miles away. Another problem was that by 1945 bombs could penetrate thicknesses of deck armour never envisaged before, thanks to improved accuracy of high-level bombing. Not even the Japanese *Yamato* and *Mushashi* could withstand the weight of bombs which could be delivered, and even if the cost of bigger ships could be justified, there was the problem of where to dock them.

During the Korean War all four of the US Navy's Iowa-Class battleships, the last to be built, were brought out of reserve to act out the same role as they had in 1944-45. In 1967-68 the *New Jersey* was refitted for service off the coast of South Vietnam. The wheel had turned full circle – aircraft bombing had proved too inaccurate and guided weapons too expensive for shore bombardment, and 16-inch shells were cheaper and more effective against underground bunkers. What was more important was that the battleship could 'loiter' in an area and resume firing if the initial bombardment had not been successful, whereas it might be twenty-four hours before a second air-strike could be laid on.

The end of the Vietnam War meant the end of the *New Jersey*'s remarkable come back, during which she fired some 6,000 shells. It was a fitting and unexpected epitaph to the age of the battleship.

The Cruiser

THE term 'cruiser' appears to have been applied by the Royal Navy for the first time in the 1880s as a description of such ships as the *Warrior* and *Black Prince*. These ships had originally been rated as 'iron frigates' and, with a displacement of some 8,800 tons each, were forerunners of the modern battleship. Gradually, however, the navies of the world came to regard as a cruiser any ship that was capable of sustained cruising for long periods without support.

There were three original classifications of cruiser: the armoured, protected and light cruisers. The absence of armour-plate in most light cruisers was compensated by their manoeuvrability and speed, and before long the cruiser category included ships of only 2,000 tons displacement, though it ranged up to 14,000 tons at the other end of the scale. The cruiser's function as a raiding vessel and as a protection for commercial shipping arose from its versatility and compact self-sufficiency at sea and, during the latter half of the last century, the leading maritime nations saw their navies undergo a swift transformation as this ship took over

more and more of the duties of an enormous range of sailing vessels.

The armoured cruiser concept reached its peak with the Royal Navy's 14,000-ton *Drake*, *Leviathan* and *King Alfred* of 1902-3. Although these ships were capable of twenty-four knots, they did not match up to the new Dreadnought battleships which arrived only four years later, and the *Minotaur*, *Defence* and *Shannon*, (completed in 1908), were the last of the classic armoured cruisers in the Royal Navy.

Powerful cruisers were also being built during the last two decades of the nineteenth century by France, America and Russia, but the launch of the *Powerful* and *Terrible*, each displacing 14,200 tons, put the British navy in a commanding position. To enable them to reach their designed speed of

twenty-two knots, however, these ships were each fitted with forty-eight boilers, and it was becoming apparent that engine design would be of great significance in cruiser technology.

It was only at Jutland that the big armoured cruisers saw any real fighting, although the *Terrible* and *Powerful* were engaged in the early days of the Boer War, and the *Kent* fought well in the Falklands in 1914. The light cruiser soon became more acceptable as a design, and the emergence of the Forward-class light cruisers really marked the evolution of the breed in its own right. With a displacement of nearly 2,900 tons and a speed of twenty-five knots, the Forward-class was completed in 1905, the same year as the larger Gem-class light cruiser of 3,000 tons. Although the latter attained a speed of less than twenty-two knots, she was armed with twelve 4-inch guns, compared with nine in the Forward class.

An important development took place when a committee of naval experts set up by the newly-appointed First Sea Lord, Fisher, recommended a design for the first true battleship, which was completed in 1908 in the form of *Invincible*, *Indomitable* and *Inflexible*. These three-funnelled 17,000-tonners were 570 feet long, and armed with eight 12-inch guns, but their fuel consumption was enormous and their range modest.

At this time Germany was involved in an arms race with Britain, and the completion of the *Blücher* in the same year revealed a somewhat pale imitation of the battlecruiser design. Displacing some 15,000 tons, she could reach a speed of twenty-six knots, compared with twenty-five knots of the Invincible class, but was armed with only 8.2-inch calibre guns. The *Von der Tann*, which followed *Blücher*, was quite different. Over thirty feet longer than the British vessels, she was armed with only eight 11-inch guns, but this allowed more weight for protection and sub-division. Unlike the British policy of designing the battlecruiser for effective chase-fire, the Germans produced a ship that could stand self-protected in a line of battle.

While the later German battlecruisers continued to improve and were capable of twenty-eight knots, the British navy's second trio, the *Indefatigable*, *Australia* and *New Zealand*, were essentially replicas of the Invincibles, and received criticism from many quarters for a lack of imagination. In 1912-13 a new trio was completed by the Royal Navy, and this design was clearly intended to impress. The *Lion*, *Queen Mary* and *Princess Royal* were massive 27,000-tonners of about 660 feet in length. The main calibre was increased to 13.5-inch guns, and all the main armament was on the centre-line. The protection, however, did not match up to that of the German ships.

The launch by Britain of the *Kongo* for Japan (immediately before completion of the *Lion*), resulted directly in the building of the *Tiger*. Similar in size and armament to the *Lion*, she was able to exceed thirty knots with ease, but her six-inch secondary armament indicated that the torpedo menace was being recognised and that she had been thus equipped to fight off destroyers during a major engagement. Amongst several other German battlecruisers laid down for the High Fleet before the outbreak of war was the *Hindenburg*, although she did not commission until 1917.

Following the declaration of war, the battlecruisers saw action in August at the Heligoland Bight, and later proved themselves in an encounter with the German China Squadron off the Falklands. In pursuit of the *Scharnhorst* and *Gneisenau*, the *Invincible* and *Inflexible* laid on a textbook demonstration of their status, and their superior speed and firepower entirely destroyed both German vessels.

Built in only eighteen months, *Repulse* and *Renown* were given horizontal protection against long-range fire, but practically no vertical protection. They had a speed of over thirty knots, but were launched with a total of only six 15-inch guns each, as there were not sufficient weapons available during the hurried building programme.

In January 1915, British battlecruisers formed the spearhead of an attack on the Germans at Dogger Bank. By no

means a disaster, this encounter nevertheless revealed highly significant weaknesses in the British force. One of the major shortcomings was a virtual breakdown in signals communication, but – more tragically – the battlecruiser's vulnerability to cordite-flash fire was exposed by the *Lion*, and although the damage was not great, the implications were disturbing. It was well over a year later that the British naval administration was to regret its failure to learn from this lesson.

In the battle of Jutland in May 1916, four ships fell victim to flash-fire explosions. *Invincible*, *Indefatigable* and *Queen Mary* were all destroyed and *Lion* only survived a direct hit on her midships turret because the magazines below had already been flooded.

It is significant that the armour of the British ships was pierced no more often than that of their enemy's, but the German ships survived at least nine turret penetrations by heavy shells, while reciprocal hits proved lethal to the British. Similar flaws in the design of the *Repulse* and *Renown* (which had not yet joined the fleet) came in for the most severe criticism.

In the meantime, progress was being made on the design of the light cruiser and, by 1918, most of these craft were easily capable of speeds exceeding thirty knots. The later ships of the British C class carried an armament of five 6-inch guns, yet they were still quite small, having a displacement of around 4,000 tons. The installation of turbine engines meant a welcome reduction in weight, and the Raleigh class of the immediate post-war years was a light vessel in spite of its 7.5-inch guns. Advances in design came so swiftly that many of the older light cruisers were converted into depot and accommodation ships or minelayers.

The end of the First World War brought the withdrawal of Germany as a naval power, but in 1919 the United States undertook a programme of six battleships and six battlecruisers, all of which were to be armed with huge 16-inch

Above: HMS 'Norfolk', a County-class missile-destroyer of the type which is largely replacing conventional cruisers.
BARNABY'S PICTURE LIBRARY

Overleaf: HMS 'Colossus', painted here by Robert H. Smith, was one of Admiral Jellicoe's dreadnoughts which faced the German High Seas Fleet at the Battle of Jutland on 31 May 1916.
IMPERIAL WAR MUSEUM, LONDON (RICHARD SHARPE STUDIOS)

guns. Before long, Japan had built some similar ships, and Britain made plans for a class of four 48,000-ton battle-cruisers, to be armed with nine 16-inch guns apiece. But this arms race was becoming expensive, and the signing of the Washington Treaty in 1922 introduced limitations on both the total and individual tonnage of future classes. The number of heavy cruisers in all the major navies dwindled in the next few years, but when the German Navy was allowed limited construction towards the end of the Twenties, she produced the three so-called pocket battleships. Officially rated by the Germans as armoured cruisers, they were essentially battlecruisers armed with six 11-inch guns, and displacing 10,000 tons. Eight twin-shaft diesel engines ensured an excellent long-range performance with a top speed of twenty-six knots. These were followed by the rebuilt *Scharnhorst* and *Gneisenau*, which were larger and capable of thirty-one knots, though they carried only nine 11-inch guns. During the early Thirties naval tacticians began to see the new battlecruiser more and more as a lone operator.

Britain entered the Second World War with only three remaining veterans from the big-gun era, and it was learnt at cost that times had changed with the emergence of highly sophisticated air power. Only the *Renown* gallantly survived to be broken up some years later.

In the mid-Thirties the Arethusa class and the three larger Amphion class (all three of which were later transferred to the Australian Navy) replaced many of the C-class cruisers of the 1917-18 period, which were destined for the scrapyard under the terms of the London Treaty. There was a general trend towards the light cruiser as Britain began building the Dido-class cruisers, which were intended to carry ten 5.25-inch guns, and the Americans built the Atlanta class, equipping them with sixteen 5-inch guns. The Southampton and Colony-class cruisers of the following years entered the Second World War armed with 6-inch guns, but by the end

of hostilities most ships in both classes had been modified to allow the installation of light anti-aircraft guns.

The American answer to the Mogami class was the Brooklyn-class light cruiser. This ship, armed with fifteen 6-inch guns, was followed by the Baltimore class which boasted nine 8-inch guns. Further American designs followed, including the Des Moines classes: easily the largest cruisers ever built, with a displacement of about 21,000 tons.

Apart from the Royal Navy's three Tiger-class ships, the only post-war-designed cruisers in the Western fleets are the Dutch *De Zeven Provincien* and *De Ruyter*, and the French *Colbert* and *De Grasse*. The American nuclear-powered cruiser *Long Beach*, completed in 1961, is armed with Talos and Tartar SAM missile systems and 5-inch guns. Various cruisers have exchanged guns for missiles since the end of the Second World War, including some of the Russian-built Sverdlov-class cruisers, a few of which have recently been shown to have a considerable minelaying capacity.

But today the cruiser is fast disappearing as a type altogether. The large missile frigate or destroyer leader seems destined to take over its role once and for all. Yet no other ship has featured so prominently over the past century in the development of the world's navies, nor has any type of warship proved more adaptable than the cruiser in meeting the changing demands of both technology and tactics.

Aircraft Carriers

THE use of aircraft at sea was quickly appreciated by far-sighted officers in the British, American, German and French navies within a very short time of the Wright brothers' historic flight in 1903. The first flight made by an aircraft from a ship was in 1910, when a Curtiss biplane took off from a platform rigged on the American cruiser *Birmingham*. The following year, the Americans landed a Curtiss biplane on the battleship *Pennsylvania*, but on both occasions the ships were at anchor.

In January 1912, a Short biplane successfully flew off the deck of the British battleship *Africa* and at King George V's Coronation Fleet Review at Portland, the following May, a Short biplane took off from the *Africa*'s sister *Hibernia* while she was steaming at ten knots. The experiment was repeated a couple of months later from the battleship *London* steaming at twelve knots.

Although thought was being given to improving the main function of naval aircraft – their effectiveness at reconnaissance – by fitting radio, and to the possibility of using the aircraft as bombers and torpedo carriers, the Navy's most important weapon remained the gun. But the flying-off platforms in battleships prevented the main armament being used, and, for that reason, it was decided to fit out the old cruiser *Hermes* as a seaplane carrier. Hydro aeroplanes, as seaplanes were first called, seemed better suited for use at sea, since they required only hangar and workshop space on board and derricks or cranes to lower them into and recover them from the water.

Although the seaplanes operated from *Hermes* proved their value for reconnaissance during fleet exercises, the need for a seaplane tender as an integral part of the fleet was still not fully established. In 1913, *Hermes* had been paid off, but a merchant ship building at Blyth was taken over for conversion to a seaplane tender and was named *Ark Royal*.

The first occasion when ship-borne aircraft were involved in hostilities occurred in January 1914, when seaplanes from the American cruiser *Birmingham* and the battelship *Mississippi* were employed on reconnaissance duties during the war with Mexico. But, by August 1914 all British naval aircraft were shore-based. France had converted the depot ship *Foudre* into a seaplane tender and Germany was concentrating almost exclusively on Zeppelin airships for use at sea.

As *Ark Royal*'s conversion could not be completed before 1915, the Admiralty commandeered three English Channel ferries, *Empress*, *Engadine* and *Riviera*, as seaplane tenders. They were fitted with hangars and a small platform served by derricks for handling seaplanes. Work was also put in hand to improve the aircraft-handling capabilities of *Hermes* because *Ark Royal*'s speed of eleven knots made her too slow to work with the fleet and neutralised the advantage of her longer deck. To meet the need for a ship with adequate length to provide a flying-off platform that was also fast enough to work with the fleet, the elderly Cunarder *Campania* was purchased in October 1914 for conversion, and work was completed late the following spring.

The first offensive action by ship-borne aircraft took place on Christmas Day 1914, when the three former Channel ferries escorted by cruisers and destroyers steamed into the Heligoland Bight to attack German airship sheds in the Hamburg area. Fog caused only one seaplane to reach its target, and its bombs missed; four seaplanes were lost. Similar attacks on German Zeppelins in their bases continued spasmodically throughout the war and culminated in the highly successful Tondern raid in 1918, when aircraft from the converted battlecruiser *Furious* destroyed two Zeppelins.

In 1915, seaplanes from the *Ark Royal* attacked a Turkish battleship in the Dardanelles and a seaplane from the converted Isle of Man ferry *Ben-my-Chree* in the same area that year made history by hitting a Turkish supply ship at 300 yards with a torpedo.

The *Campania*, on joining the Grand Fleet in the summer of 1915, was found to have too small a flight deck (it measured 120 feet) and by the end of the year, she had been taken in hand for further conversion. She had to stop to lower seaplanes into the water and an order was made that they should be launched only after the enemy had been sighted by scouting cruisers. This limitation on her use was the main reason for her being ordered to return to harbour before she could join the fleet at the Battle of Jutland in May 1916. *Engadine*, working with Beatty's battle cruisers, did get one seaplane airborne during the battle and it reported the movements of some enemy light forces.

More former ferries were converted to carry seaplanes, including *Vindex*, *Nairana*, *Manxman* and *Pegasus*. The first could carry two landplanes, but they had to be assembled before they could be flown off. As none of the conversions to that date had proved entirely satisfactory, the Admiralty decided shortly after Jutland to convert two liners then under construction for Italy. In the event, only one was converted and she was named *Argus*.

In view of the time taken to convert the *Argus*, the battlecruiser *Furious* was given a flying-off deck in place of her forward 18-in gun turret – despite fierce opposition from the naval gunnery world. The light cruiser *Yarmouth* was also given a flying-off platform for a single aircraft but, unlike those fitted in battleships before the war, the platform did not interfere with the use of the main armament. Four more cruisers were later similarly converted to give the scouting forces some means of countering German reconnaissance Zeppelins.

Towards the end of the war, *Furious* had her deck extended aft, which meant removing her other 18-in gun turret. But landing wheeled aircraft was hazardous, partly because of turbulence and smoke caused by the funnel uptakes, and because the only means of stopping an aircraft was for the flight-deck party to grab the aircraft's lower planes as it rolled onto the deck.

The successful deck landing of a Sopwith Pup on *Furious* in 1917 decided the Admiralty against ordering further seaplane carriers; in addition to fitting the after deck in *Furious*, the design of *Argus* was ordered to be modified, as was that of the new *Hermes*, which had been laid down from the keel up as an aircraft carrier. To fill the gap until those ships were ready, the new cruiser *Cavendish* (later renamed *Vindictive*) was also given a take-off and landing deck.

Because of the problems caused by the midships structures dividing the take-off and landing decks in *Furious* and *Argus*, both ships were further modified by moving the boiler-room uptakes over to the starboard side, to give a clear length of deck. The policy of fitting flying-off platforms in

H M S PEGASUS

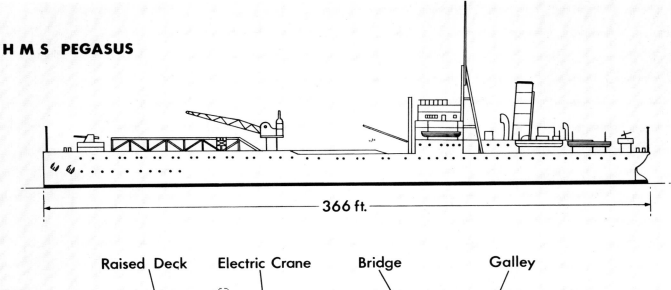

← 366 ft. →

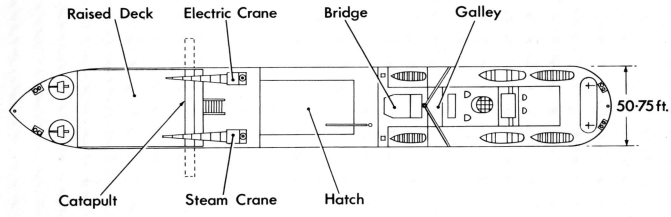

Raised Deck   Electric Crane   Bridge   Galley

Catapult   Steam Crane   Hatch

50·75 ft.

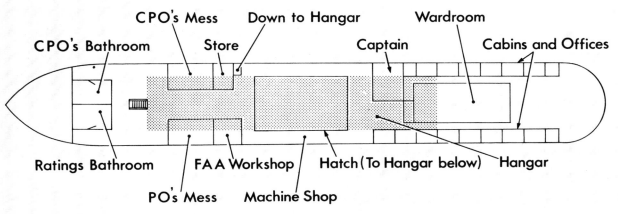

CPO's Mess   Down to Hangar   Wardroom

CPO's Bathroom   Store   Captain   Cabins and Offices

Ratings Bathroom   FAA Workshop   Hatch (To Hangar below)   Hangar

PO's Mess   Machine Shop

Above: Drawings showing the general layout and disposition of equipment for 'Pegasus' when she was a fighter catapult ship.
K. E. POOLMAN

Left: A Walrus flying-boat being lifted aboard 'Pegasus' while she was engaged in Fleet Air Arm pilot training.
IMPERIAL WAR MUSEUM, LONDON

capital ships and cruisers was continued, but only in October 1918 did the *Argus* appear as the first ship with a flight-deck similar to that in the carrier as it is known today.

Even without having to contend with funnel turbulence and smoke, landing on a carrier remained hazardous, as the first arrester wires were simply stretched across the deck and weighted at each end with sandbags.

By Armistice Day 1918, ship-borne aircraft had been employed in the North Sea and Mediterranean, off the coast of East Africa, and in the eastern Indian Ocean where the seaplane tender *Raven II* was employed hunting for the German raider *Wolf*. In numbers of ships and aircraft, not to mention experience, the Royal Naval Air Service easily led the world at the time of the merger with the Royal Flying Corps in 1918 which formed the Royal Air Force.

France and America both had seaplane tenders, and Japan had the converted merchant ship *Wakamiya* as an aircraft tender. But America particularly was to press ahead strongly with the development of carriers. In the 1919 Atlantic fleet exercises, the minelayer *Shawmut* was used as a flying-boat tender, while the battleship *Texas* had flying-off platforms for two Sopwith Camels as a result of her service with the Grand Fleet.

The Americans' use of various warships as auxiliary flying-boat tenders was extended and in 1921, the converted collier *Langley* was commissioned as a proper aircraft carrier. The former merchant ship *Wright* had the unusual distinction of being both a seaplane tender and the Asiatic Squadron flagship. The 1922 Washington Treaty resulted in the cancellation of two new American battlecruisers and their being redesigned as the aircraft carriers *Lexington* and *Saratoga*.

In France the battleship *Bearn* was also converted in the

By the early 1930s the ability to carry aircraft in some form at sea became almost *de rigueur* for all but the smallest navies. The results were some interesting designs, such as the seaplane-cruiser *Götland* in the Swedish Navy and the Australian seaplane tender *Albatross*.

The Americans, however, closely followed by the Japanese, set the pace in the development of the large aircraft carrier. Although the *Ranger* of 1933 was less than half the size of the earlier American carriers *Saratoga* and *Lexington*, she could carry seventy-five aircraft, compared to the earlier ships' maximum of ninety. The *Enterprise* and *Yorktown*, launched three years later, were able to carry 100 aircraft on a nominal displacement of 19,900 tons, compared to the *Saratoga*'s 33,000 tons.

France virtually opted out of naval aviation and built only the seaplane tender *Commandant Teste*, carrying twenty-six aircraft, in addition to the *Bearn*, between the wars. In Britain, successive disarmament conferences and political expediency resulted in the RAF putting the naval side of its responsibilities in a backwater in order to find funds for Lord Trenchard's 'omnipotent' bombers, while the Admiralty, also short of funds, concentrated available money mainly on keeping up cruiser strength for the protection of shipping. In Germany, work began in the late 1930s on two carriers, the *Graf Zeppelin* and *Peter Strasser*, although neither was destined to be completed.

Only in 1937 was the Royal Navy able to launch a new carrier, the 22,600-ton *Ark Royal*, but at least she represented about twenty years of carrier experience. By then, also, hydraulic arrester wires were in service and compressed air was used for catapulting reconnaissance aircraft from battleships and cruisers.

course of construction into a carrier and completed in 1925-26. But Japan began building a carrier designed as such from the start – the 9,500-ton *Hosho*. Two more battleship and battlecruiser designs were redrawn as carriers and emerged in the mid-1920s as the *Kaga* and *Akagi*.

Italy acquired a seaplane tender, the *Giuseppe Miraglia*, which was a converted merchant ship, like the Spanish *Dedalo* which could also carry support facilities for a small airship. Later, this ship made history when she was used to test the first rotary-wing aircraft, Cierva's Autogiro, at sea.

In Britain, the success of the conversion of *Furious* resulted in a similar conversion for her original sister ships, *Courageous* and *Glorious*, while the former Chilean battleship *Almirante Cochrane*, whose construction had been suspended throughout the war, was completed as the carrier *Eagle*.

In the year of *Ark Royal*'s launch came the laying down of the new British Illustrious-class carriers. Although nominally credited with a capacity of sixty aircraft, they carried far fewer aircraft than contemporary American carriers such as *Enterprise*, because their strength deck was the armoured flight deck, whereas in the American carriers the hangar deck was the strength deck and the flight-deck was wood planked. In addition, the British ships had enclosed forecastles, which gave them superior sea-keeping qualities, particularly when steaming fast into a head sea to launch aircraft.

Shortly before the outbreak of war, both France and Russia began constructing carriers, but in neither country did work progress very far before the war intervened. In 1939, Britain entered the war with the *Ark Royal, Courageous, Glorious,*

Eagle, *Hermes*, *Furious* and *Argus*; the last-named was assigned to a training role and at one time she had been operating 'Queen Bee' radio-controlled target aircraft. There were also two seaplane tenders, the ex-Australian *Albatross* and the *Pegasus*, former *Ark Royal*.

The first successful major action of the war using naval aircraft, that against the German cruiser *Königsberg* at Bergen in 1940, did not involve a carrier; the forerunner of the Japanese and American Pacific carrier battles was the attack on the Italian fleet at Taranto in November 1940 by aircraft from *Illustrious* and *Eagle*. At the time of her entry into the war, America had seven carriers, excluding the obsolescent *Langley*. Japan had ten, of which six were employed in the attack on Pearl Harbour in 1941.

The great carrier battles between the Americans and Japanese, starting with Midway in 1942, firmly established the carrier's position as the capital ship in place of the battleship. At first, losses on both sides were heavy, the Americans losing the *Lexington*, *Hornet*, *Wasp* and *York-town*, and later *Princeton*. But the Japanese at the end of the war had not a single carrier left.

The Royal Navy, too, suffered. The *Courageous* was torpedoed in 1939 while on anti-submarine patrol; German surface ships sank the *Glorious* the following year off Norway; and later the *Ark Royal*, *Eagle* and *Hermes* were all lost.

The loss of *Courageous* ended the use of large carriers in independent patrols against submarines, but the vital need for air support against the U-boats, particularly in the gap in mid-Atlantic which shore-based aircraft supporting convoys could not reach, was keenly felt. From this need was born the escort carrier – initially a converted German merchant ship which had been captured and renamed HMS *Audacity*. Before her conversion in 1941, the old *Pegasus* had been fitted with a catapult to launch a naval Fulmar fighter and several other ships were similarly converted in order to give convoys some means of destroying long-range German reconnaissance planes that were guiding U-boats to the convoys.

Audacity could carry twelve Martlet fighters but had no hangar and the aircraft were parked on the 460ft deck.

Audacity, which was later sunk, was the forerunner of about thirty-four escort carriers in the Royal Navy, most of them American-built converted merchant ships, and more than twice that number in the US Navy.

The Americans also converted eleven Worcester and Cleveland class cruisers during construction into light fleet carriers. One, *Princeton*, was lost and *Independence* was expended in the 1946 Bikini Atoll nuclear bomb experiments. The backbone of the American wartime carrier fleet was formed by the twenty-four Essex-class ships, although some were not completed until after the end of the war.

Although roughly comparable in size, as designed, to the British Illustrious class, they could carry up to 107 aircraft. Their wooden flight decks, which helped make this capacity possible, proved a liability, particularly during the closing days of the war when they were attacked by Japanese kamikaze aircraft. The *Franklin*, for example, was so severely damaged that she was never operational again.

Among the oddities the war produced were the first, and only, paddle aircraft carriers – the converted Great Lakes steamers *Sable* and *Wolverine*, which the Americans used for deck-landing training. In Britain, a new design of carrier intended also to serve as an aircraft repair ship was the *Unicorn*, completed in 1943. She was used mainly as an escort carrier in the war, but performed her repair and ferry carrier role in the Korean War in the early 1950s.

By 1944, with the elimination of most of the German surface fleet, the build-up of the Royal Navy's contribution to the American forces fighting the Japanese was under way. By VJ-Day 1945, all six of the fleet carriers, *Illustrious*, *Formidable*, *Victorious*, *Indomitable*, *Implacable* and *Inde-fatigable*, had played their part in fighting the Japanese and several survived hits by kamikazes. Unlike the American carriers, their armoured flight-decks allowed them to operate aircraft again within a matter of hours.

By the end of the war the first of the light fleet carriers were in the Pacific. They were built to Lloyd's specifications up to main-deck level with an eye to their post-war conversion into fast cargo ships – an option never taken up. Of sixteen of the class ordered, two were converted during construction into aircraft repair ships. One of them, the *Perseus*, was fitted with a ramp for testing the new steam catapult in the 1950s, and at Rosyth dockyard had the embarrassing experience of launching a pilotless test aircraft which failed to crash into the sea as planned and instead circled round Edinburgh and the dockyard for some minutes.

In 1946, the *Ocean*, of the same class, became the first British ship to land a jet fighter. *Ocean* also pioneered the use of helicopters at sea.

At the time of the Japanese surrender, eight larger carriers of the Polyphemus class were being built and they had a displacement of 18,000 tons, compared to the early light fleet carriers' 13,000 tons. Four of the former were never completed, as was also the case with the *Leviathan* of the smaller type. The end of the war also terminated construction of the 50,000-ton fleet carriers *Gibraltar*, *Malta* and *New Zealand*.

The light fleet carriers played their part in helping to rebuild Allied navies: *Colossus* became the French *Arromanches* and *Venerable* became the Dutch *Karel Doorman*, replacing the escort carrier *Vindex* which had been on loan, *Warrior* was lent to Canada and was replaced later by the *Magnificent* and then the *Powerful*, renamed *Bonaventure*. Australia took over the *Terrible* and *Majestic*, renaming them *Sydney* and *Melbourne*. The former, with the British *Triumph*, *Ocean*, *Glory* and *Theseus*, provided virtually all the air support the Commonwealth gave to the UN forces in Korea.

In more recent years, Argentina has acquired the former *Karel Doorman*, now the *25 De Mayo*, while Brazil has the former *Vengeance*, now the *Minas Gerais*. With the sale of the *Karel Doorman*, the Dutch abandoned carriers, as did the Canadians with the scrapping of *Bonaventure*.

The light fleet carriers' slow speed (about twenty-five knots maximum) and small capacity and flight-deck length made them unsuitable for the increasingly heavy jets that were coming into service, although *Warrior* for a time had

a rubber covering on her flight-deck aft to see if jets could be landed without undercarriages on deck. The need to find some means whereby the crash barrier to stop aircraft which failed to hook onto the arrestor wires aft would be unnecessary resulted in the angled deck, which helps an aircraft to go round again if it misses the wires.

The American carrier *Antietam* was the first to be fitted with this British invention and the first British carrier so fitted was *Centaur*, of the Polyphemus class. But the maximum desirable angle of about $8\frac{1}{2}$ degrees could only be fitted in larger carriers such as the *Victorious*, which was totally rebuilt in 1950-58, and in the new American Forrestal-class carriers, built in the 1950s. It was later fitted in the earlier three American Midway-class carriers, and in the British *Ark Royal*, of 1955, and *Eagle*, of 1951.

The *Eagle* was also the first ship to be fitted with the mirror landing aid, which was later replaced by a system of lights designed to guide the pilot approaching the deck – at about 120 knots in the case of the American Phantom fighter, for example.

The future became clear for carriers in 1961 with the completion of the American nuclear-powered *Enterprise*. On a displacement of 75,500 tons, she can carry around ninety aircraft – the same number as the *Saratoga* of thirty-five years earlier, which illustrates how the size and weight of aircraft have increased.

In 1966, the British Government, despite all the lessons of the Second World War and Korea, decided that the Royal Navy should have no more carriers; the new CVA-01 was cancelled, and the life of the remaining carriers was eventually to be ended in 1972. *Ark Royal* alone was reprieved, the announcement coming not long before the first hint that Russia had started to build carriers.

Below: The most recent 'Ark Royal' in the English Channel in 1972. J. EASTLAND

The Mammoth Tanker

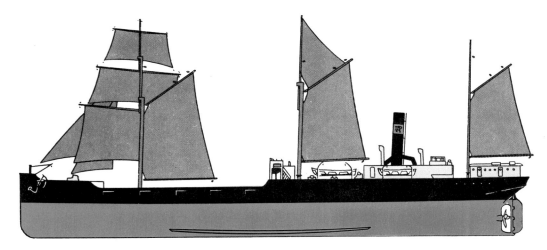

The 2,307-ton 'Gluckauf' built in 1886 for the German-American Oil Co and the prototype of the modern tanker. B. S. IRELAND

LITTLE more than a century separates the modern half-million-ton tanker from the arrival in the Thames of the 224-ton brig, *Elizabeth Watts*, with a cargo of 1,329 barrels of North American oil products; about 200 tons in all!

The specialised tanker trade developed with the increasing use of oil for illumination. However, shipment in barrels proved expensive, since the round container was uneconomic for stowage aboard and before long shippers turned to the use of rectangular cans in wooden cases. This development led to the coining of the term 'case-oil trade' to describe the shipment of paraffin (kerosene) from the United States for distribution to users throughout western Europe.

Case-oil shipment was not the complete answer, however, for there still remained the problem of economic disposal of the containers. In time, means were developed for the carriage of oil in bulk by building tanks into the hulls of ships. Among the problems encountered were the expansion and contraction of the cargo with changes in temperature, the effect upon a ship's stability of considerable liquid 'free surface' and, above all, the ever-present risk of fire or explosion presented by bulk stowage of a volatile cargo.

In due course, the idea of using the ship's hull itself as the bulk container for the cargo led to the construction of the prototype of the modern tanker, albeit miniscule by today's standards, in the shape of the 2,307-ton *Gluckauf*, built at Newcastle for the German-American Oil Co in 1886. A contemporary British-registered tank vessel, the 1,669-ton *Bakuin*, was the first to be classified by Lloyd's for the carriage of 'petroleum in bulk' but, despite prescribed precautions, she was destroyed by fire off Callao in 1902.

Thereafter, the development of the oil tanker was a process of gradual evolution, at first in step with the growth in the use of oil and its by-products, but more recently as the result of political pressures and changes in international relationships. Many and varied were the attempts to pare the costs of oil transport and in the years preceding the First World War shipbuilders devoted much design effort to meeting the requirements of the oil companies.

One solution to the problem of economics was the building for the Anglo-American Oil Co Ltd of the twin-screw steam tanker *Iroquois* and her attendant tow-barge *Navahoe* by Harland & Wolff of Belfast, a name which remains prominent in the sphere of tankship design and construction. This pair,

with respective cargo capacities of about 8,800 tons and 9,250 tons, played their part as the 'horse and cart' of the North Atlantic from 1908 until 1930, apart from a break between May 1917 and November 1918 when they were employed on Admiralty service.

However, the ship-and-trailer concept was not developed further and between the wars the oil companies evolved a series of more or less standard designs ranging from 8,000 to 17,000 deadweight tons tailored to suit the needs of individual operators. Those of the early 1920s were, in the main, steam driven, but later vessels were given diesel machinery for a service speed of eleven to twelve knots.

In passing it should be noted that it is usual to refer to the size of tankers and other bulk carriers in terms of deadweight tonnage (dwt); that is, the actual tonnage of cargo, fuel and stores that the ship is designed to carry when loaded to her marks, rather than in terms of the gross tonnage (grt) usually quoted for passenger vessels and frequently for general cargo carriers.

As has been mentioned above, the oil trade in its early days was confined largely to the North Atlantic, with European demands for paraffin and other petroleum products being met from North American sources. In the 1870s, however, Nobel Bros opened up the Caucasian oilfields around Baku in Azerbaijan and brought the first element of competition into the trade by shipping oil out from Black Sea ports, not only to meet European needs but also to satisfy demands in the Far East. The Far East traffic was developed in particular by Marcus Samuel's Shell Transport & Trading Co, which was the first organisation to be granted a concession for the shipment of petroleum products via the Suez Canal.

By the turn of the century, development of the oil industry had become more broadly based, with new sources of supply exploited in the Dutch East Indies and Persia (as it then was), followed by the opening up of oilfields in Romania, Mexico, Venezuela, Iraq, Curaçao, Trinidad and California. The major oil companies associated with the exploitation operated their own fleets, mainly under the British, Dutch, United States and French flags, but in addition large independent fleets for charter work were built up under the Scandinavian, Italian and Greek flags.

Between the wars, consumption of fuels, lubricants and

an ever-increasing variety of petroleum-based by-products grew rapidly, but the fact that, in general, cargoes were refined products processed close to the port of shipment limited the size of tankers to that sufficient to meet the economic requirements of shippers and importers. Factors to be taken into account included the rate of output at the refinery and the availability of local storage, the availability of facilities for storage of differing products at the discharge port, and the limitations imposed by the use of waterways such as the Suez Canal and the Shatt-al-Arab.

The same factors held good throughout the Second World War, but in the late 1940s, commercial and political considerations led to the construction by the established oil companies of vast refineries in the importing countries, such as those in the United Kingdom at Fawley, Stanlow in Cheshire and on the Isle of Grain in the Thames.

The change from the shipment of refined products to that of crude oil resulted in a demand for larger tankers which could be operated more economically than the then existing product carrier. The only limitation was the size of the Suez Canal, through which the greater part of the crude oil for west European refineries had to be carried. Already Suez was in the process of being widened and deepened to permit the passage of vessels drawing up to thirty-eight feet and with the early 1950s came the completion for the major fleets of numbers of so-called supertankers in the 28,000 to 30,000dwt class.

In 1953, completion by a German shipyard of the 45,750-dwt *Tina Onassis* gave rise to a claim to the title of 'largest tanker in the world' and started a growth explosion which has yet to reach the ultimate in the matters of sheer size and the economies of scale. The economic wisdom of building such vessels was soon proved, however, and each year saw the completion of new claimants to the title.

The increasing demand for oil, particularly in Japan and the United States (which had become an oil-importing country taking vast quantities from the Middle East), led to the construction by the rapidly expanding Japanese shipbuilding industry of the first tankers in the 100,000dwt class.

Closure of the Suez Canal in 1956 led to the conclusion on the part of some west European shippers, too, that large fast supertankers of 100,000 tons and more sailing round the Cape would be more economic in operation than smaller vessels, relatively more labour intensive, working via the Red Sea and a re-opened Canal. The decision to order big tankers was fully justified by the second closure of the Suez Canal in the wake of the Arab-Israeli conflict of July 1967.

The Suez Canal remained closed again for nearly ten years and giant tankers of dimensions only dreamed of in 1967 sail round the Cape from the Persian Gulf to western Europe, to the Gulf and eastern seaboard ports of the United States and also eastwards across the Indian Ocean to Australia and Japan. The expanding demand for oil has also resulted in the exploitation of new fields in Libya and Algeria to meet in part the requirements of western Europe and the United States.

In 1965, Vickers Ltd completed at Barrow the first British-built tanker in the 100,000-ton class, the 111,420dwt *British Admiral* owned by the BP Tanker Co Ltd. She was soon eclipsed, however, by the bulk of the 151,250-ton Japanese-built *Tokyo Maru* delivered in 1966, but such was progress that that giant was quickly surpassed by the 210,000-ton *Idemitsu Maru* built by Ishikawajima-Harima Heavy Industries of Yokohama. Designed for the Persian Gulf (Kuwait) to Japan (Tokuyama Refinery) trade, the *Idemitsu Maru* was propelled, in keeping with normal supertanker practice, by steam turbines geared to a single shaft and developing about 33,000shp to give a service speed of 16½ knots.

Japanese shipbuilders, with their spacious shipyards developed on assembly plant lines out of the ruins of the war, took a lead for several years in the design and construction of large crude oil and other bulk cargo carriers,

and each passing year brought the completion of another 'largest . . . in the world'! The ultimate in size has probably not yet been reached, but a definite milestone was reached in April 1972, when Ishikawajima-Harima Heavy Industries placed in position in their Kure yard the first keel section of a 'half-million ton tanker', built to the order of Globtik Tankers Ltd, London, and intended for service between the Gulf and Japan.

Built at a cost approaching £23 million, *Globtik Tokyo* was launched in October 1972 and was delivered to her owners in February 1973. The vessel has a deadweight rating of 483,644 tons and is 1,243½ feet long overall; her beam is 203½ feet and her draught nearly 92 feet when fully laden (compared with the 32½-ft draught of the 963½-ft-long Cunard liner *Queen Elizabeth 2*). Everything about the ship

is on a gigantic scale; the rudder alone weighs 250 tons and the two anchors are 29 tons apiece!

Globtik Tokyo has been chartered to the Tokyo Tanker Co, which owns a number of supertankers sailing under the Japanese flag, and operates between Kharg Island, off Bushire (Iran) in the Persian Gulf, and the Nippon Oil Group's terminal at Kiire in south-western Japan, working loaded to her marks eastwards across the Indian Ocean, passing to the south of Java and thence turning northward via the deep-water Lombok Strait to reach her discharge port. After discharge at Kiire, she is routed westwards in ballast via the South China Sea and the relatively shallow Malacca Strait.

Globtik Tokyo is propelled by a steam turbine set of 45,000shp geared to a single shaft and driving a 61-ton five-

Below: The 'Globtik Tokyo', which cost nearly £23 million and has a deadweight rating of 483,644 tons, being launched from the Kure Shipyard, Japan, in October 1972.
IH HEAVY INDUSTRIES CO LTD

bladed propeller to give a laden speed of fourteen knots. Machinery control is completely automated and surveillance is exercised by two watch engineers in the air-conditioned and sound-insulated Machinery Control Room. Passage from the Gulf to Japan takes twenty-one days and discharge at Kiire is completed in a matter of nineteen hours; it takes twenty-four hours for the complete turn-round and sixteen days at seventeen knots back to the Persian Gulf to load another half-million tons of crude oil.

Navigation of a ship almost a quarter of a mile long, and drawing ninety-two feet when fully laden, presents its own peculiar problems to the command, particularly when man-oeuvring in confined waters. When docking or negotiating narrow waterways, accurate positioning of the vessel is assisted by the use of a Doppler sonar system, which is designed to produce a visual record of the ship's position to the nearest yard and to feed signals to an auto-pilot to control speed and heading.

Once clear of land, navigation is facilitated by the use of a satellite navigation system producing a teletypewriter print-out of the ship's latitude and longitude. The system generates only a positional record and does not indicate transient navigational hazards such as other ships. As in the majority of large vessels, however, duplicate navigational radars are installed and, in *Globtik Tokyo*, one of them incorporates an anti-collision device which gives an audible warning of the presence of any other vessel or obstacle in the ship's path. In this connection, it is worth noting that with the ship in ballast, sight from the bridge of anything in the ship's path is obscured once it is within two miles!

Despite her bulk, however, the *Globtik Tokyo* has a turning circle of only 1,100 yards, that is, less than three times her length, and she is capable of an emergency stop well within three miles. The likelihood of another *Torrey Canyon* disaster as a result of navigational misjudgement is thought to be remote.

A current recommendation of the Inter-governmental Maritime Consultative Organisation (IMCO) calls for the provision in new supertankers of an inert gas system to keep to a minimum the oxygen content in the cargo tank head-space, thus reducing the chances of an accidental explosion. This is achieved in *Globtik Tokyo* by cooling and filtering the boiler uptake gases and utilising the resultant mixture of nitrogen, carbon monoxide and carbon dioxide to displace the atmospheric air in the cargo headspace.

As is usual practice in oil-tankers, tank cleaning is under-taken at sea as a routine process during the return passage in ballast to the loading terminal. Like practically every opera-tion in the new tanker, the cleaning process is automated and the resultant oil/water sullage is passed to a pair of tanks where the oil is stripped from the water before discharge overboard of the latter. Discharge of any oil or oil/water sullage is prohibited within fifty miles of any coast by inter-national convention; the latest systems are designed to ensure that cargo residues do not find their way overboard at any time.

During and after cleaning, the supply of inert gas should maintain the safety of the cargo spaces and ensure that there will be no repetition of the kind of explosion which in December 1969 wrecked the Shell tanker *Marpessa* and in similar incidents during the same month severely damaged another Shell tanker, *Mactra* (208,560dwt), and the Nor-wegian-owned *Kong Haakon VII* (219,000dwt).

All in all, everything possible has been done to ensure the safety of the ship, its cargo and the crew of only thirty-eight officers and men, but it is a truism that the sea is always master of its own environment and the possibility of disaster is always present. A tanker of half a million deadweight tons cannot ride heavy seas, but will butt its way through with the possibility of damage unless constant vigilance is exercised by the command; those on watch on the bridge have to bear in mind at all times that the huge bulbous bow is nearly a quarter of a mile distant and that motion and working of the ship cannot be felt or sensed in the manner usual in smaller vessels, which are relatively flexible.

Despite every precaution and the avoidance of risks, however, accidents can happen and in the event of some major catastrophe, either of the two boats can accommodate the entire ship's company. Survival equipment and food provided are sufficient for two months, and there are com-prehensive navigational aids.

Globtik Tankers Ltd, the London-based owners of *Globtik Tokyo*, was founded in 1967 by a former Indian Navy officer, Ravi Tikkoo, and purchased its first ship, *Globtik Sun*, in 1968. Registered in the name of Globtik Tankers Overseas Ltd, the vessel was managed on her owner's behalf by J. & J. Denholm (Management) Ltd. *Globtik Mercury* was acquired in 1969 and was registered in the name of Globtik Tankers International Ltd of Nassau, Bahamas, also managed by J. & J. Denholm.

When the firm took delivery of its first half-million-ton tanker its future profitability seemed assured, since the ship has been chartered for twenty years at £11 million a year, the owner being responsible for all aspects of operation and maintenance, including the £2 million annual insurance premium. All being well, outstanding debts should be cleared in the first eight years' operation.

The vessel is British registered and has a UK-based crew, members of which will be flown home in rotation for leave. Since the greater part of the ship's time in service will be spent at sea in tropical waters, amenities are provided on a luxurious scale. All accommodation is air-conditioned and a swimming-pool is built in on the upper deck. As is common practice senior officers may be accompanied by wives.

No other national shipbuilding industry has been in a position to compete with the Japanese in the matter of size for many years past, but recent extensive modernisation of certain west-European yards has enabled shipbuilders to offer attractive terms and satisfactory delivery dates to potential customers. Thus the Soc Maritime Shell (Shell's French tanker-operating subsidiary) has placed orders with the Chantiers de l'Atlantique for the construction of a pair of 533,000dwt twin-screw steam-turbine tankers at St Nazaire. Nearer home, Harland & Wolff Ltd, the Belfast shipbuilder, has laid claim to being the only shipyard with facilities for the construction of a 1.75-million-ton tanker!

The Globtik Tanker Co has turned again to the Japanese industry, however, with enquiries concerning the construction of a 700,000-ton giant and already, Hitachi Zosen has under construction for Greek owners another tanker in the half-million-ton class.

The scope for employment of such vessels with a draught in excess of ninety feet must of necessity be limited, however, since there are few ports or sheltered anchorages within reach of existing refineries where sufficient depth of water is available to permit provision of the appropriate terminal facilities. Certain measures are being examined to reduce the problem, such as the extra-beam reduced-draught (RD) designs. Despite the handicap of draught, economic sense dictates the employment of the largest hull possible, even if only for the relative saving in expensive manpower. The thirty-eight-man crew of *Globtik Tokyo* totals only nine more than the crew of *Tokyo Maru*, a vessel of less than one-third the deadweight tonnage!

In practice, however, the savings are not to be reckoned only in terms of manpower, as the increase in propulsive power for a specified service speed with a given hull form is not related directly to the increase in size or deadweight tonnage. Hence, savings in fuel, and a reduction in the relative weight of propulsion machinery as a function of cargo capacity, give added weight to the arguments for the largest vessel possible consistent with the limitations imposed by a particular trade route. The growth curve has yet to level off, but the indications are that any future refineries dependent upon imported supplies of crude oil will be sited within reach of deepwater discharge berths.

Nuclear Ships and Submarines

ALTHOUGH a relatively new concept in the field of marine engineering, the design and operating techniques of steam generation utilising the heat produced in a controlled nuclear reaction are already well established for warships, although it has yet to be shown that such plant can be exploited successfully on a commercial scale. The preliminary empirical work was truly international but the name particularly linked with the first practical reactor was that of Enrico Fermi who, working with a team of American and British scientists in Chicago, constructed his atomic pile which went critical for the first time on 2 December 1942. Ten days later it was run at a power level of 200 watts!

Already, in the United Kingdom, the Maude Committee had forecast in a report entitled *The Use of Uranium as a Source of Power*, published in 1941, that nuclear ship propulsion would become a practical proposition within a few years. The world was at war, however, and for the time being research was concentrated on the more immediate requirement for a nuclear fission bomb. The weapon was used with devastating effect on Hiroshima and Nagasaki early in August 1945; a few days later, on 14 August, the Japanese Government surrendered and the war was over.

Unlike the nuclear bomb, designed to produce a 'big bang' as the result of an uncontrolled chain reaction, the propulsion requirement was for a safe compact reactor to produce heat for use in some form of steam generating plant coupled to conventional steam turbine machinery. The United States, with a wealth of accumulated experience, took the lead and Vice-Admiral Hyman G. Rickover was appointed in charge of a US Navy research team. Lack of funds and facilities stifled progress, however, and little was achieved until 1949, when a vote of three million dollars was secured from the funds of the US Bureau of Ships.

It had been envisaged already that the development of a compact nuclear propulsion plant would permit the design of a true submarine, a vessel whose natural element would be beneath the surface rather than on it. The submersible torpedo craft which have featured in the navies of the world for rather more than half a century, although capable of travelling fully submerged for short distances, are still basically air dependent; the capacity of their electric storage batteries is very limited. Thus there was a long-standing incentive for the development of a true submarine, designed for optimum underwater performance without regard for surface behaviour. That was the task set for Admiral Rickover's team.

Already in 1948 the US Atomic Energy Commission, in association with the Navy Department, had awarded a contract to Westinghouse for the construction of a land-based prototype nuclear propulsion plant at Arco in Idaho. Experience with it and other reactors led to the choice of a pressurised water-cooled reactor for the first nuclear submarine, the hull of which was laid down by the Electric Boat Division of the General Dynamics Corporation at Groton, Connecticut, in June 1952.

Reactor design for a marine environment presented far greater problems than any faced in the design of land-based installations. The reactor has to be compact and adequately shielded to contain radiation, yet it has to be capable of heat transfer initially to the circulating pressurised water which acts both as a moderator, to slow down the neutrons and thus to sustain the chain reaction, and also as a primary coolant. The primary water circuit includes a steam generator

Above: USS 'Skipjack', part of the American nuclear fleet.
US NAVY

Left: The world's first nuclear submarine, the 3,530-ton USS 'Nautilus' launched in January 1954.
BARNABY'S PICTURE LIBRARY

or heat exchanger, whence the heat is transferred to a lower-pressure secondary circuit.

From that point on the geared turbine propulsion machinery is more or less conventional, although working pressures are considerably lower than those employed in modern fossil-fuelled installations. In fact the steam conditions in a nuclear plant are closer to the 'wet' steam practices of half a century ago and in service experience have necessitated the relearning of many long-forgotten lessons discussed at length in the technical press of the time.

The dispersed system, with the steam generator, primary circuit pressuriser and pumps all external to the reactor pressure vessel, is well suited to the military need, however, in that shock and damage resistance are high while reactor control is relatively simple. In addition, the radiation shielding with its attendant weight can be kept to a minimum, which is a particularly important consideration in a submarine with its low reserve of surface buoyancy compared with that of a surface vessel.

Launched as *Nautilus* on 21 January 1954, the world's first nuclear submarine was commissioned into the US Navy in April 1955. Of 3,530 tons standard (surface) displacement, she is a twin-screw vessel with a more or less conventional (pre-nuclear) submarine hull form and is capable of a submerged speed in excess of twenty knots. In May 1955 she steamed submerged from New London to San Juan, Puerto Rico, a distance of about 1,340 miles, in eighty-four hours

at an average speed of sixteen knots. In August 1958 she made the first transit from the Pacific into the Atlantic under the Arctic polar ice in the course of a voyage from Pearl Harbour to Portland, England.

The second US nuclear submarine, the somewhat similar *Seawolf*, was equipped originally with a liquid sodium-cooled reactor (Submarine Intermediate Reactor) developed by the US Atomic Energy Commission; it first went critical on 25 June 1956. The corrosive nature of the sodium-potassium alloy coolant proved an intractable problem, however, and in 1959 the original plant was replaced by a pressurised water reactor similar to that installed in the *Nautilus*.

USS *Skipjack* launched in May 1958 and later nuclear submarines, including the Royal Navy's first such craft, HMS *Dreadnought*, were built to a 'tear-drop' hull configuration with a single screw, giving greatly enhanced underwater characteristics and thus completing the initial development phase of the true submarine.

In the meantime, the USSR had also been active in the development of nuclear propulsion plant, not only for submarines but also to power a large icebreaker for service in the Soviet Arctic. The 16,000-ton vessel, laid down in the Admiralty Yard at Leningrad in 1956 and commissioned for service as the *Lenin* in September 1959, is fitted with three pressurised water reactors providing steam through heat exchangers for four steam turbogenerator sets; they provide power for three direct current electric shaft motors driving the three screws. Refuelling is necessary only at intervals of eighteen months, an obvious advantage in a ship in service in the Arctic remote from normal bunkering facilities.

The nuclear plant in the *Lenin* was extensively modified in the course of a refit at Leningrad in 1966 and the vessel now requires the use of only two of her three reactors, the third being held in reserve. Each reactor is now housed in a gas-tight containment.

A second nuclear icebreaker, named *Arktika* and of 25,000 tons, is fitted with two pressurised water reactors of the modified Lenin type. Mention has been made also of a third vessel to be named *Ledokoly*.

The first British nuclear submarine, HMS *Dreadnought*, which was completed at Barrow in April 1963, was fitted

Left: HMS 'Dreadnought'; the Royal Navy's first nuclear submarine, built in 1963. MOD (NAVY)

Below: The 75,700-ton nuclear attack aircraft carrier USS 'Enterprise' at Sydney. BARNABY'S PICTURE LIBRARY

with a US-built pressurised water reactor and propulsion machinery of the type installed in USS *Skipjack*. Later RN fleet submarines of the Valiant, Churchill and Swiftsure classes and the four ballistic missile submarines of the Resolution class have pressurised water reactors of British design. They were developed in association with the Rolls-Royce company after gaining experience with a shore-based prototype installed in the Admiralty Reactor Test Establishment (now HMS *Vulcan*) at Dounreay.

Once the feasibility of nuclear propulsion for warships had been clearly demonstrated, it was not long before consideration was given to its application to merchant ships. In the United Kingdom it took the form of a design study for a nuclear-powered fleet support tanker, but it was the United States which took the lead once again.

In 1958 an order was placed with the New York Shipbuilding Corporation of Camden, New Jersey, for the hull of a 9,900-ton twenty-one-knot single-screw passenger/cargo vessel to be powered by a pressurised water reactor with a maximum output of seventy-four megawatts. The *Savannah*

was launched on 21 July 1959, her reactor went critical in March 1962 and after sea trials the vessel was accepted for service on 1 May 1963. *Savannah* was not intended to be commercially viable although obviously a study of the economics of nuclear plant operation formed a major part of her operational programme.

The nuclear core in *Savannah*'s reactor was replaced after three years' operation and in 1970 she was laid up, having steamed in all about 470,000 miles. During her first three years' service she carried 848 passengers and 154,000 tons of cargo without incurring any claims on the grounds of nuclear liability.

After the submarine, attention was turned in both Britain and the United States to the application of nuclear power to surface warships and in December 1957 the keel was laid at Quincy, Massachussetts, of the 14,200-ton guided missile-armed cruiser (CGN) *Long Beach*. Powered by two Westinghouse pressurised water reactors, the propulsion machinery develops a total of 80,000shp for a maximum sea speed of about thirty-five knots. First commissioned in July 1961, *Long Beach* steamed about 167,000 miles before being taken in hand at Newport News for refit and refuelling in August 1965.

Eight reactors of similar design to those installed in the *Long Beach* were required for the propulsion package in the 75,700-ton nuclear attack aircraft carrier USS *Enterprise*, which commissioned for service on 25 November 1961.

The German nuclear-powered bulk carrier-research ship 'Otto Hahn'. L. DUNN

Since then the US Navy has taken delivery of four nuclear-powered guided missile frigates (USS *Bainbridge, Truxtun, California* and *South Carolina*) and currently has under construction three further frigates and three attack carriers named *Nimitz, Dwight D. Eisenhower* and *Carl Vinson*. The carriers, of 91,400 tons full-load displacement, are powered by two pressurised water reactors, compared with eight in *Enterprise*, and the nuclear cores are expected to last for at least thirteen years, or something in excess of 800,000 miles, before refuelling will be necessary.

It is the fuelling factor which plays such an important part in any decision to 'go nuclear' in ship design. Not only is frequent bunkering unnecessary, but there is no need to make provision for fuel storage or to provide the appropriate ancillary services. Against the advantages must be set the enormous capital outlay, which in the case of *Truxtun* amounted to 138 million dollars and for *Nimitz* was expected to total a staggering 594 million dollars. Moreover, to realise their full potential, nuclear capital ships need nuclear escorts if they are not to be hampered by the fuelling needs of others. With sums of such magnitude to justify, it is understandable that few navies have yet committed themselves to the construction of nuclear-powered surface warships.

In common with current practice elsewhere, pressurised water reactors, of French design, have been installed in the three completed ballistic missile submarines (Le Redoutable class) of the French Force de Dissuasion, but few details of the propulsion system have been released.

In the United Kingdom the possibilities of nuclear propulsion for merchant ships continued to receive attention throughout the 1960s and a number of design studies were undertaken.

The pressurised water reactor of the type employed in warships, with its highly enriched uranium in a zirconium-fuelled core, offers military advantages by way of compactness and resistance to shock, but running costs are higher than can be tolerated in a merchant ship, while the relative inefficiency of the saturated-steam turbine machinery further militates against economy of operation. The latter problem affected also the economic viability of *Savannah*, although her reactor core was fuelled by uranium dioxide, with a lower degree of enrichment, in stainless steel.

More recently, in Western Germany, research and development have been concentrated on the design of an integral reactor system more suited to the requirements of a competitive merchantman. The system has a once-through boiler giving some degree of superheat, that is, having the steam generator within the reactor pressure vessel and no external pressurised primary water system.

A reactor of such integral self-pressurised type, with a fuel load of 2.95 tons of uranium dioxide, was installed in the 14,040-ton-dwt bulk carrier/research ship *Otto Hahn*, which was launched by Howaldtswerke AG at Kiel in 1964 on behalf of the Gesellschaft für Kernenergieverwertung in Schiffbau und Schiffahrt (Organisation for the Evaluation of Nuclear Energy in Shipbuilding and Navigation). Preliminary trials were run in the Baltic before the installation of her reactor, but she finally commissioned for service in 1969 and in the course of the next three years steamed about 250,000 miles.

In 1972 *Otto Hahn* was refuelled with a new core which gave an increase in power density from thirty-three to fifty-two kW/litre and a considerable reduction in the overall fuel cycle cost. Like *Savannah*, *Otto Hahn* is by no means an economic proposition in commercial service, although her costs include about one million deutschmarks annually on research.

The Japanese Government decided in 1962 to build a nuclear-powered cargo/research vessel in order to gain experience in propulsion reactor design and construction, operational familiarisation and training. The vessel was laid down in November 1967 and is designed around a pressurised water reactor of the dispersed type (with a pressurised primary system and external steam generator) with a thermal output of thirty-six megawatts. Launched as *Mutsu*, the ship was completed for trials late in 1974, from which time her history developed into something of a farce. She left harbour for sea trials of the propulsion system, but radiation leaks necessitated a premature shut-down of her reactor, after which a blockade by Japanese fishermen, fearing a repetition of events which occurred a quarter of a century ago, prevented for a time her re-entry into any Japanese port.

The possibilities of the nuclear-powered merchant vessel have been demonstrated, although the state of the art has not yet reached the point where the economics of such a craft can compete successfully with the conventional fossil-fuelled merchantman. However, the great increases in the price of fossil fuels in the mid-1970s and the feared depletion of world oil reserves could force a reappraisal of the nuclear solution, particularly for the large bulk carrier and container ship. The solution might possibly be in the choice of an alternative form of reactor. The gas-cooled type is of relatively lightweight and simple construction and has a high safety factor, it could well be a contender for the future.

Index